Science and Engineering Applications Discussed in
Excel 4 for Scientists and Engineers (continued)

Computer users are not all alike.
Neither are SYBEX books.

We know our customers have a variety of needs. They've told us so. And because we've listened, we've developed several distinct types of books to meet the needs of each of our customers. What are you looking for in computer help?

If you're looking for the basics, try the **ABC's** series. You'll find short, uninitmidating turorials and helpful illustrations. For a more visual approach, select **Teach Yourself,** featuring screen-by-screen illustrations of how to use your latest software purchase.

Running Start books are really two books in one—a tutorial to get you off to a fast start and a reference to answer your questions when you're ready to tackle advanced tasks.

Mastering and **Understanding** titles offer you a step-by-step introduction, plus an in-depth examination of intermeditate-level features, to use as you progress.

Our **Up & Running** series is designed for computer-literate consumers who want a no-nonsense overview of new programs. Just 20 basic lessons, and you're on your way.

We also publish two types of reference books. Our **Instant References** provide quick access to each of a program's commands and functions. SYBEX **Encyclopedias** and **Desktop References** provide a *comprehensive reference* and explanation of all of the commands, features, and functions of the subject software.

Our **Programming** books are specifically written for a technically sophisticated audience and provide a no-nonsense value-added approach to each topic covered, with plenty of tips, tricks, and time-saving hints.

Sometimes a subject requires a special treatment that our standard series doesn't provide. So you'll find we have titles like **Advanced Techiques, Handbooks, Tips & Tricks,** and others that are specifically tailored to satisfy a unique need.

We carefully select our authors for their in-depth understanding of the software they're writing about, as well as their ability to write clearly and communicate effectively. Each manuscript is thoroughly reviewed by our technical staff to ensure its complete accuracy. Our production department makes sure it's easy to use. All of this adds up to the highest quality books available, consistently appearing on best-seller charts worldwide.

You'll find SYBEX publishes a variety of books on every popular software package. Looking for computer help? Help Yourself to SYBEX.

For a brochure of our best-selling publications:

SYBEX Inc. 2021 Challenger Drive, Alameda, CA 94501
Tel: (510) 523-8233/(800) 227-2346 Telex: 336311
Fax: (510) 523-2373

EXCEL 4

FOR SCIENTISTS AND ENGINEERS

EXCEL 4

FOR SCIENTISTS AND ENGINEERS

William J. Orvis

SYBEX ®

SAN FRANCISCO ■ PARIS ■ DÜSSELDORF ■ SOEST

Acquisitions Editor: Dave Clark
Developmental Editor: David Peal
Editor: Marilyn Smith
Technical Editor: Bruce Gendron
Project Editor: Michelle Nance
Book Designer: Suzanne Albertson
Chapter Art: Suzanne Albertson
Production Artist: Claudia Smelser
Screen Graphics: John Corrigan
Typesetter: Deborah Maizels
Production Assistant: Lisa Haden
Indexer: Paul Kish
Cover Designer: Ingalls + Associates
Cover Photographer: Mark Johann

Screen reproductions produced with Collage Plus.

Collage Plus is a trademark of Inner Media Inc.

SYBEX is a registered trademark of SYBEX Inc.

TRADEMARKS: SYBEX has attempted throughout this book to distinguish proprietary trademarks from descriptive terms by following the capitalization style used by the manufacturer.

SYBEX is not affiliated with any manufacturer.

Every effort has been made to supply complete and accurate information. However, SYBEX assumes no responsibility for its use, nor for any infringement of the intellectual property rights of third parties which would result from such use.

Library of Congress Card Number: 92-83711
ISBN: 0-7821-1196-3

Manufactured in the United States of America
10 9 8 7 6 5 4 3 2 1

For Pat and Wib.
Your dedication, perseverance,
and honesty show in the
character of your children.
I know, I married one.

CONTENTS AT A GLANCE

TABLE OF CONTENTS

PREFACE

A few years ago, I wrote *1-2-3 for Scientists and Engineers*, extolling the ease with which numerical analysis could be done using the Lotus 1-2-3 spreadsheet program. The book was about Lotus 1-2-3 because that was what most scientists and engineers had access to. However, the readers of that book might be surprised to learn that many of the book's examples were developed on the Macintosh, using the then new spreadsheet program from Microsoft known as Excel. Excel has grown since then, and is now an extremely powerful numerical analysis environment, operating on a Macintosh or on a PC under Windows.

Ever since then, I have been pushing to do the Excel version of *1-2-3 for Scientists and Engineers,* and the book you see in front of you is the result of that pushing. I hope you enjoy this book, as you watch what used to be arcane numerical methods become transparent when implemented on a worksheet.

Most numerical analysis is done using traditional programming languages such as Fortran or C. You insert the input data into a program, and the program performs some numerical magic on it and spits back the result. Using these programs, you see only the beginning and the end of a problem and miss out on the middle. With a worksheet implementation of a numerical analysis problem, you see the whole problem. When doing iterative solutions to differential equations, you get to watch the values at every node in the problem converge (or not) to the answer. Being able to see the solutions converge makes the method much more understandable, and with understanding comes new innovation and growth.

The push to write this book and develop the examples and problems was long and hard, and I want to thank Dave Clark for finally letting me do it, Michelle Nance for keeping me on track (and almost on time), Marilyn Smith and Bruce Gendron for finding and fixing all my mistakes, and all the others at SYBEX who made this book possible. And most especially, I want to thank B.J., Skye, Sierra, and Shane for staying out of my hair so I could get this done, and Julie for keeping them out.

I hope you have fun with this book—I know I did.

William J. Orvis

INTRODUCTION

The numerical calculations performed by scientists and engineers range from the simple task of determining the value of a function to the complex task of numerically integrating a differential equation—tasks that require considerable time and energy. Thus, any tool that can facilitate numerical calculations will increase a scientist's or engineer's productivity. Excel is one such tool. It offers facilities for numerical calculations, graphics, and programmability in a single, easy-to-use package.

In the past, the slide rule was the primary tool for performing numerical calculations, and graph paper was the usual data-display device. With the advent of the hand calculator, the slide rule was quickly retired to a place of nostalgic revere (most likely the bottom of a drawer). However, the graph paper still remained.

Some scientists and engineers had access to mainframe computers and could use them for their calculations and data display. These mainframe computers had tremendous computing power, and many had impressive graphics output devices. However, individuals usually needed to hire a computer scientist (or a high school student) or to learn a computer language such as Fortran or ALGOL to program them and to make the high-powered graphics work.

Microcomputers put a lot of computing power on the desktops of scientists and engineers, and the BASIC computer language included with most microcomputers provided a good environment for many numerical calculations. Many desktop computers had plotters and, with a little work, could produce good-quality graphics output. However, these computers still had to be programmed to generate and plot numbers.

Even with personal computers available, most scientists and engineers still generated their numbers with an engineering calculation sheet. An engineering calculation sheet is a piece of lined paper, much like binder paper, that also has vertical lines spaced approximately every inch or so. You put successive calculations in alternate columns until the final column contains the result. For example, if you want to calculate the function $y = 2x^2 + 3x$ for a list of x values, you place the x values in the first column, calculate $2x^2$ in the second column, calculate $3x$ in the third column, and place the sum of columns 2 and 3—the final result—in column 4.

Interestingly, these engineering calculation sheets bore a remarkable resemblance to the spreadsheets that business students used when I was in school (they must have stolen the idea from the engineers). You might occasionally have a beer or two with a business student, but you never involved yourself in their studies, so little was made of these similarities. Much of this indifference was because we used sines, cosines, and exponentials, whereas they used only addition, subtraction, multiplication, division, and percentages (they got really good with percentages: percent interest, percent penalty, percent royalty, and so on).

Many years ago, the business spreadsheet was automated with the microcomputer program VisiCalc. Some of us in science and engineering immediately saw the potential of this program as an engineering tool, especially since it could calculate scientific functions such as sines, cosines, and exponentials. Since then, spreadsheet programs have grown tremendously in power and versatility.

Microsoft Excel is currently one of the most powerful spreadsheet programs. It runs on both the PC under Windows and on the Macintosh. Excel is well suited for science and engineering calculations because it includes a high-powered worksheet, coupled with graphics, macro programmability, and database functions.

Scope of This Book

In this book, you will learn how to tap Excel's power to solve your science and engineering problems. You will not only learn how to calculate and plot simple equations, but how to perform curve fitting; to calculate statistics, numerical derivatives, and integrals; and to solve systems of equations and one- and two-dimensional differential equations. This book also explains how to create graphics and macros. These capabilities give Excel much of its power and usefulness for science and engineering.

Windows and Macintosh Versions of Excel

This book applies to both the Macintosh and Windows versions of Excel. Worksheet files can be freely transferred between these versions of Excel. The differences in their usage are minimal. The images in this book are from Excel for Windows, so Macintosh users will see a difference in some of the screens. However, the contents of the windows are the same. The implementation and worksheet methods (the location and contents of cells) employed in both the Windows and Macintosh versions of Excel are the same.

The differences between the Windows and Macintosh versions of Excel are mentioned when they affect the work at hand. The main differences are in the special keystrokes required to activate some functions. The Macintosh keyboard has a Command key, which is lacking on the PC. Thus, keystrokes that employ the Command (Cmd) key on the Macintosh are mapped onto the Control (Ctrl), Alt, and Shift keys on the PC. For example, the keystroke for the Calculate Now function is Ctrl-= on the PC and Cmd-= on the Macintosh, and the keystroke for the Store as Array function is Ctrl-Shift-Enter on the PC and Cmd-Enter on the Macintosh.

Older Versions of Excel

This book was developed with Microsoft Excel version 4.0. Readers with earlier versions of Excel will have no problem with most of the examples. The biggest differences between version 4.0 and the earlier versions of Excel are in the data-entry area and in the advanced functions.

The click-and-drag capability for moving and copying cells in version 4.0 is not available in earlier versions, nor is the fill handle for creating a data series. With earlier versions, use the Copy, Paste, Fill Down, and Fill Right commands on the Edit menu and the Series command on the Data menu to accomplish these tasks. Excel versions earlier than 3.0 do not include the Solver add-in program, so users of those versions will not be able to follow the examples that use the Solver.

Real Examples

This book was written by a practicing scientist and engineer for other practicing scientists and engineers. It is based on real uses of a spreadsheet as an engineering tool. Many of the problems were developed as part of my work or are adaptations of problems that I solved using other techniques before I realized the full potential of spreadsheets. In many cases, you will be solving real problems rather than simplified textbook problems. A few of the problems are somewhat longer than you normally find in a textbook. In those few cases, I have included abbreviated versions of the problems that still illustrate the relevant techniques.

Because this book is based on my own work in the science and engineering fields, many of the problems are electronics and solid-state physics problems, with some astronomy thrown in for fun. But the problems are used only to illustrate the calculation methods. It is the methods, not the problems, that are important. You can apply these methods to any branch of science and engineering.

This book does not teach science and engineering, nor does it teach numerical methods. I do not discuss much of the background or mathematical justification for most of the numerical techniques described here. If you are interested in background material, a number of good numerical methods books are available to sate your curiosity. I primarily depend on Curtis F. Gerald's book, *Applied Numerical Analysis*, and William H. Press' book, *Numerical Recipes*, for most of the numerical methods I use. Other books and references related to the examples are listed at the end of each chapter.

Examples on Disk

If you do not want to type all of the examples but still want to be able to run them, you can obtain the examples on disk. See the disk-offer page at the end of this book for order information. Be sure to indicate if you need a DOS or Macintosh disk and the disk size when ordering. Note that the disk does not contain the solutions to the problems at the ends of the chapters.

User Background

To use this book, you must have a background in science, engineering, or mathematics. Although the book is intended for the practicing scientist or engineer, a college student in one of these disciplines should have no trouble understanding the problems and solutions and using them to enhance his or her studies. In fact, the spreadsheet versions of the numerical methods applied in this book are much more intuitive than the same methods applied with Fortran or C, which makes the spreadsheet an excellent learning tool.

You should also know how to use your computer and the basics of working with Excel. If you do not know how to turn on a computer, put this book down, get a good tutorial, and play with the computer for a while. When you feel comfortable with the computer (when you can delete a file without cringing), then continue with this book.

If you do not know how to start up Excel, move around a worksheet, insert data in cells, save a file, and load an old file, study the tutorials and manuals that came with the software. You should also skim through the *Microsoft Excel Function Reference* to get a feel for the types of functions available in Excel. Once you understand the basics, you can continue with the problems in this book.

This book starts slowly to give you time to become comfortable with Excel. Readers who are more familiar with Excel may want to skip the first, simple example and begin with the second. From there, the worksheets quickly get increasingly complex.

Hardware Requirements

If you don't have the right hardware, Excel either won't run or won't be completely functional. The Windows version of Excel requires a machine capable of running Windows 3.0, which is a minimum of an IBM AT-class machine (80286 processor) with 2 megabytes of system memory and an EGA or better monitor. Of course, more memory and a more powerful processor (80386 or 80486) will increase the speed and functionality of Excel.

Excel will run on any Macintosh computer with System 6.02 or later, including the 128K, if you have increased its memory to 1 megabyte or more. Again, Excel works much better with more memory and with a more powerful processor.

The examples in this book were developed on a Today, 386SX-20 computer, with 4 megabytes of random-access memory (RAM) and never enough hard-disk space. The system was running DOS 5.0 and Windows 3.1. The examples were also run on a Macintosh SE computer with 4 megabytes of RAM and even less hard-disk space. Both systems were running Excel version 4.0.

Conventions Used in This Book

Many of the illustrations in this book do not show the whole worksheet, because some of the problems would fill pages. In most cases, I place the important results in the upper-left corner of the worksheet and show only that corner in the illustrations.

Excel is not case-sensitive, so functions, variable names, and formulas can be typed in uppercase or lowercase letters. In the problem descriptions, the spreadsheet functions are in uppercase, because that is how they appear in the spreadsheet, and the variables and defined names are in the case in which they were defined. You can use either uppercase or lowercase letters for your entries, and Excel will change them as appropriate.

For More Information

References to the sources of information in the examples and numerical methods used in each chapter appear at the end of each chapter, in a section like this one. Use the references in these sections if you want more information about the examples or the numerical methods.

Operating an IBM PC or Compatible Computer

J. Lasselle, C. Ramsey, *The ABC's of IBM PCs and Compatibles* (San Francisco: SYBEX, 1991).

Operating a Macintosh Computer

D. McClelland, *Macintosh System 7: Everything You Need to Know* (San Francisco: SYBEX, 1992).

Learning Excel

A. Neibauer, *The ABC's of Excel 4 for Windows* (San Francisco: SYBEX, 1992).

C. Townsend, *Mastering Excel 4 for Windows* (San Francisco: SYBEX, 1992).

Using Excel in Science and Engineering Applications

Microsoft Excel was developed to compete in the lucrative business software market. Thus, you may wonder if the program is suitable for science and engineering calculations. Can a business program do the types of calculations that are required in science and engineering? Are the precision and range of the numbers suitable for engineering calculations? Are all the standard science and engineering mathematical functions available? Can you construct useful algorithms?

As you will see, Excel is more than accurate enough for most science and engineering applications, and it has more mathematical capabilities and functions than many high-level computer languages.

Evaluating Numeric Precision and Accuracy

Probably the most important question is whether Excel's numeric precision and range are sufficient for science and engineering calculations. Numeric precision is usually not important for most simple calculations. You can calculate many science and engineering problems using a slide rule with only three places of accuracy. On the other hand, many numerical algorithms are quite sensitive to numeric precision, especially the differencing schemes used for calculating numerical solutions of differential equations.

Celestial mechanics calculations also often require an extreme number of digits of precision. In celestial mechanics, objects are often integrated for many thousands of orbits about the sun or a planet, and the cumulative round-off error can put the object on the wrong side of the sun or planet if the precision is too small.

Numeric Precision

The numeric precision of Excel meets or exceeds that of several established computational tools used in science and engineering. Excel maintains an internal numeric precision of 15 digits. A typical scientific calculator displays 10 digits and probably stores one or two more internally to reduce round-off error. A VAX minicomputer maintains only 7 digits in single-precision, floating-point numbers, and 15 in double-precision. A CRAY 1 supercomputer has 15 digits of precision in single-precision, floating-point numbers.

Excel maintains the 15 digits internally, but rounds the number for the screen display according to the format of the cell in which it appears. However, if you want to store the rounded numbers as they appear on the screen rather than the full 15 digits, select the Calculation command from the Options menu and check the Precision As Displayed check box in the Calculation Options dialog box. Reducing the precision is useful when you are working with monetary amounts and do not want to have fractional cents, but it is not usually desirable for science and engineering calculations, and it will not be used in the examples in this book. Note that using reduced precision will slow down spreadsheet recalculation slightly.

Numeric Range

Numeric range generally determines the sensitivity of the spreadsheet to overflow and underflow errors. Excel stores numbers between 2.226×10^{-308} to $1.798 \times 10^{+308}$, giving it a numeric range of $10^{\pm 308}$. A typical hand calculator handles a range of $10^{\pm 99}$. A VAX minicomputer has a range of $10^{\pm 38}$ in single-precision and $10^{\pm 308}$ in double-precision. A CRAY 1 supercomputer has a range of $10^{\pm 2500}$.

Although the largest number Excel can store is $1.798 \times 10^{+308}$, the largest number that you can type in is about $9.999 \times 10^{+307}$. If you type in a larger value, Excel treats it as a string.

Most scientific and engineering results have reasonably sized numbers, roughly in the range of 10^{-40} to 10^{+40} (reasonable for scientists and engineers, that is). However, when these numbers are used in an equation, the intermediate results can often be quite large. If the size of an intermediate result exceeds the range of the computer, the calculation overflows and returns an error. For example, consider this simple expression from quantum mechanics:

$$\frac{2m}{\hbar^2}$$

where $\hbar$ is Planck's constant divided by 2π (1.0546×10^{-34} J-s) and m is the electron rest mass (9.11×10^{-31} kg). The result of this calculation is $1.64 \times 10^{+38}$, which is also a reasonably sized number. But the intermediate result of squaring and inverting Planck's constant has a value of $8.99 \times 10^{+67}$, which is 29 orders of magnitude larger than the final result. Taking the cube of the inverse of Planck's constant will easily overflow a hand calculator, and it is far beyond the capability of single-precision numbers on a VAX.

Numeric overflow usually indicates an error in the problem setup. If that is not the case, an overflow of an intermediate value can often be corrected by reordering the equation or by splitting it into two equations to limit the size of the intermediate values. You would set up the equation above to first divide the electron mass by Planck's constant, and then divide that result by Planck's constant again. The final result would be the same, but the intermediate value would not be so large.

With a range of $10^{\pm308}$, Excel is not likely to have problems with numeric overflow. If you do manage to overflow a number, Excel stores the error value #NUM! to mark that cell and any cell that depends on it as bad. If a number underflows, because it is less than 2.225×10^{-308}, Excel stores the value as zero.

Error Numbers

In addition to the standard real numbers, Excel treats seven error values as if they were numbers:

#DIV/0!	Division by zero.
#NAME?	A variable name in a formula has not been defined.
#N/A	No value is available.
#NULL!	A result has no value.
#NUM!	Numeric overflow, underflow, or incorrect use of a number, such as SQRT(−1).
#REF!	Invalid cell reference; the cell is not on the worksheet.
#VALUE!	Invalid argument type, such as text where a number is required.

When one of these error values is used in a formula, the formula's result also has that error value. Thus, the error values propagate through a worksheet, marking any values that depends on them as bad. This propagation of error values ensures that you don't use a number calculated from bad data. If you want to use error values to test error-recovery formulas on a worksheet, you can type these values directly into a cell on the worksheet.

A Brief Review of Cell Referencing

The cells in an Excel worksheet can hold text (*labels*), numbers (*values*), or equations (*formulas*). Excel looks at what you type and converts the cell contents as appropriate. If a cell contains a number, Excel stores it as a numeric value, and you can use it for calculations. If a cell contains a mixture of text and numbers, Excel stores it as text. If the contents of a cell begin with an equal sign (=), Excel stores it as a formula.

Every cell in Excel has two parts associated with it: the contents and the value. The *contents* are what you type into a cell, and the *value* is what is visible on the screen. Cell formatting does not affect the value of a cell, although it does change how the value appears on the screen. For text and numbers, the contents and the value are the same. For formulas, the contents are the formula you typed in, and the value is the result of that formula.

You can insert the values of other cells in the worksheet into a formula by using cell references. A *cell reference* (or *address*) consists of a letter-number pair, where the letter corresponds to the column that contains the referenced cell and the number corresponds to the row. For example, G5 corresponds to the value in the cell at column G and row 5. You can also reference cells as a row-and-column pair, as in R5C7, which refers to the same cell as G5. This is called the R1C1 style.

You set the cell-referencing style you want to use by checking or unchecking the R1C1 check box in the Workspace dialog box. To display this dialog box, choose the Workspace command on the Options menu. If you created a worksheet using one style and then change the R1C1 check box setting, all your references are converted to the other style.

External Cell References

If you are referencing a cell that is on a different worksheet from the one in which you are typing a formula, you must include the worksheet name so that Excel knows where to look for the cell. This is known as an *external reference*. The worksheet containing the external reference does not need to be open for you to access the contents of one of its cells. To make an external reference, type the worksheet name, followed by an exclamation point, followed by the cell reference. If the worksheet is not in the default directory, include the path to it as well.

For example, if you want to reference cell H7 on the CARS.XLS worksheet in the default directory, you would use this reference:

`CARS.XLS!H7`

To reference cell H7 in the CARS.XLS worksheet in the D:\STATS directory, which is not the default directory, you would use this form:

`'D:\STATS\CARS.XLS'!H7`

The single quotation marks are required for a reference that includes a directory path.

The simplest way to ensure that you are correctly addressing a cell, especially a cell in another worksheet, is to have Excel insert the reference for you. Open the worksheet that contains the cell to be referenced, switch back to your worksheet, and start typing your formula. When you reach the point where you want to insert the cell reference, switch to the worksheet that contains the cell you want to reference and click on that cell with the mouse. Excel writes the correct cell reference in your formula.

Range References

You can reference a group of cells as a range. A *range* of cells is a rectangular region on the worksheet. All the cells within the rectangle are included in the range (there are no holes). You specify a range with the cell references of the cells in the upper-left and lower-right corners of the rectangular region, separated by a colon. For example, H4:J6 specifies all the cells within the rectangle that has H4 in the upper-left corner and J6 in the lower-right corner (H4, H5, H6, I4, I5, I6, J4, J5, and J6). A range reference can be as small as a single cell (H5:H5). It can also be a single row (H5:J5) or column (H5:H10).

You can combine multiple ranges in a single cell reference by separating them with commas. For example, the reference H4:J6,L2:M3 contains two ranges: the H4:J6 region and the L2:M3 region. All the cells in both regions are contained in the reference (H4, H5, H6, I4, I5, I6, J4, J5, J6, L2, L3, M2, and M3). If you use a space instead of a comma to separate two ranges, the resulting reference is to the intersection of those two regions instead of to the union. For example, H4:J6 J5:M8 is a range reference to cells J5 and J6 only, because they are the only cells that are contained in both rectangular regions.

As with single-cell references, the simplest way to reference a range is to select it with the mouse while you are typing the formula. Excel inserts the correct reference for you. To create the union of several rectangular regions into a single range reference, hold down the Ctrl key (Cmd on the Macintosh) while you select the ranges with the mouse.

Relative and Absolute References

Cell references can be relative or absolute. Relative cell references point to cells relative to the cell where the reference is typed. Absolute cell references always point to a specific cell. You can also make a mixed reference, in which just the row or column is absolute.

Relative Cell References

All of the cell references mentioned so far are relative cell references. *Relative* cell references are defined in relation to the cell that contains the typed reference.

For example, suppose that the formula in cell G5 contains the cell reference E3. The E3 does not actually refer to the contents of the cell in column E and row 3 but points to the cell that is two columns left and two rows up from cell G5, which just happens to be E3. This distinction becomes apparent when you copy or move cells. If you were to copy the contents of cell G5 into cell I8, the cell reference would change to G6, which is two columns to the left and two columns above cell I8.

In the R1C1 style of cell referencing, you enclose the row and column number in square brackets, which changes them into a distance and direction. The origin of this cell-reference system is the upper-left corner of the worksheet, so positive directions are down and to the right. For example, R[-2]C[2] is a relative cell reference to the cell two rows up and two columns right from the cell that contains the reference.

Relative cell references are extremely handy when you are copying a formula to apply it to a set of data. If you were calculating a formula for 50 different input values, it would be a tedious job to type the same formula 50 times. Instead, you can type the formula into the first cell in a column and then copy it into the cells below that one. Excel adjusts all the relative cell references according to their positions. You will see how this works as you develop some worksheets in later chapters.

Absolute Cell References

An *absolute* cell reference does not change when you copy a formula. It always points to a specific cell, no matter where it is on the worksheet. To make a cell reference absolute, precede the row and column coordinates with a dollar sign. For example, $G$5 is an absolute reference to cell G5.

The R1C1 style of cell referencing is absolute unless you use the brackets to make the reference relative. For example, R5C7 refers to the specific cell at the intersection of row 5 and column 7.

Absolute cell references are useful for pointing to the coefficients in a formula that you are going to copy into multiple cells. Specify the independent variables in a formula with relative cell references pointing to an adjacent cell, but make the coefficients of the formula absolute cell references. When you copy the formula down the column, the relative cell references will change to reference the cells in the adjacent columns. However, the coefficients will not be adjusted, so every copy will point to the cells where the coefficients are stored. This way, you need only one set of coefficients on your worksheet. No matter where you copy the formula, it will still refer to them. You can adjust a single coefficient to see what happens, and all the copies of the formula will show the results.

Mixed Cell References

A *mixed* cell reference contains an absolute reference to only the column or row coordinate and a relative reference to the other coordinate. To create a mixed reference, place a dollar sign before only the coordinate that you want to be absolute.

For example, the reference $G5 fixes the column, but the row coordinate is relative and will change if the referencing cell is copied to a different row. G$5 is just the opposite, with the row coordinate absolute and the column coordinate relative.

In the R1C1 style, R1C[4] is an absolute reference to row 1 and a relative reference to the column that is four columns right of the column containing this reference.

Range and Cell Names

You can name a range or cell and then use the name instead of the cell reference in formulas and commands. Use the Define Name or Create Names command on the

Formula menu to create, change, delete, or list named references. You can name individual cells or whole ranges of cells.

When Excel evaluates a formula that contains names, it replaces each name with its definition, and then calculates the result. Named ranges are absolute references, so they do not change when you copy cells that contain them.

Using a name is efficient when you will reference the same cell or range many times. Names also make your formulas more understandable. For example, if cell C5 contains a mass value, you could name it Mass. Then your formulas that reference this cell will contain the word *Mass*, which is much more descriptive than *C5*.

When you type a range name into a formula that requires a single value, Excel uses only a single cell in that range. The cell it uses depends on the relative locations of the cell containing the reference and the range it references. If the reference is to a column of cells to the right or left of the cell containing the reference, the cell used is the one on the same row as the cell with the reference. Likewise, if the reference is to a row that is above or below the cell containing the reference, the cell used is the one that is in the same column as the cell containing the reference. If you have more than one row or column in the reference in the same row or column as the referencing cell, you will get the #VALUE! error. You will also get the #VALUE error if none of the cells in the reference is in the same row or column as the referencing cell.

Actually, you can use the Define Name command to name just about any value, including numbers or text that are not contained in any cell. Treat the list of named ranges and values as a simple replacement table, where the value of a name is inserted into a formula before the formula is evaluated.

Copying Versus Moving Cell References

As explained earlier, when you *copy* a formula from one cell into another cell, the absolute cell references do not change, but the relative cell references change according to where the formula is copied.

When you *move* the contents of a cell, Excel assumes that you are changing only the layout of your worksheet and do not want to change the mathematical logic. Therefore, all cell references in the moved cells that point to cells outside the moved cells do not change; they still point to the same cells after the move. Any cells that refer to the moved cells are adjusted so that they still point to the cells that have the same contents as the cells that they pointed to originally. A move operation should not change any of the results of your formulas, unless you delete data by moving cells on top of it.

Using Operators in Calculations

Operators are the basic building blocks of mathematical calculations. Their action determines how numbers (or text strings) are combined to produce numeric results. Excel provides three types of operators: mathematical, text, and logical. The single text operator is concatenation (&), which is used to join two text strings together into a single string of text. Table 1.1 lists all the operators available in Excel.

Mathematical Operators

The mathematical operators consist of the standard set you would expect to find in any high-level computer language.

The unary operators are percent and negation. The percent operator divides the number to its left by 100 (/100). Excel does not provide a positive unary operator; a positive value is assumed if a unary operator is not present. In fact, if you insert a + unary operator in a value or formula, Excel removes it (except when it is in the exponent of a number in scientific notation).

The mathematical operators are addition, subtraction, multiplication, division, and exponentiation. These operators work as you would expect them to.

Logical Operators

The logical operators are used to compare two numerical values or strings. The result of the operation is the value True or the value False. When you use logical results in mathematical formulas, True has the value 1, and False has the value 0.

When Excel compares strings with the logical operators, it ignores the case (uppercase or lowercase) of the characters. However, you can use Excel's EXACT function to compare strings considering their case.

TABLE 1.1: Excel Operators and Order of Precedence

Operator	Description	Precedence in Calculations
	Unary Operators	
–	Negation (operates on the value to its right)	1
%	Percent (operates on the value to its left)	2
	Mathematical Operators	
^	Eponentiation	3
*	Multiplication	4
/	Division	4
+	Addition	5
–	Subtraction	5
	Text Operator	
&	Concatenation	6
	Logical Operators	
=	Equal to	7
<	Less than	7
>	Greater than	7
<=	Less than or equal to	7
>=	Greater than or equal to	7
<>	Not equal to	7

Operator Precedence

The precedence of the operators determines how an equation is evaluated. Table 1.1 lists the precedence along with each operator. In any calculation, the operators listed with a 1 are executed first, then the operators shown with a 2, and so on.

If there are two operations of equal precedence in a formula, they are evaluated from right to left.

If you are unsure how a formula will be evaluated, use parentheses to force the formula to be evaluated in the correct order. Parentheses always override the precedence shown in Table 1.1.

Using Worksheet Functions

An important consideration when planning to use Excel for science and engineering calculations is the availability of frequently used mathematical functions. Without these functions, relatively simple calculations can become quite tedious. For example, have you ever tried to calculate the sine of an angle using a business calculator whose most complicated function is a square root? It can be done, but it is tiresome and prone to error.

Excel provides 11 different types of worksheet functions: mathematical, engineering, logical, Boolean, string, statistical, date/time, database, financial, informational, and lookup/reference. In addition, you will find a large number of macro functions for use in creating computer programs in Excel (macro functions will be covered in Chapter 4). If the internal functions aren't sufficient for your purposes, you can create your own functions in a compiled language, such as C or FORTRAN, and call them from within Excel.

The functions that are of special interest to scientists and engineers are described here. For a complete discussion of all the functions and operators and their syntax, refer to the *Microsoft Excel Function Reference*, which is included in the Excel package.

Entering Functions

An Excel function consists of the function name, a left parenthesis, some arguments separated by commas, and a right parenthesis. Arguments of functions can be numbers, strings, cell references, or other functions (with nesting up to seven levels deep). If the argument of a function is not within the range accepted by that function, the function returns #NUM!. If the argument is not the correct type for a particular function, the function returns #VALUE!.

In this book, the function names appear in uppercase letters and the arguments are in italics. You can type the function names in either uppercase or lowercase; Excel does not distinguish between the two cases.

Note that some of the functions are in add-in macro files, which must be attached to Excel before they can be used. To attach an add-in file, use the Add-Ins command on the Options menu to access the Add-In Manager. Click on the Add button in the Add-In Manager to find and attach an add-in file. After you attach the add-in files, Excel will be able to find those functions when you use them in worksheet formulas.

Array Functions

A normal function returns a single value. However, Excel provides some array functions that return more than one value. For example, the MINVERSE(*matrix*) function returns a whole array.

An array function must be entered into a range of cells that is large enough to contain all the numbers in the result. For example, if you are using the MINVERSE function to invert a three-by-three array, the result is also a three-by-three array, so you must place the function in a three-by-three range of cells.

To insert an array function into a range of cells, select the cells and type the array function and its arguments into the upper-left cell. Then hold down the Ctrl and Shift keys and click on the check mark or press Enter (Cmd-Enter on the Macintosh). The array function, surrounded by curly braces ({}), will be placed in every cell in the range. You don't type the curly braces; Excel inserts them to mark the entry as an array function.

Actually, any formula can be applied to an array of values in the same manner. For example, this formula calculates the sum of squares of a set of values and returns a single value:

```
=SUM((A7:A15-$B$1)^2)
```

If you type this formula and then press the Ctrl and Shift keys while you click on the check mark (or press Enter), Excel will first subtract the value in cell B1 from all the values in cells A7 through A15, square the differences, and then sum them. If you enter this formula without holding down the Ctrl and Shift keys, Excel will use only one of the values in the range of cells from A7 through A15 (the one in the same row as the cell that contains the formula).

Mathematical Functions

The mathematical functions take numerical data as arguments, transform that data in some way, and produce a numerical value as a result. The mathematical functions are of four general types: basic mathematics, logarithmic, trigonometric, and matrix. Table 1.2 lists Excel's mathematical functions.

TABLE 1.2:   Excel's Mathematical Functions

Function	Returns
Basic Mathematical Functions	
ABS()	The absolute value.
BASE()	Converts a base 10 number to another base with a specific precision.
CEILING()	Rounds up to the next integer that is a multiple of the specified significance.
COMBIN()	The number of ways chosen objects may be selected from objects.
EVEN()	Rounds up to the next even integer.
FACT()	The factorial.
FACTDOUBLE()	The double factorial.
FLOOR()	Rounds down to the next integer that is a multiple of significance.
GCD()	The greatest common divisor of a list of numbers.
LCM()	The least common multiple of a list of numbers.
INT()	The integer part of a number.
MOD()	The modulus (remainder of two numbers).
MROUND()	Rounds a number to the nearest multiple of significance.
MULTINOMIAL()	The multinomial of a list of numbers.
ODD()	Rounds a number up to the nearest odd integer.
PRODUCT()	The product of a list of numbers.
QUOTIENT()	Integer division of one number by another number.
RAND()	A random number between 0 and 1.
RANDBETWEEN()	A random number between the limits of the lower and upper numbers.
ROUND()	Rounds a number to the specified number of digits.
SERIESSUM()	Sums a power series.
SIGN()	The value 1 with the sign of a number.
SQRT()	The square root of a number.

TABLE 1.2: Excel's Mathematical Functions (continued)

Function	Returns
SQRTP()	The square root of π times a number.
SUM()	Adds the numbers in a list.
SUMPRODUCT()	The sum of the products of matrix elements.
SUMSQ()	The sum of the squares of a list of numbers.
SUMX2MY2()	The sum of the difference of the squares of the elements in two matrices.
SUMX2PY2()	The sum of the sum of the squares of the elements in two matrices.
SUMXMY2()	The sum of the squares of the differences of the values in two matrices.
TRUNC()	Truncates a number to the specified number of digits.

Logarithmic Functions

Function	Returns
EXP()	Exponential of a number (power of **e**).
EXP(1)	The value **e** (2.7182818284590).
LN()	Natural logarithm of a number (base **e**).
LOG()	Logarithm of a number with the specified base.
LOG10()	Common logarithm of a number (base 10).

Trigonometric Functions

Function	Returns
COS()	Cosine of a number.
SIN()	Sine of a number.
TAN()	Tangent of a number.

Inverse Trigonometric Functions

Function	Returns
ACOS()	Arccosine of a number.
ASIN()	Arcsine of a number.
ATAN()	Arctangent of a number (from $-\pi/2$ to $+\pi/2$.
ATAN2()	Arctangent of two numbers (from $-\pi$ to $+\pi$).

Hyperbolic Functions

Function	Returns
COSH()	Hyperbolic cosine of a number.
SINH()	Hyperbolic sine of a number.
TANH()	Hyperbolic tangent of a number.

TABLE 1.2:   Excel's Mathematical Functions (continued)

Function	Returns
Inverse Hyperbolic Functions	
ACOSH()	Inverse hyperbolic cosine of a number.
ASINH()	Hyperbolic sine of a number.
ATANH()	Inverse hyperbolic tangent of a number.
PI()	The value π (3.1415926535898).
Matrix Functions	
MDETERM()	Determinant of a matrix.
MINVERSE()	The inverse of a matrix.
MMULT()	The multiple of two matrices.
TRANSPOSE()	The matrix transpose of an array.

Basic Mathematical Functions

The basic mathematical functions perform common calculations. For example, ABS(x) returns the absolute value of x.

The CEILING(x,sig), EVEN(x), FLOOR(x,sig), INT(x), MROUND(x,sig), and ODD(x) functions convert x to an integer, each using different logic to perform the conversion. The argument *sig* is the significance, which is the value whose multiple you want to round to. Table 1.3 shows examples of the results of using these functions.

The function SIGN(x) returns the value 1.0, with the same sign as x, or 0 if x is 0. The function MOD($x1$,$x2$) returns the modulus or remainder of the quotient $x1/x2$. It is most commonly used to map a large angle ($x1>2\pi$) back onto the unit circle ($0<x1<2\pi$), as in this example:

```
MOD(2.703*PI(),2*PI())=.703π
```

The MOD function is also often used as part of a logical formula to determine when a value is an even multiple of some other value, as in this formula:

```
(MOD(X,10)=0)=TRUE for X=…,-10, 0, 10, 20,…
```

TABLE 1.3: Rounding and Truncating Numbers

x	n	CEILING (x,n)	EVEN (x)	FLOOR (x,n)	INT (x)	MROUND (x,n)	ROUND (x,n)	TRUNC (x,n)
1.5263	0	0	2	#DIV/0!	1	0	2	1
−1.5263	0	0	−2	#DIV/0!	−2	0	−2	−1
2.48554	0	0	4	#DIV/0!	2	0	2	2
2.61756	0	0	4	#DIV/0!	2	0	3	2
−2.48554	0	0	−4	#DIV/0!	−3	0	−2	−2
−2.61765	0	0	−4	#DIV/0!	−3	0	−3	−2
1.5263	2	2	2	0	1	2	1.53	1.52
−1.5263	−2	−2	−2	0	−2	−2	0	0
132.4855	2	134	134	132	132	132	132.49	132.48
642.6176	2	644	644	642	642	642	642.62	642.61
−132.486	−2	−134	−134	−132	−133	−132	−100	−100
−642.618	−2	−644	−644	−642	−643	−642	−600	−600
1.5263	0.01	1.53	2	1.52	1	1.53	2	1
−1.5263	−0.01	−1.53	−2	−1.52	−2	−1.53	−2	−1
2.48554	0.01	2.49	4	2.48	2	2.49	2	2
2.61756	0.01	2.62	4	2.61	2	2.62	3	2
−2.48554	−0.01	−2.49	−4	−2.48	−3	−2.49	−2	−2
−2.61765	−0.01	−2.62	−4	−2.61	−3	−2.62	−3	−2

The SQRT(*x*) function returns the value of the square root of *x*. SQRTPI(*x*) returns the square root of *x*π.

The functions SUM(*list*), PRODUCT(*list*), QUOTIENT(*x1,x2*), SERIESSUM(*x,n,m,coefs*), SUMPRODUCT(*matrix1,matrix2*), SUMSQ(*list*), SUMX2MY2(*matrix1,matrix2*), SUMX2PY2(*matrix1,matrix2*), and SUMXMY2(*matrix1,matrix2*) perform different summations of lists of terms. The RAND() and RANDBETWEEN(*lower,upper*) functions both return random numbers.

The function COMBIN(*n,chosen*) calculates the number of ways *chosen* objects can be selected from a pool of *n* objects. The FACT(*n*) and FACTDOUBLE(*n*) functions calculate the factorial of a number (*n!*=1*2*3*...*n*) and the double factorial of a number (*n!!*). The GCD and LCM functions calculate the greatest common divisor and the least common multiple of a list of numbers.

Logarithmic Functions

The logarithmic functions calculate the natural and common logarithms of a number. LN(x) and EXP(x) calculate the natural logarithm of x, and the exponential of x (e^x) respectively. Theoretically, the value of x in the exponential function can take on any value. However, a value of x greater than about 709 will cause numeric overflow, and the function will return the value #NUM!.

EXP(1) returns the base e of the natural logarithm (2.71828182845904). LOG10(x) returns the common logarithm (base 10) of x. LOG(x,b) returns the logarithm of x to any base b.

Trigonometric Functions

The trigonometric functions SIN(x), COS(x), and TAN(x) return the sine, cosine, and tangent, respectively, of the angle x. The angle x must be in radians, so convert an angle in degrees to one in radians by multiplying by $\pi/180$. For example, if y is in degrees, this is the formula for the sine of y:

```
SIN(Y*PI()/180)
```

Because of Excel's numeric precision, the sine or cosine of π, 2π, ..., or the cosine of $\pi/2$, $3\pi/2$, ..., are not exactly zero. Therefore, you must be careful not to write equations that depend on the results of these functions being exactly zero, as in the following:

```
SIN(PI())=1.22x10⁻¹⁶
SIN(2*PI())=-2.45x10⁻¹⁶
COS(PI()/2)=6.12x10⁻¹⁷
TAN(2*PI())=-2.45x10⁻¹⁶
```

In most cases, these values are close enough to zero. However, they can cause problems in some equations.

The trigonometric functions for calculating the secant, cosecant, and cotangent are not available in Excel. However, you can use other Excel functions to obtain the results:

- To calculate the secant of the angle x, SEC(x), use the formula

  ```
  1/COS(x)
  ```

- To calculate the cosecant of the angle x, CSC(x), use the formula

  `1/SIN(x)`

- To calculate the cotangent of the angle x, COT(x), use the formula

  `1/TAN(x)`

Inverse Trigonometric Functions

The inverse trigonometric functions ASIN(x) and ACOS(x) return the arcsine and arccosine, respectively, in radians of x. Since the arctangent is multivalued, Excel provides two different versions of that function. The first version, ATAN(x), does not have enough information to be able to determine which quadrant the result should be in, so it returns a value in the range of $-\pi/2$ to $+\pi/2$. The second version, ATAN2(x,y), has sufficient information to determine the correct quadrant, so it returns a value in the range of $-\pi$ to $+\pi$. The function PI returns the value of π (3.141592653589879).

You can calculate the inverse trigonometric functions that are not supplied with Excel as follows:

- To calculate the arcsecant of x for $x > 0$, ASEC(x), use the formula

  `ATAN(SQRT(x^2-1))`

- To calculate the arcsecant of x for $x < 0$, ASEC(x), use the formula

  `ATAN(SQRT(x^2-1))-PI()`

- To calculate the arccosecant of x for $x > 0$, ACSC(x), use the formula

  `ATAN(1/SQRT(x^2-1))`

- To calculate the arccosecant of x for $x < 0$, ACSC(x), use the formula

  `ATAN(1/SQRT(x^2-1))-PI()`

- To calculate the arccotangent of x, ACOT(x), use the formula

  `PI()/2-ATAN(x)`

Hyperbolic Functions

Excel provides the three hyperbolic functions SINH(x), COSH(x), and TANH(x). These functions calculate the hyperbolic sine, cosine, and tangent of x, respectively.

The rest of the hyperbolic functions can be calculated from the existing functions, as follows:

- To calculate the hyperbolic secant of x, SECH(x), use the formula

  `1/COSH(x)`

- To calculate the hyperbolic cosecant of x, CSCH(x), use the formula

  `1/SINH(x)`

- To calculate the hyperbolic cotangent of x, COTH(x), use the formula

  `1/TANH(x)`

Inverse Hyperbolic Functions

The inverse hyperbolic functions in Excel are ASINH, ACOSH, and ATANH. These functions calculate the inverse hyperbolic sine, cosine, and tangent, respectively. The other inverse hyperbolic functions can be calculated as follows:

- To calculate the inverse hyperbolic secant of x (dual-valued), ASECH(x), use the formula

  `LN((1±SQRT(1-x^2))/x)`

- To calculate the inverse hyperbolic cosecant of x (dual-valued), ACSCH(x), use the formula

  `LN((1±SQRT(1+x^2))/x)`

- To calculate the inverse hyperbolic cotangent of x, ACOTH(x), use the formula

  `0.5*LN((x+1)/(x-1))`

Matrix Functions

Four matrix functions are supplied with Excel: MDETERM(*matrix*), MINVERSE(*matrix*), MMULT(*matrix1,matrix2*), and TRANSPOSE(*array*). The MDETERM function calculates the determinant of a matrix. MINVERSE calculates the inverse of a matrix. MMULT calculates the matrix product of two matrices. The primary use for the matrix functions is for solving matrix equations, particularly those that result from solving systems of linear equations.

MINVERSE and MMULT are array functions; they return an array of values rather than a single value. While entering these functions, you must hold down the Ctrl and Shift keys (Cmd-Enter on the Macintosh) to insert them into an array of cells instead of just one cell, as explained earlier in the chapter.

The TRANSPOSE function performs the matrix transpose operation on its argument. That is, it exchanges the rows and columns. This function is useful for changing horizontal vectors into vertical vectors and vice versa.

Engineering Functions

Excel's engineering functions include the following types:

- Bessel functions
- Base conversion functions
- Angular conversion functions
- Error functions
- Numeric comparison functions
- Complex arithmetic functions

Complex numbers are stored as strings in the form $x + yj$, where x is the real part and y is the imaginary part.

Table 1.4 lists Excel's engineering functions.

Logical Functions

The logical functions are those that return the values True or False as their result. Table 1.5 lists Excel's logical functions.

The logical values True and False are equivalent to the numerical values 1 and 0, respectively. That is, for all values of x True $* x = x$ and False $* x = 0$. Functions that expect a logical argument will interpret all nonzero values as True and the value zero as False.

The IF(*logical*,*x*,*y*) function tests logical values, but it does not necessarily return a logical result. If the value of *logical*, which may be a logical formula, is True or

TABLE 1.4: Excel's Engineering Functions

Function	Returns
	Bessel Functions
BESSELJ()	Bessel function $J_n\,x$).
BESSELI()	Modified Bessel function $I_n\,x$).
BESSELK()	Modified Bessel function $K_n\,x$).
BESSELY()	Weber's Bessel function $Y_n\,x$).
	Base Conversion Functions
BIN2DEC()	Converts a binary number to a decimal number.
BIN2HEX()	Converts a binary number to a hexadecimal string.
BIN2OCT()	Converts a binary number to an octal string.
CONVERT()	Converts a number from one measurement system to another.
DEC2BIN()	Converts a decimal integer to a binary string.
DEC2HEX()	Converts a decimal integer to a hexadecimal string.
DEC2OCT()	Converts a decimal integer to an octal string.
HEX2BIN()	Converts a hexadecimal number to a binary string.
HEX2DEC()	Converts a hexadecimal number to a decimal number.
HEX2OCT()	Converts a hexadecimal number to an octal string.
OCT2BIN()	Converts an octal number to a binary string.
OCT2DEC()	Converts an octal number to a decimal number.
OCT2HEX()	Converts an octal number to a hexadecimal string.
	Angular Conversion Functions
DEGREES()	Converts an angle in radians to degrees.
RADIANS()	Converts an angle in degrees to radians.
	Error Functions
ERF()	Error function.
ERFC()	Complementary error function.

TABLE 1.4: Excel's Engineering Functions (continued)

Function	Returns
Numeric Comparison Functions	
DELTA()	Delta function; returns 1 if both numbers are the same or 0 if they are different.
GESTEP()	Step function; returns 1 if the number is greater than the step or 0 if the number is less than or equal to the step.
Complex Arithmetic Functions	
COMPLEX()	Converts the two coefficients into a complex number in a string "$x + yj$".
IMABS()	The absolute value of a complex number in a string.
IMAGINARY()	The imaginary coefficient y of a complex number in a string.
IMARGUMENT()	The angle, in radians, in the complex plane of a complex number in a string.
IMCONJUGATE()	The complex conjugate of a complex number in a string.
IMCOS()	The cosine of a complex number in a string.
IMDIV()	Quotient of two complex numbers in strings.
IMEXP()	Exponential of a complex number in a string.
IMLN()	Natural logarithm of a complex number in a string.
IMLOG2()	Base 2 logarithm of a complex number in a string.
IMLOG10()	Common logarithm (base 10) of a complex number in a string.
IMPOWER()	Complex number in a string raised to an integer power.
IMPRODUCT()	Product of two complex numbers stored in strings.
IMREAL()	Real coefficient of a complex number in a string.
IMSIN()	Sine of a complex number in a string.
IMSQRT()	Square root of a complex number in a string.
IMSUB()	Difference of two complex numbers stored in strings.
IMSUM()	Sum of two or more complex numbers stored in strings.

nonzero, the function returns the value x. If *logical* is False or zero, the function returns the value y.

A common use of the IF function is to watch for invalid numeric calculations (such as dividing by zero) and select an alternate calculation. When x or y are formulas,

TABLE 1.5:   Excel's Logical Functions

Function	Returns
	Logical Value Functions
TRUE()	TRUE or 1
FALSE()	FALSE or 0
	Logical Test Functions
IF()	Selects one of two values depending on a logical value.
ISBLANK()	TRUE if the argument is a reference to a blank cell.
ISERR()	TRUE if the argument is any error value but #N/A.
ISERROR()	TRUE if the argument is one of the error values (#N/A, #REF!, #DIV/0!, #NUM!, #VALUE!, #NAME?, or #NULL!).
ISEVEN()	TRUE if the argument is an even number.
ISLOGICAL()	TRUE if the argument is a logical value.
ISNA()	TRUE if the argument is the error value #N/A.
ISNONTEXT()	TRUE if the argument is not text string.
ISODD()	TRUE if the argument is an odd number.
ISREF()	TRUE if the argument is a cell reference.
ISTEXT()	TRUE if the argument is a text string.

they will be evaluated only if they are needed. For example, to calculate the value of $SIN(x)/x$ for all values of x, use the following formula:

```
IF(x=0,1,SIN(x)/x)
```

If x is equal to 0, the function returns the correct value, 1; otherwise, it calculates and returns the value of $SIN(x)/x$. If you do not use the IF function, you will get the error value #DIV/0! when x equals zero, even though $SIN(0)/0$ is equal to 1.

The other logical test functions—ISBLANK, ISERR, ISERROR, and so on—test the content of values for specific types. They return True if the value is the specified type and False if it is not.

Boolean Functions

The three Boolean functions provided by Excel are AND(*A,B*), OR(*A,B*), and NOT(*A,B*). They combine logical values according to the rules of Boolean algebra to produce a logical result. Table 1.6 lists Excel's Boolean functions.

TABLE 1.6: Excel's Boolean Functions

Function	Returns
AND()	Logical AND of logical values.
NOT()	Returns TRUE if the argument is FALSE or FALSE if the argument is TRUE.
OR()	Logical OR of logical values.

A complete set of Boolean functions should also contain the functions NAND (not-AND), NOR (not-OR), and XOR (exclusive-OR). You can create these functions by combining the three available functions, as follows:

- For the NAND function, use the formula

  `NOT(AND(A,B))=OR(NOT(A),NOT(B))`

- For the NOR function, use the formula

  `NOT(OR(A,B))=AND(NOT(A),NOT(B))`

- For the XOR function, use the formula

  `OR(AND(A,NOT(B)),AND(B,NOT(A)))`

Table 1.7 is a truth table for the six Boolean functions.

TABLE 1.7: Truth Table for Boolean Functions

A	*B*	AND(*A,B*)	OR(*A,B*)	NOT(*A*)	NAND(*A,B*)	NOR(*A,B*)	XOR(*A,B*)
T	T	T	T	F	F	F	F
T	F	F	T	F	T	F	T
F	T	F	T	T	T	F	T
F	F	F	F	T	T	T	F

String Functions

A string is an ordered sequence of text characters, such as a word or sentence. The string (or text) functions manipulate or create strings. Table 1.8 lists Excel's string functions.

The functions DOLLAR(*number,digits*) and FIXED(*number,digits,no-commas*) both round the value *number* to *digits* decimal places, and then convert it into a string of characters. If the *no-commas* argument is true, FIXED does not insert commas in the resulting string. The difference between them is that DOLLAR produces a number in currency format. As with the ROUND function, negative values of *digits* are rounded to the left of the decimal.

The function LEN(*text*) determines the length of the text string *text*. The functions MID(*text,start,number*), LEFT(*text,number*), and RIGHT(*text,number*) extract characters from within a string or from the ends. Characters are numbered with the first character as 1, the second as 2, and so on. The SUBSTITUTE(*text,old,new,num*) and REPLACE(*text,start,num,new*) functions replace substrings within a string. The SEARCH(*text1,text2,start*) and FIND(*text1,text2,start*) functions locate a substring within a string. The SEARCH function's search is not case sensitive; the FIND function's search is case sensitive.

Date and Time Functions

The date and time functions perform calculations and transformations of dates, times, and combinations of dates and times. Excel performs these calculations by converting the dates into a serial date number. A *serial date number* for a date is the number of days since January 1, 1900. All dates, whether entered by hand or returned by a formula, are stored in terms of these serial date numbers. To see the actual date that a number represents, format the cell containing it as a date.

A time is also stored as a serial date number. Excel calculates times as the fractional part of a day, with midnight being time 0, noon being time 0.5, and so on. All times are stored as this fraction. To see the time associated with a fractional time number, format the cell as a time.

Since dates and times are both expressed in days, you can combine them simply by adding them. To find the difference between any two dates and times, subtract one date-time number from the other. The result is in days and fractional days.

TABLE 1.8: Excel's String Functions

Function	Returns
Numeric-String Conversion Functions	
DOLLAR()	A number as text in currency format.
FIXED()	A number as text, rounded the specified number of digits.
T()	Converts the value to text.
TEXT()	A number as a string using a specified string format.
VALUE()	The value of a string representation of a number contained in the text.
String Manipulation Functions	
CLEAN()	Removes nonprintable characters from text.
FIND()	Locates a substring (case-sensitive).
LEFT()	Extracts characters from the left.
LEN()	The number of characters in a string.
LOWER()	Converts text to lowercase.
MID()	Extracts a substring.
PROPER()	Capitalizes the first letter of each word in a string.
REPLACE()	Replaces a substring.
RIGHT()	Extracts characters from the right.
SEARCH()	Locates a substring (not case-sensitive).
SUBSTITUTE()	Replaces multiple substrings.
TRIM()	Removes leading and trailing spaces.
UPPER()	Converts text to uppercase.
String Creation Functions	
CHAR()	The character specified by the ASCII code.
CODE()	The ASCII code of a character.
REPT()	Repeats a string.
String Comparison Function	
EXACT()	Case-sensitive string comparison.

Table 1.9 lists Excel's date and time functions. The NOW and TODAY functions return the current date and time, or the current date as a serial date number.

TABLE 1.9: Excel's Date and Time Functions

Function	Returns
	Current Date Functions
NOW()	The serial date number of the current date and time.
TODAY()	The serial date number for today's date.
	Date Functions
DATE()	Serial date number for the year, month, and day.
DATEVALUE()	Converts a date in text format to a serial date number.
DAY()	The day of the month corresponding to the serial date number.
DAYS360()	The number of days between two dates assuming a 360-day year.
EDATE()	The serial date number for the day that is the specified months before or after the specified date.
EOMONTH()	The serial date number for the last day of the month that is the specified months before or after the specified date.
MONTH()	The month of the year corresponding to the serial date number.
NETWORKDAYS()	The number of workdays between two dates.
WEEKDAY()	The day of the week corresponding to the serial date number. Sunday is 1 and Saturday is 7.
YEAR()	The year corresponding to the serial date number.
YEARFRAC()	The fraction of a year the difference between two dates represents.
	Time Functions
HOUR()	The hour of the day corresponding to the serial date number.
MINUTE()	The minute of the hour corresponding to the serial date number.
SECOND()	The second of the minute corresponding to the serial date number.
TIME()	The serial date number for the hour, minute, and second.
TIMEVALUE()	Converts a time in text format to a serial date number.

Date Functions

The function DATE(*year,month,day*) converts the specified date into a serial date number. Use this function to create a serial date-time number from the year, month, and day in number format.

The DATEVALUE(*text*) function converts the text representation of a date into a serial date number. Excel will also convert these two strings to serial date numbers when they are enclosed in quotation marks:

- *"month/day/year"*, where *month*, *day*, and *year* are numbers.
- *"day-month-year"*, where *day* and *year* are numbers and *month* is the spelled-out name or abbreviation of the name of the month.

You can use the DATEVALUE function or text string, as appropriate for your situation.

The functions YEAR(*number*), MONTH(*number*), and DAY(*number*) return the numeric value of the year, month of the year, and day of the month of the date specified by *number*. These three functions perform the inverse of the DATE function. The function WEEKDAY(*number*) returns a numeric value for the day of the week of the date specified with *number*. For this function, Sunday is 1 and Saturday is 7.

Time Functions

The time functions are similar to the date functions, except that they deal with the time of day rather than the date. The function TIME(*hour,minute,second*) returns the specified time as the decimal fraction of a day. Note that the arguments must be integers. Any fractional parts of these arguments will be ignored. Thus, the smallest time that you can manipulate with these functions is the second.

The TIMEVALUE(*text*) function converts a time stored in a string into a serial date number. You could also use either of these strings, enclosed in quotation marks:

- *"hour:minute:second"*, for 24-hour time, where *hour*, *minute*, and *second* are integers.
- *"hour:minute:second PM"*, for 12-hour time, where *hour*, *minute*, and *second* are integers.

The functions HOUR(*number*), MINUTE(*number*), and SECOND(*number*) are the inverse of the TIME function. They return the hour, minute, and second corresponding to the time stored as *number*. Excel rounds all numbers to the nearest second.

Statistical Functions

The statistical functions are generally applied to sets of numbers, and they return statistical values. The statistical values not only include sums and deviations, but also some simple linear and exponential curve fitting. Several of the functions return an array as a result. Table 1.10 lists Excel's statistical functions.

Basic Statistics

The functions AVERAGE(*numlist*), SUM(*numlist*), and COUNT(*numlist*) operate on lists of values and return the average, sum, and number of values in *numlist*, respectively. The functions MIN(*numlist*) and MAX(*numlist*) simply locate and return the minimum or maximum value in *numlist*. Cells containing blank, text, or logical values are ignored.

In addition to the average, the geometric mean is calculated with GEOMEAN(*numlist*), and the harmonic mean is calculated with HARMEAN(*numlist*). The median value in a distribution is returned by MEDIAN(*numlist*).

STDEV(*numlist*) calculates the sample standard deviation of the values in *numlist*. That is, it gives the best estimate of the standard deviation of a population, given the sample *numlist*. This value is computed using the following equation:

$$\sqrt{\frac{\sum_{i=1}^{N}\left(x_i - \overline{x}\right)^2}{N-1}}$$

where $\overline{x}$ is the average of the n values x_i.

TABLE 1.10: Excel's Statistical Functions

Function	Returns

Basic Statistics Functions

Function	Returns
AVERAGE()	The average of a list of values.
COUNT()	The number of values in a list.
COUNTA()	The number of nonblank cells in a list.
DEVSQ()	Sum of squares of the deviations of the values in a list from their mean.
GEOMEAN()	Geometric mean of the values in a list.
HARMEAN()	Harmonic mean of the numbers in a list.
MAX()	The maximum value in a list.
MEDIAN()	Middle value in a list after it is ranked from high to low.
MIN()	The minimum value in a list.
STDEV()	The standard deviation of the values in a list.
STDEVP()	The standard deviation of the values in a list, assuming it is the entire population.
SUM()	The sum of the values in a list.
VAR()	Variance of the numbers in a list.
VARP()	Variance of the numbers in a list, assuming it is the entire population.

Advanced Statistics Functions

Function	Returns
AVEDEV()	Average deviation of the points in a list from their mean.
CORREL()	Correlation coefficient between two lists.
CONFIDENCE()	Population confidence interval.
COVAR()	Covariance between two lists.
FISHER()	Fisher transformation of a number.
FISHERINV()	Inverse of the Fisher transformation of a number.
FREQUENCY()	Frequency distribution of the values in a list.
KURT()	Kurtosis of the values in a list.
LARGE()	The kth largest value in a list.
MODE()	The most common value in a list.
PEARSON()	Pearson product moment correlation coefficient of two arrays.
PERCENTILE()	Value from the kth percentile in a list.

TABLE 1.10: Excel's Statistical Functions (continued)

Function	Returns
PERCENTRANK()	Percentage rank of the number in a list.
PERMUT()	Number of permutations for objects chosen at a time from a specified number of objects.
PROB()	Probability that the values in a list are between the lower and upper numbers.
QUARTILE()	Quartile limits from a list.
RANK()	The rank of a number in a list.
SMALL()	The kth smallest value in a list.
STANDARDIZE()	Normalizes a number with the mean and standard deviation.
TRIMMEAN()	Mean of a list with specified percent points removed from the ends of the distribution.

Curve-Fitting Functions

Function	Returns
FORECAST()	Extrapolates a value with a linear fit.
GROWTH()	Extrapolates a value with an exponential fit.
INTERCEPT()	The y-intercept of the linear-regression line.
LINEST()	The slope and y-offset of a linear curve fit.
LOGEST()	The parameters of an exponential curve fit.
RSQ()	The goodness of the fit; r^2 value for a linear-regression line.
SLOPE()	Slope of a linear-regression line.
STEYX()	Standard error of the predicted y value for each x in a linear-regression line.
TREND()	A list of predicted values from a linear curve fit.

Distribution Functions

Function	Returns
BETADIST()	Cumulative beta probability density function.
BETAINV()	Inverse of the cumulative beta probability density function.
BINOMDIST()	Individual term in the binomial distribution.
CHIDIST()	One-tailed probability of the Chi-squared distribution.
CHIINV()	Inverse of the Chi-squared distribution.
EXPONDIST()	Exponential distribution.
FDIST()	F probability distribution.
FINV()	Inverse of the F probability distribution.

TABLE 1.10: Excel's Statistical Functions (continued)

Function	Returns
GAMMADIST()	Gamma distribution.
GAMMAINV()	Inverse of the gamma cumulative distribution.
GAMMALN()	Natural logarithm of the gamma function.
HYPGEOMDIST()	Hypergeometric distribution.
LOGINV()	Inverse of the lognormal distribution.
LOGNORMDIST()	Lognormal distribution.
NEGBINOMDIST()	Negative binomial distribution.
NORMDIST()	Normal cumulative distribution.
NORMINV()	Inverse of the normal cumulative distribution.
NORMSDIST()	Standard normal cumulative distribution.
NORMSINV()	Inverse of the standard normal cumulative distribution.
POISSON()	Poisson probability distribution.
SKEW()	Skewness of the distribution represented by the numbers in the list.
TDIST()	Student's T-distribution.
TINV()	Inverse of the Student's T-distribution.
WEIBULL()	Weibull distribution.

Significance Test Functions

CHITEST()	Chi-squared test for the independence of two distributions.
CRITBINOM()	Smallest value for which the cumulative binomial distribution is less than or equal to the criterion value.
FTEST()	F-test on two distributions.
TTEST()	Student's T-test for the significance of a coefficient.
ZTEST()	Z-test, two-tailed P-value.

If *numlist* is the whole population rather than a sample of the population, use STDEVP, which is computed using this equation:

$$\sqrt{\frac{\sum_{i=1}^{N}\left(x_i - \overline{x}\right)^2}{N}}$$

The variance function VAR(*numlist*) is just the square of the standard deviation. Thus, it gives the sample variance of a population. To get the population variance when *numlist* is equal to the whole population, use the VARP(*numlist*) function, which is the square root of the population standard deviation.

Advanced Statistical Functions

Excel's statistics functions include many of the more advanced functions for testing relationships between lists of numbers. For example, the CORREL(*numlist1,numlist2*) function calculates the correlation between two lists of numbers, and the COVAR(*numlist1,numlist2*) function returns the covariance.

Some of the advanced statistics functions work with ranked lists of values. For example, the LARGE(*numlist,k*) and SMALL(*numlist,k*) functions select values from the top and bottom of the list, respectively. The PERCENTRANK(*numlist,num,sig*) function gives the ranking of a new value.

Curve-Fitting Functions

Excel provides two types of curve fitting: linear and exponential. The functions, LINEST(*yarray,xarray*), TREND(*yarray,xarray,xlist*), and FORECAST(*x,yarray, xarray*) calculate a linear least-squares curve fit to the *x,y* data in *xarray* and *yarray*.

The LINEST function returns a two-element horizontal array containing the slope (*m*) and *y*-intercept (*b*) of the line: $y = mx + b$. The TREND and FORECAST functions return the estimated *y* values obtained by inserting the *x* values in *xlist* (or *xarray* if *xlist* is not supplied) into the equation of the line. The TREND function returns an array of *y* values; FORECAST returns only one value. In both functions, if *xarray* is not supplied, it is assumed to be equal to the list of values: 1, 2, 3,.... As with other functions that return arrays of values, you must hold down the Ctrl and Shift keys when entering them to place the function into a list of output cells rather than a single cell.

Exponential curve fits are calculated with the functions LOGEST(*yarray,xarray*) and GROWTH(*yarray,xarray,xlist*). These two functions operate in the same manner as the linear curve fitting functions, except that they calculate the fit to the exponential growth curve rather than to a linear curve: $y = bm^x$.

The growth curve coefficients are calculated by taking the natural logarithm of the *yarray* data, applying the LINEST function, and then taking the exponential of the results after getting the coefficients *m* and *b*:

```
EXP(LINEST(LN(yarray),xarray))
```

This formula must be inserted into two cells as an array function. It gives the same result as the GROWTH function.

However, if the range of values in *yarray* is large (with orders of magnitude between the largest and smallest values), the curve fit will be skewed. The smaller values will have more weight (be more closely fitted) than the larger values. This is because the fit is to the logarithm of the *y* data rather than to the data itself.

The least-squares method minimizes the residual error (the difference between the data and the curve fit). In this case, the formula minimizes the difference in the logarithms of the *y* data rather than the *y* data itself. Since the logarithm is a non-linear function, the residual error will be larger for larger values of the *y* data. On the other hand, the percent error will be roughly constant for all values of the *y* data.

Distribution and Significance Test Functions

Excel's distribution functions produce values for most of the common distributions used for testing the significance of values, as well as for predicting the lifetime or failure rate of products. The distributions include binomial (BINOMDIST), Chi-squared (CHIDIST), F (FDIST), gamma (GAMMADIST), hypergeometric (HYPGEOMDIST), normal (NORMSDIST), Poisson (POISSON), T (TDIST), and Weibull (WEIBULL).

Along with the distribution functions are functions for significance tests based on the Chi-squared, F, T, and Z distributions. These tests check the significance of values, the regression coefficients, and the dependence or independence of different distributions of values.

Database Functions

The calculations of the database functions are the same as those of the basic statistical functions. However, the database functions are applied to values selected from a database using selection criteria. A *database* is a rectangular area of cells on a worksheet. Each row in the database is a *record*, and each column is a *field*.

Table 1.11 lists Excel's database functions. These functions all take the same three arguments: the database name, the field name or the column number of the field to act on, and the criteria. Only records that match the criteria are processed by the database functions. Working with Excel databases will be discussed in Chapter 5.

TABLE 1.11:   Excel's Database Functions

Function	Returns
CROSSTAB()	Creates a cross-tabulation table.
DAVERAGE()	The average of the values in a field for records that match criteria.
DCOUNT()	The number of records in a database that match criteria.
DCOUNTA()	The number of records in a database that match criteria and contain values in a field, ignoring blanks.
DGET()	Extracts a single record that matches criteria.
DMAX()	The maximum of the values in a field for records that match criteria.
DMIN()	The minimum of the values in a field for records that match criteria.
DPRODUCT()	Multiplies the values in records that match criteria.
DSTDEV()	The sample standard deviation of the values in a field for records that match criteria.
DSTDEVP()	The population standard deviation of the values in a field for records that match criteria.
DSUM()	The sum of the values in a field for records that match criteria.
DVAR()	The sample variance of the values in a field for records that match criteria.
DVARP()	The population variance of the values in a field for records that match criteria.

Financial Functions

The financial functions are useful for keeping track of your investments or calculating the cost of refinancing your mortgage. Excel's financial functions are listed in Table 1.12.

TABLE 1.12: Excel's Financial Functions

Function	Returns

Annuity Functions

Function	Returns
CUMIPMT()	Cumulative interest paid between the specified starting and ending periods.
CUMPRINC()	Cumulative principal paid between the specified ending and starting periods.
FV()	Future value of an annuity.
FVSCHEDULE()	Future value of an annuity after a scheduled series of interest rates.
NPER()	Number of periods of an annuity.
PMT()	Payment of an annuity.
PPMT()	Principal paid in a specific payment.
PV()	Present value of an annuity.
RATE()	Interest rate returned of an annuity.

Investment Functions

Function	Returns
ACCRINT()	Accrued interest for a security that pays periodically.
ACCRINTM()	Accrued interest for a security that pays at maturity.
COUPDAYBS()	Days from the beginning of the coupon period to the settlement date.
COUPDAYS()	Days in the coupon period that contains the settlement date.
COUPDAYSNC()	Days from the settlement date to the next coupon date.
COUPNCD()	Next coupon date after the settlement date.
COUPNUM()	Number of coupons payable between the settlement date and maturity date.
COUPPCD()	Coupon date before the settlement date.
DISC()	Discount rate for a security.
DURATION()	Macauley duration for a security with periodic interest payments and an assumed par value of $100.
EFFECT()	Effective annual interest rate.
INTRATE()	Interest rate for a fully invested security.
MDURATION()	Modified Macauley duration for a security with an assumed par value of $100.
NOMINAL()	Nominal annual interest rate.
ODDFPRICE()	Price per $100 face value of a security with a short or long first period.
ODDFYIELD()	Yield of a security with a short or long first period.

TABLE 1.12: Excel's Financial Functions (continued)

Function	Returns
ODDLPRICE()	Price per $100 face value of a security with a short or long last period.
ODDLYIELD()	Yield of a security with a short or long last period.
PRICE()	Price per $100 face value of a security that pays periodic interest.
PRICEDISC()	Price per $100 face value of a discounted security.
PRICEMAT()	Price per $100 face value of a security that pays interest at maturity.
RECEIVED()	Amount received at maturity for a fully invested security.
TBILLEQ()	Bond-equivalent yield for a Treasury bill.
TBILLPRICE()	Price per $100 face value for a Treasury bill.
TBILLYIELD()	Yield for a Treasury bill.
YIELD()	Yield on a security that pays periodic interest.
YIELDDISC()	Annual yield for a discounted security.
YIELDMAT()	Annual yield of a security that pays interest at maturity.

Depreciation Functions

Function	Returns
DB()	Declining-balance depreciation for an asset using a fixed rate.
DDB()	Double-declining-balance depreciation for an asset.
SLN()	Straight-line depreciation for an asset.
SYD()	Sum-of-years'-digits depreciation for an asset.
VDB()	Variable-declining-balance depreciation for an asset.

Other Business Functions

Function	Returns
DOLLARDE()	Converts a dollar price expressed as a fraction into a dollar price expressed as a decimal number (for example, $1\frac{1}{8}$ to 1.125).
DOLLARFR()	Converts a dollar price expressed as a decimal number into a dollar price expressed as a fraction (for example, 1.125).
IRR()	Internal rate of return for the payments.
MIRR()	Modified internal rate of return for the payments.
NPV()	Net present value of the values.
XIRR()	Internal rate of return for cash flows on the specified dates.
XNPV()	Net present value of the cash flows on the specified dates.

You can refer to a book about accounting for more information about the calculations of the financial functions.

Information Functions

You can use the information functions in combination with the logical functions to examine the contents of a cell, to check its type, or to get its location or reference. Excel's information functions are listed in Table 1.13.

The function TYPE(*value*) returns the type of *value*: 1 for a number, 2 for text, 4 for a logical value, 16 for an error value, and 64 for an array. You can use the TYPE function to ensure that values are of the correct type before performing operations with them.

TABLE 1.13: Excel's Information Functions

Function	Returns
CELL()	Gets information about the contents, formatting, or location of a cell.
ERROR.TYPE()	An error number that corresponds to the type of error value the error is.
INFO()	Gets information about the operating environment.
N()	Converts values to numbers.
NA()	Returns the error value #N/A.
TYPE()	Gets information about the type of number stored in the value.

Lookup and Reference Functions

The lookup and reference functions allow you to manipulate or examine areas on the worksheet. These functions are listed in Table 1.14.

Table and Vector Lookup Functions

The CHOOSE(*index,value1,value2,...*) function uses the value *index* to pick a value from the list *value1,value2,...*. If *index* is 1, *value1* is returned, if *index* is 2, *value2* is returned, and so forth. If *index* is less than 1 or larger than the number of values, the function returns #VALUE!.

TABLE 1.14:   Excel's Lookup and Reference Functions

Function	Returns
CHOOSE()	Selects a value from a set of values, based on an index value.
FASTMATCH()	Searches an array for a value and returns its reference.
HLOOKUP()	Looks up a value in a horizontal array.
INDEX()	Selects a value in the specified row, column, and area.
LOOKUP()	Locates a value in an array.
MATCH()	Locates the position of a value in a vector.
VLOOKUP()	Looks up a value in a vertical array.
Reference Characteristics	
ADDRESS()	The reference as text to the cell at the intersection of a specified row and column.
AREAS()	The number of areas in a cell reference.
COLUMN()	A vector of column numbers, one for each column in a cell reference.
COLUMNS()	The number of columns in an array.
INDIRECT()	The contents of a reference to a reference.
OFFSET()	A reference that is offset from a cell.
ROW()	A vector of row numbers, one for each row in a reference.
ROWS()	The number of rows in a reference.
TYPE()	The type of a value.

The table lookup functions are HLOOKUP, VLOOKUP, and LOOKUP. Use them to search a tabular function or data table for particular values. HLOOKUP(*value,array, index*) and VLOOKUP(*value,array,index*) search the first row or column of *array* for the greatest value that is less than or equal to *value*. They then move down that column or row by *index* cells and return the value there. *Value* can be a numeric value, text string, or logical value. HLOOKUP looks from left to right, so the values in the first row of *array* must be in ascending order. VLOOKUP searches from the top down, so the values in the first column of *array* must be in ascending order as you move down the column. Ascending order is numbers first, then text, then logical false values, then logical true values.

The LOOKUP (*value,vector1,vector2*) function scans *vector1* for the largest value that is less than or equal to *value* and returns the corresponding value from *vector2*. As with VLOOKUP and HLOOKUP, the values in *vector1* must be in ascending order.

Another version of the LOOKUP function is included to make Excel compatible with Microsoft Multiplan. The LOOKUP(*value,array*) function searches the first row or column of *array* for the greatest value that is less than or equal to *value* and returns the corresponding value in the last row or column of *array*. It looks in the longest side of *array*. If *array* has more columns than rows, its first row will be searched. If *array* has more rows than columns, the first column will be searched. If the array is square, it is searched along its first column.

The MATCH(*value,vector,type*) and FASTMATCH(*value,vector,type*) functions are similar to the LOOKUP function, except that they return the index number of the looked-up value. The argument *type* determines how *value* is compared to the values in *vector* to determine a match. If *type* is 1, the largest value that is less than or equal to *value* is located. If *type* is −1, the smallest value that is greater than or equal to *value* is located. If *type* is 0, the value that is equal to *value* is located. Use 0 for *type* to search text strings for matching strings. Locate a string that contains a specific substring by using the wildcard characters * and ?. The function matches only the first occurrence of the string or substring, not any later occurrences. Use FASTMATCH instead of MATCH to search an ordered array.

One of the more useful lookup functions is INDEX(*ref,row,column*), which returns the value at the intersection of *row* and *column* of *ref*. Use it to select values in an array according to the row and column indices. If *ref* contains multiple areas, add a fourth argument *area*, to determine which area of *ref* to use. If *ref* is a simple vector, only one index is needed. The indices are all base one, so the first row is number 1, the second column is number 2, and so on. If the requested row or column number is negative, the function returns #VALUE!. If the requested number is too large, INDEX returns #N/A.

Reference Characteristics Functions

The AREAS(*ref*) function returns the number of areas in the cell reference *ref*. An area is a continuous rectangular region on the worksheet.

The functions COLUMN(*ref*), COLUMNS(*array*), ROW(*ref*), and ROWS(*array*) return information about the rows and columns in a cell reference. COLUMN returns a vector containing the column references for each column in *ref*. ROW returns a vector containing the row references for each row in *ref*. COLUMNS and ROWS return the number of columns or rows in *array*.

Macro Functions

Excel provides macro functions that are equivalent to the commands and structures in a high-level computer language. You can create custom functions as macros. Although functions implemented as macros will not operate as quickly as the built-in functions, they can perform almost any calculation. Of special interest to scientists and engineers are the scientific, engineering, and statistical macro functions, listed in Table 1.15.

TABLE 1.15: Excel's Science, Engineering, and Statistical Macro Functions

Function	Returns
ANOVA1()	Single-factor analysis of variance.
ANOVA2()	Two-factor analysis of variance with replication.
ANOVA3()	Two-factor analysis of variance without replication.
DESCR()	Descriptive statistics.
EXPON()	Forecasting with error analysis.
FOURIER()	Fourier transform.
FTESTV()	Two-sample F-test.
HISTOGRAM()	Calculates the data for a histogram chart.
MCORREL()	Calculates correlation coefficients.
MOVEAVG()	Moving average.
PTTESTM()	Two-Sample student's T-test for means.
PTTESTV()	Two-sample Student's T-test for unequal variances.
RANDOM()	Generates random numbers from selected distributions.
RANKPERC()	Table of ranking of a data set.
REGRESS()	Multiple linear regression.
SAMPLE()	Samples a data set.
TTESTM()	Two-sample Student's T-test for equal variances.
ZTESTM()	Two-sample Z-test for means and known variances.

The macro functions can only be called from a macro sheet, but you can pass the data they return to a worksheet by using user-defined macro functions. Macro programming is described in Chapter 4.

External Functions

In addition to internal functions and functions coded in macro sheets, Excel can access subroutines stored in external Dynamic Link Libraries (DLLs). It can also pass values to and from other programs by using Dynamic Data Exchange (DDE). You can create a custom function in another program and then access it from within Excel.

Use the CALL(*file,function,type,args*) function to access external functions. *File* is the DLL file name, *function* is the name of the function in the DLL file, *type* is the data type of the returned value, and *args* are the arguments to be passed to the function.

You need to know how the external function operates in order to call and use it. Generally, you must test the values you plan to pass to ensure that they are valid and of the correct type. If you use bad arguments, you may hang the program in the external library and crash your system. The advantage of external functions is that they operate much faster than functions implemented as macros.

Summary

Excel is well-equipped to handle calculations in science, engineering, mathematics, and statistics. Its numeric precision and range compare well with the other computation methods for scientific and engineering calculations.

This chapter briefly discussed the functions available in Excel. You have seen that the program includes all the standard mathematical functions available in high-level computer languages, plus many more that are usually found only in expensive engineering subroutine libraries. Refer to the *Microsoft Excel Function Reference* for more information about the functions and their arguments. If you are unsure how a function works, experiment with it on the worksheet by trying different values as arguments to see the result. Better yet, experiment with the functions even if you *do* think you know how they work, because the documentation may be wrong. As in science and engineering, the final proof is in the experiment.

For More Information

Mathematical Formulas

S. M. Selby, *CRC Standard Math Tables*, (Cleveland, OH: The Chemical Rubber Co., 1970).

Statistical Formulas

C. Lipson and N. J. Sheth, *Statistical Design and Analysis of Engineering Experiments* (New York: McGraw-Hill, 1973).

R. M. Bethea, B. S. Duran, and T. L. Boullion, *Statistical Methods for Scientists and Engineers* (New York: Marcel Dekker, 1975).

Problems

1. Cell G5, which contains a reference to cell H2, is copied to cell J7.

   a. How is the reference adjusted when cell G5 is copied to another location?

   b. How should the reference to cell H2 be written so that it will not be adjusted when it is copied?

   c. How should the reference to cell H2 be written so that the row number will be adjusted but the column letter will not?

   d. How should the reference to cell H2 be written so that the column letter will be adjusted but the row number will not?

   e. How is the reference adjusted if you move the contents of the cell instead of copying the cell?

2. With what character must a formula begin?

3. If cell G5 contains a formula with a reference to cell H2, and you copy it to cell B25, to what cell will the reference in the copy point?

4. To what cells does the cell range B4:C8 refer?

5. If A1 = True, and B1 = False, what are the results of the following formulas?

   ```
   =AND(OR(AND(A1,A1),A1),B1)
   =OR(AND(A1,A1),AND(A1,B1))
   ```

6. Write a string formula that combines the strings "My name is" and "Bill".

7. Write a formula that calculates the common logarithm (base 10) of the value in cell A7.

8. Write a formula that calculates the secant of 10 degrees.

9. Write two different formulas that both add the contents of cells B1, B2, B3, B4, and B5.

10. Cell A1 contains the string "Excel for Scientists and Engineers".

    a. Write a formula that extracts the string "Excel" from cell A1.

    b. Write a formula that extracts the string "Engineers" from cell A1.

    c. Write a formula that extracts the string "Scientists" from cell A1.

    d. Write a formula that replaces the string "Scientists" with the string "Dogs" and the string "Engineers" with the string "Horses".

Engineering Tables

T he first chapter described Excel's potential to be an exceptional engineering tool. You can learn how to put all of this power to use by starting with simple calculations. In this chapter, you will explore calculating values for analytical equations and generating engineering tables. As you develop each example, you will slowly expand your repertoire of modeling methods to use more of the power and functionality of Excel.

As scientists and engineers, we frequently must take an analytical equation, put numbers into it, and calculate the result. This task is not difficult, and calculators do it well. You don't need to resort to an expensive worksheet to calculate the value of a single equation. A hand calculator can do this long before your computer even finishes booting. If you want to use the same equation with many sets of numbers, creating a table of inputs and results from the equation, you can use a calculator, but a worksheet is designed for problems of this type, and it will do the problem faster, easier, and more accurately.

Calculating a Simple Analytical Equation

Thermal Conductivity of Silicon   The temperature dependence of the thermal conductivity of silicon for temperatures between 200 and 700 K can be described with an analytical equation:

$$K(T) = \frac{K_0}{(T - T_0)}$$

where $K_0 = 350$ W/cm, and $T_0 = 68$ K.

This is a simple equation that you can calculate quickly with your hand calculator. However, recalculating the equation for many temperatures takes a lot more time and is prone to errors. Use this example to examine the methods of calculating values for analytical equations with Excel.

You should begin with a blank worksheet. Start Excel, or if you have been experimenting, close the worksheet by selecting the Close command from the File menu or by double-clicking in the window's Control box in the upper-left corner of the worksheet window (single-click on the window's close box on the Macintosh). If there is something on the worksheet that you want to keep, save it with the Save command on the File menu before you close its window. Select the New command from the File menu, and choose Worksheet. Your screen should now look like Figure 2.1.

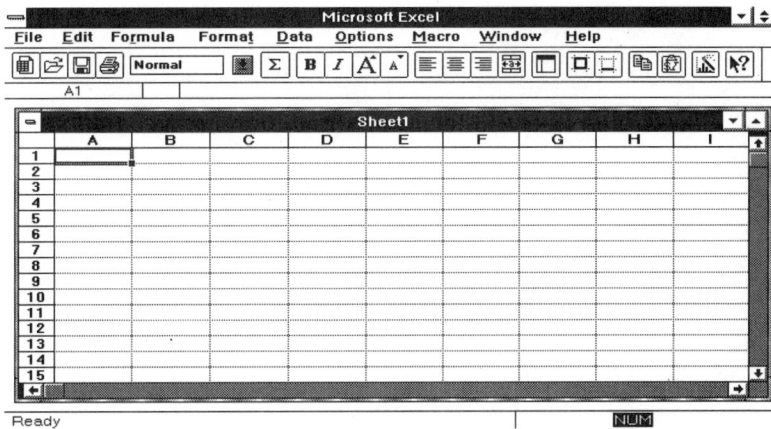

Along the top of the screen is the menu bar, and just below it is the toolbar. Each of the icons on the toolbar executes a different command, as if it were selected from a menu or dialog box. Table 2.1 shows the tools on Excel's toolbar.

To see what a tool does, place the mouse pointer on it and hold down the left mouse button. The function of the tool appears in the status bar along the bottom of the screen. If you want to execute the command, just release the mouse button. If you don't want to execute the command, drag the mouse pointer off the tool before releasing the mouse button.

Below the toolbar is the formula bar. The formula bar is where you type values and formulas into cells. Whatever you type in the formula bar is inserted in the active cell on the worksheet. While you are editing a formula in the formula bar, two buttons appear on its left side. The button with an x in it is an undo button, which returns the contents of the cell to what they were before you started editing. The second button has a check mark in it, and clicking on it accepts the changes you made and stores the contents of the formula bar in the active cell. Clicking on the check box is the same as pressing the Enter key on the keyboard.

TABLE 2.1: Excel's Standard Toolbar

Tool	Description
	New worksheet
	Open
	Save
	Print
Σ	Insert SUM() function
B	Bold text
I	Italic text
Á	Increase font size
A	Decrease font size
	Left-justify text
	Center text
	Right-justify text

TABLE 2.1: Excel's Standard Toolbar (continued)

Tool	Description
	Center text across multiple columns
	Reapply previous table format
	Outline cells
	Underline cells
	Copy
	Paste formats
	Chart Wizard
	Context-sensitive help

Calculating a Single Value

First calculate a single value: the thermal conductivity at room temperature.

1. Click on the Maximize button of the new worksheet window (in its upper-right corner) to expand it to full size.

2. Move down to cell B5 by clicking on it with the mouse or by using the down-arrow key.

3. Type **=350/(300−68)**.

4. Press Enter.

As soon as you press Enter, the number 1.508621 appears in cell B5, as shown in Figure 2.2. This is the result of letting *T* be 300 K (room temperature) in the thermal-conductivity equation. You can check it with your hand calculator (or your slide rule if you can find it).

You can insert other temperatures into this formula by selecting cell B5 and editing the value of the temperature in the formula bar. When you press Enter or click on the check mark, Excel recalculates the formula using the new value. However, this method of changing the temperature is a bit cumbersome. To make it easier to change the value, you will move the temperature from the formula to an adjacent cell and reference that cell in the formula.

5. Select cell B5.

6. Change the 300 in the formula to the cell reference **A5** and press Enter. The formula in cell B5 should now be

=350/(A5-68)

7. Select cell A5.

8. Type **300** and press Enter.

Cell B5 again has the value 1.508621 in it. Changing the temperature is now simple. Whatever temperature you type into cell A5 is inserted into the formula in cell B5, and the formula is recalculated. Using cell references instead of values in formulas

FIGURE 2.2:

Calculating the thermal-conductivity equation for a single value

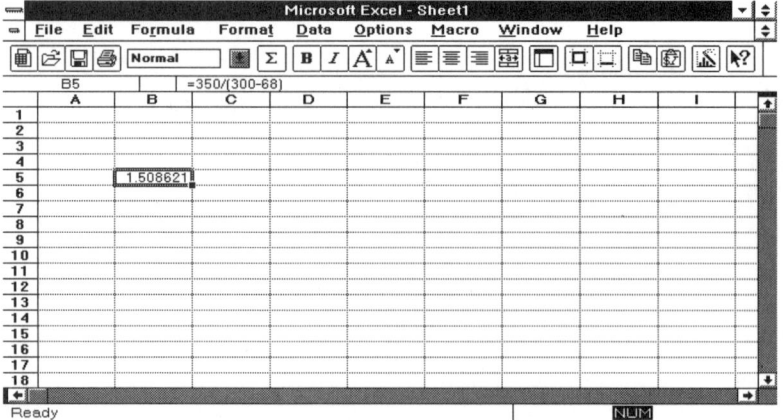

is much easier than editing the formula every time you want to change values. This formula structure is the basis for building engineering tables with Excel.

Calculating a List of Values

Suppose you want to calculate the thermal-conductivity equation for a number of different temperatures. You could enter the list of temperature values in cell A5 and then write down the results of each calculation, but working with lists of data is what a spreadsheet does best.

Now use Excel to calculate the temperatures every 50 degrees between 200 and 700 K. First you need to create the list of temperatures to be inserted in the formula.

9. Select cell A5.

10. Type **200** and press Enter.

Instead of typing in each value, highlight the range of cells and use the Series command on the Data menu to fill the cells with evenly spaced data.

11. To select cells A5 through A15, place the mouse pointer on cell A5 and hold down the left mouse button while dragging down the column. When you reach cell A15, release the mouse button.

12. Choose the Series command on the Data menu.

13. In the Series dialog box, set the step value to **50** and the series type to Linear.

14. Click on OK, or press Enter.

The cells are filled with a range of numbers from 200 to 700 in steps of 50. Now you need to copy the formula in cell B5 down into the cells adjacent to the temperature data.

15. Select cells B5 through B15 by dragging down from cell B5 and releasing the mouse button when you reach cell B15.

16. Choose the Fill Down command on the Edit menu.

Your worksheet should now look like Figure 2.3. Excel copied the formula from cell B5 down into the range of cells B5:B15 and then evaluated each formula. If you look at the contents of cells B5 through B15, you will see that the relative cell reference

FIGURE 2.3:
Calculating the thermal-
conductivity equation for a
list of data

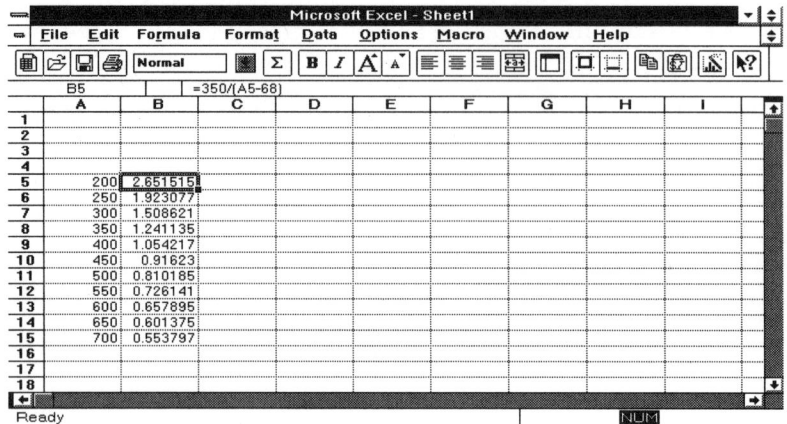

that you used for the temperature was adjusted to always point to the cell immediately to the left of the cell containing the formula.

Extracting the Coefficients

Now suppose you want to change the coefficients in the formula to see what happens to the thermal conductivity. You could change the values in cell B5 and then
copy the new formula down into the rest of the cells (copying into a cell that already
has data causes the old data to be replaced by the new data). However, this becomes
cumbersome if you want to try several different values for the coefficients. A better
way is to take the coefficients out of the formula and replace them with absolute cell
references.

17. In cell B5, type **=\$B\$2/(A5−\$B\$3)** and press Enter.

18. In cell B2, type **350** and press Enter.

19. In cell B3, type **68** and press Enter.

You made the cell references for the coefficients absolute so that you can copy the
formula down into cells B6 through B15. The cell references for the coefficients will
not be adjusted in the copies; they will still point to the coefficients in cells B2 and B3.

20. Select cells B5 through B15 and use the Fill Down command on the Edit menu to copy the contents of cell B5 into the cells below it.

The worksheet should now look like Figure 2.4. You can insert other values of K_0 and T_0 by changing the contents of cells B2 and B3. Your change is applied to all the formulas in cells B5 through B15.

FIGURE 2.4:
Calculating the thermal-conductivity equation for a list of data with modifiable coefficients

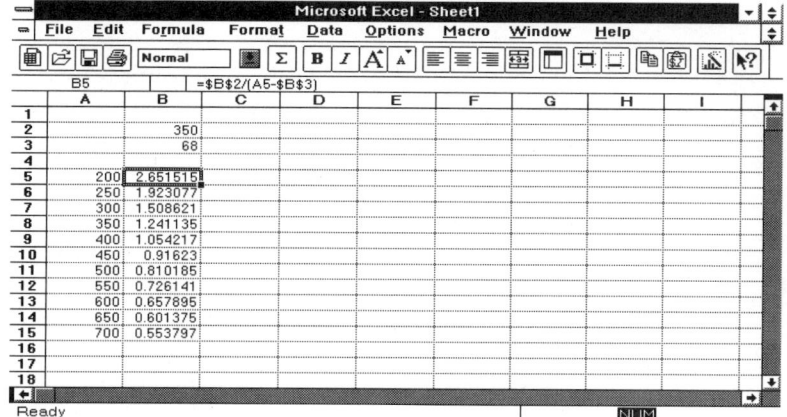

Dressing Up the Worksheet

To anyone but us, the worksheet shown in Figure 2.4 is meaningless, and even we will not know what it is all about in a month or two. You need to add some titles and labels so that anyone (including us) will know what is being calculated.

By now, you know that you must press the Enter key or one of the arrow keys to enter a value into a cell or to complete a command. The instructions will indicate the Enter keypresses only when they are not obvious.

21. In cell A1, type the title: **Thermal Conductivity of Silicon**.

22. Type **K0** in cell A2.

23. Type **T0** in cell A3.

You need to right-align the labels in cells A2 and A3. The commands for formatting cells, such as for setting the font, size, and color, are on the Format menu. Many of the more common formatting commands are also available on the toolbar (see Table 2.1).

24. Select cells A2 and A3.

25. Click on the right-alignment tool in the toolbar. Alternatively, choose the Alignment command on the Format menu, select the Right radio button in the dialog box, and then click on OK.

Put centered headings on the two columns of data.

26. Type **T (K)** in cell A4.

27. Type **K (W/cm⁻K)** in cell B4.

28. Select cells A4 and B4.

29. Click on the centered tool in the toolbar. Alternatively, choose the Alignment command on the Format menu, select Centered, and click on OK.

Notice that the label in cell B4 does not fit within the cell, and that the numbers in column B are displayed with far too many decimal places. You will widen the column of cells to make the title fit and format the numbers with fewer decimal places.

30. Move the mouse pointer to the vertical line that separates the B and C column headings. The pointer changes to a vertical line with two opposing horizontal arrows.

31. Hold down the left mouse button and drag the right edge of the column B heading until you can see the whole title, and then release the mouse button. While you are dragging the column, its width shows on the left side of the formula bar.

32. Select cells B5:B15, and then choose the Number command on the Format menu.

33. Select the numeric style 0.00 from the list box, or type it in the box at the bottom of the dialog box, and click on OK.

Next you will add some lines and remove the worksheet gridlines to make the table more readable.

34. Select cells A4 and B4.

35. Choose the Border command on the Format menu, click on the Outline button, and then click on OK.

36. Select cells A5:B15, choose the Border command, and select Outline again.

37. Select cells B4:B15, choose the Border command, and select the Left button.

38. Hide the worksheet gridlines by choosing the Display command on the Options menu, unchecking the Gridlines checkbox, and clicking on OK.

Your completed worksheet should look like Figure 2.5. All the data cells are labeled and boxed to make the meaning of the table clear to anyone who might use it. You could also have typed in the formula as a label, so that a user could see exactly what is being calculated without having to look at the contents of the cells containing the formulas. At this point, if you want to keep the worksheet, you should save it by using the Save command on the File menu.

Figure 2.6 shows the contents of all the cells in the worksheet. To see the worksheet's formulas instead of their results, choose Display from the Options menu and check the Formulas check box in the dialog box.

FIGURE 2.5:

The completed worksheet for the simple thermal-conductivity equation

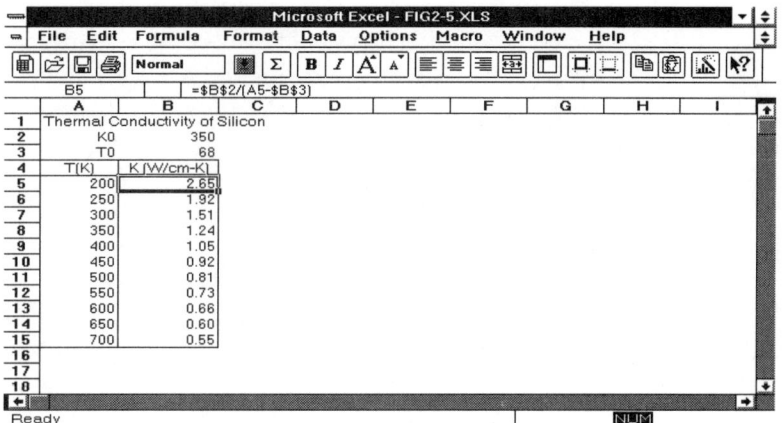

FIGURE 2.6:

The contents of the cells in the Thermal Conductivity worksheet

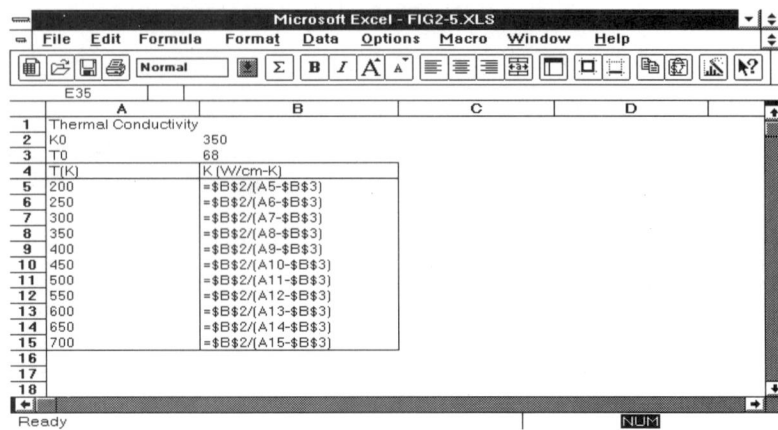

Creating Tables with Copied Formulas

In the previous section, you created an engineering table of values of the thermal conductivity of silicon. Creating tables of values like this is probably the second most common numerical task of a scientist or engineer (the first is calculating individual values of a function with a calculator). You can create tables for simple formulas or for complicated calculations.

Excel provides two ways to create tables of values: by copying the formulas or with the Table command. You used the former method for the thermal-conductivity equation, and it is probably the most versatile way to create tables of values on a worksheet. The following sections describe several engineering tables generated in this manner. Using the Table command is discussed later in this chapter.

Setting Up Single-Input Tables

Precession of the North Celestial Pole   In astronomy, two common frames of reference are used for locating the positions of celestial objects: the equatorial system and the ecliptic system. The celestial reference systems are illustrated in Figure 2.7.

The *equatorial system* is based on the orientation and rotation axis of Earth. Imagine taking a world globe with latitude and longitude lines on it, but no continents, with

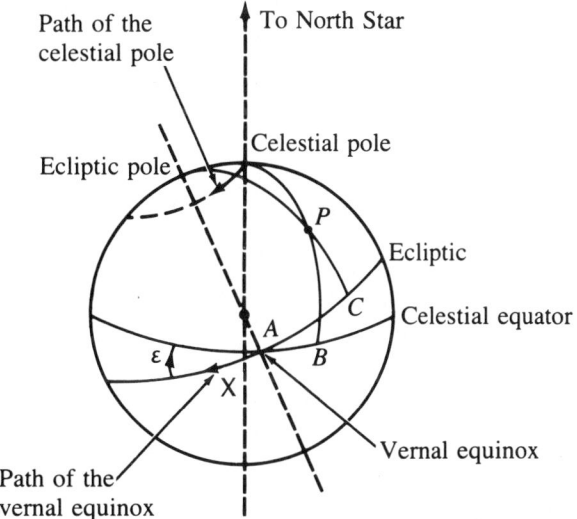

FIGURE 2.7:

Orientation of the equatorial and ecliptic coordinate systems and the motion of the equatorial system due to precession of Earth's rotational axis

the same orientation as Earth. If you expand the size of that globe to infinity, you will have the celestial sphere, overlaid with the equatorial reference system.

The plane of Earth's equator is also the plane of the reference system's equator and is known as the celestial equator. If you extend the axes of rotation of Earth through the North Pole and South Pole and out to the celestial sphere, they would form the celestial poles. The north celestial pole is near the North Star, which has been used for navigation for centuries.

Specification of the location of a star (point P in Figure 2.7) in the equatorial system is much the same as latitude and longitude on Earth's surface. Similar to latitude, the declination of a celestial object is the angular measurement of that object's position north or south of the celestial equator (the angle from B to P in Figure 2.7). The equator is 0 degrees, and the north and south celestial poles are at 90 degrees north or south declination.

The second coordinate is similar to the longitude, and it is known as the right ascension. An object's right ascension is measured in hours, minutes, and seconds from the vernal equinox (point A, in the constellation Aries, in Figure 2.7), eastward to the meridian passing through the star (the angle from A to B in Figure 2.7). The meridian is a line from the celestial equator to the celestial pole, much like a longitude line on Earth's surface.

The *ecliptic system* of measurement is similar to the equatorial system, but it is based on the plane of Earth's orbit around the sun rather than the plane of Earth's equator. If Earth's orbit is expanded to the celestial sphere, it forms a great circle known as the ecliptic. Ninety degrees above or below the ecliptic are the ecliptic poles. Measurement is in ecliptic longitude and ecliptic latitude (angles A to C and C to P, respectively, in Figure 2.7). This measurement system is also similar to latitude and longitude on Earth's surface, but it is oriented to the ecliptic rather than the equator.

The great circles that are the ecliptic and the celestial equator intersect at the vernal and autumnal equinoxes at an angle of about 23½ degrees. This is the well-known 23½-degree tilt of Earth with respect to the plane of its orbit, and it is known as the obliquity of the ecliptic.

The equatorial system is useful for Earth-based observational astronomy, and the ecliptic system is useful for sun-based celestial mechanics calculations. Both systems are equally relevant, being related by a simple 23½-degree rotation of coordinate systems. Unfortunately, nature is not so simple. The relationship between these two systems is not static but variable.

The action of the sun and the moon cause the rotation of Earth to wobble, like a spinning top when you give it a push. This wobble is known as precession, and causes the North Pole, and hence the north celestial pole, to move in a small circle with a radius of 23½ degrees about the north ecliptic pole. While the plane of the ecliptic does not change, the location of the vernal equinox, which is the origin of the right ascension and the ecliptic longitude, does.

The action of the planets causes precession in the ecliptic, which makes the ecliptic pole move as well. Now, if you are not an astronomer, you might think that these are really atrocious coordinate systems, wobbling around the universe as they do. But the period of this movement is about 26,000 years, which makes the movement tolerable. The following two equations calculate the annual change in the ecliptic longitude (X) and the value of the obliquity of the ecliptic (ε).

$$X = 50.2564'' + 0.00222''t$$
$$\varepsilon = 23^0 27' 8.26'' - 0.4684''t$$

where t is the number of years since 1900. While these changes will not cause large changes in a star's coordinates, they must be accounted for by any Earth-based observatories that are fixed to this wobbly coordinate system.

Now you will create a table of the annual change in the ecliptic longitude and the obliquity of the ecliptic, for every ten years between 1900 and 2000.

1. Start with a new worksheet, expanded to full size.

2. Change the widths of columns A through P according to the following list:

A = 3	I = 1
B = 5	J = 5.43
C = 8.43	K = 2
D = 9.57	L = 1
E = 3	M = 7
F = 3	N = 2
G = 1	O = 8.43
H = 7	P = 4.57

3. Type **Precession of the North Pole** in cell A1.

4. Type **Annual Precession** in cell C3.

5. Type **in Longitude** in cell C4.

6. Type **Obliquity of the** in cell E3.

7. Type **Ecliptic** in cell E4.

8. In cell B4, type **Date** and right-justify it.

9. Type **Annual Precession in Longitude** in cell J3.

10. Type **Obliquity of the Ecliptic** in cell J6.

11. Type **For t in years after 1900** in cell M9.

You are writing the equations as text so that anyone reading the worksheet can tell what is being calculated. However, the coefficients of the equations in the text representations are the actual values that the worksheet formulas will reference.

12. Type **X =** in cell J4.

13. Type **50.2564** in cell M4.

14. Type **" +** in cell N4.

15. Type **0.000222** in cell O4.

16. Type **″ * t** in cell P4.

Your next cell entry includes a degree symbol (°), which is part of the DOS extended character set. On most computers, you access these characters by holding down the Alt key and typing the ASCII code number (248 in this case) on the numeric keypad. Some computers require you to hold down the Shift and Alt keys while typing the code. See your DOS manual if these methods don't work, or substitute some other text for the symbol.

17. Type **e = 23°** in cell J7.

18. Type **27** in cell K7.

In cell L7, you will enter two single quotation marks. Excel uses the first one as an alignment symbol (to be compatible with Lotus 1-2-3). The second one is the abbreviation for minutes, to go with the value in cell K7.

19. Type **″** in cell L7.

20. Type **8.26** in cell M7.

21. Type **″** in cell N7.

22. Type **−0.4684** in cell O7.

23. Type **″ * t** in cell P7.

Next enter the values of the dates to be calculated. Instead of using the Series command on the Data menu, use Excel 4's shortcut for filling a cell with a series of numbers.

24. Type **1900** in cell B5.

25. Type **1910** in cell B6.

26. Select cells B5:B6.

27. Using the mouse, grab the fill handle on the lower-right corner of the selection rectangle (the rectangle surrounding the selected cells), drag it down to cell B15, and release it.

The values 1900 through 2000, in steps of 10, should now fill those cells. Excel used the arithmetic relationship you established in the first two cells to fill the rest of the range.

Now enter the formula for the annual precession in longitude.

28. In cell C5, type the following formula:

=$M$4+$O$4*(B5−1900).

29. Type " in cell D5.

Your next entries are the formula for the obliquity of the ecliptic. The value of the number of degrees does not change over this short amount of time, so type in the value.

30. Type **23°** in cell E5.

The number of minutes will change, so you need to calculate the number of seconds, divide it by 60, and take the integer part to get the number of minutes.

31. In cell F5, type this formula:

=($K$7)+INT(($M$7+$O$7*(B5−1900)/60)

32. In cell G5, type " (two single quotation marks).

Now calculate the number of seconds and then use the MOD function to map the total number of seconds back onto the range 0 to 60, since seconds in excess of 60 have already been carried over into the minutes column.

33. In cell H5, type this formula:

=MOD($M$7+$O$7*(B5−1900)+60,60)

34. Type " in cell I5.

You need to copy all these cells down into the rest of the table. Excel 4 provides a shortcut for filling a range. Instead of selecting B5:I15 and using the Fill Down command on the Edit menu, you can select the top row of the range and use the fill handle to fill the rest.

35. Select cells B5:I5.

36. Grab the fill handle in the lower-right corner of the selection, drag it down to cell I15, and release it. The formulas and values are copied down into the rest of the table.

Now you can format your worksheet. Give the cells a numeric format with four decimal places, add boxes around the tables, and turn off the gridlines.

37. Select cells H5:H15, choose the Number command on the Format menu, and type the format **0.0000** into the box at the bottom of the Number Format dialog box. Then click on OK.

38. Change the format of cells C5:C15 to 0.0000.

39. Select cells C5:I15 and click on the outline tool on the toolbar this time to outline the cells.

40. Select cells B3:B15 and outline them.

41. Select cells B3:I4 and outline them.

42. Select cells J3:P9 and outline them.

43. Choose the Display command on the Options menu, uncheck the Gridlines check box in the dialog box, and click on OK.

44. Use the Save command on the File menu to save the worksheet.

Your worksheet should now look like Figure 2.8.

FIGURE 2.8:

The tables for annual precession of the celestial longitude and the obliquity of the ecliptic between the years 1900 and 2000

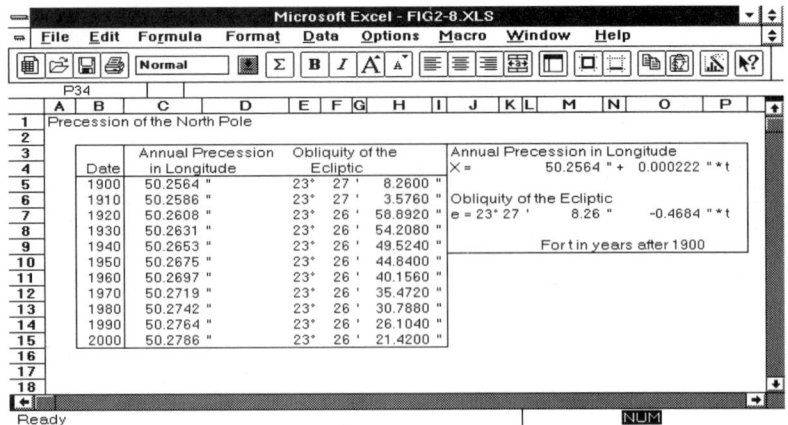

Temperature Dependence of the Intrinsic Carrier Density   The intrinsic carrier density of silicon is the density of electrons or holes in intrinsic silicon at equilibrium. It is an important parameter for the modeling of silicon solid-state devices. Intrinsic silicon is defined as silicon where the electron density equals the hole density at equilibrium. This situation is satisfied in extremely pure silicon at room temperature, or in less pure silicon at higher temperatures. Holes are places in the electronic structure of silicon where an electron could be but is not. A hole can be treated as if it were an electron with a positive charge.

The intrinsic carrier density (n_i) is defined with the following equation:

$$n_i = \left(4M_c \left(\frac{2\pi m_0 k}{h^2} \right)^3 \right)^{1/2} \left(\frac{m_e^* m_h^*}{m_0} \right)^{3/4} T^{3/2} e^{-E_g/2kT}$$

The coefficients have the following values:

M_C	6	The number of equivalent electron valleys in silicon
m_0	0.91095×10^{-30} kg	Electron rest mass
k	1.38066×10^{-23} J/kg	Boltzmann's constant
h	6.62618×10^{-34} J-s	Planck's constant
m_e^*	$0.33\ m_0$	Electron effective mass
m_h^*	$0.56\ m_0$	Hole effective mass

E_g is the value of the energy gap in silicon. The following equation has been fitted to the experimental data for the energy gap versus temperature:

$$E_g = \left(EG0 - \frac{EG1 \cdot T^2}{T + EG2} \right) q$$

where $EG0$ is 1.17 eV, $EG1$ is 4.73×10^{-4} eV/K, $EG2$ is 636 K, and q is 1.60219×10^{-19} coulombs (the electron charge).

You could algebraically insert the equation for the energy gap into the equation for the intrinsic carrier density. This insertion would give you a single complicated equation for the intrinsic carrier density. However, it is simpler, and just as valid, to calculate the value of the energy gap separately and then insert that value into the equation for the intrinsic carrier density.

The intrinsic carrier density equation has numerous constants that precede the temperature coefficients. Calculating these constants every time you use the equation is a needless waste of computational effort, which will slow down the worksheet calculation. To make the worksheet more efficient, combine all the constants into a single value, and then reference that value whenever you write a formula for the equation. You should also name the constants to make the formulas more readable.

You will now create a table for calculating the intrinsic carrier density of silicon.

1. Start with a new worksheet expanded to full size.

2. Type **Intrinsic Carrier Density in Silicon** in cell A1.

3. Type **EG0 =** in cell A3.

4. Type **EG1 =** in cell A4.

5. Type **EG2 =** in cell A5.

6. Type **cons =** in cell A7.

7. Type **1.17** in cell B3.

8. Type **4.73E-4** in cell B4.

9. Type **636** in cell B5.

Now calculate the coefficient of the intrinsic carrier density equation and change the units from $1/(m^3\text{-}K)$ to $1/(cm^3\text{-}K)$.

10. In cell B7, type the following formula:

$$\text{=SQRT}(4*6*(2*\text{PI}()*0.91095\text{E-30}*1.38066\text{E-23}/(6.62618\text{E-34})^\wedge2)^\wedge3)*$$
$$(0.33*0.56)^\wedge(.75)*1.0\text{E-6}$$

At this point, you could calculate this formula, and then replace the formula with its result so that the cell contains that value. To replace a formula with its value, select the entire formula in the formula bar and press Ctrl-= (Cmd-= on the Macintosh). When you click on the check mark or press Enter, your formula will be replaced with the value. If you click on the x box instead, the formula will be restored. You can also replace part of a formula by selecting just that portion in the formula bar and pressing Ctrl-=. You can use this technique when you need to see the current value, not the formula, or when you are debugging your worksheet.

Next name the cells so that you can use the names in the formulas. You can use the Create Names or Define Name command on the Formula menu to name cells. The Create Names command uses the entries in adjacent cells to name a group of cells. The Define Name command names single cells or ranges. The Define Name command also allows you to name a value. For example, if you type the name ONE, insert the value 1, and click on Add, you will have defined the name ONE as the number 1. Then when you use that name in a formula, Excel inserts the value you defined for it before calculating the formula.

11. Select cells A3:B7 and choose the Create Names command on the Formula menu.

12. In the Create Names dialog box, make sure the Left Column check box is checked, and then click on OK.

The selected cells in column B now have the names of the entries in the left column (column A), but without the equal signs. You can see which names have been assigned to different cells on a worksheet in the Define Name dialog box (choose the Define Name command on the Formula menu). If you select a name, you will see its definition in the dialog box. To see the name of a specific cell, select it, and its name (if one has been assigned) appears on the left side of formula bar.

In the Define Name dialog box, you would see that cells B4 and B5 are named EG1_ and EG2_ instead of EG1 and EG2. Excel added the underscore because EG1 is a valid cell reference (column EG, row 1), and cannot be used as a name. If you use names such as A1 and C7 for variables in algebraic equations, they must also include underscores or some other symbol so they won't be cell references. If you don't like the underscore, you can rename the cells.

Your next steps are to enter the titles for the table.

13. Type **T (K)** in cell D3.

14. Center the contents of cell D3.

15. Type **Eg (eV)** in cell E3.

16. Type **ni (cm^−3)** in cell F3.

Now you will enter the range of temperatures to use in the formulas.

17. Type **300** in cell D4.

18. Type **350** in cell D5.

19. Select cells D4:D5, grab the fill handle in the lower-right corner of the selection, drag it down to cell D14, and release it.

Next enter the energy-gap equation. When you are typing a formula that includes a name, you can either type the name or use the Paste Name command on the Formula menu to insert the name.

20. In cell E4, type the following formula:

   =EG0−EG1_*D4^2/(D4+EG2_)

Now you need to type the formula for the intrinsic carrier density, using the values of the temperature and the energy gap.

21. In cell F4, type the following formula:

   =cons*(SQRT(D4)^3)*EXP(−E4*1.60219E-19/(2*1.38066E-23*D4))

Your final tasks are to copy the formulas down into the rest of the table, format the numeric results, and draw some boxes to make the table more readable.

22. Select cells E4:F4.

23. Grab the fill handle in the lower-right corner of the selection, drag it down to cell F14, and release it.

24. Select cells E4:E14 and format them in the 0.00 numeric style.

25. Select cells F4:F14 and format them in the 0.00E+00 numeric style. You can select the format from the Scientific format category, or type it in the box at the bottom of the Number Format dialog box.

26. Choose the Display command on the Options menu and turn off the worksheet gridlines (uncheck the Gridlines check box in the dialog box).

27. Save the worksheet.

Your completed worksheet should look like Figure 2.9.

FIGURE 2.9:

The Intrinsic Carrier Density in Silicon engineering table

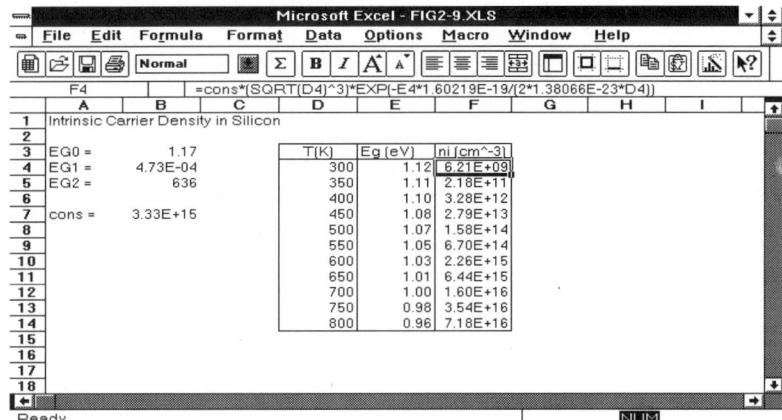

Hyperbolic Functions   As explained in Chapter 1, you can calculate the hyperbolic functions that Excel does not provide with equations that use the available hyperbolic and logarithmic functions. In the following example, use those equations to calculate the values of the hyperbolic functions for several different arguments. You will also calculate the inverse hyperbolic functions to see if they return the original argument.

The arc hyperbolic secant and arc hyperbolic cosecant are both double-valued, so you need to calculate both values for these functions.

1. Start with a new worksheet expanded to full size.

2. In cell A1, type **Hyperbolic Functions**.

3. In cell A2, type **x**.

4. In cell B2, type **Sech(x)**.

5. In cell C2, type **ASech+**.

6. In cell D2, type **ASech−**.

7. In cell E2, type **Csch(x)**.

8. In cell F2, type **ACsch+**.

9. In cell G2, type **ACsch−**.

10. In cell H2, type **Ctanh(x)**.

11. In cell I2, type **ACtanh**.

12. In cells A3:A17, type in values as follows:

   A3: **−5**   A11: 0.1
   A4: **−4**   A12: **0.5**
   A5: **−3**   A13: **1**
   A6: **−2**   A14: 2
   A7: **−1**   A15: **3**
   A8: **−0.5**   A16: 4
   A9: **−0.1**   A17: 5
   A10: **0**

13. Select cells A3:A17 and name them x with the Define Name command on the Formula menu.

14. In cell B3, type

   =1/COSH(x)

15. In cell C3, type

   =LN((1+SQRT(1−B3^2))/B3)

16. In cell D3, type

   =LN((1−SQRT(1−B3^2))/B3)

17. In cell E3, type

   =1/SINH(x)

18. In cell F3, type

   =LN((1+SQRT(1+E3^2))/E3)

19. In cell G3, type

   =LN((1−SQRT(1+E3^2))/E3)

20. In cell H3, type

   =1/TANH(x)

21. In cell I3, type

    =0.5*LN((H3+1)/(H3−1))

22. Select cells B3:I3, grab the fill handle, and drag it down to cell I17 to copy the formulas into the rest of the table.

23. Outline cells A2:I2.

24. Outline cells A3:I17.

25. Turn off the gridlines with the Display command on the Options menu.

26. Save the worksheet.

Your worksheet should now look like Figure 2.10. Note that even though cells A3:A17 are all named x, the formulas that use x always get the value from the cell that is in the same row as the formula.

You will notice that many cells contain error values, which result from the functions that are undefined. The CSCH and CTANH functions have poles at 0, which means that their values go to ±infinity, making the function undefined. The ACSCH and ACTANH functions depend on the values of CSCH and CTANH, so they show the error values as well. The ACSCH function is also double-branched, with one formula that is valid only for negative arguments and one that is valid only for positive values.

FIGURE 2.10:

The table for calculating hyperbolic and inverse hyperbolic functions

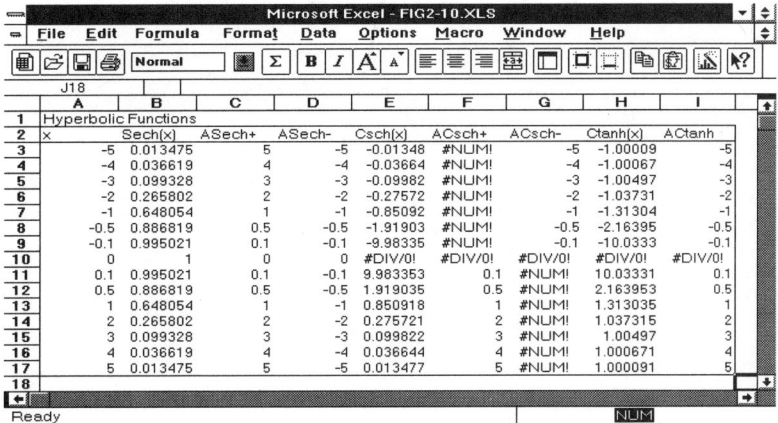

The inverse hyperbolic functions give the original arguments back. Be sure to use the correct formula for the dual-valued functions, or they may return the negative of the original argument.

Creating Two-Input Tables

The previous examples all have one independent variable (the input) and one or more dependent variables (the output, or result of the equation). However, some equations require two or more input variables, which must be handled separately. You can handle equations with two input variables in either of two ways:

- Put the input variables in parallel columns.

- Use a square array with one variable in a column on the left side and the other in a row along the top.

In the next two examples, you will examine both methods.

Van der Waals Equation of State　The ideal gas law shows the relationship between pressure (p), volume (V), and temperature (T) of an ideal gas. The law is expressed as $pV = \mu RT$, where μ is the number of moles of gas and R is the universal gas constant. To develop this equation, the volume of the individual gas molecules and the range of the intermolecular forces were ignored. The equation works well for low-density gases, but it becomes less and less accurate as the gas density increases. In a real gas, molecules have a definite volume, and the intermolecular forces are not localized to the volume of the molecules.

In an attempt to better model the behavior of a real gas, J. D. van der Waals modified the ideal gas law to account for these facts. His modified equation of state takes the following form:

$$\left(p + \frac{a}{v^2}\right)(v - b) = RT$$

where v is the volume per mole (V/μ), and a and b are constants, derived from experiments. For carbon dioxide gas, the constants have these values:

a	3.59 l^2-atm/mole^2
b	0.0427 l/mole

This equation has three variables, any one of which could be solved in terms of the other two. In the following example, you will calculate the pressure for different values of the volume and temperature.

1. Start with a new worksheet expanded to full size.

2. In cell A1, type **Van der Waals Equation of State**.

3. Type **a =** in cell A3.

4. Type **3.59** in cell B3.

5. Type **l^2atm/mole^2** in cell C3.

6. Type **b=** in cell A4.

7. Type **0.0427** in cell B4.

8. Type **l/mole** in cell C4.

9. Select cells A3:B4 and choose the Create Names command on the Formula menu.

10. In the Create Names dialog box, make sure the Left Column check box is checked, and then click on OK.

11. Type **T (K)** in cell A6.

12. Type **v (l/mole)** in cell B6.

13. Type **P (atm)** in cell C6.

14. Type **264** in cell A7.

15. Using the Fill Down command or the fill handle, copy the contents of cell A7 into cells A8:A14.

16. Type **0.05** in cell B7.

17. Type **0.1** in cell B8.

18. Select cells B7:B8, grab the fill handle, drag it down to B14, and release it.

Now enter the van der Waals equation, solved for the pressure. You will convert the universal gas constant from J/mole-K to l-atm/mole-K with the factor 101.3.

19. In cell C7, type the following equation:

$$=(8.3143/101.3)*A7/(B7-b)- a/(B7\text{^}2)$$

20. Copy the contents of cell C7 into cells C8:C14.

21. Type **304** in cell A15.

22. Copy the contents of cell A15 into cells A16:A22.

Next you want to copy the data series in column B and the formulas in column C down into the range B15:C22. Use the shortcut for the Copy and Paste commands on the Edit menu, which is to select the cells, hold down the Ctrl key (Cmd key on the Macintosh), and drag the selection by its edge to where the copy is to appear. (Dragging a selection without holding down the Ctrl key moves the selection.)

23. Select cells B7:C14.

24. Place the mouse pointer on the edge of the selection, hold down the Ctrl key, press the left mouse button, and drag the selection by its edge down into the range B15:C22.

25. Type **344** in cell A23.

26. Copy the value in cell A23 into cells A24:A30.

27. Copy cells B15:C22 into cells B23:C30.

28. Outline the following cell ranges: A7:C7, A6:A30, B6:B30, and C6:C30.

29. Select cells A14:C14 and choose the Border command on the Format menu. Select Bottom and click on OK to underline the range.

30. Underline the range A22:C22.

31. Change the numeric format of cells B7:B30 to 0.00.

32. Change the numeric format of cells C7:C30 to 0.0.

33. Turn off the worksheet gridlines.

34. Save the worksheet.

Your worksheet should now look like Figure 2.11. The table works well for this number of values for the different variables, but it could get quite long and difficult to understand if you input many values. A more efficient way to set up two-input

FIGURE 2.11:

The table for van der Waals equation of state

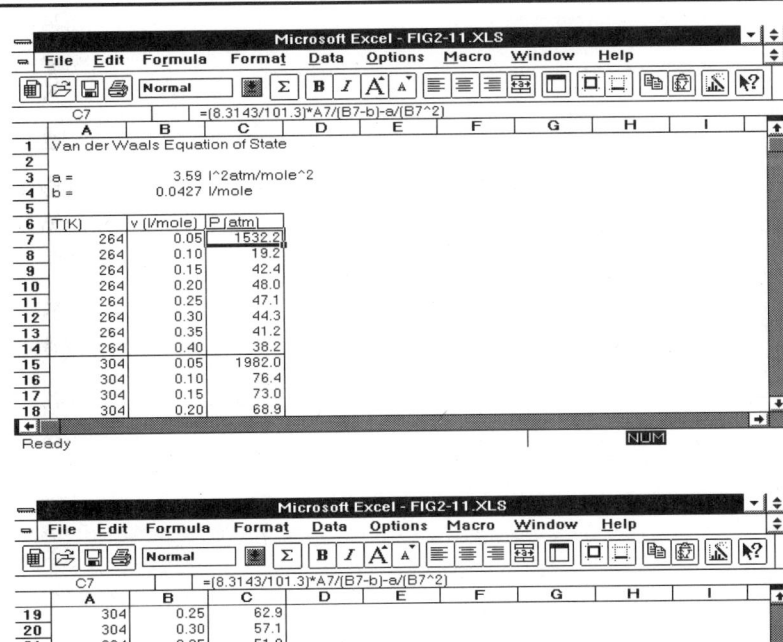

tables is to have one variable in a column and the second variable in a row, as demonstrated in the next example.

Absolute Magnitude of a Star   In astronomy, the apparent brightness of a star is measured in magnitudes. This system of measurement was first used by Hipparchus, an early Middle Eastern astronomer. He called the brightest stars in the sky first magnitude and the dimmest visible ones sixth magnitude. Differences in magnitude were based on a person's ability to discern a difference in brightness between two stars. That is, if you could just barely discern a difference in brightness between two stars, they differed by one magnitude. Since that time, the magnitude scale has been formalized, mathematically, for more precise measurement of a star's brightness. Currently, a difference in magnitude of 5 is equal to a measured 100 times increase in brightness. This leads to a simple formula for the relative magnitude of any two stars based on their measurable difference in brightness:

$$(m_2 - m_1) = \frac{1}{0.4} \text{Log}\left(\frac{b_1}{b_2}\right)$$

where m_1 and m_2 are the magnitudes of the two stars and b_1 and b_2 are the brightnesses of the two stars. With at least one star as a standard, the magnitude of any other star can be calculated from its brightness relative to the standard.

The magnitude of objects visible from Earth range from −26.7 for the sun to +23 for the dimmest object discernible in the 200-inch Hale telescope, or possibly dimmer for some of the new multiple-mirror telescopes. Two of the brightest stars are Sirius at a magnitude of −1.58 and Vega with a magnitude of +0.14. After astronomers agreed on a zero point for the magnitude system, they found that some stars were brighter. This is why the magnitudes of the sun and some of the brighter stars are negative.

The brightness of a star as we see it from Earth's surface is its apparent magnitude, which is dependent on the actual brightness of a star and the distance of the star from Earth. Apparent magnitude does not tell us a lot about a star's characteristics, nor does it allow us to make meaningful comparisons between stars. To remedy this, astronomers have defined the absolute magnitude as the magnitude that a star would have if it were 10 parsecs (192 trillion miles) from Earth. Using absolute magnitudes, the brightness of different stars can be compared. The relationship between apparent magnitude and absolute magnitude is expressed as $M = m + 5 - 5\text{Log}(r)$, where, M is the absolute magnitude, m is the apparent magnitude, and r is the distance to the star in parsecs.

In 1913, Hertzsprung in Germany and Russell in the United States compared the absolute magnitude with the spectral class (essentially the color) of stars and came up with a nearly linear relationship. The now classic Hertzsprung-Russell diagram allows astronomers to determine the absolute magnitude of a star from its spectral class (color). Knowing the absolute magnitude and the apparent magnitude, you can use the equation above to calculate the distance to a star.

In the following example, you will create a table of distances, based on the absolute and relative magnitudes of a star. First, solve the following equation for the distance:

$$r = 10^{\left(\frac{5+m-M}{5}\right)}$$

Now you will create a two-input table with apparent magnitude on the left, absolute magnitude on the top, and distance in the body.

1. Start with a new worksheet expanded to full screen.

2. Set the width of column A to 9 and column B to 3.

3. In cell A1, type **Distance to a star based on its absolute and apparent magnitudes**.

4. In cell B2, type **Distance in parsecs (1 parsec = 3.26 lightyears)**.

5. In cell G3, type **Absolute Magnitude**.

6. In cell A9, type **Apparent**.

7. In cell A10, type **Magnitude**.

8. Type **−5** in cell C4 and **−3** in cell D4. Select cells C4 and D4, and drag the fill handle to M4 to fill C4:M4 with the set of integers from −5 to 15 in steps of 2.

9. Type **−5** in cell B5 and **−3** in cell B6. Select cells B5 and B6, and drag the fill handle to B18 to fill B5:B18 with the set of integers from −5 to 21 in steps of 2.

10. In cell C5, type the following formula

    =10^((5+$B5−C$4)/5)

You are using mixed cell references to keep the arguments pointing to the correct row or column when the cells are copied into the rectangular body of the table.

11. Select cell C5 and drag the fill handle to cell C18. Select the fill handle again and drag it to M18 to fill cells C5:M18 with the formula in C5.

12. With C5:M18 still selected, outline those cells. Then change their format to 0.0E+0.

13. Outline ranges B4:B18, B4:M4, and C5:M18.

14. Turn off the worksheet gridlines.

15. Save the worksheet.

Your worksheet should now look like Figure 2.12.

FIGURE 2.12:

The table for calculating distance to a star based on its absolute and relative magnitudes

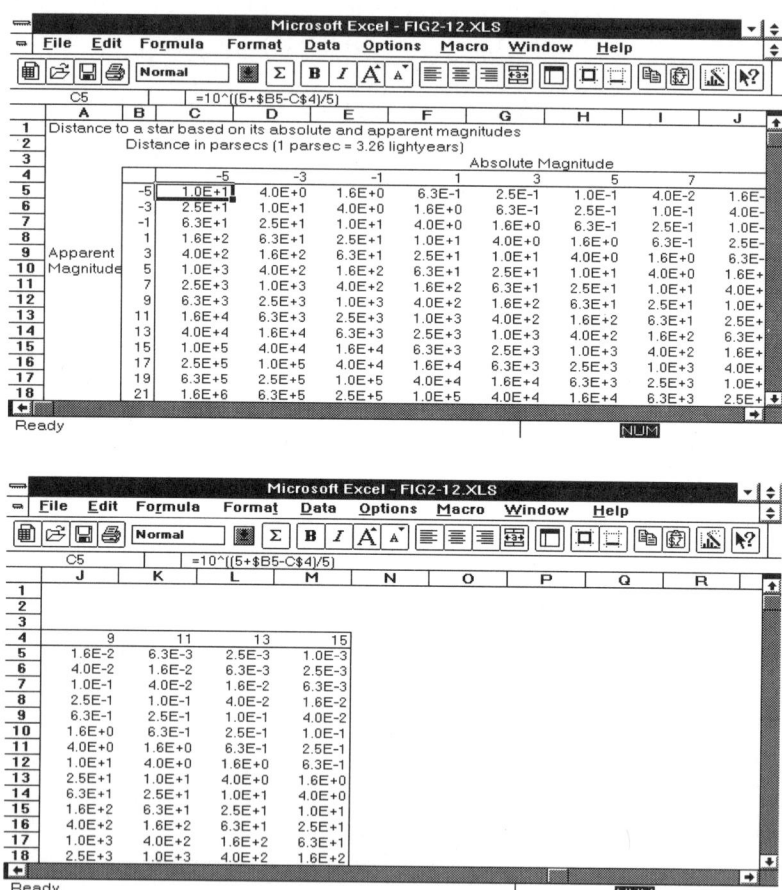

Creating Multiple-Input, Multiple-Column Tables

Many functions have more than one or two input values. You cannot create tables of these functions in the simple rectangular format used in the previous example. Instead, you can put a different variable in alternate columns, with the function in the last column, as for the van der Waals equation (Figure 2.11). Another way to handle multiple input is to place one of the variables in a row and the others in alternate columns, which would tend to compact the table somewhat. How you set up a particular table depends on what you are calculating and how you want to view the results.

Electron Mobility in Silicon   The next example calculates the electron mobility in silicon versus electric field, doping density, and temperature. The formula requires three input values to get the one output value. You will set up the table as three columns of independent variables, two columns of intermediate values, and one column for the calculated mobility value.

The mobility equation was developed for use in a large-scale computer model that calculates the effects of high-power electrical transients in semiconductor devices. It consists of curve fits of mobility versus electric field, doping density, and temperature. It is expressed as follows:

$$\mu_0 = \frac{\mu_{max} - \mu_{min}}{1 + \left(N/N_r\right)^\alpha} + \mu_{min}$$

$$E_c = \frac{2.319V_m}{\left(1 + 0.8\exp\left(T/600\right)\right)\mu_0\left(T/T_0\right)^\delta}$$

$$\mu = \frac{\mu_0\left(T/T_0\right)^{-\delta}}{\left(1 + \left(E/E_c\right)^\beta\right)^{1/\beta}}$$

The coefficients have the following values:

μ_{max}	$0.1330 \ \text{m}^2/\text{V-s}$
μ_{min}	$0.0065 \ \text{m}^2/\text{V-s}$
N_r	$8.5 \times 10^{22} \ \text{m}^{-3}$

V_m	$1.1\text{x}10^5$ m/s	
α	0.72	
β	2	
δ	2.42	
T_0	300 K	

where N is the net positive doping density (that is, the donor density minus acceptor density) in inverse cubic meters, T is the temperature in Kelvin, E is the electric field in volts per meter, and μ is the electron mobility in meters squared per volt-second.

The formula is in three parts, which you could combine into a single formula. However, it is much simpler to assemble the table in columns and then calculate each part of the formula in a separate column.

1. Start with a new worksheet expanded to full size.

2. Select columns A through F by placing the mouse pointer in the column heading of column A and clicking and dragging to column F. Select one of the lines between two column headings and adjust the column width to 10 characters wide. All the selected columns will be adjusted to the same width.

3. In cell A1, type **Electron Mobility in Silicon**.

4. Type the following entries in the specified cells. The μ is part of the extended character set and is created by holding down the Alt key while typing 230 on the keypad. Some computers require that you hold down the Shift key as well as Alt.

		C2: **Nr**
A3: μ**max**	B3: **0.133**	C3: **Vm**
A4: μ**min**	B4: **0.0065**	C4: **T0**
A6: **Doping**	B6: **Temp.**	C6: **Electric**
A7: **Density**		C7: **Field**
A8: **(m^−3)**	B8: **(K)**	C8: **(V/m)**
D2: **8.5e22**	E2: **alpha**	F2: **0.72**
D3: **1.1E5**	E3: **beta**	F3: **2**
D4: **300**	E4: **delta**	F4: **2.42**

D6: $\mu 0$	E6: **Ec**	F6: μ
D8: **(m^2/V-s)**	E8: **(V/m)**	F8: **(m^2/V-s)**

5. Select and right-align the contents of the ranges A3:A4, C2:C4, and E2:E4.

6. Select and center the contents of the cells in A6:F8.

7. Select cell B4, choose the Define Name command on the Formula menu, and name this cell as **umin**.

8. Select cell B3 and name this cell as **umax**.

9. Select C2:D4, choose the Create Names command on the Formula menu, click on Left Column, and then click on OK.

10. Select E2:F4 and use the Create Names command to name the cells with the labels in the left column.

Now that the table is set up, you can put some data in the range.

11. In cell A9, type **1.0e19**, and then copy it into A10:A16.

12. In cell B9, type **300**, and then copy it into B10:B12.

13. In cell B13, type **600**, and then copy it into B14:B16.

14. Type **1e4** in cell C9, **1e5** in cell C10, **1e6** in cell C11, and **1e7** in cell C12.

15. Copy cells C9:C12 into cells C13:C16.

16. In cell D9 type the following equation:

    =(umax−umin)/(1+(A9/Nr)^alpha)+umin

    Then copy it into D10:D16.

17. In cell E9, type the following equation:

    =2.319*Vm/((1+0.8*EXP(B9/600))*D9*(B9/T0)^delta)

    Then copy it into E10:E16.

18. In cell F9, type the following equation:

    =(D9*(B9/T0)^delta)/((1+(C9/E9)^beta)^(1/beta)

    Then copy it into F10:F16.

19. Format cells C9:C16 as 0E+00.

20. Format cells D9:F16 as 0.000E+00.

21. Copy cells F9:F16 to cells A17:F24.

22. In cell A17, type **1.0e21** and copy it into A18:A24.

23. Outline the following ranges:

A3:B4	C6:C8	B9:B24
C2:D4	D6:D8	C9:C24
E2:F4	E6:E8	D9:D24
A6:A8	F6:F8	E9:E24
B6:B8	A9:A24	F9:F24

24. Turn off the worksheet gridlines.

Now split the screen horizontally and lock the titles so that you can better view the table. To split the screen, you can use the split handle, which is the black bar just above the up arrow at the top of the vertical scroll bar.

25. Grab the split handle, drag down between rows 8 and 9, and release the handle.

26. Lock the area above the scroll bar by choosing the Freeze Panes command on the Window menu.

27. Save the worksheet.

Your worksheet should now look like Figure 2.13. Because you split the screen and locked the titles, you can click above or below the thumb on the scroll bar to switch between the two blocks of the table. You could add more blocks for different doping densities, and they will also scroll under the labels fixed at the top. To remove the split, use the Remove Split or Unfreeze Panes command on the Window menu, and then drag the split handle off the top or the bottom of the screen.

Using the Table Command to Create Tables

Excel's Table command on the Data menu allows you to produce single- and two-input tables from a single copy of a formula, instead of copying the formula into

FIGURE 2.13:

The table for calculating electron mobility in silicon

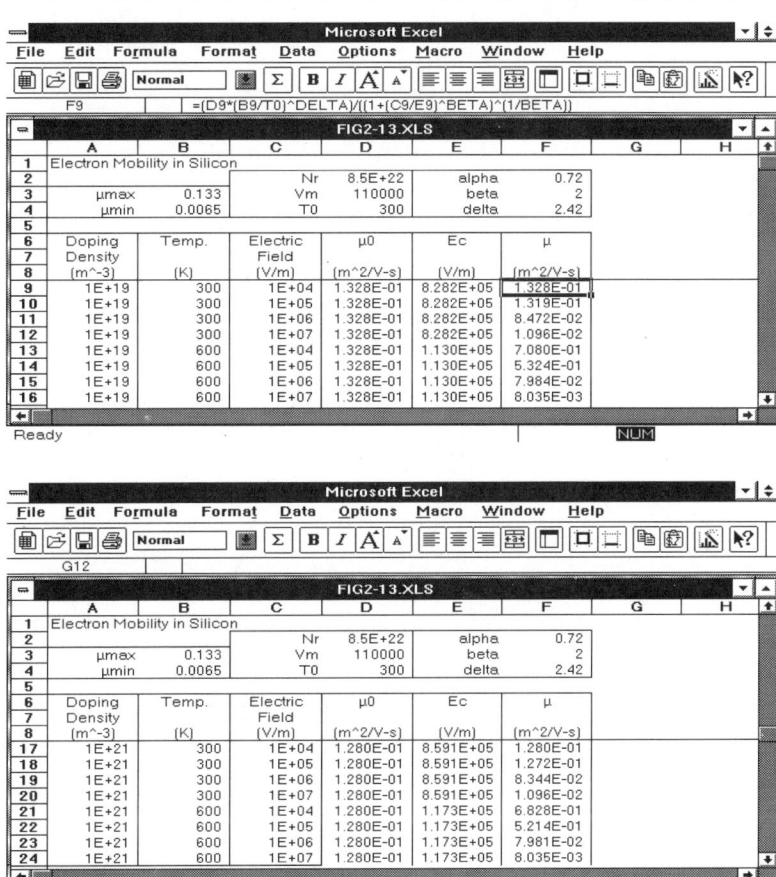

every cell. With a single input cell, you can actually create a table for several single-input formulas, placed in adjacent columns. With two input cells, you can calculate a two-input table for a single formula.

Using the Table command on the Data menu has several advantages over copying formulas. Because you need only one copy of a formula, you have less to type in, and you can quickly alter a formula and see the results in the table. Another advantage is that the table does not need to be recalculated every time you make a change to the worksheet. You can use the Calculation command on the Options menu to set recalculation to automatic for all cells except those that are part of a data table. Then your tables will be recalculated only when you press F9.

A disadvantage of using the Table command is that you must use a single formula, rather than a set of formulas for the function. For example, in the previous section, you used three formulas to calculate the final result. In order to perform this calculation with a data table, you would need to combine all three formulas into one. Another disadvantage is that you cannot have special formulas for different parts of the table. For example, you cannot use the Table command to create a table that contains a different formula for the areas where the arguments are zero.

Whether or not you use the Table command is largely a matter of preference. The time required to set up tables using copied equations or the command is about the same, so there is no advantage there. The speed with which the table is calculated is also about the same for both methods. If you frequently change individual equations or groups of equations to better handle a part of the range of the input variable, you will need to use copied equations since this cannot be done with the Table command. You will probably prefer to use copied equations if the equations you calculate are not available as a single formula, but as a set of formulas that each calculate an intermediate value leading to the final result. Although you could probably do all the algebra to make these into single formulas, you would be doing extra work, and the equations would quickly become unwieldy.

The Table Command's Single-Input Table

To create a single-input table with the Table command, you must first set up the worksheet, following this general procedure:

- Put the list of input values in the column immediately to the left of the body of the data table.

- Select a convenient cell outside the table to use as the input cell. Use this cell in all your formulas for the input variable.

- Put the formula to be evaluated in a cell that is one row above the body of the table, in the same column as the table. You can calculate several single-input tables at the same time, as long as they use the same set of input data. Just put the formulas in adjacent columns.

- Select the range containing the input values and the formulas.

After setting up the worksheet, you can select the Table command on the Data menu. In the Table dialog box, specify the input cell. Excel then calculates the table by inserting the input values into the input cell, calculating the formula, and listing the results in the column below the formula and in the same row as the input value. You can also create a horizontal table, with the input data in the top row and the formula on the left side. Transpose the setup described here for vertical tables.

Stress and Deflection in a Cantilever Beam   Calculating stress and strain in beams is a common requirement in mechanical and civil engineering. In most cases, standard beams can be modeled with a set of simple analytical equations. You can find lists of these equations for different beams and methods of support in a number of handbooks.

Stress (S) in a cantilever beam with a single-point load, illustrated in Figure 2.14, can be calculated at any point x with the following equation:

$$S = \frac{W}{Z}(l - x) \quad (\textbf{for } x < l)$$

where W is the applied load, l is the location of the load, and Z is the section modulus of the beam. The deflection (y) of the beam is calculated with the equations:

$$y = \frac{Wx^2}{6EI}(3l - x) \quad (\textbf{for } x \leq l)$$

FIGURE 2.14:

Cantilever beam with a single-point load

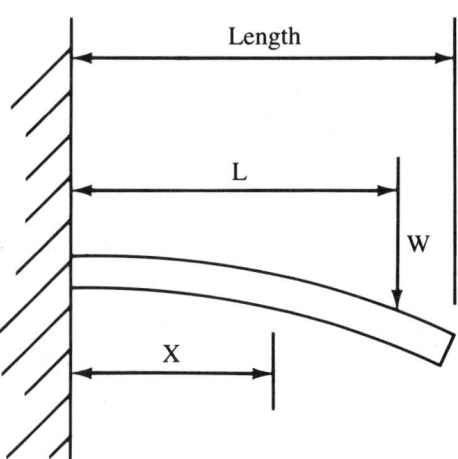

$$y = \frac{Wl^2}{6EI}(3x - l) \quad \left(\textbf{for } x \geq l\right)$$

where E is the modulus of elasticity and I is the moment of inertia.

Suppose you have a 12-foot cantilever beam with a 15,000-pound load located 2 feet from the end. You want to calculate the stress in the beam and the deflection at every point. The beam is a type W 12 x 53 beam (a form of I beam) that is 12 inches deep and has a weight of 53 pounds per foot. A beam of this type has a section modulus (Z) of 70.7 in^3, a moment of inertia (I) of 426 in^4, and a modulus of elasticity (E) of 2.9x10^7 psi.

Create an engineering table that shows the stress and deflection of the cantilever beam every foot along its length. Actually, this table is two engineering tables applied to the same set of input data with the Table command. The first table is the stress calculation, and the second is the deflection calculation.

1. Start with a new worksheet expanded to full size, and set the widths of columns A through G as follows:

A = 9	E = 3
B = 4	F = 19
C = 9	G = 9
D = 9	H = 5

2. In cell A1, type **Cantilever Beam**.

3. In cell C3, type **Stress**.

4. In cell C4, type **(psi)**.

5. In cell D3, type **Deflection**.

6. In cell D4, type **(in)**.

7. In cell A10, type **Distance**.

8. In cell A11, type **from Wall**.

9. In cell A12, type **(in)**.

Now mark the input cell to emphasize its location. You are only marking the cell to clarify how the Table command operates. You don't need to do this in your own tables.

11. In cell A6, type **^^input^^**.

12. In cell A7, type **cell**.

13. Center the contents of cells C3, C4, D3, D4, A6, A7, A10, A11, and A12.

14. Enter the data describing the beam in cells F3 through H11 as follows:

F3: **Length of Beam**	G3: **144**	H3: **in**
F4: **Location of Load**	G4: **120**	H4: **in**
F5: **Weight of Load**	G5: **15000**	H5: **lbs**
F7: **Beam Designation**	G7: **W 12 x 53**	
F8: **Section Modulus**	G8: **70.7**	H8: **in^3**
F9: **Moment of Inertia**	G9: **426**	H9: **in^4**
F10: **Modulus of**		
F11: **Elasticity**	G11: **2.9e7**	H11: **psi**

15. Right-justify the contents of cell F11.

16. Name cells as follows:

G4: **L**

G5: **W**

G8: **Z**

G9: **I**

G11: **E**

Next you will enter the input data for the calculation. You want to calculate the stress and deflection every 12 inches along the beam.

17. Type **0** in cell B6.

18. Type **12** in cell B7.

19. Select cells B6 and B7, grab the fill handle, and drag it to cell B18.

This problem uses two stress and two deflection equations: one each for x between the wall and the location of the weight, and the other for x beyond the location of the weight. Use the logical IF statement to select the correct equations for the input range.

20. In cell C5, type the following equation:

$$=IF(A5<L,(W/Z)*(L-A5),0)$$

21. In cell D5, type this equation:

$$=IF(A5<G4,(G5*A5\wedge2)*(3*G4-A5)/(6*G11*G9),(G5*A5\wedge2)*(3*A5-G4)/(6*G11*G9))$$

The table is now set up for execution of the Table command. Note that the range of the table includes the column of input values and the formulas, but not the input cell.

22. Select cells B5:D18 and choose the Table command on the Data menu.

23. Place the cursor in the Column Input Cell text box and click on cell A5 to insert its reference in the dialog box as the input cell. Click on OK to make the table.

24. Format cells C5:C18 as 0.

25. Format cells D5:D18 as 0.0000.

26. Format cell G11 as 0.00E+00.

27. Outline the following ranges: C6:D18, B6:B18, B5:D5, and F3:H11.

28. Turn off the worksheet gridlines.

As your final step, hide the values calculated by the formulas at the top of the columns.

29. Select cells C5:D5 and format them as ;;; with the Number command on the Format menu. This format hides the cell values.

30. Save the worksheet.

Your worksheet should now look like Figure 2.15. If you look at any of the cells in the body of the table, you will see that they are all array formulas (the formulas are surrounded by curly brackets). You can now use the values in other formulas, but you cannot change any cell's value independently of the rest of the table.

FIGURE 2.15:

Single-input table for calculating the stress and deflection in a cantilever beam

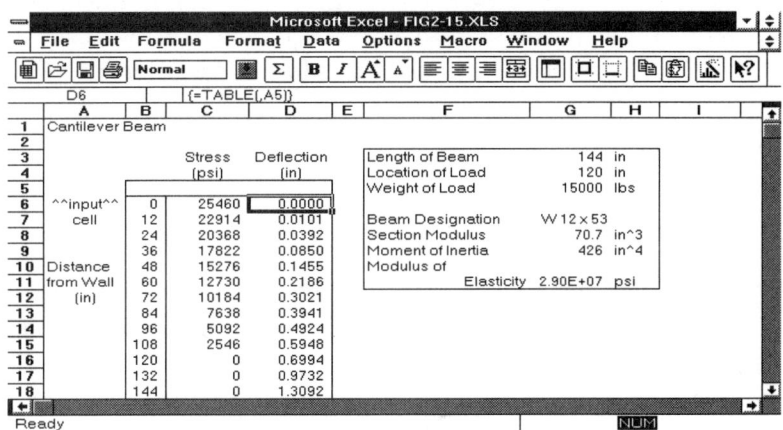

The Table Command's Two-Input Table

You create a two-input table with the Table command in much the same manner as a single-input table. Put the values of the first variable in the column immediately to the left of the body of the table. Place the second variable in the row immediately above the body of the table, and insert the formula at the intersection of the row and column containing the input data. Define two input cells outside the table area and reference them in the Table dialog box.

Linear Variable Differential Transformer   As part of this nation's nuclear safety program, laboratories conduct tests to stress nuclear reactors and reactor components to failure in order to determine the nominal failure levels. As fuel rods are heated and cooled, their length changes. Rod length also changes drastically when a fuel rod breaks, which often happens in the destructive tests. A linear variable differential transformer (LVDT) is used to measure the change in length.

An LVDT consists of two identical secondary coils of wire spaced symmetrically about a primary coil. The secondary coils are wired in a series-opposed circuit. When the primary coil is excited with an AC source, the magnetic field is coupled to the secondary coils through a movable core. If the core is centered in the device, the coupling to each of the secondary coils is identical. Since they are wired in a series-opposed configuration, the resultant voltage is zero. If the movable core is displaced in either direction, a differential voltage is produced. The series-opposed configuration also helps to reduce thermal- and radiation-induced noise.

The LVDTs are calibrated at several different temperatures, and then linear curve fits are performed on the voltage versus displacement data. Then you can fit the coefficients of the curve fit to a linear function of the temperature to get the temperature sensitivity. Combining these curve fits results in this calibration equation:

$$x = a_0 + a_1 V + a_2 (T - 608) + a_3 V (T - 608)$$

where x is the fuel-rod elongation in millimeters, V is the transducer voltage, and T is the transducer temperature in Kelvins. For a particular device, the coefficients are as follows:

a_0	0.3347 mm
a_1	10.6592 mm/V
a_2	-2.19701×10^{-3} mm/K
a_3	-6.32662×10^{-4} mm/K-V

You will use these values to create a table of fuel-rod elongation versus transducer voltage and temperature.

1. Start with a new worksheet expanded to full size.

2. Change the widths of columns A through G as follows:

A = 13	E = 9
B = 7	F = 9
C = 10	G = 9
D = 9	

3. Type **LVDT Calibration Table** in cell A1.

4. Type **a0** in cell D1.

5. Type **a1** in cell E1.

6. Type **a2** in cell F1.

7. Type **a3** in cell G1.

8. Type **Coefficients** in cell C2.

9. Type **0.3347** in cell D2.

10. Type **10.6592** in cell E2.

11. Type **−0.00219701** in cell F2.

12. Type **−0.000632662** in cell G2.

13. In cell A3, type **Fuel rod elongation.**

14. In cell A4, type **in millimeters.**

15. In cell C4, type **Transducer Temperature (K).**

16. In cell A12, type **Transducer.**

17. In cell A13, type **Voltage.**

18. In cell A14, type **(V).**

19. Center cells D1:G1 and A8:A14.

Next enter the values for the column input across the top of the table. You could insert the four values by using the Series command, but here it is faster to just type them in.

20. Type **300** in cell C5, **400** in cell D5, **500** in cell E5, and **600** in cell F5.

Now mark the input cells to clarify how the table works. Use the Shaded option in the Border dialog box to shade the contents of those cells, and also add labels to identify them.

21. Select cell A7, choose the Border command on the Format menu, check the Shade check box, and click on OK.

22. In cell A8, type **^Column Input**.

23. Select cell A9 and use the Border command on the Format menu to shade the contents of this cell.

24. In cell A10, type **^Row Input**.

In the left column of the table, enter the values for the first input.

25. Type **1.2** in cell B6 and **1.0** in cell B7. Then select cells B6:B7, grab the fill handle, and drag it to B18.

The final setup task is to enter the two-input function in the table at the intersection of the row and column containing the input values. Remember, the formula must reference the two input cells.

26. In cell B5, type the following formula:

$$=D2+E2*A7+F2*(A9-608)+G2*(A9-608)*A7$$

Now you can use the Table command to create the table and then format the table. You will hide the contents of the cell containing the formula so that it will not detract from the rest of the table.

27. Select cells B5:F18 and choose the Table command on the Data menu. Click on cell A9 to insert the row input cell into the dialog box. Click on Column Input Cell, and then on cell A7 for the column input cell.

28. Format cells B6:B18 as 0.0.

29. Format cells C6:F18 as 0.00.

30. Format cell B5 as ;;;.

31. Outline the following ranges:

C1:C2	G1:G2
D1:D2	B5:F5
E1:E2	B5:B18
F1:F2	C6:F18

32. Turn off the worksheet gridlines.

33. Save the worksheet.

Your worksheet should now look like Figure 2.16. You could now change one of the values in an input row or column, or change the table formula. Excel will automatically recalculate the table, unless you have executed the Calculation command on the Options menu and set the Update option to Automatic Except Tables or to Manual. To update a table that is not automatically recalculated, press the F9 key.

If you want to add rows to the bottom or columns to the right of the table, you must issue the Table command again to include them in the table. If you want to insert rows or columns within the body of a table, you must first select and clear the body of the table (not the input values or the formula), insert the new rows, select the new table, and use the Table command again.

FIGURE 2.16:
The table for calculating LVDT calibration data

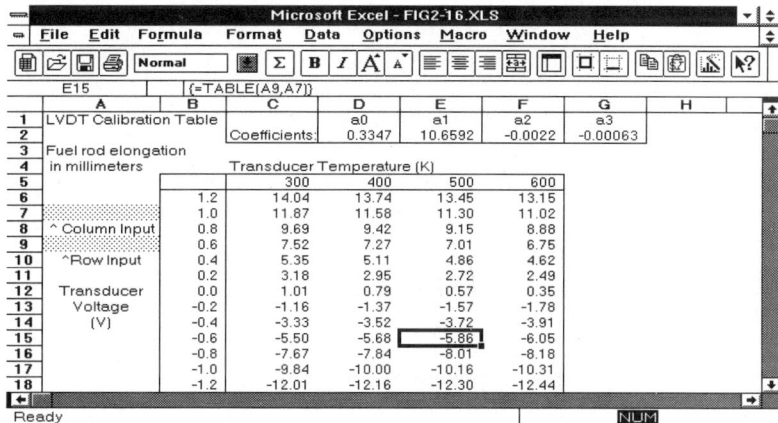

Using Function Calculators

Function calculators work similarly to the first example in this chapter, in which you calculated the values for a simple analytical equation. You place one or several input values in a formula and calculate the results. This approach is in contrast to the tables of values you have created in this chapter.

A function calculator contains an input area where the user types the input values and an output area where the results are calculated and presented. You can also protect parts of the worksheet so that users can enter values only in the input area, not in other areas of the worksheet.

Creating a Simple Function Calculator

A function calculator need not be complex. In this first example, you will generate a function calculator that has a single input value and a single output value, calculated with a single simple formula.

Julian Day Calculator One of the principle tasks of astronomers is recording the dates and times of events, measurements, and sightings. Although the dates can be in conventional days, months, and years, the irregularity of months and years makes calculations difficult. If you need to know the difference in time between two different events, you must take into account the lengths of the years (how many were regular years and how many were leap years) and the lengths of the months between the events.

Astronomers do not want to spend time calculating the lengths of months and years when there is a clear night sky and the seeing (the amount of twinkle in starlight) is good. Therefore, they use a system of time measurement known as the Julian Day, proposed by Joseph Scalinger in 1582. The Julian Day calendar consists of consecutively numbered days, starting with January 1, 4713 BC. (I don't have any idea why he chose this particular date, but it is well before any accurately recorded history.) To find the difference in time between two events, you simply subtract their Julian Days.

Time of day is also incorporated into the Julian Day calendar as decimal fractions of a day. Since astronomers generally work at night, the Julian Day starts at noon rather than midnight. Therefore, midnight between December 31, 1979, and January 1, 1980, is Julian Day 2,444,239.5.

Julian Days work well with Excel's date and time functions, which calculate with consecutive days and fractions of days. All you need to do is to add the offset from a known date.

In the following example, you will create a simple function calculator that converts a standard date into a Julian Day. To be compatible with Lotus 1-2-3, Excel counts a day for 2/29/1900, even though that day does not exist. To handle this, restrict dates to those after 3/1/1900.

1. Start with a new worksheet expanded to full size, and set the width of column A to 12 and the width of column B to 11.

2. In cell A1, type **Julian Day Calculator**.

3. In cell A3, type **Input the date to be converted as 'MM/DD/YYYY**.

4. In cell A4, type **The date must be between 3/1/1900 and 12/31/2078**.

5. In cell A6, type **Date:**.

6. In cell A8, type **Julian Day:**.

7. Right-justify cells A6 and A8.

The Julian Day for 1/1/80 in the afternoon is JD 2,444,240. Use this date to synchronize the Julian Day calendar with the Excel date and time functions. You don't need to apply the DATEVALUE function to the contents of cell B6, because Excel automatically converts the date you type into a serial date number.

8. In cell B6, type the following formula:

   =B6−DATEVALUE("1/1/80")+2444240

9. Outline cell B6, and set the numeric format to mm/dd/yyyy.

10. Type the explanation of how the calendar works in cells A10 through A12, as follows:

    A10: **Julian days go from noon to noon rather than midnight to midnight,**

    A11: **so this is the Julian day of the evening of the date specified**

    A12: **in the input cell. The Julian day calendar starts at noon on Jan. 1, 4713BC.**

The text in cells A10:A12 looks a bit ragged. You can use the Justify command on the Format menu to form a compact paragraph. The text to be justified must be in a single column. The range you select determines the width of the text when it is justified.

11. Select A10:D18 and choose the Justify command on the Format menu.

12. Turn off the worksheet gridlines.

Finally, protect this worksheet so that other users cannot ruin your work. You want to protect all cells except the one in which the user enters the date to be converted to a Julian Day. You use the Cell Protection command on the Format menu to mark cells as *not* protected, then the Protect Document command on the Options menu to protect the worksheet. If a user tries to change a protected part of the worksheet, Excel beeps and displays a dialog box explaining that the cell cannot be changed. Another option here is to use a password to protect the document. If you use a password, the user cannot unprotect the document and make changes. If you check the Hidden check box in the Cell Protection dialog box as well, the user won't be able to see your formulas either.

13. Select cell B6, choose the Cell Protection command on the Format menu, uncheck the Locked check box, and click on OK.

14. Choose the Protect Document command on the Options menu. In the dialog box, the Cells check box should be checked. Click on OK.

15. Save the worksheet.

Now you can type a date into cell B6, and the Julian Day will appear in cell B8. For example, if you input 1/19/87, the worksheet would look like Figure 2.17.

Setting Up a Complicated Function Calculator

Thermoelectric Cooler A thermoelectric cooler is a solid-state heat pump. It is a semiconductor device that uses electrons to carry heat from one side of the device to the other. When you apply a voltage to a thermoelectric cooler, one side gets hot and the other side gets cold (the opposite of a thermocouple). In fact, if you drive a thermoelectric cooler with heat on one side and cold on the other, it generates an electric current. If you reverse the current through the thermoelectric cooler, the opposite sides of the device are heated and cooled.

Thermoelectric coolers have been used for a number of years to cool small volumes in restricted spaces, such as a single integrated circuit in the middle of a large circuit board. More recently, they have been used to heat or cool a food chest, so that you can have hot food and cold beer at a picnic.

FIGURE 2.17:

A Julian Day function calculator

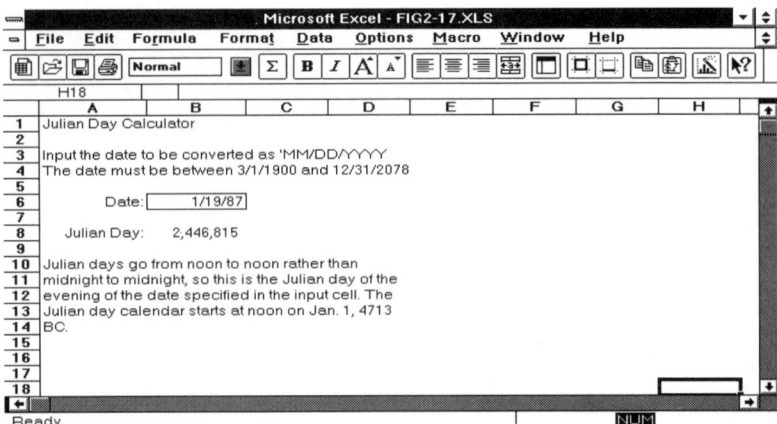

In the next example, you will apply a complicated function calculator to the problem of analyzing a thermoelectric cooler. You will calculate all the relevant design and operational parameters for the problem.

The input parameters for a thermoelectric cooler consist of material parameters and device parameters. The material parameters are the Seebeck coefficient (α), the resistivity (ρ), and the figure of merit (Z), for the n-type and p-type semiconductor materials that make up the two legs of the cooler. Here are the material parameters for two semiconductor materials commonly used in thermoelectric coolers:

Parameter	n-type	p-type
Composition	75% Bi_2Te_3	25% Bi_2Te_3
	25% Bi_2Se_3	75% Sb_2Te_3
Seebeck coefficient (α)	-1.65×10^{-4}	2.10×10^{-4} V/K
Resistivity (ρ)	1.05×10^{-3}	9.8×10^{-4} ohm-cm
Figure of merit (Z)	2.0×10^{-3}	3.5×10^{-3} $(K)^{-1}$

The thermal conductivities (λ) of the materials can be calculated using this equation:

$$\lambda = \frac{\alpha^2}{\rho Z}$$

The junction Seebeck coefficient is calculated by this equation:

$$\alpha = |\alpha_n| + |\alpha_p|$$

The device parameters start with the ratios of the areas to the lengths of the n- and p-legs of the thermoelectric cooler: γ_n and γ_p. These are the design parameters. In the following ratio, the parameters optimize the coefficient of performance (β):

$$\frac{\gamma_n}{\gamma_p} = \left(\frac{\rho_n\lambda_p}{\rho_p\lambda_n}\right)$$

The figure of merit for the junction is given by this equation:

$$Z = \frac{\alpha^2}{RK}$$

where R is the device resistance and K is the device thermal conductance.

$$R = \frac{\rho_n}{\lambda_n} + \frac{\rho_p}{\lambda_p}$$

$$K = \lambda_n \gamma_n + \lambda_p \gamma_p$$

The optimized figure of merit is given by this equation:

$$Z^* = \frac{\alpha^2}{\left[\left(\rho_n \lambda_n \right)^{1/2} + \left(\rho_p \lambda_p \right)^{1/2} \right]}$$

The driving current is another design parameter, and the value that optimizes the coefficient of performance is derived by this equation:

$$I = \frac{\alpha \Delta T}{R \left[\left(1 + Z^* T_{av} \right)^{1/2} - 1 \right]}$$

where T_{av} is the average and ΔT is the temperature difference of the hot (T_h) and cold (T_c) junction temperatures.

The heat pumping rate from the cold junction is as follows:

$$q = \alpha T_c I - \tfrac{1}{2} I^2 R - K \Delta T$$

The coefficient of performance is the ratio of the heat pumped from the cold junction to the electrical energy required to pump it:

$$\beta = \frac{\alpha T_c I - \tfrac{1}{2} I^2 R - K \Delta T}{\alpha T_c \Delta T + I^2 R}$$

The maximum value of β is found by inserting the optimized values of I, K, and R:

$$\beta_{max} = \frac{T_c}{\Delta T}\left[\frac{\left(1+Z^*T_{av}\right)^{1/2} - T_h/T_c}{\left(1+Z^*T_{av}\right)^{1/2} - 1}\right]$$

Finally, the power input into the device is as follows:

$$P = \alpha I \Delta T + I^2 R$$

If the device was completely optimized, this would equal the optimized power input:

$$P = \frac{q}{\beta_{max}}$$

Using these equations, you will create a function calculator that calculates all the device parameters. You will calculate two sets of values: one for input device parameters, and the other for the optimized values of the device parameters. Begin by entering the material type and material parameters described above.

1. Start with a new worksheet expanded to full size, and set the widths of columns A through E as follows:

    A = 16   D = 12

    B = 12   E = 9

    C = 12

2. In cell A1, type **Thermoelectric Cooler Calculator**.

3. In cell A2, type the following text:

    n-type: 75% Bi2Te3 25% Bi2Se3   p-type: 25% Bi2Te3 75% Sb2Te3

The entries you will make in the cells in column A show a simple way to hide descriptive material in a worksheet. For example, in cell A3, you will type a few spaces, then the name of the value, then some spaces, and then descriptive text. When the number is typed in cell B3, all the text but the name of the value is hidden. (Adjust the number of blank spaces at the beginning of cell A3 as necessary.) The user can see a description by moving the cursor into a cell, which puts its contents in the formula bar. This makes descriptive material available to the user without cluttering the worksheet with an excessive amount of text.

You could also attach a note to the cell by using the Note command on the Formula menu. When a note is attached to a cell, a small red dot appears in the cell's upper-right corner.

4. Make the following entries in cells A3:A5:

A3:	**alpha =**	**Material Seebeck Coefficient**
A4:	**Rho =**	**Material Resistivity**
A5:	**Z =**	**Material Figure of Merit**

Then make these entries in cells B3:E5:

B3: **1.65E-4**	C3: **V/K**	D3: **2.1E-4**	E3: **V/K**
B4: **1.05E-3**	C4: **ohm-cm**	D4: **9.8E-4**	E4: **ohm-cm**
B5: **2.0E-3**	C5: **1/K**	D5: **3.5E-3**	E5: **1/K**

Next enter the calculations for the thermal conductivities.

5. In cell A6, type **lambda =** **Material Thermal Conductivity**.

6. Type **=B3^2/(B4*B5)** in cell B6.

7. In cell C6, type **watt/cm-K**.

8. Type **=D3^2/(D4*D5)** in cell D6.

9. In cell E6, type **watt/cm-K**.

Enter the hot and cold junction temperatures. Assume that you want to keep the cold junction at freezing (273 K) and the hot junction at 327 K, so that the average is at room temperature (300 K).

10. In cell A7, type **T-hot, T-cold =** **Hot Leg and Cold Leg Temperatures**.

11. Type **327** in cell B7.

12. Type **K** in cell C7.

13. Type **273** in cell D7.

14. Type **K** in cell E7.

Now enter the area-to-length ratios. The optimized value of γ_p will be calculated in cell D11.

15. In cell A8, type   **gamma =**   **Ratio of the Leg Area to Leg Length**.

16. Type **1** in cell B8.

17. Type **cm** in cell C8.

18. Type **1** in cell D8.

19. Type **cm** in cell E8.

20. In cell A9, type   **Tav =**   **Average Temperature**.

21. Type **=(B7+D7)/2** in cell B9.

22. In cell C9, type **K**   **Alpha =**   **Junction Seebeck Coefficient**.

23. Type **=ABS(B3)+ABS(D3)** in cell D9.

24. In cell B10, type **General Values**.

25. In cell D10, type **Optimized Values**.

26. In cell A11, type   **gamma p opt =**   **Optimized p-type A/l Ratio Using the n-type A/l**.

27. Type **'** in cell B11.

28. Type **=SQRT(D4∗B6/(B4∗D6))** in cell D11.

29. In cell E11, type **cm**.

30. In cell A12, type   **Z =**   **Junction Figure of Merit**.

31. Type **=D9^2/(B13∗B14)** in cell B12.

32. In cell C12, type **1/K**.

33. In cell D12, type this formula:

    =D9^2/((SQRT(B4∗B6)+SQRT(D4∗D6))^2)

34. In cell E12, type **1/K**.

35. In cell A13, type   **K =**   **Device Thermal Conductance**.

36. Type **=B6∗B8+D6∗D8** in cell B13.

37. In cell C13, type **watt/K**.

38. Type **=B6*B8+D6*D11** in cell D13.

39. In cell E13, type **watt/K**.

40. In cell A14, type   **R =   Device Resistance**.

41. Type **=B4/B8+D4/D8** in cell B14.

42. In cell C14, type **ohm**.

43. Type **=B4/B8+D4/D11** in cell D14.

44. In cell E14, type **ohm**.

In the unoptimized calculation, the value of I is an input parameter. In the optimized calculation, I is calculated.

45. In cell A15, type   **I =   Device Current**.

46. Type **29** in cell B15.

47. In cell C15, type **amps**.

48. In cell D15, type this formula:

$$\text{=D9*(B7−D7)/(D14*(SQRT(1+D12*B9)−1))}$$

49. In cell E15, type **amps**.

50. In cell A16, type   **qc =   Heat Flow into the Cold Side**.

51. In cell B16, type this formula:

$$\text{=D9*D7*B15−0.5*B15\^2*B14−B13* B7−D7)}$$

52. In cell C16, type **watts**.

53. In cell D16, type this formula:

$$\text{=D9*D7*D15−0.5*D15\^2*D14−D13* B7−D7)}$$

54. In cell E16, type **watts**.

55. In cell A17, type   **beta =   Coefficient of Performance**.

56. In cell B17, type this formula:

   =(D9*D7*B15−0.5*B15^2*B14−B13* B7−D7))/(D9* 15* B7−D7)+B15^2*B14)

57. In cell D17, type this formula:

   =(D7/(B7−D7))*(SQRT(1+D12*B9)−B7/D7)/(SQRT(1+D12 *B9)+1)

58. In cell A18, type   **P =   Input Power**.

59. In cell B18, type this formula:

   =D9*B15*(B7−D7)+B15^2*B14

60. In cell C18, type **watts**.

61. Type **=D16/D17** in cell D18.

62. In cell E18, type **watts**.

63. Format the following cells as 0.000E+00:

   B3:B6

   B12:B14

   D3:D6

   D9

   D12:D14

64. Format these cells as as 0.000:

   B15:B18

   D11

   D15:D18

65. Unprotect the following cells by selecting them, choosing the Cell Protection command on the Format menu, and unchecking Locked:

A2	B15
B3:B5	D3:D5
B7	D7
B8	D8

66. Make the following cells bold by using the Font command on the Format menu or by clicking on the bold button on the toolbar:

   A2   B15
   B3:B5   D3:D5
   B7   D7
   B8   D8

67. Turn off the worksheet gridlines.

68. Select cells A2:F2 and underline them by using the Border command on the Format menu or the bottom border tool on the toolbar.

69. Select cells A10:F10 and place a line at the top and bottom of each cell by using the Border command on the Format menu.

70. Protect the worksheet by choosing the Protect Document command on the Options menu.

71. Save the worksheet.

Your worksheet should now look like Figure 2.18. The unprotected cells (the ones whose values you can change) stand out because they are in a bold font and have a dotted underline.

FIGURE 2.18:

A function calculator for analyzing a thermoelectric cooler

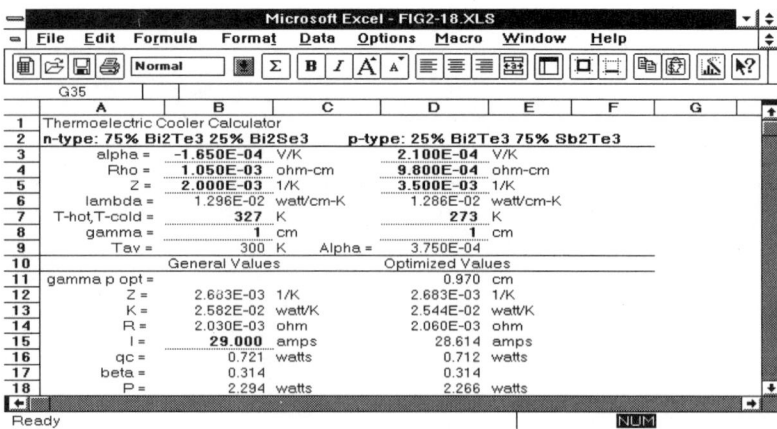

Summary

This chapter covered at least 50 percent of the worksheet techniques that a practicing scientist or engineer would normally use in the course of his or her work. Much of the numerical work that we do involves putting simple numbers into relatively simple equations and calculating the results. As you have seen, the worksheet format is quite suitable for this type of work. All that is missing is graphical presentation of the data, which is discussed in the next chapter.

In this chapter, you explored the various ways to create engineering tables and function calculators with Excel. Engineering tables allow you to calculate single or multiple values from scientific and engineering equations. Function calculators calculate values for complex sets of equations. With them, you can model a complex system, and then perform what-if analyses with the system parameters and see the results immediately. While creating these tables and calculators, you have used many of the commands and techniques that simplify the creation of a worksheet and define how the completed worksheet will look. As you use the program to solve your own problems and gain experience in building worksheets, you will find many more ways to calculate and present useful results.

For More Information

Thermal Conductivity

E. L. Heasell, "The Heat Flow Problem in Silicon," *IEEE Trans. on Elec. Dev.*, ED-25, 12 (Dec. 1978):1382.

Precession of the North Celestial Pole

A. E. Roy, *The Foundations of Astrodynamics* (New York: Macmillan, 1969), p. 53.

Temperature Dependence of the Intrinsic Carrier Density

S. M. Sze, *Physics of Semiconductor Devices*, 2nd. ed. (New York: Wiley, 1981), p. 19.

Van der Waals Equation of State

D. Halliday, R. Resnick, *Physics* (New York: Wiley, 1967), pp. 611-615.

Absolute Magnitude of a Star

D. S. Birney, *Modern Astronomy* (Boston: Allyn and Bacon, 1969), pp. 168-174.

Electron Mobility in Silicon

W. J. Orvis, *Semiconductor Device Modeling with BURN42; a One-Dimensional Code for Modeling Solid State Devices*, UCID-20602 (Livermore, CA: Lawrence Livermore National Laboratory, 1985), p. 8.

D. M. Canghey, R. E. Thomas, "Carrier Mobilities in Silicon Empirically Related to Doping and Field," *Proc. IEEE* (Dec. 1967): 2192.

C. Jacoboni, C. Canali, G. Ottaviani, A. A. Quaranta, "A Review of Some Charge Transport Properties of Silicon," *Solid State Electronics*, 20 (1977): 77.

Stress and Deflection in a Cantilever Beam

E. Oberg, F. D. Jones, H. L. Horton, *Machinery's Handbook*, 20th ed. (New York: Industrial Press, 1978).

T. Baumeister, E. A. Avallone, T. Baumeister III, *Standard Handbook for Mechanical Engineers* (New York: McGraw-Hill, 1979).

Julian Days

G. Ottewell, *The Astronomical Companion* (Greenville, SC: Furman University, 1979), p. 23.

Thermoelectric Coolers

S. W. Angrist, *Direct Energy Conversion*, 4th. ed. (Boston: Allyn and Bacon, 1982), pp. 148-153.

Problems

1. Create a table of sine, cosine, tangent, arcsine, arccosine, and arctangent for the angles 0 through 180 degrees in steps of 10 degrees. Use degrees instead of radians.

2. Create a table of common logarithms, log(x); natural logarithms, ln(x); exponentials, e^x; and powers of ten, 10^x for the values 0, .1, .3, .5, .9, 1.0, 2.0, 5.0, 8.0, and 10.0. Automatically insert the text *INF* for log(0) and ln(0) by testing the argument with an IF statement.

3. Create a simple function calculator that, when you input an angle in degrees, will calculate all six of the trigonometric functions (sine, cosine, tangent, secant, cosecant, and cotangent) and their logarithms.

4. The Lemniscate of Bernoulli, also known as a two-leaf rose curve, is a figure-eight shaped curve aligned with the x-axis. It is defined by the equation

$$\left(x^2 + y^2\right) = a^2\left(x^2 - y^2\right) \qquad or \qquad r^2 = a^2\cos(2\theta)$$

Let $a = 2$ and calculate a table of 50 values of x and y to use to draw the complete curve (that is, let θ range from 0 to 2π).

5. Create a table comparing the pressure for a given temperature and volume of gas using the van der Waals equation of state for nitrogen, ammonia, and helium. Make the table for 10 different combinations of temperature and volume.

Gas	a (l2−atm/mol2)	b (l/mol)
N2	1.39	0.0391
NH3	4.17	0.037
He	0.0341	0.0237

6. Create a function calculator for a thermoelectric cooler that uses 75%−PbTe 25%−SnTe and AgSbTe2.

	75%−PbTe 25%−SnTe	AgSbTe2	
type	n	p	
α	80	240	μV/K
π	0.8×10^{-3}	4.3×10^{-3}	ohm−cm
Z	0.8×10^{-3}	1.8×10^{-3}	K^{-1}

7. The bending (stress and deflection) of a uniformly loaded (W/l pounds/unit length) cantilever beam is described in the equations

$$S = \frac{W}{2Zl}(l-x)^2$$

$$y = \frac{Wx^2}{24EIl}\left(2l^2 + (2l-x)^2\right)$$

Use the same beam as the example with the cantilever beam loaded at a single point. Using the Table command, create a single-input table that shows the stress and deflection along the beam for different total loadings. Include the weight of the beam in the loading.

8. Create a function calculator that converts ecliptic coordinates (ecliptic latitude β and ecliptic longitude λ) to equatorial coordinates (right ascension α and declination δ). Input the date and the ecliptic coordinates and output the equatorial coordinates. Don't forget to convert degrees to hours for the right ascension. (Use the ATAN2 function to get the quadrant correct.)

$$\delta = \arcsin\left[\sin(\beta)\cos(\varepsilon) + \cos(\beta)\sin(\varepsilon)\sin(\lambda)\right]$$

$$\cos(\alpha) = \left[\frac{\cos(\beta)\cos(\lambda)}{\cos(\delta)}\right]$$

$$\sin(\alpha) = \left[\frac{\cos(\beta)\cos(\varepsilon)\sin(\lambda) - \sin(\beta)\sin(\varepsilon)}{\cos(\delta)}\right]$$

$$\alpha = \arctan\left(\frac{\sin(\alpha)}{\cos(\alpha)}\right)$$

9. The escape velocity (v) is calculated with the equation

$$v^2 = G(m_1 + m_2)\frac{2}{r}$$

where

G = gravitational constant (6.67×10^{-11} nt–m^2/kg^2)

m_1 = mass of planet (kg)

m_2 = mass of escaping body (kg)

r = radius of planet (m)

Create a table of escape velocities for a rifle bullet escaping from the following bodies ($m_1 \gg m_2$; that is, ignore m_2).

	Radius (km)	Mass (kg)
Sun	695,300	1.97×10^{30}
Mercury	2,439	2.39×10^{23}
Venus	6,050	4.91×10^{24}
Earth	6,378	5.98×10^{24}
Moon	1,738	7.35×10^{22}
Mars	3,396	6.58×10^{23}
Jupiter	71,398	1.90×10^{27}
Saturn	60,330	5.70×10^{26}
Uranus	25,900	8.80×10^{25}
Neptune	24,750	1.04×10^{26}
Pluto	1,500	1.41×10^{22}

10. Make a table of drift velocities (v) and mobility (μ) for electrons in GaAs (Gallium arsenide) moving under applied fields (E) ranging from 0 to 10 KV/cm.

$$v = \frac{\mu_1 E \left(1 + BF^k\right)}{1 + F^k}$$

$$\mu = \frac{v}{E}$$

$$F = \frac{E}{E_0}$$

where

$E_0 = 4{,}000$ V/cm

$\mu_1 = 8{,}000$ cm^2/V-s

$k = 4$

$B = 0.05$

Plotting Data and Functions

Once you have generated a set of numbers, your next task usually is to analyze them. The simplest form of analysis is to plot the numbers and see what kind of curve they form. A lot of good scientific insight has been obtained by simply looking at the shape of a plot of data. In this chapter, you will examine the plotting capabilities of Excel and how to adapt them to scientific and engineering uses.

Excel's Chart Types

Two types of charts exist in Excel: charts embedded in worksheets and those on separate chart sheets. Embedded charts are physically attached to an Excel worksheet. They are embedded in a worksheet in the same manner as a table of values is a part of the worksheet. Chart sheets are separate Excel documents that contain a single chart. In both types of charts, the points plotted are linked to the cells of a worksheet. Which type you use depends on what you are doing.

When you are analyzing data on a worksheet, you most likely will use small embedded charts. You can place a chart on the worksheet, near the data used to create it. Embedded charts are usually too small for a printed presentation, but they are more than sufficient for analysis purposes. When you are preparing a chart for a presentation or document, you will probably use a chart sheet to create a large, good-quality graph.

Using the Chart Wizard

Creating a chart in Excel generally involves executing four or five different commands to create the basic chart, set its type, add labels, and so on. To simplify this process, Excel 4 provides the Chart Wizard, a single command that walks you through most of the steps needed to create a chart.

Selecting the Data and Chart Location

The Chart Wizard has five screens, each of which gathers more of the information needed to create a chart. The first step in creating a chart is to select the data to be plotted, as follows:

- If x data and one or more columns of y data are in adjacent columns on a worksheet, select those columns.

- If the first cell in each column contains the text to use in a legend, select those cells as well.

- If the columns of data are not adjacent, select the column of x-data first, hold down the Ctrl key, and select the first column of y-data. Continue until you have selected all the data to be plotted.

- If the data is in rows instead of columns, select the data as described for non-adjacent columns, but by rows instead of by columns.

After you select the data, choose the Chart Wizard command by clicking on the Chart Wizard button (the one that looks like a small chart with a wand being waved over it) on the toolbar. When you click on the button, the cursor changes into a cross. Drag the cross to select a range on the current worksheet where you want the chart to appear.

As soon as you select a location for the chart, the Chart Wizard's first window appears, as shown in Figure 3.1. The first window asks you to verify that the selected data is the data you want to plot. If the data is correct, click on Next > to move to the second window, shown in Figure 3.2.

FIGURE 3.1:
The Chart Wizard's first step: selecting the data for the chart

FIGURE 3.2:

The Chart Wizard's second step: choosing a chart type

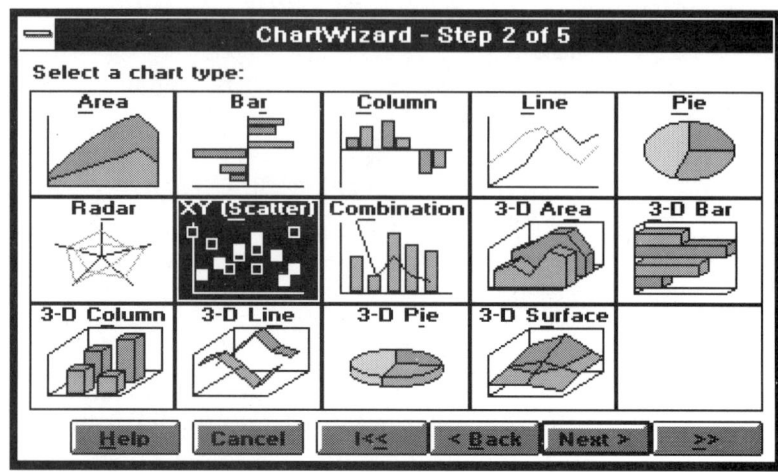

Selecting the Chart Type

In the Chart Wizard's second window, you pick a chart type from the 14 types available. Of all the chart types, only the XY and 3-D Surface charts are really useful for scientific and engineering purposes.

The XY chart type is a true x-y plot, with linear or logarithmic scales on the axes. The XY chart type is the only type that actually plots the x range of data. All the other chart types use the x data for labels, so no matter what values you use for the x data, the plotted points are are all equally spaced in the x direction. Unless all of your data is equally spaced and ordered, the other chart types are not particularly useful for science and engineering tasks.

A 3-D surface chart plots a rectangular grid of data as a 3-D surface. The data for the x- and y-axes is above and to the right of the grid of z data. The chart plots only the values of the z data, and equally spaces the plotted points along the x and y directions. The x and y data are used only for labels.

Click on the type of chart you want to create, and then click on Next >. The next Chart Wizard window presents the available styles for the chart type you chose.

Selecting the Chart Style

When you choose the XY chart type, the window shown in Figure 3.3 appears. It shows five standard styles for XY charts: data markers only, markers and lines, markers and grids, markers and vertical semilog grids, and markers and logarithmic grids.

If you select a 3-D Surface chart type, the window shown in Figure 3.4 appears. It shows the four standard styles for 3-D charts: 3-D surface, 3-D wire-frame, colored contour chart (looking straight down on a surface chart), and wire-frame contour chart.

FIGURE 3.3:
The Chart Wizard's third step: choosing an XY chart style

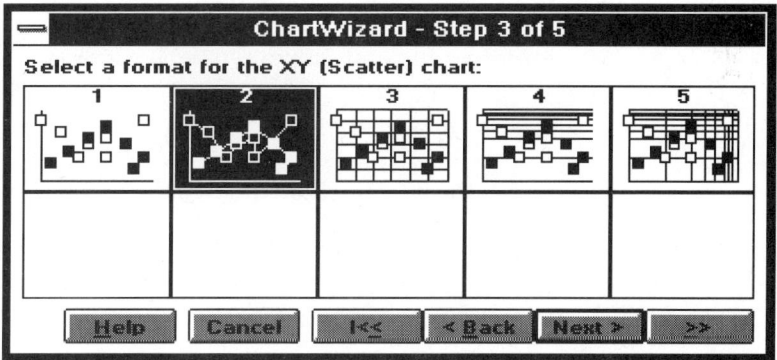

FIGURE 3.4:
The four 3-D Surface chart styles

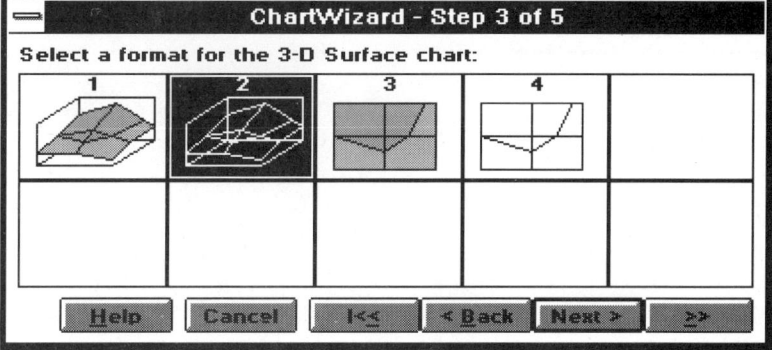

Select the style that most closely resembles how you want your final chart to appear. It doesn't need to be exactly what you want, just pick the closest one. You can adjust most of the chart elements after you create the chart. Click on Next > to move the the fourth step.

Determining the Data Layout

The data for an XY chart type is normally organized in adjacent columns or rows. If the data is in columns, the first column contains the x data and the columns to the right contain the y data for one or more plots. The y data for each plot is known as a data series and may also include the x data and a label for a legend. If the x data is missing, the values 1, 2, 3,... are used.

The fourth Chart Wizard window, shown in Figure 3.5, displays a sample chart and asks for information about how the data is organized on the worksheet. With this information, the Chart Wizard combines the x and y data and the labels and produces the chart. For the XY chart type, there are three questions to answer:

- How is the data organized, by columns or by rows?

- Does the first column or row contain x data, or is it the first series of y data?

- Does the first cell in each column or row contain a label for the series, or does it contain the first data point?

The organization of 3-D chart types is quite different from the 2-D chart types. In a 3-D chart, the z data forms a rectangular region on the worksheet. The first row above this rectangular region can contain the x data, and the first column to the left

FIGURE 3.5:

The Chart Wizard's fourth step: specifying the data organization

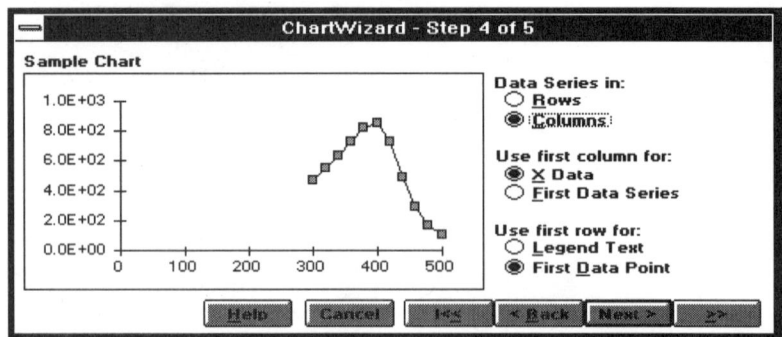

can contain the y data. The x and y data values that apply to a z value are the ones that are in the same row and column as the z value. If the y values are omitted, the labels s1, s2, s3,… are used. If the x values are omitted, the values 1, 2, 3,… are used as labels. For 3-D charts, the Chart Wizard asks questions similar to those for the XY plot type:

- Is the data in columns or rows? This option does not make a lot of difference in a 3-D chart type, but serves to identify whether the x data is in the first column or the first row.

- Does the first column or row contain x data, or is it the first series of z data?

- Does the first row or column contain the y data, or is it the first data point in each series?

Click on the buttons next to the correct answers, then on Next >.

Adding Titles

The last Chart Wizard window, shown in Figure 3.6, lets you add a title, axis labels, and a legend to the chart. In XY charts, the legend shows the series name and samples of the line and marker used to represent it. Use a legend on multiseries XY charts to mark the different series. In 3-D charts, the legend shows the range of z values that apply to a color on the chart.

Type the text you want for the title and axes labels into the text boxes. Click on OK to finish the last Chart Wizard step and place the graph on the worksheet.

FIGURE 3.6:
The Chart Wizard's fifth step: entering a legend and titles

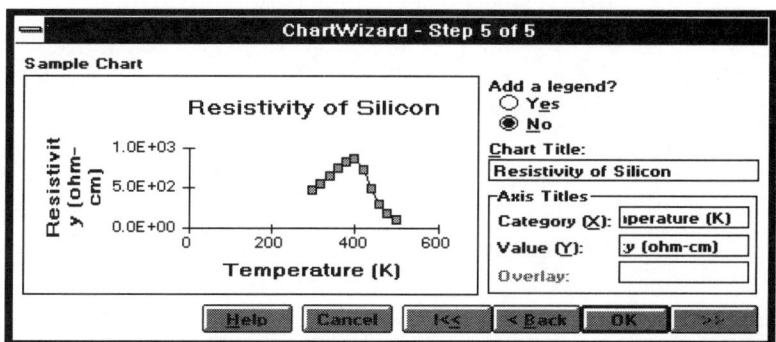

Plotting an Engineering Table

The following example demonstrates how to create charts of engineering functions. First calculate the table of values, and then make an XY chart of those values.

Resistivity of Silicon   A plot of the resistivity of silicon versus temperature is a multivalued curve that peaks at some temperature between 300 and 1000 K, depending on the doping density. This curve is important to solid-state device engineers because devices that operate beyond the peak are likely to fail.

At low temperatures, the resistance of silicon increases with temperature. Thus, any heating of a device due to high currents is self-limiting; the increasing resistance reduces the current, which reduces the heating. If, on the other hand, the temperature of a device passes a threshold value, the resistance starts to decrease with temperature. As the resistance decreases, more current can flow, which increases the heating and decreases the resistance even more. The effect grows exponentially until the device melts. This is the thermal-runaway state known as thermal second breakdown in semiconductor devices.

The resistivity of silicon due to electron motion (ignore hole motion for this example) is defined with the following equation:

$$\rho = \frac{1}{qn\mu}$$

where ρ is the resistivity in ohm-meters, q is the charge on an electron, n is the electron density, and μ is the electron mobility. The electron equilibrium density in doped silicon is obtained from this equation:

$$n = \frac{1}{2}\left[N + \sqrt{N^2 + 4n_i^2} \right]$$

where N is the doping density in m^{-3}, and n_i is the intrinsic carrier density. In Chapter 2, you calculated the intrinsic carrier density, as well as the mobility for all fields, temperatures, and doping densities. However, for this problem, you will be dealing with low fields and doping densities, so the mobility equation can be approximated with:

$$\mu = \mu_0 \left(\frac{T}{T_0} \right)^{-2.42}$$

which is much simpler than the formula that you used in the previous chapter. If you still have the intrinsic carrier density problem available, you can use it as a starting point for this problem. Otherwise, you will need to type it all in again.

Calculate the resistivity of silicon versus temperature for three doping densities: 1.0×10^{13}, 1.5×10^{13}, and 1.0×10^{14} cm^{-3}. You may want to use the Calculation command on the Options menu to turn off recalculation while you are typing this worksheet, and then turn it back on when you are finished. You can recalculate the worksheet at any time by pressing F9 or Ctrl-= (Cmd-= on the Macintosh).

1. Start with a new worksheet expanded to full size.

2. In cell A1, type **Resistivity of Silicon vs. Temperature**.

3. In cells A2:B3, type the following entries:

   A2: **EG0**   B2: **1.17**
   A3: **EG1**   B3: **4.73E-4**

4. Select cells A2:B3, choose the Create Names command on the Formula menu, make sure the Left Column option button is checked, and click on OK. This names cells B2 and B3 as EG0 and EG1_, respectively. The name for cell EG1 is followed by an underscore to differentiate it from the valid cell reference for cell EG1.

5. In cell C2, type **EG2**.

6. In cell D2, type **636**.

7. In cell C3, type **CONS**.

8. In cell D3, type the following formula:

   =SQRT(4*6*(2*PI()*0.91095E−30*1.38066E-23/(6.62618E−34^2))^3)*(0.33*0.56)^(0.75)*1E−6

9. Select cells C2:D3, and use the Create Names command to set the names in the left column. This names cells D2 and D3 as EG2_ and CONS, respectively.

10. In cells E2:F3, type the following entries (use Alt-230 on the numeric keypad to type the μ):

   E2: **Q**   F2: **1.6E-19**

   E3: μ0   F3: **1330**

11. Select cells E2:F3, and use the Create Names command to set the names in the left column. This names cells F2 and F3 as Q and _0, respectively. (Excel doesn't know to handle the μ, so it uses an underline instead.)

12. Select cell F3, choose the Define Name command on the Formula menu, name the cell **u0**, and delete the name _0.

13. In cell G2:H3, type the following entries:

   G2: **T0**   H2: **300**

   G3: **GAMMA**   H3: **2.42**

14. Select cells G2:H3, and use the Create Names command to set the names in the left column. This names cells H2 and H3 as T0 and GAMMA, respectively.

15. In cells A6:F7, type the following entries:

   A6: **T**   B6: **Eg**   C6: **ni**

   A7: **(K)**   B7: **(eV)**   C7: **(cm^-3)**

   D6: μ   E6: **n**   F6: **rho**

   D7: **(cm^2/V-s)** E7: **(cm^-3)**   F7: **(ohm-cm)**

16. Center the contents of cells A6:F7.

17. Copy cells E6:F7 to G6:H7 and I6:J7.

18. Type the following in cells D5:J5:

   D5: **Doping:**   E5: **1E13**   F5: **(cm^-3)**

   G5: **1.5E13**   H5: **(cm^-3)**   I5: **1E14**

   J5: **(cm^-3)**

19. In cell A8, type **300**, and in cell A9, type **320**.

20. Select cells A8:A9, grab the fill handle, drag it down to cell A18, and release it.

21. In cell B8, type this formula:

$$=EG0-EG1\_*A8\wedge2/(A8+EG2\_)$$

22. In cell C8, type the formula:

$$=CONS*SQRT(A8\wedge3)*EXP(-B8\ 1.60219E-19/(2\ 1.38066E-23\ *A8))$$

23. In cell D8, type the formula:

$$=u0*(A8/T0)\wedge(-GAMMA)$$

24. In cell E8, type the formula:

$$=0.5*(E\$5+SQRT(E\$5\wedge2+4*\$C8\wedge2))$$

25. In cell F8, type the formula:

$$=1/(Q*E8*\$D8)$$

26. Format cell B8 as 0.00.

27. Format cells C8:F8 as 0.0E+00.

28. Copy cells E8:F8 into cells G8:H8 and I8:J8.

29. Select cells B8:J8, grab the fill handle, and drag it down to cell J18. This copies the formulas down into the body of the table.

30. Outline the following cells:

A2:B3   A5:J5

C2:D3   A8:J18

E2:F3   A5:D18

G2:H3   G5:H18

31. Turn off the gridlines with the Display command on the Options menu.

If you turned off automatic recalculation, turn it on again now. Your worksheet should look like Figure 3.7. You are now ready to plot these three sets of data. First move the table out of the way to make room for the chart.

32. Select cell A5, hold down the Shift key, and double-click on the bottom border of the selection rectangle. This extends the selection down to the next, nonblank cell. Continue holding the Shift key down as you double-click on

FIGURE 3.7:

Table for calculating the resistivity of silicon versus temperature

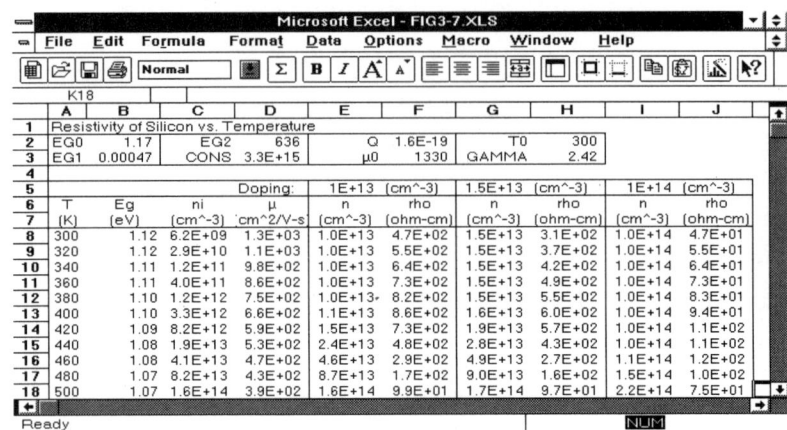

the right side of the selection rectangle. This extends the selection to the right to the first nonblank cell, selecting the rest of the table.

33. Grab the top edge of the selection rectangle with the mouse and drag the upper-left corner down to cell A18. This moves the whole table down.

34. Select cells A21:A31 (the *x* data), hold down the Ctrl key and select cells F21:F31 (the first set of *y* data).

35. Select the Chart Wizard command by clicking on the Chart Wizard button. Outline cells C5:H16 to define the chart area. You should see the first Chart Wizard window (Figure 3.1). Click on Next > to continue.

36. In the second Chart Wizard window (Figure 3.2), select the XY (Scatter) chart type and click on Next >.

37. In the third window (Figure 3.3), select number 2, lines and symbols, and click on Next >.

38. The fourth window (Figure 3.5) appears showing a sample chart. Click on Next > to accept the default settings and go to the next dialog box.

39. In the last Chart Wizard window, type **Resistivity of Silicon** in the Chart Title box, type **Temperature (K)** in the Category (X) box, and type **Resistivity (ohm-cm)** in the Value (Y) box. The titles should look like those in Figure 3.6.

40. Click on OK to leave the Chart Wizard and place the chart on the worksheet.

Your worksheet should look like Figure 3.8, with a chart below the list of coefficients. If you change any of the coefficients, Excel will recalculate the worksheet and change the chart to reflect the different value.

You will notice that the chart created by the Chart Wizard isn't quite right. The y-axis crosses the x-axis at a bad spot. Also, it needs two more curves and a legend to mark the three curves. You will modify the chart after reviewing the techniques for editing Excel charts.

FIGURE 3.8:

The Resistivity of Silicon versus Temperature worksheet with an embedded chart

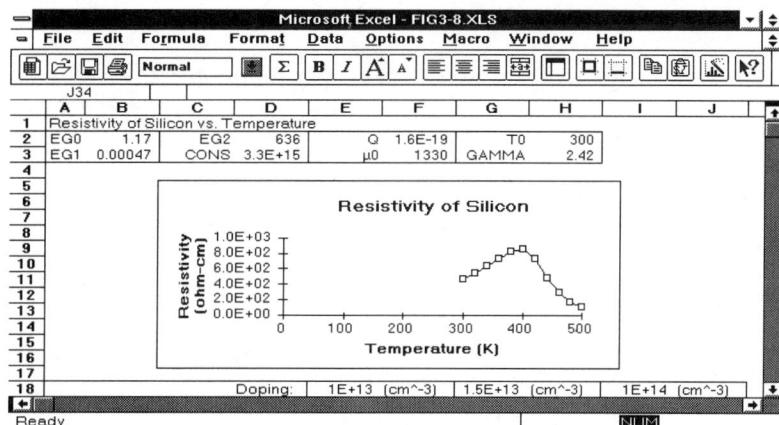

Editing Charts

To edit an embedded chart, double-click on it to put it in its own chart window. When you are finished editing the chart, double-click on the Control box (the close box on the Macintosh) in the upper-left corner of the chart window (not the Excel window) to reinsert the chart into the worksheet.

In the chart window, you can select parts of the chart and edit them individually, as follows:

- Click on the plotted points to change the cells being plotted, the symbols and lines being used, and any attached text.
- Click on an axis to change its style, limits, and label text format.

- Click on the whole chart to change all the text styles and the background and foreground colors and patterns.

When a chart window is open and selected, three special menus appear on the menu bar: Gallery, Chart, and Format.

Changing the Chart Type

The Gallery menu lists all the standard chart types. When you choose one of these types, Excel displays the list of subtypes. Select one of the subtypes to change the active chart.

At the bottom of the Gallery menu are the Preferred and Set Preferred commands. Use Set Preferred to define the style of the active chart as the preferred, or default, style. Everything you put on a chart but the data itself is part of the preferred chart style. You apply the preferred type to an existing chart with the Preferred command.

Adding and Changing Objects on a Chart

Use the Chart menu to add or change objects attached to a chart, as follows:

- The Attach Text command adds or changes chart titles, axis labels, and data labels.
- The Add Arrow command places an arrow on the chart to point out some specific piece of data.
- The Add Legend command places a legend on the chart.
- The Axes command determines which of the two or three axes are displayed on the screen.
- The Gridlines command sets whether or not gridlines are displayed within the body of the chart.
- The Add Overlay command attaches a second graph to the current one. An overlay graph can be a different chart type, with its own axes and range.
- The Edit Series command allows you to select a data series to edit.

To add unattached text, click on the chart, then click in the formula bar. Whatever you type appears on the chart, and you can drag it to anywhere you want it to appear.

Formatting a Chart

The Format menu contains commands to change the format or style of objects on a chart. The command you choose is applied to the selected chart object:

- The Patterns command displays a different dialog box depending on which object is selected. If a data series is selected, the Patterns command controls the color and shape of the lines and symbols on the screen. If a chart is selected, the Patterns command changes the foreground and background colors and the border style and color.

- The Font command changes the font, size, and style of the selected text.

- The Scale command allows you to change the scale limits for a selected chart axis.

- The Legend command determines where the legend appears on the chart.

- The Main Chart and Overlay commands set style parameters for the different chart types. Style parameters govern the appearance of chart elements, such as the amount of overlap of the columns on a column chart.

- The 3-D View command changes the viewpoint for the 3-D charts.

- The Move and Size commands are for changing the location and size of a chart without using the mouse.

You can also simply drag the chart where you want it, or drag the chart by its edge to change its size and shape. In Excel 4, you can reorient a 3-D chart by selecting it, grabbing one of the handles that appear around it, and rotating the chart to the orientation that most suits its purpose.

Adding Curves to a Chart

The simplest way to add more curves to a chart is to select the data, copy it, and then paste it on the chart using the Paste Special command on the Edit menu. You need to use the Paste Special command so that you can designate the first column of data as the x data. If you use Paste instead of Paste Special, Excel will plot the x data and the y data as two separate curves, with the integers 1, 2, 3, … as the x data.

Excel attaches curves to charts with series formulas. To see a series formula, put the chart in a chart window (double-click on the chart) and click on the curve. The series formula will appear in the formula bar. A series formula has four arguments separated by commas: the name of the series, surrounded by double quotation marks, which is used in a legend; a range reference to the x data; a range reference to the y data; and a series number, which determines the order in which the data is plotted.

You can edit a series formula to change the data that is plotted. If you paste a series formula into the formula bar, the data it points to will be plotted on the current chart.

One reason to edit the series formula is to keep the chart from being updated when you enter new data in the worksheet. Normally, a chart displays the contents of the attached cells. If the contents of the cells change, the chart changes to reflect the new values. If you have a chart that you want to keep, but you want to continue changing the data on the worksheet, you need to change the references in the chart's series formula into values. You can have Excel do this for you so that you don't have to type in the values. Simply select the reference in the series formula, press Ctrl-= (Cmd-= on the Macintosh) to replace the reference with its values, and click on the check button. After you change the data to values, you can continue to work with the worksheet without affecting that chart. You can develop some new data and plot another chart, or add another curve to an existing chart.

Modifying an XY Chart

Now you are ready to edit the Resistivity of Silicon chart you created earlier in the chapter. Your first step toward improving this XY chart is to plot the other two curves.

1. Select the two other series to be plotted: first the x data in the range A21:A31, then, while holding down the Ctrl key, H21:H31 and J21:J31.

2. Choose the Copy command on the Edit menu.

3. Double-click on the chart to expand it into a chart window.

4. Choose the Paste Special command on the Edit menu. Click on the Columns button to indicate the data is in columns, click on the Categories (X Values) in First Column check box to indicate that the first column contains x data, and then click on OK.

All three series are now on the chart, as shown in Figure 3.9. Now you need to adjust the point where the y-axis crosses the x-axis. Use the Scale command on the Format menu to change the limits and type (linear or log) of the selected axis.

5. Click on the x-axis to select it.

6. Choose the Scale command on the Format menu. Change the value in the Min box from Automatic to **300**, as shown in Figure 3.10, and click on OK.

7. Double-click on the chart window's Control box (the close box on the Macintosh) to return the chart to the worksheet.

FIGURE 3.9:
Two more curves added to the Resistivity of Silicon chart

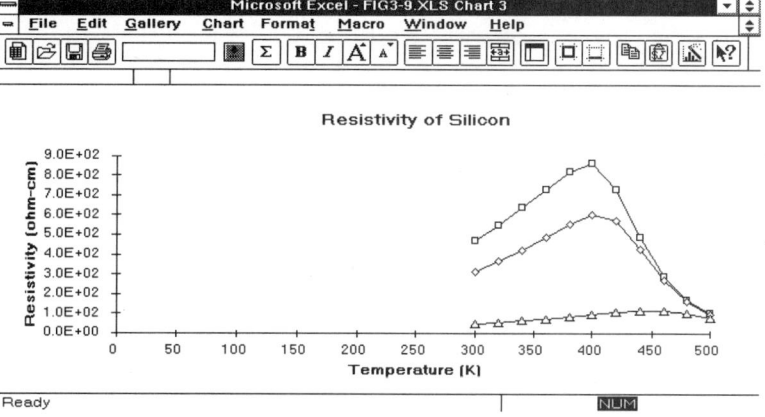

FIGURE 3.10:
Changing the scale of an axis

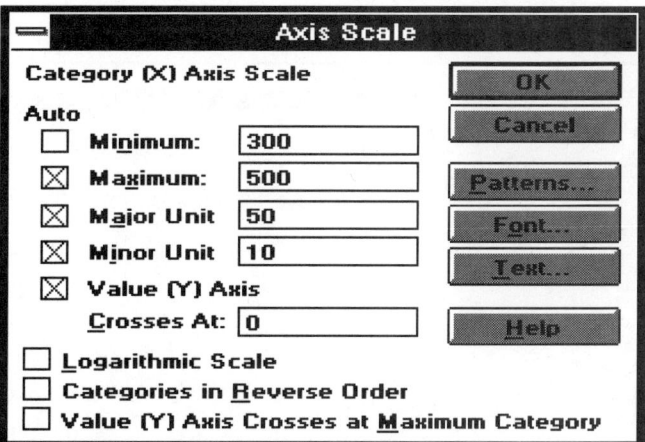

The chart now looks like the one shown in Figure 3.11. Your next task is to add labels to identify the three curves. You can add a label as a legend, as attached text, or as unattached text. First try a legend to see how it looks.

The series formulas for the three curves do not contain series names for the curves. You will begin by adding the series names to the series formulas.

8. Double-click on the chart to open the chart window.

9. Select the upper curve.

10. In the series formula, before the first comma, type **'1.0E13 (cm^−3)'**.

Your screen should look like Figure 3.12. Now add names for the other two curves.

11. Select the middle curve and type **'1.5E13 (cm^−3)'** in the series formula.

12. Select the lower curve and type **'1.0E14 (cm^−3)'** in the series formula.

13. Choose the Add Legend command on the Chart menu.

14. Double-click on the chart window's Control box to return the chart to the worksheet.

The modified chart looks like the one in Figure 3.13. If you don't like how the legend appears, use the Legend command on the chart window's Format menu to change its location and layout, or drag the legend to a new location.

FIGURE 3.11:

The Resistivity of Silicon chart with its scale adjusted

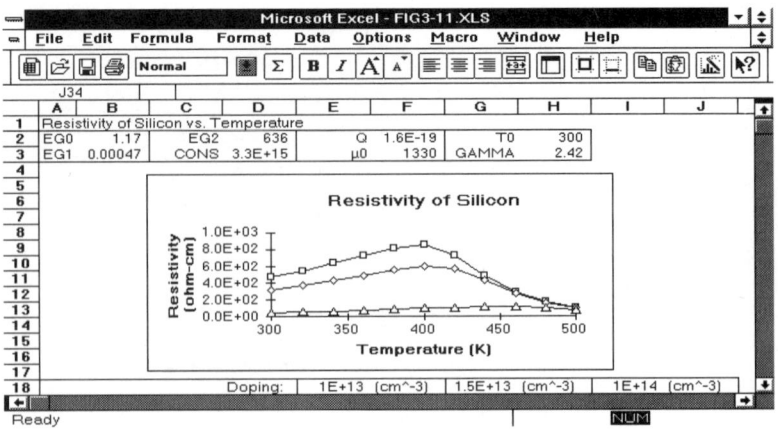

FIGURE 3.12:

Adding a series name to a
series formula

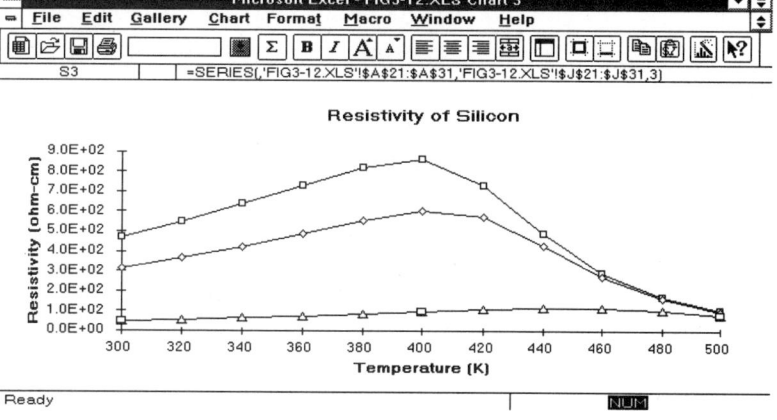

FIGURE 3.13:

The Resistivity of Silicon chart
with a legend

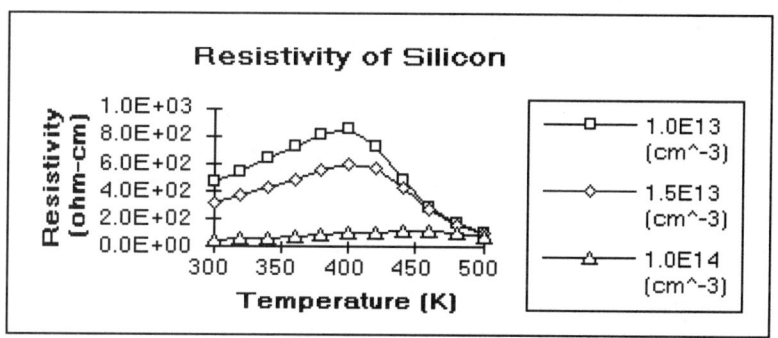

The second method for labeling the curves on a chart is by using attached text. You
attach text to a data point with the Attach Text command on the Chart menu. Any
text attached to a data point appears to the right of that data point. If you move the
data point, the attached text moves along with it. Now replot your data using attached text instead of a legend.

15. Double-click on the chart to open its chart window.

16. Choose the Delete Legend command on the Chart menu to remove the
legend.

17. Hold down the Ctrl key and click on the seventh data point on the top curve
to select it.

129

18. Choose the Attach Text command on the Chart menu. The Series and Data Point box should be checked, with series 1 and data point 7 listed in the text boxes. Click on OK.

At this point, a number is attached to the data point. The number is the current value of the data point. Change the number to the series name.

19. With the attached text selected, edit it in the formula bar to read **1.0E13 (cm^-3)**.

20. Choose the Patterns command on the Format menu. Click on the Custom Border button (black lines on white background), then on the Custom Area option with a white foreground and background, and then on OK.

21. Hold down the Ctrl key and click on the fourth data point in the second series and use the Attach Text command on the Chart menu to attach text to this series' data point. Edit the attached text in the formula bar to read **1.5E13 (cm^-3)**. Then use the Patterns command on the Format menu to choose a Custom Border and Custom Area as you did for the other attached text.

22. Attach text to the fifth data point in the third curve and change the text to **1.0E14 (cm^-3)**. Set a Custom Border and Custom Area, as you did for the other text.

23. Double-click on the Control box to put the chart back into the worksheet.

The worksheet and chart should now look like Figure 3.14, with the three data series labeled with attached text.

FIGURE 3.14:

The Resistivity of Silicon chart with the curves labeled with attached text

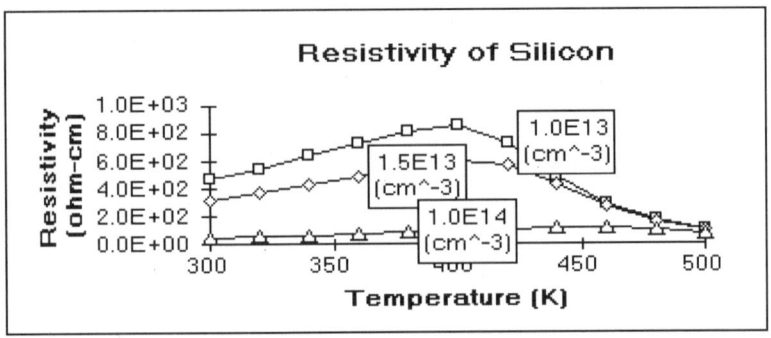

Now see how the chart looks with unattached text and arrows. Unattached text is attached to the chart background, and it stays in the same relative location no matter what size you make the chart. However, since the text is not attached to a data point, it will not move if the data is changed. You shouldn't use unattached text to label a curve until you are finished changing the data.

To add unattached text, enter it into the formula bar of the chart window, and then drag it from its current position in the window to where you want it to appear. You can type additional lines of unattached text by holding down the Ctrl key while pressing Enter (Cmd-Option-Enter on the Macintosh).

24. Double-click on the chart to open its chart window.

25. Select one of the attached data labels and press the Delete (Backspace on the Macintosh) key to remove it. Delete the other two labels in the same way.

26. Click in the formula bar and type **1.0E13 (cm^−3)**. Press Ctrl-Enter (Cmd-Option-Enter on the Macintosh) to move down a line, then type **1.5E15 (cm^−3)**, press Ctrl-Enter, and type **1.0E14 (cm^−3)**.

27. Grab the unattached text at the center of the chart and drag it to the open area in the upper-right corner of the chart.

28. Choose the Add Arrow command on the Chart menu to add an arrow to the chart.

29. Select the arrow and drag the selection boxes on each end of the arrow until it points to the top curve, with its tail near the top piece of unattached text.

30. Add two more arrows, one pointing from the middle text to the middle curve, and the other pointing from the bottom text to the bottom curve.

31. Double-click on the chart window's Control box to close the window.

Your worksheet should now look like Figure 3.15. Unattached text is also useful for placing notes and other information on a graph. But keep in mind that if you change the chart, the text and arrows may no longer point to the right objects.

FIGURE 3.15:

The Resistivity of Silicon chart
with the curves labeled with
unattached text and arrows

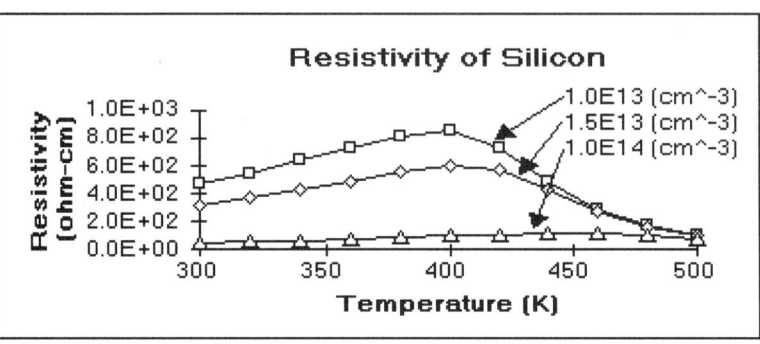

Creating Log and Semilog Charts

The XY chart type includes both linear and logarithmic axes. To switch the axes from linear to logarithmic, choose a logarithmic chart type from the Chart Gallery dialog box (accessed from the Gallery menu), or use the Scales command on the Format menu to change the axes. In the next example, you will calculate another equation and graph it as a logarithmic chart.

Electron Avalanche Coefficient in Silicon   When a voltage is applied across a semiconductor device, electrons in the semiconductor material are accelerated. If the voltage is high enough, the electrons are accelerated to the point where they generate additional electrons through impact ionization. Device designers usually like to keep avalanche out of their devices, except in special devices such as the avalanche transistor.

The avalanche rate can be calculated with empirical equations that have been fit to experimental data. For example, you can calculate the silicon avalanche coefficients versus electric field and temperature with the following equation:

$$\alpha = AVN\,1 \cdot \exp\left[\frac{AVN\,2 + AVN\,3(T - 300)}{|E|}\right]$$

where α is in m^{-1}, T is the temperature in Kelvin, and E is the electric field in V/m. The avalanche rate is then calculated by multiplying this coefficient by the electron density and by the electron velocity. These are the coefficients of the equation:

E (V/m)	AVN1 (m-1)	AVN2 (V/m)	AVN3 (V/m-K)
$E < 2.4 \times 10^7$	2.6×10^8	1.43×10^8	1.3×10^5
$2.4 \times 10^7 < E < 4.2 \times 10^7$	6.2×10^7	1.08×10^8	1.3×10^5
$E > 4.2 \times 10^7$	5.0×10^7	9.90×10^7	1.3×10^5

In this example, you will calculate the avalanche coefficients versus electric field at 300, 600, and 900 K.

1. Start with a new worksheet expanded to full size.

2. Set the column widths as follows:

   A = 2   D = 12
   B = 12   E = 12
   C = 12

3. In cell A1, type **Electron Avalanche Coefficients in Silicon**.

First create the table of values for the avalanche coefficient equation. Each set of coefficients is for a different range of electric field values.

4. In cells B3:E6, type the following entries:

B3: **E (V/m)**	C3: **AVN1 (1/m)**	D3: **AVN2 (V/m)**	E3: **AVN3 (V/m−K)**
B4: **0**	C4: **2.6E8**	D4: **1.43E8**	E4: **1.3E5**
B5: **2.4E7**	C5: **6.2E7**	D5: **1.08E8**	E5: **1.3E5**
B6: **4.2E7**	C6: **5.0E7**	D6: **9.9E7**	E6: **1.3E5**

5. Right-justify the contents of cells B3, C3, D3, and E3.

6. Name cells in the table as follows:

	C4: **AVN11**	D4: **AVN21**	E4: **AVN31**
B5: **ECUT1**	C5: **AVN12**	D5: **AVN22**	E5: **AVN32**
B6: **ECUT2.**	C6: **AVN13.**	D6: **AVN32**	E6: **AVN33**

7. Name the whole table, B4:E6, as **COEFFS**.

8. Outline ranges B3:E3 and B4:E6.

Next create the avalanche coefficient table.

9. In cell B8, type **T (K) =** and right-justify it.

10. Type **300** in cell C8, **600** in cell D8, and **900** in cell E8.

11. In cell B9, type **E (V/m)** and right-justify it.

12. In cell C9, type **alpha (1/m)** and right-justify it.

13. Select cell C9 and copy it into cells D9:E9 by grabbing its fill handle and dragging right to cell E9.

14. Type **5.0E+06** in cell B10, and **1.0E+07** in cell B11.

15. Select cells B10:B11, grab the fill handle, and drag it down to cell B29.

You can choose the correct values from the table according to the applied field in two ways. The first is to use nested IF functions. Two nested IF functions will divide the problem into three ranges. The second method is to use the VLOOKUP function, which scans the table automatically. You will use both methods in this example. The next step illustrates the nested IF function method.

16. In cell C10, type the following formula:

> **=IF($B10>ECUT1,IF($B10>ECUT2,AVN13,AVN12),AVN11)***
> **EXP(−(IF($B10>ECUT1,IF($B10>ECUT2,AVN23,AVN22),AVN21)+**
> **IF($B10>ECU T1,IF($B10>ECUT2,AVN33,AVN32),AVN31)*(C$8−**
> **300))/$B10)**

The lookup functions result in a more compact formula than the nested IF functions, especially if there are more than two ranges in the table. The next step uses the VLOOKUP function method.

17. In cell D10, type the following formula:

> **=VLOOKUP($B10,COEFFS,2)*EXP(−(VLOOKUP($B10,COEFFS,3)**
> **+VLOOKUP($B10,COEFFS,4)*(D$8−300))/$B10)**

Use the lookup function method for the rest of the worksheet.

18. Select cell D10, grab its fill handle, and drag it right to E10.

19. Select cells C10:E10, grab the fill handle, and drag it down to E29.

20. Format cells B4:E6 and B10:E29 as 0.00E+00.

21. Outline cells B8:E8, B9:E9, B10:E29, B8:B29, and D8:D29.

22. Turn off the worksheet gridlines with the Display command on the Options menu.

23. Save the worksheet as **FIG3-16.XLS**.

This completes the worksheet, which should look like Figure 3.16. This worksheet calculates the electron avalanche coefficient versus electric field for the temperatures 300, 600, and 900 K, listed along the top.

The values of the avalanche coefficient span many orders of magnitude, which is difficult to plot on a linear scale. A logarithmic scale gives a much more reasonable graph. This time, create the chart using the menu commands instead of the Chart Wizard.

24. Select cells B10:E29 and choose the Copy command on the Edit menu.

25. Choose the New command on the File menu and select a Chart document.

26. Choose the Paste Special command on the Edit menu, and select the Values (Y) in Columns and the Categories (X-Labels) in First Column options. Then click on OK.

Excel creates a bar chart of the data. Interesting, but definitely not what you want.

27. Select the XY (Scatter) chart type from the Gallery menu. Select chart type number 2 from the Scatter dialog box.

28. Click on the y-axis and choose the Scale command on the Format menu. Click on the Logarithmic Scale box.

29. Change the Category (X) Axis Crosses At box to **1E-11** and click on OK.

30. Choose the Add Legend command on the Chart menu.

FIGURE 3.16:
Electron avalanche coefficients in
silicon versus electric field and
temperature

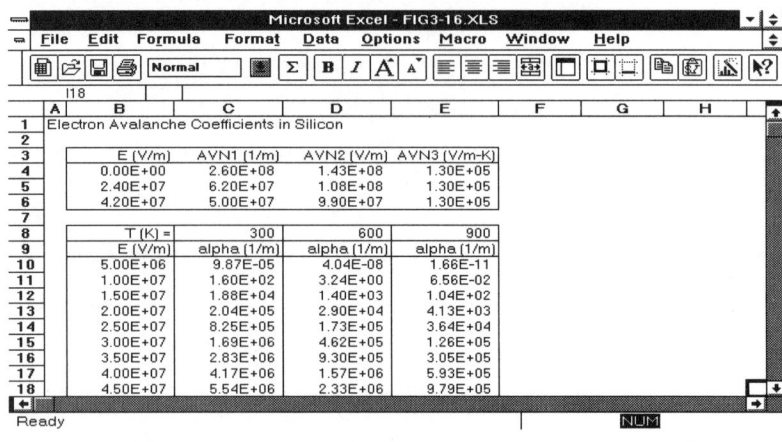

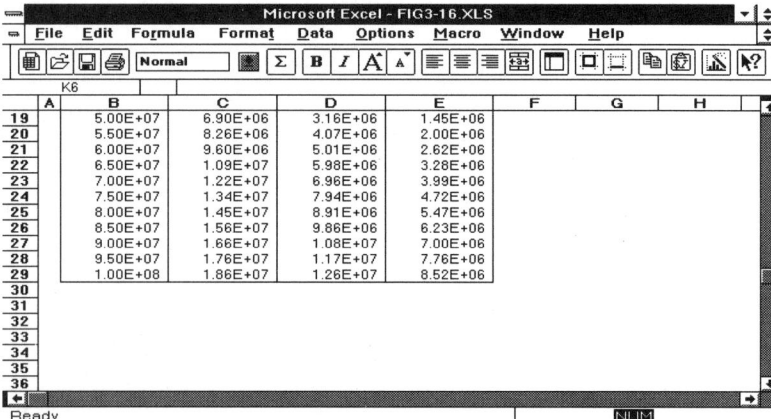

31. Grab the legend and drag it under the curve.

32. Select the top curve on the graph and add the name of the curve "T = 300
    (K)" (including the double quotation marks) as the first argument of the
    series formula, so that it reads:

    =SERIES("T = 300 K",'FIG3-16.XLS'!$B$10:$B$29,'FIG3-
    16.XLS'!$C$10:$C$29,1)

33. Select the center curve and add **"T = 600 (K)"** to the series formula, so that it reads:

    =SERIES("T = 600 K",'FIG3-16.XLS'!$B$10:$B$29,'FIG3-16.XLS'!$D$10:$D$29,2)

34. Select the bottom curve and add **"T = 900 (K)"** to the series formula, so that it reads:

    =SERIES("T = 900 K",'FIG3-16.XLS'!$B$10:$B$29,'FIG3-16.XLS'!$E$10:$E$29,2)

35. Choose the Attach Text command on the Chart menu, click on Chart Title, and then click on OK.

36. Edit the new chart title in the formula bar so that it reads **Electron Avalanche Coefficient in Silicon**.

37. Choose the Attach Text command on the Chart menu, click on Value (Y) Axis, and then click on OK.

38. Edit the new y-axis title in the formula bar, so that it reads **Avalanche Coeff. (1/m)**.

39. Choose the Attach Text command on the Chart menu, click on Category (X) Axis, and then click on OK.

40. Edit the new x-axis title in the formula bar, so that it reads **Electric Field (V/m)**.

41. Select the x-axis and choose the Scale command on the Format menu. Change the major unit to **20000000** (2×10^7).

The completed chart is shown in Figure 3.17. This chart is currently on a separate chart sheet, which can be saved independently from the worksheet. If you want to attach the chart to the worksheet, select the whole chart, choose Copy on the Edit menu, select a cell on the worksheet, and then choose Paste. A copy of the chart will be attached to the worksheet.

FIGURE 3.17:

Electron avalanche coefficient in silicon for three different temperatures: a semilog plot

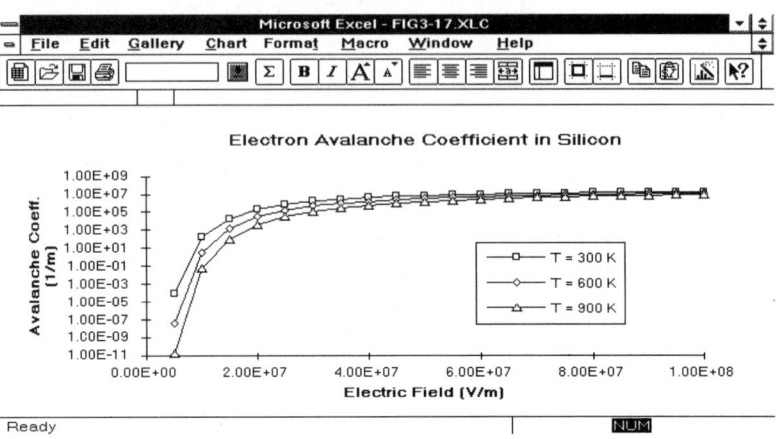

Creating Three-Dimensional Charts

Excel's three-dimensional charts all have equally spaced grids in both the x and y directions, so that the gridding is uniform no matter what values you supply for the x- and y-axes. This uniform gridding can be a problem in some cases, such as when the gridding distorts the results. However, by plotting consecutive slices through the data and offsetting them by an appropriate amount, you can produce a reasonable three-dimensional wire-frame plot using the two-dimensional XY chart type.

First you need to define a new rectangular coordinate system u, v, and w. Plot the u axis horizontally, the v axis at an angle ϕ, and the w axis vertically, as illustrated in Figure 3.18. Next you map these three axes onto the two-dimensional plane, with these transform equations: $x = u + v\cos(\phi)$ and $y = w + v\sin(\phi)$. To plot a three-dimensional data point (u, v, w), insert it into the transform equations and calculate the two-dimensional (x,y) data point.

To create the worksheet, you need to put the three-dimensional data into three columns so that you can map them into two columns that can then be plotted on an XY chart. Data for this type of chart usually appears as slices through the domain

FIGURE 3.18:

FIGURE 3.18:

Mapping the three-dimensional axes onto the two-dimensional surface

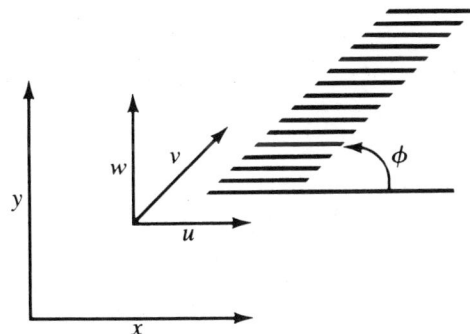

to be plotted. Each slice goes from one boundary to the other. You stack these data sets, so that the first data point of one section comes after the last data point of the previous section.

A problem with the layout of the chart is that a line will be drawn from the last data point of each section to the first data point of the next section. These lines cut across the middle of the graph, which is definitely not what you want. But you can stop Excel from drawing the return lines by inserting a blank row between each section of data. Excel considers the blank line as a data point missing from the middle of a data range, and will not draw a data marker or lines to that point.

Temperature Profile in an Overstressed Silicon Diode   When a small silicon diode is pulsed with a high-power pulse of electricity, it heats up. If it heats up too much, it will be damaged. Of course, if you really pour on the power, you will see smoke and fire where the diode used to be, and there will not be much question that it failed. On the other hand, if you use only a small amount of power, the diode may only be degraded and may still operate, at least for a while.

One way to evaluate the type of damage that a diode may sustain is to mathematically model its operation and see where the damaging heating occurs. This type of modeling is usually done on a Cray or VAX computer, however the analysis of the results can be done on a desktop computer, as you will do in the next example. The data in Table 3.1 comes from just such a diode simulation, and it shows the temperature at different positions in the diode. The data is in the form of y and z position data, and T temperature data.

TABLE 3.1: Temperature Data versus Position in a Small Signal Diode

								$y(\mu)$							
T(K)	0	10	20	30	35	40	43.3	46.6	50	55	60	110	155	200	250
0	300	300	300	300	300	300	486	329	308	303	301	300	300	300	300
1	425	429	441	474	528	779	414	327	307	302	301	300	300	300	300
2	462	465	478	512	569	766	419	332	309	303	301	300	300	300	300
3	463	465	476	505	554	659	448	342	312	303	301	300	300	300	300
4	453	456	466	495	542	659	461	352	316	304	301	300	300	300	300
5	440	443	453	480	522	617	459	360	320	305	301	300	300	300	300
6	424	426	435	460	497	572	451	365	324	306	301	300	300	300	300
7	405	407	415	436	467	527	443	370	328	308	301	300	300	300	300
8	389	390	397	416	443	496	440	377	333	309	301	300	300	300	300
9	380	382	388	406	430	482	442	384	338	311	301	300	300	300	300
10	381	383	389	407	430	480	448	392	344	313	302	300	300	300	300
11	385	387	395	413	435	480	452	398	350	316	302	300	300	300	300
12	391	393	401	420	439	476	451	403	356	319	302	300	300	300	300
13	376	378	384	400	415	449	440	404	360	322	303	300	300	300	300
14	444	447	457	477	494	518	492	442	385	333	305	300	300	300	300
15	444	448	459	484	503	520	493	449	399	349	323	301	300	300	300
16	344	346	354	373	391	414	410	397	376	352	338	302	300	300	300
17	331	333	339	354	369	386	386	378	365	348	335	302	300	300	300
18	330	332	337	351	363	375	375	369	359	344	333	302	300	300	300
19	330	331	337	349	359	368	367	362	353	341	331	302	300	300	300
20	330	331	336	347	355	362	361	356	348	337	328	302	300	300	300
31	325	325	327	329	330	329	328	326	323	319	314	302	300	300	300
42	319	319	319	319	318	317	316	315	314	312	309	302	300	300	300
53	315	315	314	314	313	312	311	311	310	309	307	302	300	300	300
64	312	312	311	310	310	309	309	308	308	307	306	301	300	300	300
75	310	310	309	308	308	308	307	307	306	306	305	301	300	300	300
86	308	308	308	307	307	307	306	306	306	305	305	301	300	300	300
97	307	307	307	306	306	306	306	305	305	305	304	301	300	300	300
108	307	307	306	306	306	305	305	305	305	304	304	301	300	300	300
119	306	306	306	306	305	305	305	305	305	304	304	301	300	300	300
130	300	300	300	300	300	300	300	300	300	300	300	300	300	300	300

$z(\mu)$

The data at $y = 0$ is the centerline of the device (that is, only half of the diode was modeled). The bottom conductor is at $z = 130$ microns, and it covers the whole bottom of the diode. The top conductor is at $z = 0$, and it extends from $y = 0$ to $y = 40$ microns. The diode junction, where all of the action takes place, is at $z = 10$ microns, and extends from $y = 0$ to about 50 microns. The layout of the diode is illustrated in Figure 3.19.

As you can tell from Table 3.1, a large amount of data has to go into this worksheet. However, you will find that it does not take too much time to type it in. Now create the table, and then use the data in a three-dimensional graph.

1. Start with a blank worksheet expanded to full-screen size.

2. Select columns A:AF and change their width to 4.

3. In cell A1, type **Temperature Profile in an Overstressed Silicon Diode**.

4. In cell A3, type **T (K)**.

5. In cells A4:A18, type the y values (from Table 3.1):

A4: **0**	A9: **40**	A14: **60**
A5: **10**	A10: **43.3**	A16: **110**
A6: **20**	A11: **46.6**	A17: **155**

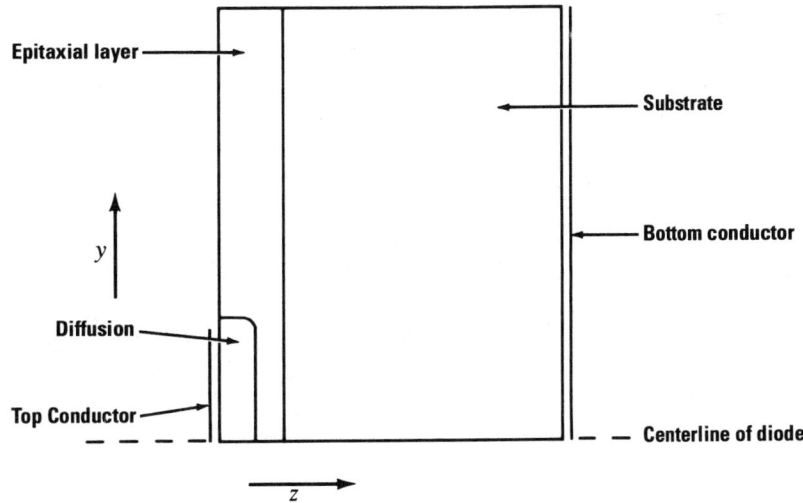

FIGURE 3.19:

The layout of the small signal diode used to generate the temperature data

| A7: **30** | A12: **50** | A18: **200** |
| A8: **35** | A13: **55** | A19: **250** |

6. In cells B3:AF3, type the z values (from Table 3.1):

B3: **0**	J3: **8**	R3: **16**	Z3: **64**
C3: **1**	K3: **9**	S3: **17**	AA3: **75**
D3: **2**	L3: **10**	T3: **18**	AB3: **86**
E3: **3**	M3: **11**	U3: **19**	AC3: **97**
F3: **4**	N3: **12**	V3: **20**	AD3: **108**
G3: **5**	O3: **13**	W3: **31**	AE3: **119**
H3: **6**	P3: **14**	X3: **42**	AF3: **130**
I3: **7**	Q3: **15**	Y3: **53**	

7. In cells B4:AF18, type the temperature values from Table 3.1. Note that the values you are typing in the worksheet are the transpose of the values in the table. That is, as you move across the table you move down the worksheet.

Your worksheet should now look like Figure 3.20. Now see how Excel's built-in 3-D wire-frame plotter does with the data.

8. Select cells A3:AF18 and choose the Copy command on the Edit menu.

9. Choose the New command on the File menu and create a new chart sheet.

10. Choose the Paste Special command on the Edit menu. In the dialog box, select Columns, Series Names in First Row and Categories (X-Labels) in First Column, and then click on OK.

What you see on the screen is definitely not what you wanted. This is what happens when you try to plot a three-dimensional data set as the default column chart type.

11. Choose the 3-D Surface command on the Gallery menu and select chart type 2.

12. Click on the axes until the black squares appear on the corners of the 3-D box surrounding the plot. Grab one of these squares and rotate the plot to the left a little until it looks better.

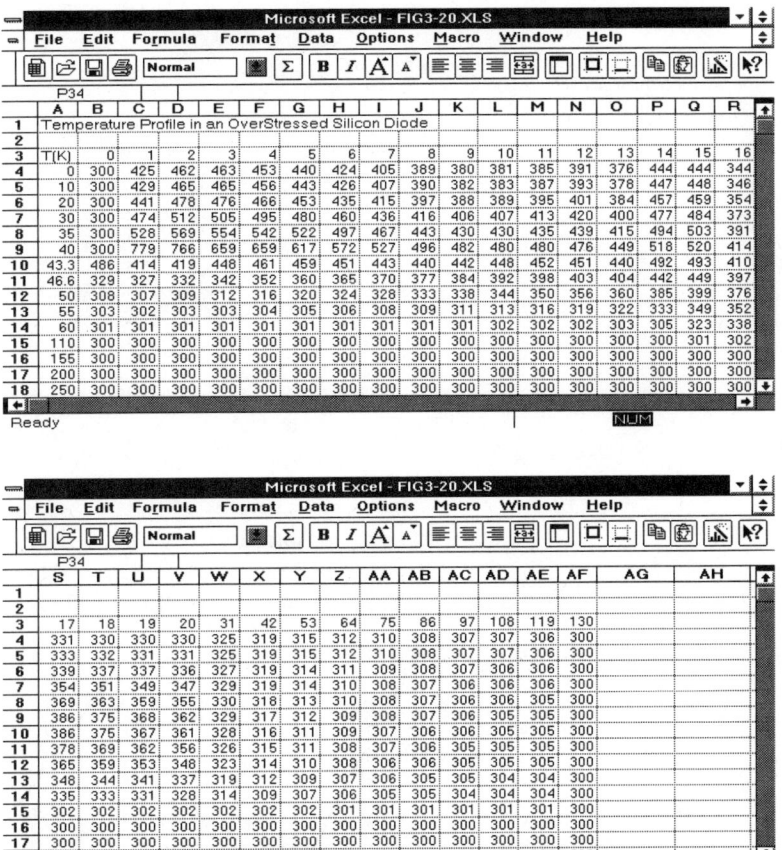

FIGURE 3.20:

The worksheet for the temperature profile in an overstressed silicon diode

13. Select the vertical axis, choose the Scale command on the Format menu, and change the minimum to **300**.

This chart, shown in Figure 3.21. is more like what you expected to see. The only problem is that, with the uniformly spaced grids, the temperature data in the upper-left corner of the plot is spread out over most of the plot. It is a bit difficult to get a good idea of where the heating is taking place because of the distortion in the chart. Plot this data again, but this time you will calculate your own lines and correctly space the gridlines. Save the existing chart and worksheet if you want to keep them.

FIGURE 3.21:

The 3-D wire-frame chart of the temperature profile in an overstressed silicon diode

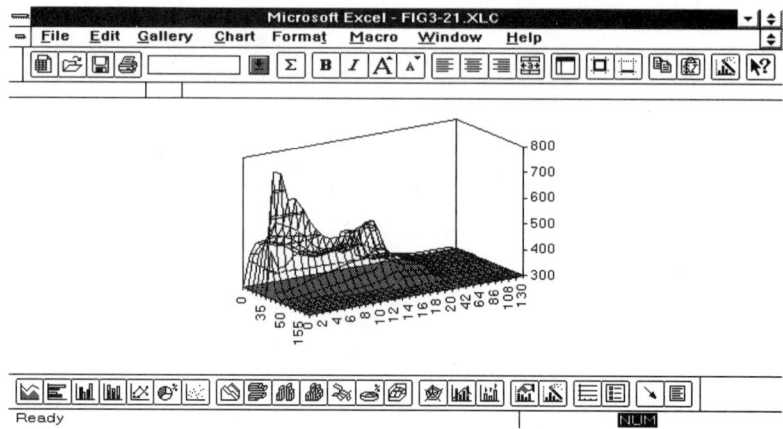

First place the y, z, and T data into three parallel columns on a worksheet, and then map this data onto the x-y plane in two more columns.

14. Open a new worksheet and expand it to full size.

15. In cell A1, type **Temperature Profile in an Overstressed Silicon Diode**.

16. In cell D2, type **Plot Angle:** and right justify it.

17. Type **60** in cell E2.

You need both the sine and cosine of the plot angle in every mapping. Instead of recalculating them again and again, calculate them here and use the numbers in the rest of the worksheet. First convert the degrees to radians, and then use them in the functions.

18. Type **=SIN(E2*PI( )/180)** in cell F2.

19. Type **=COS(E2*PI( )/180)** in cell G2.

20. In cell A3, type **Y (μ)** and right-justify it.

21. In cell B3, type **Z (μ)** and right-justify it.

22. In cell C3, type **T (K)** and right-justify it.

23. In cell D3, type **x** and right-justify it.

24. In cell E3, type **y** and right-justify it.

Now you are ready to insert the y values. Fill the cells by typing in the first value and then copying it to the rest of the range. You can use the Copy and Paste commands, the Fill Down command, or the fill handle to copy the values.

25. In the following ranges, type the value in the first cell and copy it into the other cells in the range:

A4:A34: **0**	A260:A290: **50**
A36:A66: **10**	A292:A322: **55**
A68:A98: **20**	A324:A354: **60**
A100:A130: **30**	A356:A386: **110**
A132:A162: **35**	A388:A418: **155**
A164:A194: **40**	A420:A450: **200**
A196:A226: **43.3**	A452:A482: **250**
A228:A258: **46.6**	

Next put in the z data values. Again, you enter the data once and then copy it into ranges. You can either type in the first set or copy it from the other 3-D chart worksheet. To copy the first data set, switch to the worksheet for the last example, copy the data there, switch back to this worksheet, select the range, use the Paste Special command on the Edit menu, and check the Transpose box.

After the first set of values is on the worksheet, copy the values into the other ranges by holding down the Ctrl key (Option on the Macintosh), placing the pointer on the edge of the range, pressing the mouse button, and dragging it to the new range.

26. In the following ranges:

B4:B34	B164:B194	B324:B354
B36:B66	B196:B226	B356:B386
B68:B98	B228:B258	B388:B418
B100:B130	B260:B290	B420:B450
B132:B162	B292:B322	B452:B482

type and copy this list of data into each cell range:

0	8	16	64
1	9	17	75

2	10	18	86
3	11	19	97
4	12	20	108
5	13	31	119
6	14	42	130
7	15	53	

Now put in the temperature data. Be sure that you put the correct temperature value with each y, z value, and don't forget to insert blank lines between the sets of data. The quickest way to do this is to copy this data from the last example. Select a row of data in the last example, switch to this worksheet, select the first cell of the range, and use the Paste Special command on the Edit menu with the Transpose box checked. If you don't want to type the 464 data values (it only takes about 15 minutes), you can plot the formula shown in the next step instead. The formula has no special significance other than it makes an interesting graph.

27. Using the data in Table 3.1, type or copy in the 464 temperature values in cells C4:C482. Alternatively, you can type and then copy this formula:

=300+500*COS(A4*3*PI()/250)*COS(B4*3*PI()/130)* EXP(−A4/62) * EXP(−B4/33)

The next step is to put in the mapping functions.

28. In cells D4:D468, type and copy **=B4+A4*$G$2.**

29. In cells E4:E468, type and copy **=C4+A4*$F$2.**

30. Choose the Clear command on the Edit menu and check All to erase the data copied into the following rows: 35, 67, 99, 131, 163, 195, 227, 259, 291, 323, 355, 387, 419, and 453.

Insert some extra data values to draw lines around the edges of the plot at the minimum temperature (300 K), to provide a visual cue to the perspective of the graph.

31. Type **130** in cell D483, **0** in D484, **300** in E483, and **300** in E484.

32. Type **=0+250*$G$2** in cell D485.

33. Type **=130+250*$G$2** in cell D486.

34. Type **=300+250*$F$2** in cells E485 and E486.

The worksheet should now look like Figure 3.22. You are ready to plot the data in columns D and E.

35. Select cells D4:E486.

36. Click on the Chart Wizard button and select cells K2:R17 for the graph.

37. In the first Chart Wizard window, click on OK to accept the data.

38. In the second Chart Wizard window, select the XY (Scatter) chart type, and then choose XY chart type number 2 in the third window.

39. In the fourth window, select the Columns, Use First Column for X Data, and Use First Row for First Data Point options.

40. In the fifth window, type the title **Temperature Profile in a Silicon Diode**, the x-axis label **z (microns)**, and the y-axis label **Temperature (K)**.

Now mark the y-axis with labels. Add the labels by creating a new hidden plot and attaching a label to each point.

41. Copy the contents of cells A354:E354 to L19:P19.

42. Copy the contents of cells A418:E418 to L20:P20.

43. Copy the contents of cells A482:E482 to L21:P21.

FIGURE 3.22:

The remapped worksheet for the temperature profile in an overstressed silicon diode

	A	B	C	D	E	F	G	H	I	J
1	Temperature Profile in an Overstressed Silicon Diode									
2			Plot Angle:		60	0.86603	0.5			
3	y (µ)	z (µ)	T (K)	x	y					
4	0	0	300	0	300					
5	0	1	425	1	425					
6	0	2	462	2	462					
7	0	3	463	3	463					
8	0	4	453	4	453					
9	0	5	440	5	440					
10	0	6	424	6	424					
11	0	7	405	7	405					
12	0	8	389	8	389					
13	0	9	380	9	380					
14	0	10	381	10	381					
15	0	11	385	11	385					
16	0	12	391	12	391					
17	0	13	376	13	376					
18	0	14	444	14	444					

Microsoft Excel - FIG3-22.XLS

File Edit Formula Format Data Options Macro Window Help

Normal

S23

Ready   NUM

147

44. Select the range O19:P21 and choose Copy from the Edit menu.

45. Double-click on the chart to open the chart window.

46. Choose the Paste Special command on the Edit menu, select Columns, select Categories (X Labels) in First Column, and then click on OK.

47. Hold down the Ctrl key, click on the leftmost data point of the new curve, and choose the Attached Text command on the Chart menu.

48. Change the newly attached text to **60**.

49. Ctrl-click on the middle data point, choose Attached Text, and change the text to **155 (microns)**.

50. Ctrl-click on the right data point, choose the Attach Text command, and change the text to **250**.

51. Click on the line, choose the Patterns command on the Format menu, and click on None under Lines and None under Marker.

52. Double-click on the Control box (the close box on the Macintosh) to close the chart window and put the chart back on the worksheet.

Your 3-D chart should look like the one in Figure 3.23, unless you plotted the formula (in step 27) instead of the data. If you plotted the formula, your chart should look like the one in Figure 3.24. You can change the value of the plot angle and see how it changes the view of the chart.

FIGURE 3.23:
The replotted 3-D chart of the temperature profile in an overstressed silicon diode

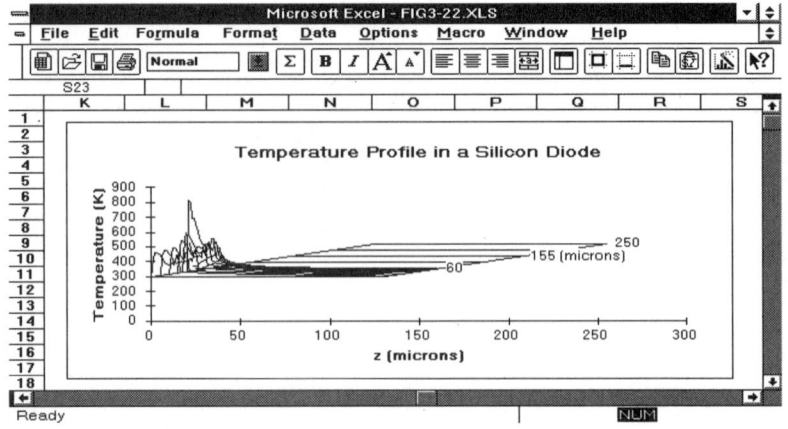

FIGURE 3.24:
The 3-D chart of the
alternative formula

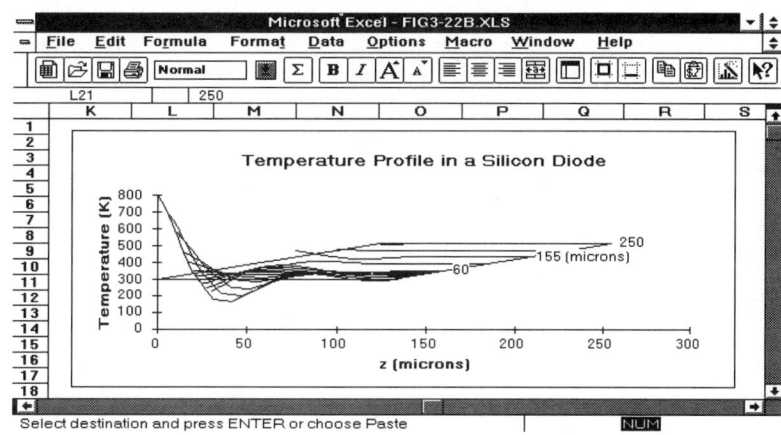

Drawing Pictures

Along with its charting tools, Excel also provides tools for drawing shapes. If you activate the drawing toolbar, you can draw lines circles and boxes in various colors to highlight different results and calculations on your worksheets. To display the drawing toolbar, use the Toolbar command on the Options menu. The drawing toolbar contains the tools listed in Table 3.2 (from left to right).

In addition, you can use Excel's data-plotting capability to draw complex figures on the screen. Figure 3.25 shows a segmented line drawing created with approximately 425 data pairs that form 53 discrete line segments. Digitizing the drawing by hand and typing the data pairs into the worksheet took an evening, which is not an unreasonable amount of time to produce a figure of this complexity. Of course, this does not include the amount of time that Julie, my wife, spent drawing the original figure.

A drawing on a chart can help illustrate the function being plotted. For example, if you are plotting the output of an electronic circuit, adding a simple drawing of the circuit in the corner of your chart makes the results more meaningful to a reader. Unfortunately, Excel's drawing tools work only on worksheets, not on chart sheets. You can either create a chart embedded in a worksheet and use the drawing tools to add a graphic, or you can place a drawing on a chart sheet by using line segments, as in Figure 3.25.

FIGURE 3.25:

A drawing created as line segments with Excel's data plotter (*an osprey in flight, by Julie Stephens Orvis, D.V.M*)

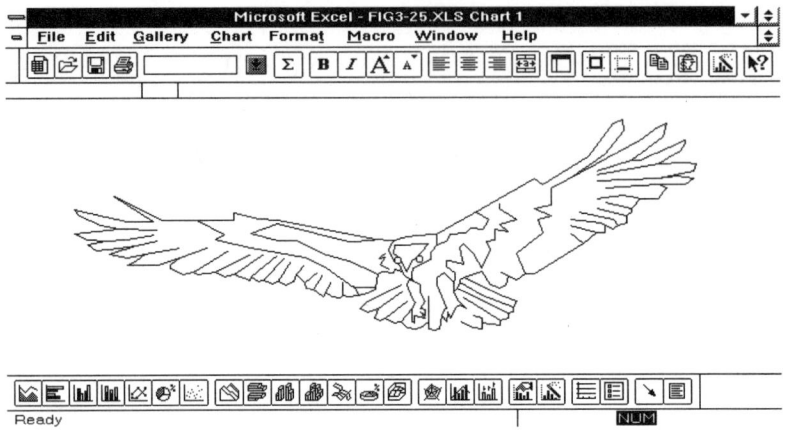

TABLE 3.2: Excel's Drawing Toolbar

Tool	Description
	Straight line
	Arrow
	Freehand line
	Unfilled rectangle
	Unfilled oval
	Unfilled arc
	Unfilled polygon

TABLE 3.2: Excel's Drawing Toolbar (continued)

Tool	Description
	Filled rectangle
	Filled oval
	Filled arc
	Filled polygon
	Text box
	Selection rectangle
	Edit polygon
	Group objects
	Ungroup objects
	Bring to front
	Move to back

TABLE 3.2: Excel's Drawing Toolbar (continued)

Tool	Description
	Color object
	Shadow object

Delyiannis Bandpass Filter   The Delyiannis bandpass filter is an active electronic filter network that passes frequencies within a particular range and filters out all others. Figure 3.26 shows the circuit diagram. The transfer function (the ratio of the output to the input) is defined with this equation:

$$|G(i\omega)| = \frac{\dfrac{\omega}{R_1 C_2 (1 - 1/k)}}{\sqrt{\left(\omega_p^2 - \omega^2\right)^2 + \omega^2 \left(\omega_p / Q_p\right)^2}}$$

Here, ω is the angular frequency:

$$k = 1 + \frac{R_A}{R_B}$$

$$\omega_p^2 = \frac{1}{R_1 R_2 C_1 C_2}$$

$$\frac{\omega_p}{Q_p} = \frac{1}{R_2 C_1} + \frac{1}{R_2 C_2} - \frac{1}{k-1}\frac{1}{R_1 C_2}$$

FIGURE 3.26:

A diagram of the Delyiannis
bandpass circuit

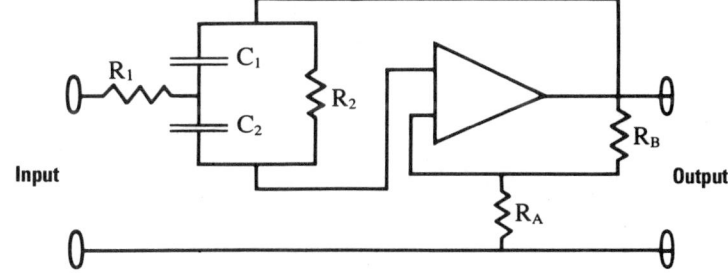

Let $C_1 = C_2 = \mu f$, $R_1 = R_2 = R_B = 10$ ohms and $R_A = 32$ ohms, which yields a bandpass frequency centered on 100 kHz. Now plot the transfer function and then draw the circuit on the graph.

1. Set the column widths as follows:

   A = 3   E = 9

   B = 10   F = 9

   C = 10   G = 9

   D = 20

2. Type **Delyiannis Bandpass Circuit** in cell A1.

3. In cell B3, type **RES1** and left-justify it.

4. In cell B4, type **RES2** and right-justify it.

5. Type **10** in cell C3.

6. Type **10** in cell C4.

7. In cell D3, type **CAP1** and right-justify it.

8. In cell D4, type **CAP2** and right-justify it.

9. Type **1E-6** in cell E3.

10. Type **1E-6** in cell E4.

11. In cell F3, type **RESA** and right-justify it.

12. In cell F4, type **RESB** and right-justify it.

13. Type **32** in cell G3.

14. Type **10** in cell G4.

15. Name cells as follows:

      C3: **RES1**   E4: **CAP2**

      C4: **RES2**   G3: **RESA**

      E3: **CAP1**   G4: **RESB**

16. In cell B5, type **K** and right-justify it.

17. Type **=1+RESA/RESB** in cell C5.

18. In cell D5, type **WP** and right-justify it.

19. In cell E5, type the following formula:

$$=SQRT(1/(RES1*RES2*CAP1*CAP2))$$

20. In cell F5, type **WPQP** and right-justify it.

21. Name cells as follows:

      C5: **K**

      E5: **WP**

      G5: **WPQP**.

22. In cell G5, type this formula:

$$=1/(RES2*CAP1)+1/(RES2*CAP2)-(1/(K-1))*1/(RES1*CAP2))$$

23. In cell B8, type **Frequency** and right-justify it.

24. In cell C8, type **|G(s)|** and right-justify it.

25. Type **Comments** in cell D8.

26. Select cell B9 and type **1E4**.

27. Select cells B9:B49, choose the Series command on the Data menu, set the step value to **1E4**, and click on OK.

28. In cells C9:C49, type and copy the following formula:

$$=(B9/(RES1*CAP2*(1-1/K)))/SQRT((WP^2-B9^2)^2+WPQP^2*B9^2)$$

29. In cell D9, type **Begin filter calculation**.

30. In cell D49, type **End filter calculation**.

31. Format cells B9:B133, E3:E5, and G5 as 0.00E+00 and cells C9:C135 as 0.00.

32. Outline these ranges: B3:C5, D3:E5, F3:G5, B8:D8, B8:B133, C8:C133, and D8:D133. Underline cells B49:D49.

This completes the data for the transfer function. Your worksheet should look like Figure 3.27. Now you will create the chart of the function.

33. Select cells B9:C49, click on the Chart Wizard button, and select I1:Q18 for the chart.

34. In the first Chart Wizard window, accept the data to plot.

35. In the second window, select XY (Scatter plot).

36. In the third window, select plot type 2.

37. In the fourth window, select the Data Series in Columns, Use First Column for X-Data, and Use First Row for First Data Point options.

38. In the fifth window, type the chart title **Delyiannis Bandpass Circuit**, the category axis label **Angular Frequency (Rad/s)**, and the value axis label **Transfer Function**. Then click on OK.

39. Select the chart and choose the Copy command on the Edit menu.

40. Select cell I20 and choose the Paste command on the Edit menu. You will use this other copy of the chart later.

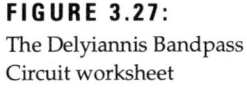

FIGURE 3.27:

The Delyiannis Bandpass Circuit worksheet

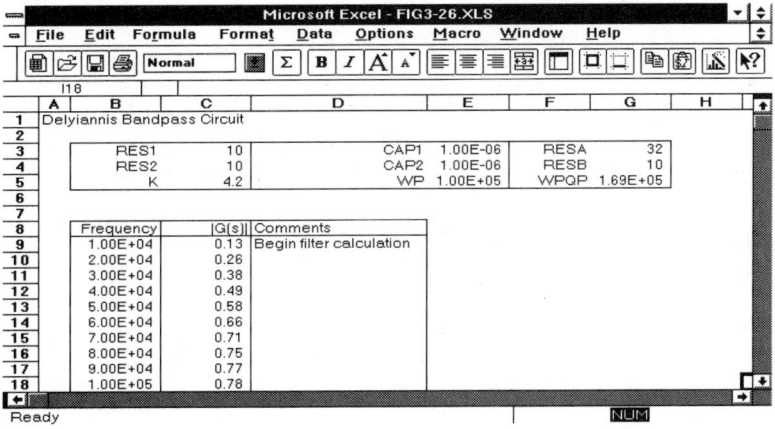

Now switch to the drawing toolbar and use the drawing tools (see Table 3.2) to draw the circuit on the figure. Instead of trying to work with a very small drawing, magnify the image to make the drawing tools easier to use.

41. Place the pointer on the edge of the standard toolbar and drag it down until it turns into a smaller rectangle.

42. Double-click on the Close box in the upper-left corner of the toolbar to remove the toolbar.

43. Use the Toolbar command on the Options menu and select the Drawing toolbar.

44. Drag the drawing toolbar to the top of the screen and release it, so that it replaces the standard toolbar.

45. With the chart showing, use the Zoom command on the Window menu. Set 200% magnification and click on OK.

46. Use the drawing tools to draw the circuit as shown in Figure 3.28. Most of this is done with the Line tool. Use the Oval tool to draw the four circles, and the Text Box tool to label the parts. Use the Patterns command on the Format menu to remove the border on the text box.

47. Use the Zoom command on the Window menu and change back to 100%.

48. Use the Multiselection tool to select the whole drawing, including the chart. Start dragging outside the chart, so that you don't grab the chart and move it around instead of selecting the drawing.

49. Click on the Group tool (the sixth from the right). This groups the figure and the drawing so that they move together. You must ungroup them if you want to edit the drawing.

The chart should look like the one shown in Figure 3.28.

Now try the same thing with the copy of the chart, but do the drawing with a second data set. I sketched the circuit on grid paper to determine the x-y coordinates of the lines to type into the worksheet. All of the drawing must be done in the scale of the plot already on the graph. Alternatively, you could determine the x-y pairs on a regular grid (say 100 by 100), and then use a simple function to map the values onto the scale of the plot on the chart.

FIGURE 3.28:
The Delyiannis Bandpass
Transfer function chart with
a circuit drawn with the
drawing tools

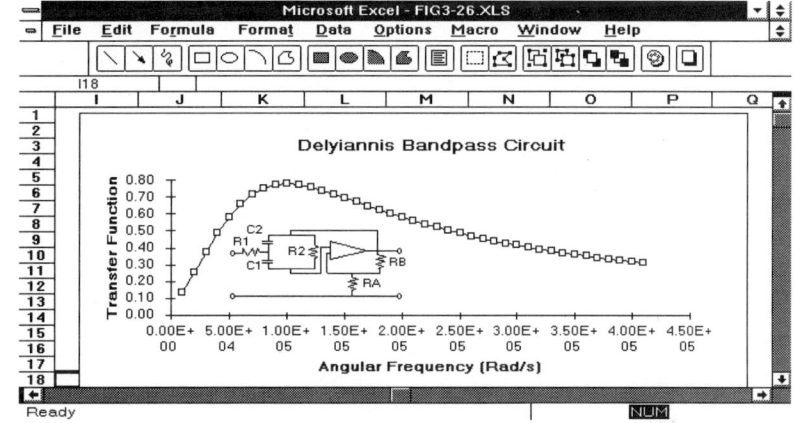

50. In cells B52:D133, make the following entries:

		D52: **'Begin circuit plot**
B54: **5.0E4**	C54: **0.1**	D54: **Ground line**
B55: **3.0E5**	C55: **0.1**	
B57: **2.3E5**	C57: **0.1**	D57: **Resistor B**
B58: **2.3E5**	C58: **0.12**	
B59: **2.35E5**	C59: **0.13**	
B60: **2.25E5**	C60: **0.14**	
B61: **2.35E5**	C61: **0.15**	
B62: **2.25E5**	C62: **0.16**	
B63: **2.35E5**	C63: **0.17**	
B64: **2.3E5**	C64: **0.18**	
B65: **2.3E5**	C65: **0.2**	
B67: **2.0E5**	C67: **0.2**	D67: **Operational amplifier**
B68: **2.5E5**	C68: **0.3**	
B69: **2.0E5**	C69: **0.36**	
B70: **2.0E5**	C70: **0.2**	
B72: **2.0E5**	C72: **0.2**	D72: **Resistor C and wire**
B73: **1.9E5**	C73: **0.2**	D73: **from input network**

B74: **1.9E5**	C74: **0.2**	D74: **to operational amplifier**
B75: **2.8E5**	C75: **0.2**	
B76: **2.8E5**	C76: **0.2**	
B77: **2.85E5**	C77: **0.2**	
B78: **2.75E5**	C78: **0.2**	
B79: **2.85E5**	C79: **0.2**	
B80: **2.75E5**	C80: **0.2**	
B81: **2.85E5**	C81: **0.2**	
B82: **2.8E5**	C82: **0.2**	
B83: **2.8E5**	C83: **0.42**	
B84: **1.25E5**	C84: **0.42**	
B85: **1.25E5**	C85: **0.39**	
B87: **1.0E5**	C87: **0.35**	D87: **Resistor 2**
B88: **1.0E5**	C88: **0.39**	
B89: **1.5E5**	C89: **0.39**	
B90: **1.5E5**	C90: **0.33**	
B91: **1.45E5**	C91: **0.32**	
B92: **1.55E5**	C92: **0.31**	
B93: **1.45E5**	C93: **0**	
B94: **1.55E5**	C94: **0.29**	
B95: **1.45E5**	C95: **0.28**	
B96: **1.5E5**	C96: **0.27**	
B97: **1.5E5**	C97: **0.21**	
B98: **1.0E5**	C98: **0.21**	
B99: **1.0E5**	C99: **0.25**	
B101: **8.5E4**	C101: **0.25**	D101: **Capacitor 1**
B102: **1.15E5**	C102: **0.25**	
B104: **8.5E4**	C104: **0.26**	
B105: **1.15E5**	C105: **0.26**	
B107: **8.5E4**	C107: **0.34**	D107: **Capacitor 2**
B108: **1.15E5**	C108: **0.34**	

B110: **8.5E4**	C110: **0.35**	
B111: **1.15E5**	C111: **0.35**	
B113: **5.0E4**	C113: **0.3**	D113: **Resistor 1**
B114: **6.0E4**	C114: **0.3**	
B115: **6.5E4**	C115: **0.31**	
B116: **7.0E4**	C116: **0.29**	
B117: **7.5E4**	C117: **0.31**	
B118: **8.0E4**	C118: **0.29**	
B119: **8.5E4**	C119: **0.31**	
B120: **9.0E4**	C120: **0.3**	
B121: **1.0E5**	C121: **0.3**	
B123: **2.5E5**	C123: **0.3**	D123: **Output terminal**
B124: **3.0E5**	C124: **0.3**	
B126: **1.0E5**	C126: **0.2**	D126: **Wire from C1 to C25**
B127: **1.0E5**	C127: **0.34**	
B129: **1.25E5**	C129: **0.21**	D129: **Wire from input network**
B130: **1.25E5**	C130: **0.18**	D130: **to operational amplifier**
B131: **1.8E5**	C131: **0.18**	
B132: **1.8E5**	C132: **0.33**	
B133: **2.0E5**	C133: **0.33**	

51. Underline cells B53:D53.

52. Select cells B54:C133 and choose the Copy command on the Edit menu.

53. Select the copy of the chart you made around cell I20 and double-click on it to open the chart window.

54. Choose the Paste Special command on the Edit menu, select Values (Y) in Columns and Categories (X Values) in First Column, and click on OK.

55. Select the circuit drawing and choose the Patterns command on the Format menu. Set Marker to None and Line to Black. Then click on OK.

56. Use unattached text (type in the formula bar while the chart is visible) to create the four circles at the left and right (use a lowercase *o*) and to label the

resistors and capacitors. Use the Font command on the Format menu to reduce the size of the text to 8 points.

57. Close the chart window to return the chart to the worksheet.

The chart should look like Figure 3.29. There is actually a much easier way to place a graphic on a chart: use a drawing program to draw it, copy the drawing, and paste it on the worksheet. The features in most drawing programs are easier to use than the drawing tools in Excel.

Summary

In this chapter, you created graphs of worksheet data and enhanced those graphs with data labels, markers, legends and titles. In addition to these normal plotting functions, you investigated ways to use Excel's graphics capabilities to perform other common science and engineering graphics tasks, such as creating log or semi-log charts, plotting three-dimensional charts, and enhancing those charts with simple drawings.

FIGURE 3.29:

The Delyiannis Bandpass Transfer function chart and circuit drawn with worksheet data

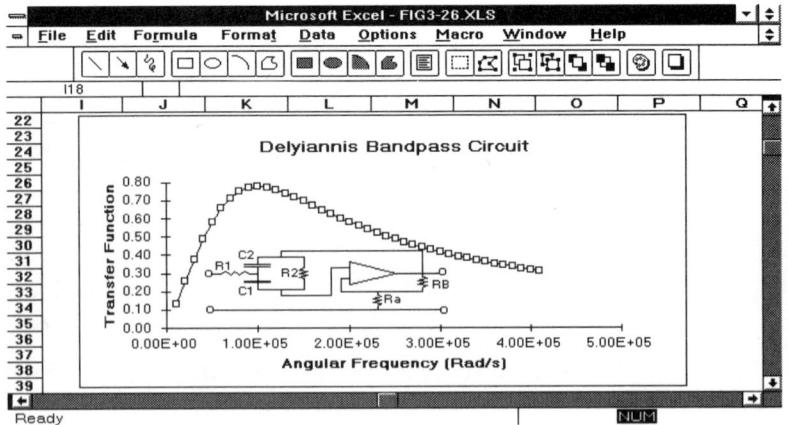

Using the techniques presented in this chapter plus a little ingenuity, you should be able to manage most of your data-plotting and presentation tasks. For any new plot type, such as polar, create a linear transform to transform your data onto the linear x- and y-axes in Excel. Plot your data, and then use Excel's tools to add any required axis lines or labels.

For More Information

Resistivity of Silicon

S. M. Sze, *Physics of Semiconductor Devices*, 2nd ed. (New York:Wiley, 1981), Ch. 1.

Electron Avalanche Coefficient in Silicon

W. N. Grant, "Electron and Hole Ionization Rates in Epitaxial Silicon at High Electric Fields," *Solid State Electronics 16* (1973):1189-1203.

Delyiannis Bandpass Filter

D. G. Fink and D. Christiansen, *Electronics Engineers' Handbook* (New York: McGraw Hill, 1982).

Problems

1. Plot the results of the first engineering table in the previous chapter (thermal conductivity of silicon). Don't forget to label the axes.

2. The hyperbolic sine (sinh) of an angle in radians is calculated by

$$\sinh(x) = \frac{e^x - e^{-x}}{2}$$

    a. Using this equation, calculate the value of the sinh of x for 40 values of x between 0 and 2π radians. Plot those values and label the axes.

    b. Add plots of the hyperbolic cosine (cosh) and hyperbolic tangent (tanh) to the plot of the hyperbolic sine. Label the curves with a legend.

$$\cosh(x) = \frac{e^x + e^{-x}}{2} \qquad \tanh(x) = \frac{\sinh(x)}{\cosh(x)}$$

    c. Label the curves with data labels attached to the respective curves instead of the legend.

3. Modify the van der Waals example from the previous chapter to calculate a table of three isotherms of the van der Waals equation of state for carbon dioxide. Let the volume range from 0.06 to 0.4 1/mole in steps of 0.01. In three columns, calculate the pressure for the temperatures 264 K, 304 K, and 344 K. Plot the pressure versus volume for these three isotherms, and label them with the temperature.

4. Complete problem 3 using the ideal gas law instead of the van der Waals equation.

5. Complete problem 2 as a semilog plot. Plot the log of the hyperbolic functions for x ranging from 0 to 10.

6. Create a template for polar plots. On the screen, draw x- and y-axes that range from −2.5 to +2.5 with the origin at the center. Draw a circle of radius 1 and a circle of radius 2, centering both on the origin. Create a transfer function to convert a function of r and v to x and y values that can be plotted on the template.

7. Plot the four-leaved rose function on the polar template created in problem 6:

$$r = a\sin(2\theta) \qquad 0 < \theta < 2\pi \qquad a = 2$$

8. For the bending beam example in the previous chapter, plot the stress as a function of the position along the beam. Draw a picture of a cantilever beam (see Figure 2.14) in the corner of the plot. (Draw a straight beam instead of the curved one shown in the figure.)

9. For the LVDT (linear variable differential transformer) calibration table in the previous chapter, plot the four calibration curves versus the transducer voltage. Label the curves on the plot with a legend.

10. For the intrinsic carrier density example in the previous chapter, plot the energy gap and the log of the intrinsic density as a function of the temperature. Label the curves.

11. Make a three-dimensional plot of the function sin($x*y$) for x and y ranging from $-\pi$ to $+\pi$.

12. Make a wire-frame plot of the three-dimensional plot example in the text. (On a wire-frame plot, the data points are connected in both directions, rather than in just the one illustrated in the example.) Plot the data first along the y direction, as in the example, and then again along the z direction. The result should look like a net draped over the data points, creating a surface in three-dimensional space.

Using Macros

4

Originally, macros were intended to be simply a playback of keystrokes to save you time when performing repetitive actions. However, in Excel, macros have evolved into a complete programming language. Excel macros cannot only play back keystrokes, they also can be used to create custom worksheet functions or even complete computer programs. Excel's macro language contains most of the functions and control structures you would expect to find in a high-level language.

Using Macro Commands

Excel macros are placed on a separate macro sheet, which behaves quite differently from a worksheet. On a worksheet, cells are calculated in the natural recalculation order, in which a cell's precedents (the cells a cell depends on) are always calculated before a cell is calculated, no matter where those precedents are located on the worksheet. On a macro sheet, calculation proceeds down a column, one cell at a time, executing each cell in order.

All macro commands are functions; that is, they always return a value. Action-taking macro functions often return True or False, depending on whether the action they were supposed to take occurred or not. Most macro commands cannot be used on a worksheet, but all worksheet commands can be used on a macro sheet.

Most command-equivalent macro commands are named for the command, or command and menu they inhabit. For example, the FORMAT.NUMBER function executes the Number command on the Format menu.

Some useful macro commands are described in this chapter. See the *Microsoft Excel Function Reference* included in the Excel package for a complete description of each macro command.

Creating Command Macros to Automate Worksheets

The most basic set of macro commands are for automating repetitive actions on a worksheet. Macros of this type are known as command macros, because they are executed like menu commands. Almost every repetitive task can be performed by a macro. The main uses for these macros are to save you time when you have to perform repetitive actions and to create automated worksheets for people who are not experts at Excel. They are also good for amazing your friends, because worksheets appear to create themselves without your touching the keyboard.

Command macros are simple to create and even simpler to use. To create a command macro, set up a worksheet as it will be before the macro is executed, and choose the Record command on the Macro menu. The Record Macro dialog box appears, as shown in Figure 4.1.

In this dialog box, type a name for your macro and, optionally, enter a key to be used in combination with the Ctrl key (Option-Cmd on the Macintosh) as a shortcut for playing back the macro. You don't need to specify a shortcut key, but it will allow you to execute a macro faster. The dialog box also includes the choice between recording the macro on a macro sheet or on the global macro sheet. Put macros that you use frequently on the global macro sheet, because it is opened whenever you run Excel. Put project-specific macros on regular macro sheets, which must be opened before the macros on them can be used. Then open the appropriate macro sheet when you are working on the associated project.

As soon as you click on OK, Excel begins recording your actions. Everything you do is recorded on the macro sheet—opening and closing files, typing formulas, and so on. When you are finished, choose the Stop Recorder command on the Macro menu.

If you recorded your macro on a regular macro sheet, switch to the macro sheet using the Window menu, and you will see your new macro. If your macro is on the global macro sheet, use the Unhide command on the Window menu to make it visible.

FIGURE 4.1:
The Record Macro dialog box

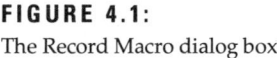

Record Macro	
Name: `Record1`	OK
Key: Ctrl+ `a`	Cancel
┌─Store Macro In───────	Help
○ **G**lobal Macro Sheet	
◉ **M**acro Sheet	
To edit the global macro sheet, choose Unhide from the Window menu.	

To record a second macro on a macro sheet, select the cell on the macro sheet where you want to start recording and choose the Set Recorder command on the Macro menu. Then use the Start Recorder and Stop Recorder commands on the Macro menu to start and stop recording. When you are finished recording, select the first cell of the macro again and use the Define Name command on the Formula menu to name the macro, set its type, and assign a shortcut key.

When you are recording macros, cell references are recorded in absolute mode, which makes them access the same cells every time. But some macros require relative references. For example, you want a macro that formats a cell to format the cell you are in, not the cell you were in when you recorded the macro. To change to recording in Relative mode, choose the Relative Record command on the Macro menu. Use the Absolute Record command on the Macro menu to change back.

Instead of giving a macro a shortcut key or executing it from the Macro menu, you can assign a macro to an object, such as a button, and execute the macro by clicking on the object. You can create a button with the button tool on the utility toolbar, but any object on a worksheet can be attached to a macro, including an embedded chart or a drawing element, such as a rectangle or line. To assign a macro to an object, select the object, choose the Assign to Object command on the Macro menu, select the macro to attach from the dialog box, and click on OK.

To run a command macro, hold down Ctrl (Option-Cmd on the Macintosh) and press its shortcut key (if you assigned one), click on its object (if you assigned a macro to an object), or select Run from the Macro menu and choose its name from the Run Macro dialog box.

Cell-Formatting Macro   As an example, create a command macro to format and outline cells. This is a simple macro that formats the contents of the selected cell or cells as 0.00E+00 and draws a box around the cells. Attach the macro to a button on the worksheet.

1. On a new worksheet, type a number in a cell to format while recording the macro.

2. Choose the Record command on the Macro menu.

3. In the Record Macro dialog box, name the macro **FormatIt**, set the shortcut key to **f**, and click on OK to start recording.

4. Choose the Relative Record command on the Macro menu if it appears. If the Absolute Record command is on the menu, the recorder is already in Relative mode.

5. Click on the cell containing the number, choose the Number command on the Format menu, select the 0.00E+00 format, and click on OK.

6. Select the Border command on the Format menu, click on Outline, and click on OK.

7. Choose the Stop Recorder command on the Macro menu.

8. Select the macro sheet from the Window menu.

The macro appears on the macro sheet, as shown in Figure 4.2. Note the RETURN() at the end of the macro. All macros must end with a RETURN function to return control to the user. Without RETURN, Excel continues executing cells in the column until it can't find anymore.

If you look at this macro closely, you will see that it isn't exactly what you want. It has a SELECT function in line 2, which was written when you selected the cell to be formatted. Since you want this macro to format whatever cell you have selected and not move to some other cell, you must remove this function.

FIGURE 4.2:

The FormatIt macro recorded on the macro sheet

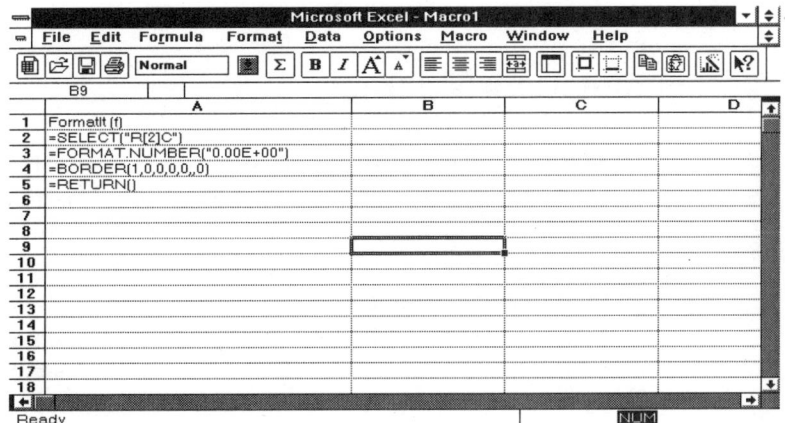

9. Select cell A2 and use the Delete command on the Edit menu to delete the cell and move up the cells below it.

10. Select the worksheet from the Window menu.

11. Choose the Toolbar command on the Options menu and select Utility to display the utility toolbar.

12. Click on the button tool (the icon looks like a gray rectangle with round corners and a shadow) and draw a button on the worksheet by clicking and dragging in a convenient place.

13. Choose the Assign to Object command on the Macro menu. In the dialog box, select the FormatIt macro and click on OK.

14. Use the mouse pointer to select the text on the face of the button and type **Format It**.

The macro is now ready to use. Type some numbers in a cell and click on the Format It button to see what happens.

Once created, a macro sheet is saved or opened just like a worksheet. To use a macro, the macro sheet that contains it must be open. The macros you create are portable; you can use the macros on an open macro sheet with any open worksheet, not just the one that was active when they were created.

Programming with Macros

Macros need not be as simple as the one in the last example. You can write complete programs that include custom dialog boxes and menus, repetitive calculations, file access and creation, and custom control of a worksheet. Excel's main failing is its speed. Since it is an interpreted language, it does not run terribly fast, although it is more than fast enough for most simple applications. If you have a custom function that needs the speed of a compiled language, create it as a module in a Dynamic Link Library (DLL) (a CODE resource on the Macintosh) and then use the CALL or REGISTER function to access it.

Laying Out Macros

It is customary (but not required) to lay out macros in a three-column format:

- The first column is used to label the named cells in the macro. In this column, enter a name for each cell in the second column that you want to name. These consist of the macro names and any named cells used for data storage.

- The second column contains the macro and the named ranges for data storage.

- The third column is for comments.

Manipulating Cell References

Since the macro language was designed to manipulate worksheets, many of the commands return cell references. Be careful when designing a program to manipulate references. If you store a reference in a cell, the value of that cell will be the contents of the reference, not the reference itself. A problem most often occurs when you have a function that takes a reference as an argument, and you use another function that returns a reference as that argument. For example, suppose you are using two functions, FUNCTIONA( ) and FUNCTIONB( ). FUNCTIONA( ) requires a reference for an argument, and FUNCTIONB( ) returns a reference. If you place this formula in a cell:

=FUNCTIONA(FUNCTIONB( ))

it works as expected. However, if you store the result of FUNCTIONB( ) in a cell, such as in A1, and then use that value as an argument to FUNCTIONA( ) in another cell, as in this formula:

=FUNCTIONA(A1)

it won't work, because cell A1 contains the contents of the reference, not the reference.

If you must store a reference in a cell for further manipulation, first convert it to a string and store the string, rather than the actual reference. Many functions already return a reference as a string. For those that do not, use the REFTEXT function to change the reference into text. When you need to use the reference, change it back into a reference with the TEXTREF function. For example, if you entered this formula in cell A1:

=REFTEXT(FUNCTIONB( ))

and this formula in cell A2:

=FUNCTIONA(TEXTREF(A1))

the reference will work correctly.

When you convert a reference into text, it is almost always in the R1C1 style of cell referencing. In the R1C1 style, the location of a cell is by its row and column number instead of the letter and number style. For example, R7C3 stands for row 7, column 3, which is cell C7. Keep this in mind if you plan to manipulate a cell address.

Macro Sheet Variables

A macro sheet can contain two types of variables: named values and cells. You create named values at design time with the Define Name command on the Formula menu, or with the SET.NAME function in an executing macro. For example, this function:

```
=SET.NAME("theLength",5)
```

defines the name theLength as the number 5. If you use a cell reference as the second argument, the name is defined as the cell reference, not the contents of the cell. Thus, when you use the name, it is evaluated as the cell reference, which evaluates to the current contents of the cell.

Cells can hold values on the macro sheet in the same manner as cells on a worksheet contain values. When a cell is calculated, it gets the value of the function it contains. Additionally, the value of a cell can be set from another cell using the SET.VALUE function. For example, these functions:

```
=SET.VALUE(B7,6)
=SET.VALUE(I,I+1)
```

set the value of cell B7 on the macro sheet to 6, and the cell named I to the value I + 1. Both of these refer to cells on the macro sheet.

To change a value on a worksheet, use the FORMULA function. The FORMULA function works the same as typing in the formula bar of the worksheet. It takes one or two arguments. The first argument must be text and is what you want inserted into the cell. The second is the reference of the cell in which to insert the text. If you omit the second argument, the currently selected cell is used.

Handling Input and Output

To get input from the user, use the INPUT function, which displays a dialog box and asks the user to type something. To simply send the user a message, use the ALERT function. You can create custom dialog boxes with Excel for both input and output. Custom dialog boxes are designed with the Dialog Editor and displayed with the DIALOG.BOX function, as described later in this chapter.

You can access data in ASCII disk files with the FOPEN, FCLOSE, FREAD, FWRITE, FPOS, FREADLN, and FWRITELN functions. You can also get the file size with FSIZE. These commands allow you to open and close text files and to read and write data from them.

Controlling Program Flow

You control the flow of operations in an operating macro with loop commands, jumps, conditionals, and subroutine calls. Loops are controlled with the FOR, FOR.CELL, WHILE, and NEXT functions. The FOR function starts a counted loop, in which a counter is incremented each time the loop is executed. The FOR.CELL function is similar to the FOR function, but loops over the cells in a cell reference instead of incrementing a number. The WHILE function repeatedly executes a loop until a condition turns False. All of these loops are terminated with a NEXT function.

Your macro can perform an unconditional jump, similar to GOTO in Fortran or BASIC, with the GOTO function. A conditional branch is performed with an IF function when GOTO functions are used as its arguments. To call another macro program as a subroutine, simply place its name in your macro, followed by its arguments within parentheses. Subroutines return to the next cell in the calling routine when they encounter a RETURN function. Use the ARGUMENT function to specify where subroutine's parameters are stored.

Creating Dialog Boxes

You use the Dialog Editor to create custom dialog boxes. The Dialog Editor generates a dialog definition table, which contains a description of each item on the dialog box.

Each row of the dialog definition table describes a different item. The first line is special, because it describes the dialog box itself. If you include a name for the dialog box in the text field of the first row, the dialog box will be movable; otherwise, it will be fixed. If you place a file reference to a Help file in the first column of row one, that file will be opened as a Help topic if you add a Help button to the dialog box.

The first column of the dialog definition table contains a code that identifies the item type. Table 4.1 lists the codes and item types available in Excel.

The second and third columns contain the x-y location of the upper-left corner of the item, measured in points (1 point equals $\frac{1}{72}$ inch) from the upper-left corner of the dialog box. The fourth and fifth columns contain the width and height of the item measured in points. The sixth column contains the text attached to the object. The text is the caption of a button, the contents of a text box, or the label of an option button or check box.

The seventh column contains the initial value and the result for each item. When the user makes selections in a dialog box and clicks on a button to exit, the item number of the button selected (counting down from the top of the dialog definition table) is returned by the DIALOG.BOX function, and all the selections made are returned in the seventh column of the dialog definition table.

Creating Function Macros

When you define a name on a macro sheet with the Define Name command on the Formula menu, you have the choice of defining it as a command macro or a function macro. As you have seen, command macros usually perform an action. Function macros calculate and return one or more values. The simplest and most common type of function macro returns a single value. However, function macros can return an array of values, and they are treated in the same manner as any of the other functions that return an array.

TABLE 4.1: Item Type Codes for a Dialog Definition Table

Code	Item
1	Default OK button; selected automatically if the user presses Return
2	Cancel button
3	OK button
4	Default Cancel button; selected automatically if the user presses Return
5	Text label; static text used to label items in the dialog box
6	Text edit box; used to get text from the user
7	Integer edit box; used to get an integer value from the user
8	Number edit box; used to get a number from the user
9	Formula edit box; used to get a formula from the user
10	Reference edit box; used to get a reference from the user (clicking on a cell when editing this box inserts the reference to that cell)
11	Option button group; used to define an option button group (all option buttons that immediately follow this item are in the same option button group)
12	Option button
13	Check box
14	Frame; used to draw a frame in the dialog box
15	List box; used to display a list of items for selection (place a reference to the list in the text column of the dialog definition table)
16	Linked list box; when preceded with a text edit box, the item selected in the list is placed in the text edit box
17	Icon; put a 1 (choose), 2 (information), or 3 (alert) in the text column to select the icon
18	Linked file list box (Windows only); when preceded with a text edit box and followed with a linked drive and directory list box, the pattern in the text edit box is used to select the files listed
19	Linked drive and directory list box (Windows only); when preceded with a linked file list box and followed with a text label, the text label will contain the drive
20	Directory text (Windows only); used to display the current directory only
21	Drop-down list box; used to have the list drop down when selected (place a reference to the list in the text column of the dialog definition table)
22	Drop-down combination list box; when preceded with a text edit box, the item selected in the list is inserted in the text edit box
23	Picture button; a button created with a picture drawn with the drawing tools
24	Help button; used to display the Help topic for this dialog box (the name of the Help file goes in the top-left cell of the dialog box definition table)

Energy Gap in Silicon   Use function macros to provide functions that are not available in the Excel function language and special-purpose functions that cannot be constructed with Excel functions easily. In Chapter 2, you needed the energy gap in silicon in order to calculate the intrinsic carrier density. The energy gap in silicon is not a built-in Excel function, although it would be handy for those of us doing a lot of solid-state physics. In Chapter 2, you calculated it in one column of a worksheet and used it in the adjacent column. However, if it were available as a function, you could eliminate a whole column of data on the worksheet.

Referring to the equations in the last chapter, the energy gap in silicon is a simple function of the temperature. Create a function macro that returns the energy gap for any temperature used as an argument. Omit the q from the equation to return the value in electron volts instead of Joules.

1. Select the New command on the File menu, choose Macro Sheet, and click on OK.

2. Set the widths of column A to 3, column B to 14, and column C to 9.

3. Make the following entries in cells A1:B9:

A1: EGap	B1: **Energy Gap**	
	B2: =ARGUMENT("T",1,B6)	C2: **Store the argument**
A3: **Eg**	B3: =(EG0− (EG1_*T^2)/(T+EG2_))	C3: **Calculate Eg**
	B4: =RETURN(B3)	C4: **Return the result**
A6: **T**		C6: **The argument**
A7: **EG0**	B7: **1.17**	C7: **Coeffs.**
A8: **EG1_**	B8: **0.000473**	
A9: **EG2_**	B9: **636**	

4. Select cells A1:B9, choose the Create Names command on the Formula menu, make sure only the Left Column check box is checked, and click on OK.

5. Outline the following cells:

A1:A4   A6:A9

B1:B4   B6:B9

C1:C4   C6:C9

A1:C1

6. Turn off the gridlines with the Display command on the Options menu.

7. Select cell B1 and choose the Define Name command on the Formula menu. In the Define Name dialog box, set the name to **EGap**, click on the Function Macro option button, and click on OK.

8. Save the macro sheet as **EGAP.XLM**.

This completes the function macro, which should look like Figure 4.3. The macro is defined to start in cell B1, but it just contains text, so the macro ignores it and starts processing in cell B2.

The ARGUMENT function in cell B2 gets the argument from the calling program and stores it in cell B6 on the macro sheet. The syntax of the ARGUMENT function is

`=ARGUMENT(name,type,reference)`

You must include the *name* or *reference* argument. If you use only *name*, Excel stores the value as a named value. If you include *reference*, the value is stored in the reference, and the reference is named. The *type* argument determines the type of the argument (number, string, and so on). If the supplied argument is of the wrong type, the function returns #VALUE!.

FIGURE 4.3:

The energy-gap function macro

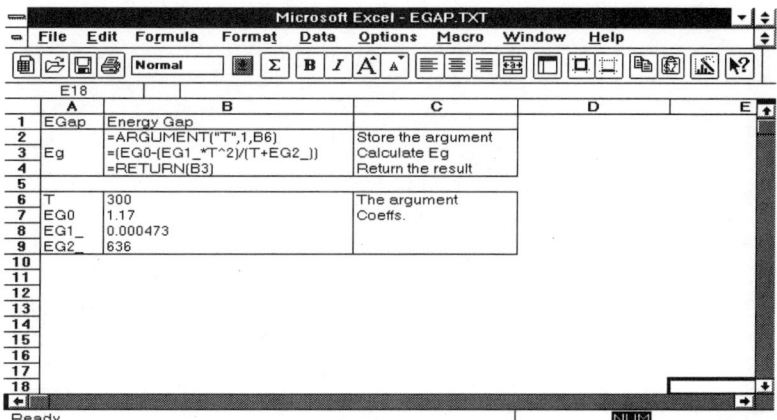

In cell B3, the value of the energy gap is calculated using the coefficients in the table below. Finally, in cell B4, the RETURN function returns the value in cell B3 to the cell in the worksheet that called it.

To use this function in a worksheet, simply enter its name as an external reference, followed by its argument enclosed in parentheses. If cell A4 contains a temperature, the following formula in some other cell executes the macro and returns the energy gap in eV:

```
=EGAP.XLM!EGap(A4)
```

The form of the external reference is the same as the form for referencing values in some other worksheet. The simplest and most accurate way to insert this function in a formula is to use the Paste Function command on the Formula menu. The function will be in the Function Category: User Defined section of the Paste Formula dialog box.

Creating a Macro Program

As well as calculating simple functions, you can create complete programs with macro and worksheet commands. The programs can pause for keyboard input, store values, calculate values, test for errors, print error messages, and so on. In the next example, you will create a macro program that converts worksheets to another format.

Excel to Fortran   The work involved in converting a large worksheet into another program format is tedious, time-consuming, and prone to error. Suppose that you need to convert a worksheet with several thousand filled cells into a compiled Fortran program. Instead of doing it by hand, you can create an Excel macro program to do the job for you. The macro in this example does not completely convert a worksheet to Fortran, but it comes close.

The macro creates and opens a text file, and then displays a custom dialog box that asks the user to select the cells to convert. After the cells are selected, the macro scans the cells row by row looking for cells with numeric values, formulas, or text.

If a cell contains text, the macro converts it to a Fortran comment (a **c** in column 1). If a cell contains a value or a formula, the macro creates a Fortran statement by inserting six spaces, followed by the cell reference and finally the formula or value. The new statement is then scanned for an up arrow (for exponentiation), which must be replaced with the ** used in Fortran. Finally, the statement is written to the text file.

One thing this program does not do is to make sure that values are defined prior to use. However, since most worksheets are generated down and to the right, the statements are usually in the correct order. You will need to check the order yourself after the conversion is complete. You could probably write a macro to do this part as well, or at least flag statements that are out of order.

Begin by using the Dialog Editor to draw the custom dialog box shown in Figure 4.4. The commands for placing items in the current dialog box window are on the Item menu. After you add items, you can use the mouse to move and resize them.

1. Start with a new macro sheet.

2. Switch to the Program Manager (the Finder on the Macintosh) and run the Dialog Editor.

3. Use the mouse to enlarge the box that appears in the dialog box window.

4. Choose the Text command on the Item menu to create a text label, and type **Input the cell range**.

5. Choose the Text command on the Item menu to create another text label, and type **to process into Fortran**.

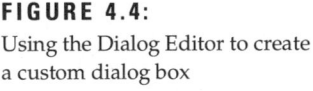

FIGURE 4.4:

Using the Dialog Editor to create a custom dialog box

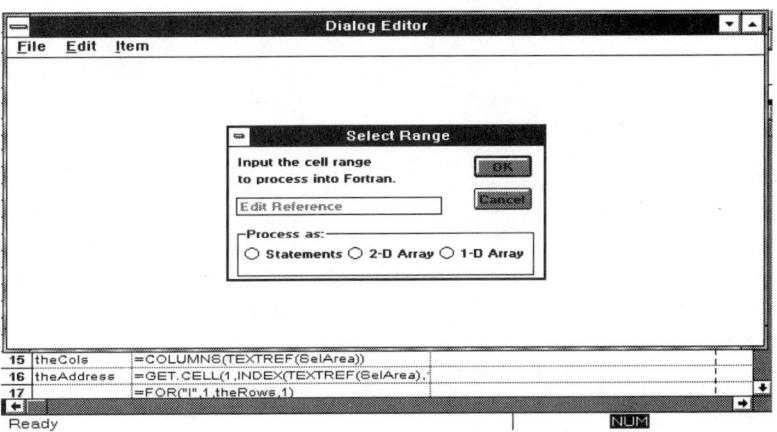

6. Select the Edit Box command on the Item menu, select Reference, and click on OK to create a text edit box.

The macro will allow for three types of formulas: normal assignment statements, 2-D array assignment statements, and 1-D array assignment statements. Next add option buttons for selecting the type of conversion and OK and Cancel buttons. Make the OK button the default button, so it is executed if the user presses Enter.

7. Choose the Group Box command on the Item menu to create a group box for the option buttons, and type **Process as:**.

8. Select the Button command on the Item menu to create an option button, and type **Statements.**

9. Use the Button command on the Item menu to create an option button, and type **2-D Array.**

10. Create a third option button, and type **1-D Array.**

11. Choose the Button command on the Item menu to create a default OK button. Click on the button type OK, make sure Default is checked, and then click on OK.

12. Choose the Button command on the Item menu to create a Cancel button. Click on the button type Cancel, and then click on OK.

13. Move the items until they are arranged as in Figure 4.4. To move the option buttons, double-click on them to display the Option Button Info dialog box, then uncheck the Auto check box for *X* and *Y*.

14. Choose the Select Dialog command on the Edit menu.

15. Select the Copy command on the Edit menu, switch back to Excel, select cell E3 on the macro sheet, and choose the Paste command on the Edit menu to create the dialog definition table.

16. Select the Border command on the Format menu, click on Outline, and then click on OK.

17. Use the Define Name command on the Formula menu to name the dialog definition table as **Conversion Dialog**.

18. Type the column titles in row 2 above the dialog definition table as shown in Figure 4.5. Also adjust the column widths until your dialog definition table looks like the one in the figure.

19. In cell J3, type **Select Range**. This names the dialog box and makes it movable.

In the dialog definition table shown in Figure 4.5, each row of the table describes a dialog box item: row 1 of the table indicates the dialog box is 350 points wide and 133 points high and is named *Select Range*, row 2 describes a type 5 text label that contains the text *Input the cell range*, row 3 describes another text label containing *to process into Fortran*, row 4 describes a text edit box that must contain a reference, row 5 describes a text label containing *Process as:*, and row 6 describes an option button group.

An option button group command does not appear as a button on the screen, but combines the following frame and option buttons into a group. Since only one option button in a group can be selected at a time, this control defines which option buttons are in the group. Rows 7 through 9 describe the three option buttons. Row 10 describes the default OK button, and row 11 describes the Cancel button,

20. Make the following entries in cells B1:B6

B1: **This macro sheet converts worksheets**

B2: **to Fortran. Run the Macro, select the area**

FIGURE 4.5:

The dialog definition table on the macro sheet

	D	E	F	G	H	I	J	K	L
1		Conve							
2		item	x	y	w	h	Text	init/result	row
3					350	133	Select Range		1
4			5	10	8		Input the cell range		2
5			5	10	25		to process into Fortran		3
6			10	9	50	225			4
7			14	11	80	326	49	Process as:	5
8			11						6
9			12	17	99		Statements		7
10			12	130	99		2-D Array		8
11			12	230	100		1-D Array		9
12			1	270	9	64	OK		10
13			2	271	42	64	Cancel		11
14									
15									
16									
17									
18									

B3: **to be converted and it does the rest.**

B4: **Press Cancel when done.**

Then type **ToFortran** in cell A6 and **Excel to Fortran** in cell B6.

Now use the SAVE.DIALOG function to get the file name and directory for the Fortran file from the user. The SAVE.DIALOG function displays a standard Save As dialog box. The SAVE.DIALOG function is an add-in file, so you may need to install the FILEFNS.XLA file in the Excel library before you can use it. Use the Add-Ins command on the Options menu to add the file.

21. In cell B7, type this formula:

=SAVE.DIALOG("PROG.FOR")

22. In cell B8, type this formula:

=IF(B7="FALSE",GOTO(Quit))

23. Type **OutputID** in cell A9.

24. Type **=FOPEN(B7,3)** in cell B9.

The following step is the top of the loop. The DIALOG.BOX function displays the dialog box you created with the Dialog Editor. The DIALOG.BOX function returns FALSE if the Cancel button was pressed; otherwise, it returns the number of the button pressed. If Cancel was pressed, the macro should jump to the end and quit.

25. Type **Top** in cell A10.

26. In cell B10, type this formula:

=DIALOG.BOX(ConversionDialog)

27. In cell B11, type this formula:

=IF(B10=FALSE,GOTO(Done))

The formula in cell B12 combines the sheet name and path, surrounded with single quotation marks, followed by an ! and the selected range returned by the dialog box. The values returned by the dialog box are stored in cells K6 and K8 in the dialog definition table. Cell B13 gets the type of the conversion to do (statement, 2-D array, 1-D array) from K8 in the dialog definition table.

28. Type **SelArea** in cell A12.

29. In cell B12, type this formula:

="'"&GET.DOCUMENT(1)&"'!"&K6

30. Type **ConvType** in cell A13.

31. Type **=K8** in cell B13.

32. Type **1=Statements, 2=2-D Array, 3=1-D Array** in cell C13.

The next few cells extract the size of the selected area (rows, columns), the reference to the first cell in the selected area. The two FOR loops scan over all the cells in the selection. The reference contained in cell SelArea (B12) is stored in text form, so you need to use the TEXTREF function to convert it back into a reference.

33. Type **theRows** in cell A14.

34. In cell B14, type this formula:

=ROWS(TEXTREF(SelArea,FALSE))

35. Type **theCols** in cell A15.

36. In cell B15, type this formula

=COLUMNS(TEXTREF(SelArea))

37. Type **theAddress** in cell A16.

38. In cell B16, type this formula:

=GET.CELL(1,INDEX(TEXTREF(SelArea),1,1))

39. In cell B17, type this formula:

=FOR("I",1,theRows,1)

40. In cell B18, type this formula:

=FOR("J",1,theCols,1)

The formula in cell B19 gets the contents of a cell. The next few cells examine those contents to see if the cell contains a value, a formula, or text. If it starts with an = sign, assume it is a formula. The TYPE command will tell you if it is a value; otherwise, it is text.

41. Type **theFormula** in cell A19.

42. In cell B19, type this formula:

> **=GET.CELL(6,INDEX(TEXTREF(SelArea),I,J))**

43. In cell B20 type this formula:

> **=IF(ConvType=1,SET.VALUE(theAddress,GET.CELL(1, INDEX(TEXTREF (SelArea),I,J))),0)**

44. Type **theType** in cell A21.

45. In cell B21, type this formula:

> **=IF(LEFT(theFormula,1)="=",1,IF(TYPE(INDEX(TEXTREF(SelArea), I,J))=1,2,3))**

46. Type **1=formula, 2=value,3=label** in cell C21.

Next see if there is a note attached to the cell, and if there is, turn it into a Fortran comment statement. Notes are short pieces of descriptive text attached to a cell with the Note command on the Formula menu. The formula in cell B24 takes the current cell address, turns it into a relative reference, and prefaces it to any note found in the cell. Then the macro writes the contents of the note to the output file.

Although some of the formulas may look complicated, if you examine them piece by piece from the inside out, you will see that they are straightforward. For example, in the formula in cell B24, the cell named theAddress contains a string with the external address of a cell, including the sheet name and cell reference. You want to extract a string containing only the cell reference converted to relative form. The portion

```
FORMULA.CONVERT(theAddress,TRUE,TRUE,4)
```

converts all cell references in theAddress into relative references and returns the resultant string. The portion

```
LEN(FORMULA.CONVERT(theAddress,TRUE,TRUE,4))
```

gets the length of that string. The part

```
FIND("!",FORMULA.CONVERT(theAddress,TRUE,TRUE,4))
```

gets the number of characters from the beginning of the string to the first ! symbol, which separates the sheet name from the reference. The portion

```
LEN(FORMULA.CONVERT(theAddress,TRUE,TRUE,4))-
FIND("!",FORMULA.CONVERT(theAddress,TRUE,TRUE,4))
```

gets the number of characters from the ! symbol to the end of the string, which is the length of the cell reference at the right side of the string. The part

```
RIGHT(FORMULA.CONVERT(theAddress,TRUE,TRUE,4),
LEN(FORMULA.CONVERT(theAddress,TRUE,TRUE,4))-
FIND("!",FORMULA.CONVERT(theAddress,TRUE,TRUE,4)))
```

extracts the cell reference from the right side of the string. The portion

```
"c  "&RIGHT(FORMULA.CONVERT(theAddress,TRUE,TRUE,4),
LEN(FORMULA.CONVERT(theAddress,TRUE,TRUE,4))-
FIND("!",FORMULA.CONVERT(theAddress,TRUE,TRUE,4)))&
": Note: "&theNote
```

combines the string "c   ", plus the cell reference, plus the string *Note:* , plus the text contained in theNote. Finally, the part

```
=SET.VALUE(theNote,"c  "&RIGHT(FORMULA.CONVERT(theAddress,
TRUE,TRUE,4),LEN(FORMULA.CONVERT(theAddress,TRUE,TRUE,4)
)-FIND("!",FORMULA.CONVERT(theAddress,TRUE,TRUE,4)))&
": Note: "&theNote)
```

inserts the resulting string back into the cell named theNote.

47. Type **theNote** in cell A22.

48. In cell B22, type

> =GET.NOTE(INDEX(TEXTREF(SelArea),I,J))

49. In cell B23, type

> =   IF(theNote<>"")

50. In cell C23, type **Get any notes and print as a comment.**

51. In cells B24, type

> =   SET.VALUE(theNote,"c   "&RIGHT(FORMULA.CONVERT(
> theAddress,TRUE,TRUE,4),LEN(FORMULA.CONVERT(
> theAddress,TRUE,TRUE,4))−FIND("!",FORMULA.CONVERT(
> theAddress,TRUE,TRUE,4)))&": Note: "&theNote)

52. In cell B25, type

> =   FWRITELN(OutputID,theNote)

53. In cell B26, type

    = END.IF()

The next six statements calculate some values needed by the blocks starting in cell B33. In cell B33, the IF function breaks the following section into three parts: one for statements, one for values, and one for text strings. These statements convert the formula, number, or value into a Fortran statement. The three statements in each block select the type of conversion: a normal Fortran statement, a 2-D array element, or a 1-D vector element. For example, cell B34 adds six spaces to the line, followed by the cell reference, an equal sign, and the formula. Cells B35 and B36 do the same as B34, but convert it into a 1-D or 2-D array element, with the array named after the top-left cell of the array. These formulas are very similar, so you can use the Copy and Paste commands on the Edit menu to copy parts.

Convert the address into relative references in the A1 style, then extract the cell reference from the right side of theAddress. Use the relative A1 style, because that creates a legal Fortran variable name from the cell reference.

54. Type **absAddr** in cell A27.

55. In cell B27, type

    = FORMULA.CONVERT(theAddress,TRUE,TRUE,4)

56. In cell C27, type

    Convert references in theAddress

57. Type **lenAddr** in cell A28.

58. In cell B28, type

    = LEN(absAddr)

59. In cell C28, type

    Length of address string

60. Type **lhsAddr** in cell A29.

61. In cell B29, type

    = FIND("!",absAddr)

62. In cell C29, type

    length of left side

63. Type **lenRef** in cell A30.

64. In cell B30, type

= lenAddr–lhsAddr

65. In cell C30, type

Length of the cell reference

66. Type **theRef** in cell A31.

67. In cell B31, type

= RIGHT(absAddr,lenRef)

68. In cell C31, type

Extract the reference

Convert all references in the formula into relative references in the A1 style.

69. Type **theForm** in cell A32.

70. In cell B32, type

= FORMULA.CONVERT(theFormula,TRUE,TRUE,4)

71. In cell C32, type

Convert references in theformula

72. In cell B33, type

= IF(theType=1)

73. In cell C33, type

Print formulas as fortran statements

74. In cell B34, type

= IF(ConvType=1,SET.VALUE(theFormula," "&theRef&
" "&theForm))

75. In cell B35, type

= IF(ConvType=2,SET.VALUE(theFormula," "&theRef&
"("&TEXT("0",I)&","&TEXT("0",J)&")"&theForm))

76. In cell B36, type

= IF(ConvType=3,SET.VALUE(theFormula," "&theRef& "("&TEXT("0",I+(J−1)*theRows)&")"&theForm))

77. In cell B37, type

= ELSE.IF(theType=2)

78. In cell C37, type

Print values as fortran statements

79. In cell B38, type

= IF(ConvType=1,SET.VALUE(theFormula," "&theRef& "="&theForm))

80. In cell B39, type

= IF(ConvType=2,SET.VALUE(theFormula," "&theRef& "("&TEXT("0",I)&","&TEXT("0",J)&")="&theForm))

81. In cell B40, type

= IF(ConvType=3,SET.VALUE(theFormula," "&theRef& "("&TEXT("0",I+(J−1)*theRows)&")="&theForm))

82. In cell B41, type

= ELSE()

83. In cell B42, type

= IF(ConvType=1,SET.VALUE(theFormula,"c "&theRef& ":"&theFormula))

84. In cell C42, type

Print anything else as a comment

85. In cell B43, type

= IF(ConvType=2,SET.VALUE(theFormula,"c "& theRef&"("&TEXT("0",I)&","&TEXT("0",J)&"):"&theFormula))

86. In cell B44, type

 = IF(ConvType=3,SET.VALUE(theFormula,"c "&
theRef&"("&TEXT("0",I+(J− 1)*theRows)&"):"&theFormula))

87. In cell B45, type

 = END.IF( )

The Fortran symbol for exponentiation is two asterisks (**), rather than the caret (^) used by Excel, so scan for any carets in the formula and replace them with double asterisks. Finally, write the new line to the output file.

88. In cell B46, type

 = IF(theType=1)

89. In cell B47, type

 = SET.VALUE(theFormula,SUBSTITUTE(theFormula,"^","**"))

90. In cell C47, type

 Replace ^ with **

91. In cell B48, type

 = END.IF()

92. In cell B49, type

 = FWRITELN(OutputID,theFormula)

If this is an array element, include a second formula that equates the array element to the cell name so that any formulas that depend on the value of this cell have access to it. The formulas are created much like those described previously.

93. In cell B50, type

 = IF(ConvType<>1)

94. Type **theAddress2** in cell A51.

95. In cell B51, type

 = GET.CELL(1,INDEX(TEXTREF(SelArea),I,J))

96. Type **absAddr2** in cell A52.

97. In cell B52, type

= FORMULA.CONVERT(theAddress2,TRUE,TRUE,4)

98. Type **lenAddr2** in cell A53.

99. In cell B53, type

= LEN(absAddr2)

100. Type **lhsAddr2** in cell A54.

101. In cell B54, type

= FIND("!",absAddr)

102. Type **lenRef2** in cell A55.

103. In cell B55, type

= lenAddr2−lhsAddr2

104. Type **theRef2** in cell A56.

105. In cell B56, type

= RIGHT(absAddr,lenRef)

106. Type **theForm2** in cell A57.

107. In cell B57, type

= FORMULA.CONVERT(theFormula,TRUE,TRUE,4)

108. In cell B58, type

= IF(theType=1)

109. In cell C58, type

Add cross reference formulas

110. In cell B59, type

= IF(ConvType=2,SET.VALUE(theFormula," "&theRef2&
"="&theRef&"("&TEXT("0",I)&","&TEXT("0",J)&")"))

111. In cell B60, type

= IF(ConvType=3,SET.VALUE(theFormula," "&theRef2&
"="&theRef&"("&TEXT("0",I+(J−1)*theRows)&")"))

112. In cell B61, type

    =   **ELSE.IF(theType=2)**

113. In cell B62, type

    =   **IF(ConvType=2,SET.VALUE(theFormula,"   "&theRef2& "="&theRef&"("&TEXT("0",I)&","&TEXT("0",J)&")"))**

114. In cell B63, type

    =   **IF(ConvType=3,SET.VALUE(theFormula,"   "& theRef2&"="&theRef&"("&TEXT("0",I+(J−1)*theRows)&")"))**

115. In cell B64, type

    =   **ELSE()**

116. In cell B65, type

    =   **IF(ConvType=2,SET.VALUE(theFormula,"c "& theRef2&"="&theRef&"("&TEXT("0",I)&","&TEXT("0",J)&")"))**

117. In cell B66, type

    =   **IF(ConvType=3,SET.VALUE(theFormula,"c "& theRef2&"="&theRef&"("&TEXT("0",I+(J−1)*theRows)&")"))**

118. In cell B67, type

    =   **END.IF()**

Finally, see if the cell has been named. If it has, write another statement that equates the name to the value of the cell.

119. In cell A68, type **theName**.

120. In cell B68, type

    =   **GET.DEF(REFTEXT(INDEX(TEXTREF(SelArea),I,J)))**

121. In cell C68, type

    See if the cell is named

122. In cell B69, type

    =   **IF(NOT(ISERROR(theName)))**

123. In cell C69, type

Print the definition as a fortran statement

124. In cell B70, type

= SET.VALUE(theName,"" ""&theName&""="""&theRef)

125. In cell B71, type

= FWRITELN(OutputID,theName)

126. In cell B72, type

= END.IF()

127. In cell B73, type

= NEXT()

128. In cell B74, type

=NEXT()

129. In cell B75, type

=FWRITELN(OutputID,""c ******************""")

130. In cell C75, type

Separate this section from the next

131. In cell B76, type =GOTO(Top).

132. In cell A77, type **Done.**

133. In cell B77, type =FCLOSE(OutputID).

134. In cell A78, type **Quit.**

135. In cell B78, type =RETURN( ).

136. Select cells A9:B80, choose the Create Names command on the Formula menu, make sure the Left Column check box is checked, and click on OK.

137. Select cell B6, choose the Define Name command on the Formula menu. In the dialog box, enter **ToFortran** as the name, click on Command Macro, enter **a** as the speed key, and click on OK.

This completes the macro. The beginning of your worksheet should look like Figure 4.6. You can now open a worksheet and apply the macro to it. The macro should work if you have not made any typing errors. If it does not work properly, you can debug it, as described in the next section.

138. Open the Delyiannis Bandpass Circuit worksheet you created in Chapter 3 (Figure 3.27).

139. Choose the Run command on the Macro menu, select the ToFortran macro, and click on OK.

140. When the Save dialog box appears, accept the default file name and click on OK to save the output in that file.

141. When the custom dialog box appears, click in the edit box and then click and drag through cells B3:C5 on the Delyiannis Bandpass circuit worksheet, as shown in Figure 4.7.

142. Click on Statements, and then click on OK.

143. When the dialog box reappears, select cells B9:C11, click on 2-D Array, and click on OK.

144. When the dialog box reappears, click on Cancel to close the file and end the macro.

FIGURE 4.6:

The Excel to Fortran conversion macro

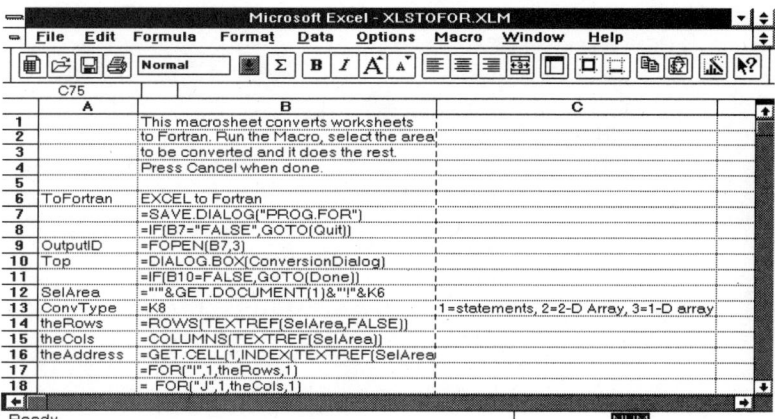

FIGURE 4.7:

Selecting cells to process
into Fortran

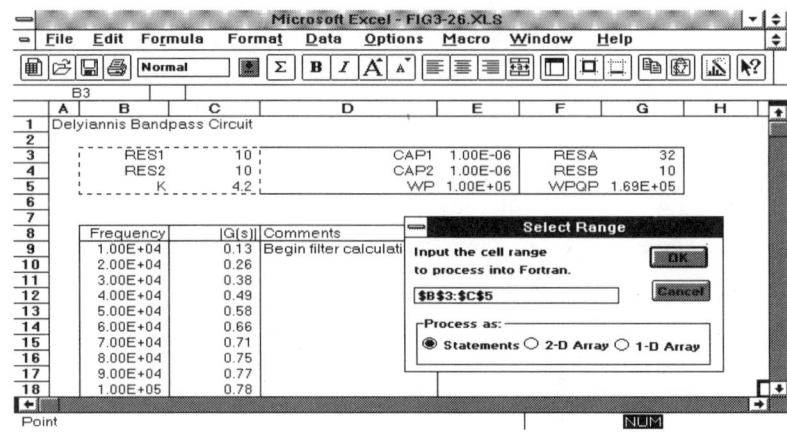

The text file created by the macro contains the following:

```
c   B3:  RES1
    C3=10
c   B4:  RES2
    C4=10
c   B5:  K
    C5  =1+G3/G4
c   *******************
    B9(1,1)=10000
    B9=B9(1,1)
    B9(1,2)=(B9/(C3*E4*(1-1/C5)))/SQRT((E5**2-
B9**2)**2+G5**2*B9**2)
    C9=B9(1,2)
    B9(2,1)=20000
    B10=B9(2,1)
    B9(2,2)=(B10/(C3*E4*(1-1/C5)))/SQRT((E5**2-
B10**2)**2+G5**2*B10**2)
    C10=B9(2,2)
    B9(3,1)=30000
    B11=B9(3,1)
    B9(3,2)=(B11/(C3*E4*(1-1/C5)))/SQRT((E5**2-
B11**2)**2+G5**2*B11**2)
    C11=B9(3,2)
c   *******************
```

Note that it is all good Fortran, which could be compiled by most generic compilers.
You still need to check the order of the statements to ensure that the values are not

used before they are assigned. You also need to rewrite IF statements and look for lines longer than 72 characters, although your Fortran compiler will find most of these problems.

Debugging Macro Programs

In many cases, a macro program will not work correctly the first time. To figure out where you went wrong, you need to determine what the macro is doing at each step. If you get a macro error of some type, note the cell and the type of error. A #REF! error is caused by an invalid reference. A #VALUE! error is caused by the incorrect or invalid use of a number.

Open the macro sheet and select the Display command on the Options menu. Remove the check in the Formulas check box and click on OK to display the values in the cells. If you click on a cell, the formula in it is displayed in the formula bar. Look at the values and see if there are error values where there should be numbers or text. See if those error values are used by the cell where the error occurred.

If you cannot find the problem, run the macro again using the Run command on the Macro menu, but click on the Step button instead of OK. This option lets you step through the macro, one line at a time. The current line and its value are displayed in the Single Step dialog box, as shown in Figure 4.8. If you click on the Step Into button, the contents of the displayed cell are executed, and the next cell is displayed. If the current statement is a subroutine call, use the Step Over button to execute all the commands in that subroutine and stop at the next cell in the current routine.

FIGURE 4.8:
The Single Step dialog box

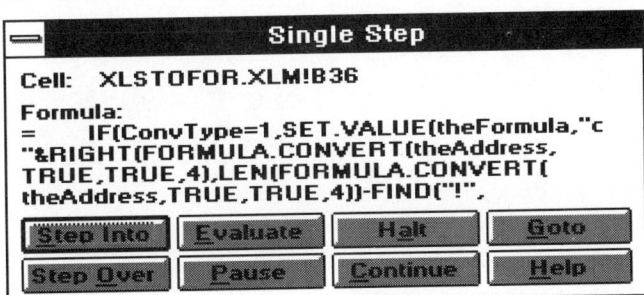

The Evaluate button executes the current cell piece by piece and displays the results. Using Evaluate, you can see how a cell calculates its result. This is especially useful in formulas like the one in Figure 4.8. If you click on Evaluate seven times, the dialog box should look like Figure 4.9.

For more difficult situations, Excel includes a Macro Debugger add-in program. To install the add-in file, use the Add-Ins command on the Options menu, click on the Add button in the dialog box, and select the DEBUG.XLA file in the LIBRARY directory.

To use the Macro Debugger, switch to the macro sheet and choose the Debug command on the Macro menu. The menu bar will change to the Debug menu bar. You can now set breakpoints and trace points in your macro code, and display the values of variables. A trace point is a cell in your macro where you want to switch to single-step mode. By setting a trace point, you can run a macro full speed up to the point just before a problem occurs, rather than single-stepping all the way to the problem. A breakpoint pauses the macro at the step you indicate and displays the values of variables you selected with the Breakpoint Output command on the Debug menu. Figure 4.10 shows the result of running the macro program described in the previous section with a breakpoint set at cell B20 and several variables selected for display.

FIGURE 4.9:

The Single Step dialog box after selecting Evaluate seven times

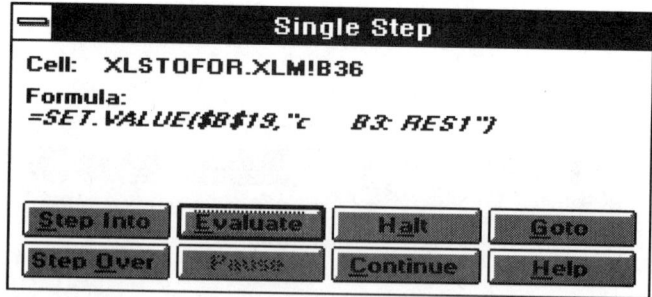

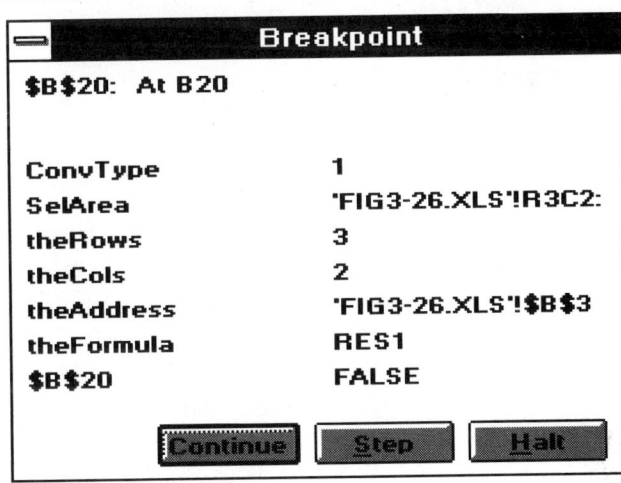

Using a breakpoint with the
Macro Debugger add-in program

Summary

Macros tremendously increase the power of Excel. With macros, you can automate most repetitive tasks. You can also create custom functions for use in the worksheet, as well as complete macro programs to automate complex tasks.

Excel's macro recorder records every step you make as a list of macro commands. You can edit this list of commands into the macro program you need. For debugging macro programs, Excel includes a Macro Debugger add-in program.

The add-in includes many high-level debugging capabilities, including breakpoints, trace points, and variable display.

For More Information

Energy Gap in Silicon

S. M. Sze, *Physics of Semiconductor Devices*, 2nd ed. (New York: Wiley, 1981).

Problems

1. Write a macro to automatically create the worksheet shown in Figure 2.5.

2. Write a macro to automatically create the worksheet shown in Figures 3.22 and 3.24. Use the alternative formula rather than the temperature data.

3. Write a macro that displays the question "Do you want to save this worksheet (Y or N)?" in a dialog box, and waits for you to type Y, y, N, or n and press Enter. If y or Y is typed, your macro should save the worksheet in the current directory, replacing any old version, and display "Worksheet saved" in the formula bar. If n or N is typed, "Worksheet not saved" should appear in the formula bar. The macro should ignore anything else that is typed and redisplay the dialog box.

4. Write a macro that displays the question "What is your birth date?" in a dialog box, accepts the date, and then displays how many days old you are.

5. Write a macro that automatically creates a table of angles x and values of the hyperbolic sine for 10 angles from 0 to 4, using the following equation:

$$\sinh(x) = \frac{e^x - e^{-x}}{2}$$

6. Write a macro to create a plot of the data in problem 5. Label both axes and set the data ranges and plot type.

7. Write a macro to create the worksheet shown in Figure 2.8.

8. Write a macro to transpose a 3x3 matrix (**A**). A transposed matrix (**A^t**) has the values in the rows and columns exchanged. Don't use the Transpose command in the Paste Special dialog box.

$$\mathbf{A} = \begin{vmatrix} a & b & c \\ d & e & f \\ g & h & i \end{vmatrix} \quad \mathbf{A^t} = \begin{vmatrix} a & d & g \\ b & e & h \\ c & f & i \end{vmatrix}$$

9. Write a macro that combines two numbers in two cells and creates a cell reference as a text value. The first number specifies the column, and the second

specifies the row. The column numbers will need to be converted to the corresponding letter (1 to A, 2 to B, and so on). For example, for the numbers 3 and 5, your macro should produce the string C5.

10. Write a macro to scroll the cursor down by 20 lines (one screen) and then scroll the worksheet to leave the cursor in the upper-left corner. Write a second macro to scroll the worksheet up one screen, again leaving the cursor in the upper-left corner. Write two more macros to move the worksheet left and right by one screen.

CHAPTER

FIVE

Analyzing Experimental Data

5

Analysis of experimental data can be as simple as averaging a few numbers or as complex as searching a large database for records that match some criterion. With Excel, you can handle simple to very complex data analysis.

Your first step is to bring the experimental data into Excel. After the data is in a worksheet, you can use Excel's commands and functions to calculate averages, fit data to lines, or plot data. For example, many experimental devices output voltages and currents that are proportional to the physical quantities being measured. Using a simple equation and the engineering table format, you can easily convert those voltages and currents into the physical quantities they represent.

Bringing Experimental Data into a Worksheet

You can use several methods to get your data into a worksheet, depending on the format of the data. If it is in the form of data in an experimental notebook, you will need to type it directly into a worksheet. If it is already in your computer in a text file, you can load it into a worksheet and separate it into cells without retyping it. If the data is in an external database, Excel can access it directly.

Manually Entering the Data

Much experimental data is available only in written form. Notes in an engineering notebook and data tables in reports or journal articles are good examples of printed experimental data. You must manually type this data into the worksheet, unless you happen to have access to an optical character reader (or a graduate student).

An optical character reader (OCR) can read printed (but not handwritten) characters and turn them into editable text in a disk file. If the data is printed, even the inexpensive hand scanners bundled with OCR software do a credible job scanning in data and converting it into editable text. Make sure you compare the printed data with the scanned data to ensure there are no mistakes (it's a good idea to check graduate-student scanned data as well).

You can type data into Excel quickly. Select a column in a worksheet and begin typing. When you press Enter or Tab, the active cell moves down to the next cell so you can continue with the next number. Be careful that you don't reach the end of the selected range before you type the last data value, because when the active cell reaches the end of the selection, it wraps back to the top of the selection and begins overwriting the data you just typed.

If you select two or more columns and press Enter (Return on the Macintosh) after each value, the active cell moves down the first column before going down the next. Press Tab (or Enter on the Macintosh) after each value to move left to right across all the columns in the selected range before moving down to the next row. If you hold down Shift when pressing Tab or Enter, the active cell moves in the opposite direction (up for Shift-Enter and left for Shift-Tab).

Inputting Data from a Disk File

Getting data into a worksheet is much simpler if your data already exists in a disk file. This includes data created by numerical simulations or data you receive from another source. You can use several methods to read the data in the disk file into the worksheet.

Excel can directly open all the file formats listed in Table 5.1. In addition, Excel contains a capability known as Q&E, which allows it to manipulate other database programs from within Excel.

Computer modeling of physical phenomena and devices produces large amounts of data that needs to be analyzed and plotted. As long as that data is written out into an ASCII data file (a text file printable with the DOS PRINT or TYPE command), you can easily load it into the worksheet for further analysis.

If the data is in a binary file, you must write a small program to read that binary file and write an ASCII file. For easy conversion, the data in the ASCII file should be in the form of a table, with multiple columns of data values or text separated by tabs, with carriage returns at the end of each line. This is Excel's default text file format. Excel can also read text files with the data delimited by commas, semicolons, spaces, or any single character, but you must specify the delimiter in the Open dialog box.

Terminal-emulation programs make your computer behave like a terminal for communications with another computer. You can use these programs to receive the results of a simulation on a mainframe computer or to receive data from another

TABLE 5.1: File Formats Accepted by Excel

Format	File Extension
Excel version 3.0	.XL?
Excel version 2.x	.XL?
Symbolic Link format (Multiplan)	.SLK
Text format	.TXT
Comma-separated values format	.CSV
1-2-3 Release 1A	.WKS
1-2-3 Release 2.x	.WK1
1-2-3 Release 3.x	.WK3
1-2-3 for Windows	.WK3
Data Interchange Format	.DIF
dBASE II	.DBF
dBASEIII	.DBF
dBASE IV	.DBF

person at a remote desktop computer. Most terminal-emulation programs have the capability to receive and store data in ASCII files. Terminal-emulation programs are also useful for connecting two computers with incompatible storage media and allowing them to share ASCII files.

Using Delimited Files

If your data is in a tab-delimited text file, simply open the file with the Open command on the File menu. This format—data values separated with tab characters and with a carriage return at the end of each line—is Excel's default text file format. When you open a tab-delimited text file, Excel opens a new worksheet, and places characters from the file into cell A1 until it reaches the first tab character. Excel then moves the active cell right one cell and places the characters following the tab character in cell B1 until it reaches the next tab character. Excel continues moving right one cell at each tab until it reaches a carriage return, which causes the active cell to move down one row and left to column A again.

If your data is delimited with a different character, such as a comma, space, or semi-colon, click on the Text button in the Open dialog box and select the delimiter from the list shown in Figure 5.1. You can also select the file origin, which corrects for different end-of-line characters used by different operating systems.

FIGURE 5.1:
File delimiter options in Excel

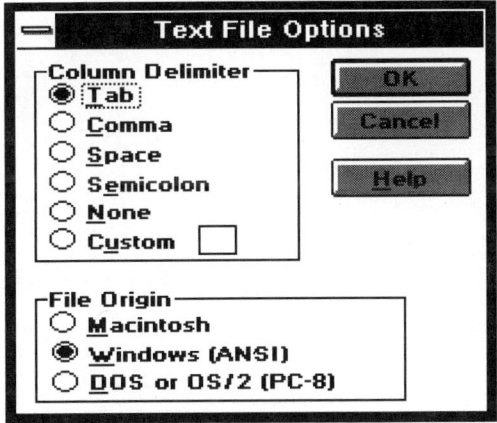

Spark Gaps   As an example, consider the text file in Figure 5.2, which consists of some spark-gap data. The text file was created with the Notepad application included with Windows. On the Macintosh, use Teach Text to create the file.

1. Using the Notepad application (Teach Text on the Macintosh), create the text file shown in Figure 5.2, using spaces to align the columns.

2. Save the file as **FIG5-2.DOC**.

3. Switch to Excel and open the file using the Open command on the File menu.

4. In the Open dialog box, click on the Text button.

5. In the Text File Options dialog box (Figure 5.1), click on Space, then on OK.

6. Select the FIG5-2.DOC file and click on OK.

The worksheet that opens looks like Figure 5.3. As you can see, this worksheet is nearly useless, because each space marks a new cell.

7. Close the file without saving it.

FIGURE 5.2:

Spark-gap sizes: a text file created with the Windows Notepad application

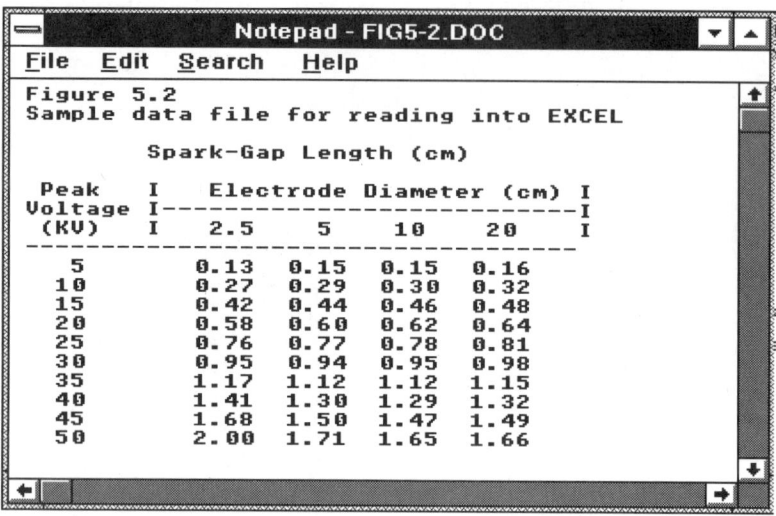

FIGURE 5.3:

Excel's conversion of a space-delimited file

8. Open the file in the Notepad application and place tab characters between each column of data, as shown in Figure 5.4.

9. Save the file as **FIG5-4.DOC.**

10. Switch to Excel and open the file, but use tab delimiters this time. (You don't need to click on the Text button and choose Tab because it is the default.)

The worksheet now looks like Figure 5.5. Most of the data and titles are in the right place; only a few labels at the top need to be moved a little to make the worksheet look good. What's important is that the columns of data are now in separate columns, where they can be used in calculations.

FIGURE 5.4:
Changing the text file to tab-delimited format

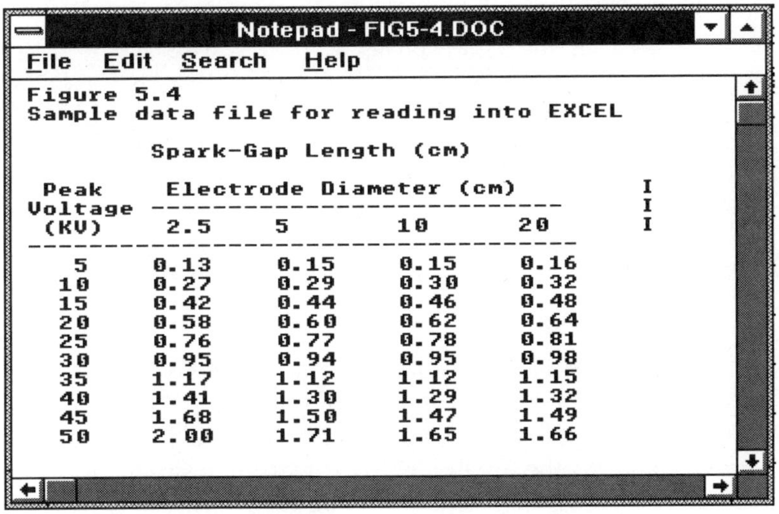
Notepad - FIG5-4.DOC
File Edit Search Help
Figure 5.4
Sample data file for reading into EXCEL
Spark-Gap Length (cm)
Peak Electrode Diameter (cm) I
Voltage I
(KV) 2.5 5 10 20 I
5 0.13 0.15 0.15 0.16
10 0.27 0.29 0.30 0.32
15 0.42 0.44 0.46 0.48
20 0.58 0.60 0.62 0.64
25 0.76 0.77 0.78 0.81
30 0.95 0.94 0.95 0.98
35 1.17 1.12 1.12 1.15
40 1.41 1.30 1.29 1.32
45 1.68 1.50 1.47 1.49
50 2.00 1.71 1.65 1.66

FIGURE 5.5:
The tab-delimited text file loaded into Excel

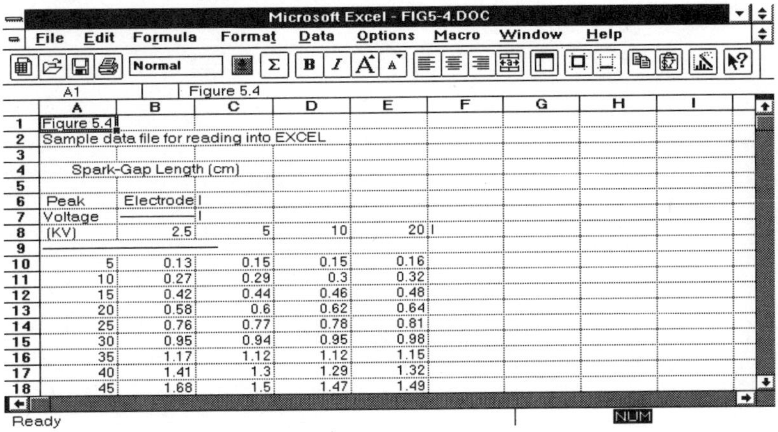
Microsoft Excel - FIG5-4.DOC
File Edit Formula Format Data Options Macro Window Help
Normal
A1 Figure 5.4
A B C D E F G H I
1 Figure 5.4
2 Sample data file for reading into EXCEL
4 Spark-Gap Length (cm)
6 Peak Electrode I
7 Voltage I
8 (KV) 2.5 5 10 20 I
10 5 0.13 0.15 0.15 0.16
11 10 0.27 0.29 0.3 0.32
12 15 0.42 0.44 0.46 0.48
13 20 0.58 0.6 0.62 0.64
14 25 0.76 0.77 0.78 0.81
15 30 0.95 0.94 0.95 0.98
16 35 1.17 1.12 1.12 1.15
17 40 1.41 1.3 1.29 1.32
18 45 1.68 1.5 1.47 1.49
Ready NUM

Using Tabular Data

If your data is in columns (as in Figure 5.2), you can still load it into Excel and place the data values in separate columns by parsing, without having to change all the spaces into tabs. Many DOS applications create tabular data, using a monospaced font to make the numbers line up. In a monospaced font, each letter is the same width. Data parsing will not work correctly if the font is not monospaced. In Windows, most fonts are not monospaced; they are proportionally spaced like the text in this book. The letter *i* uses less space than the letter *w*.

When you load a text file that does not contain tab spaces, lines of the text file are placed into consecutive cells down column A of the worksheet. Each cell in the column contains a complete line of text stored as a long label. Beware of text files created by word processors that word wrap at the end of lines. Most modern word processors store a complete paragraph as a long line with a carriage return at the end. When you load such a file in Excel, the whole paragraph (up to the 255-character limit) is stored in a single cell.

Word processors also place hidden formatting characters within a file, which cause problems when loading the file into Excel. Before opening such a file in Excel, load it into the word processor that created it and save it as text only, with line breaks (refer to the application's manual for instructions). The saved file will open properly in Excel.

Elementary Particles Figure 5.6 is a table of elementary particles and some of their characteristics. This is a more complicated (and slightly out of date) table, containing a mixture of text, numbers, and rational fractions.

FIGURE 5.6:

Particle physics constants: a text file created with the Notepad

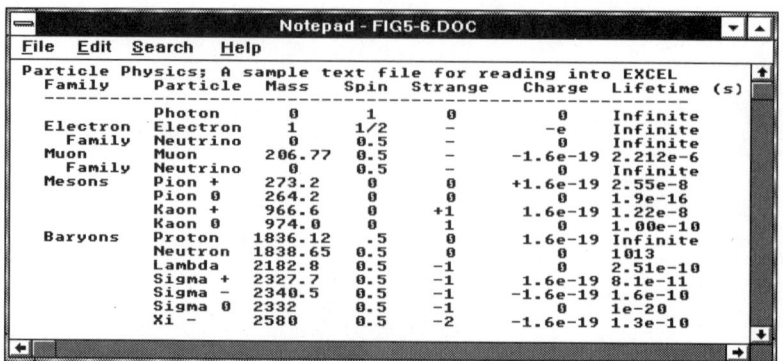

Figure 5.7 shows the result of using Excel's Open command to load the data file in Figure 5.6 into Excel, without specifying delimiters. In Excel, the file was changed to a monospace font. While it may look like it has been divided into separate cells, each line is actually in a single cell in column A. To be able to access this data, you must now parse it into separate cells.

To parse the text, select the cells to parse, choose the Parse command on the Data menu, and create a parse line to tell Excel where the different columns begin and end.

1. Create the disk file shown in Figure 5.6 using the Notepad application (Teach Text on the Macintosh).

2. Start Excel and open the file you created in step 1, with the default delimiters.

3. Select column A and choose the Font command on the Format menu. Select Courier or some other monospaced font.

The worksheet should look like Figure 5.7. Now parse the data into columns.

4. Select cells A2:A20 and select the Parse command on the Data menu. The Parse dialog box appears, as shown in Figure 5.8.

In the parse line, the square brackets mark the beginning and ending characters of the fields that will be parsed into different cells. Click on Guess, and Excel will guess where the fields begin and end from the contents of the first line in the selection. You can then select and edit the position of the brackets if Excel guesses wrong

FIGURE 5.7:

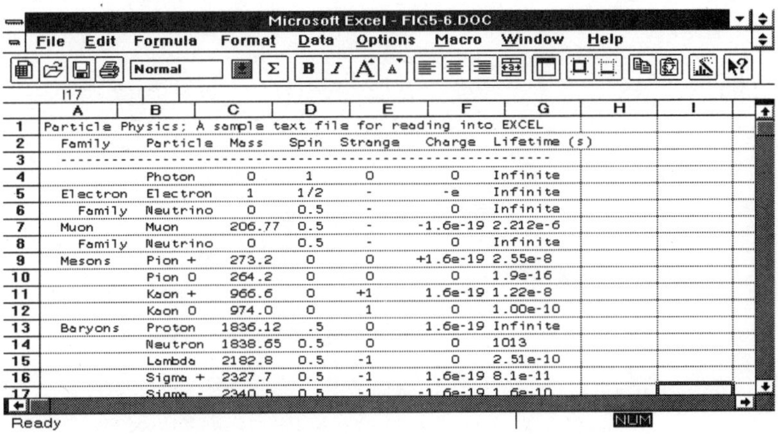

Particle physics constants loaded into Excel as text, with all the data in column A

about where they should go. In this case, the brackets to the right of the Particle and Strange columns are in the wrong place, so move them one space left.

5. In the Parse dialog box, select the two square brackets to the right of *Particle*, delete them, and type two new ones one space to the right of *Particle*.

6. Select the two square brackets to the right of *Strange*, delete them, and place two new brackets to the right of the *e* in *Strange*.

7. Click on OK to parse the data.

The data is now in columns, as shown in Figure 5.9. Now you can correct the worksheet as necessary and then use the data in other calculations. Only cells D5 and F5 are incorrect. In cell D5, Excel interpreted the 1/2 as a Date, not a number. In cell F5, Excel was confused by the -*e* in that column.

FIGURE 5.8:

The Parse dialog box with the parse line

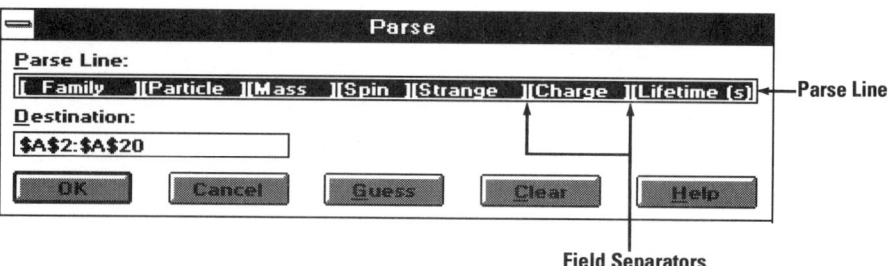

FIGURE 5.9:

Particle physics constants parsed into cells

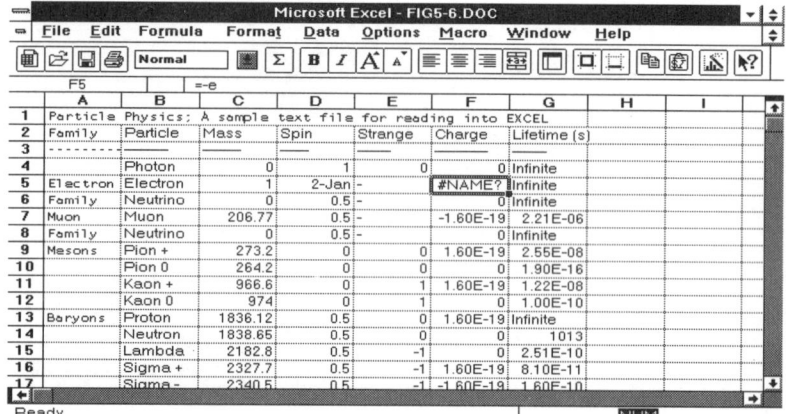

8. Change the entry in cell D5 to **0.5** and change the cell format back to General.

9. Change the entry in cell F5 to **−1.6E-19**.

Using Macros

Excel's macro facility can open text files and read characters or lines of data into the worksheet. If you need to import complex data, and you cannot parse the data in Excel, you can use the macro facility to bring in the file. For more information, see the *Microsoft Excel Function Reference* (the FOPEN, FCLOSE, FREAD, FREADLN, FWRITE, and FWRITELN functions) and Chapter 4 of this book.

Storing and Accessing Data

Once you get all of this data into Excel, you need to store it where you can find it. You can use a data table or an Excel database.

The simplest data storage methodology is the data table, which you have used in previous chapters. Data for a particular parameter is stored in columns, with particular instances of that data in the rows. This is how scientists and engineers usually store data in laboratory notebooks. Each line contains a particular measurement, with the columns containing the parameters measured. You will store most of your data in a worksheet data table.

For large amounts of data that you need to selectively analyze, (for example, selectively averaging cells that satisfy some criteria), the database format is much more flexible. The remainder of this chapter describes how to store and work with data in an Excel database.

Working with Excel Databases

In an Excel database, a range of cells is designated the database. Each column in the database is a field, and each field can contain up to 255 characters of text or a value (or formula). Each row of the range is a record of the database. Records contain related data. For example, the parameters measured in a single experimental measurement would be stored in a single record. Each field contains the data for a different parameter. For example, a particular parameter from many experimental measurements would be stored in the same field in many records, one record for each measurement.

The format of a database is similar to that of a data table. The difference is that Excel has special commands and methods for accessing data in a database.

Defining the Database Range

The first record in the database range contains the field names. These are like the column headings in the data table. Field names should be simple. They cannot consist of more than one line, nor be separated from the rest of the records of the database by any blank records or lines. The database records follow below the field names.

To define the database range, select the database, including the first row with the field names, and choose the Set Database command on the Data menu. This command names those cells Database.

Defining the Criterion Range

The next part of the database is the criterion range. The criterion range consists of a copy of the first record of the database containing the field names, plus one or more lines for inserting search criteria. Search criteria are labels or values to search for, or logical expressions for searching for ranges of values. You can put search criteria under any of the field names to further restrict the search. Criteria placed in the same row are assumed to be connected with a logical AND. Criteria placed in alternate rows are assumed to be connected with a logical OR.

Two wildcard characters are available for searching label fields: ? and *. The question mark stands for any single character. For example, C?T will match *CAT*, *COT*, and *CUT*. The asterisk matches any number of characters. For example, C* matches *common*, *creation*, or *continue*.

To define the criterion range, select the cells that contain the criteria, and then choose the Set Criteria command on the Data menu.

Defining the Extract Range

A few database commands also need an extract range, which consists of a copy of the first record of the database containing the field names. The extract range does not need to contain all the field names. Include only the names of the fields that you want in the output.

The extract range can consist of one or many rows. If your extract range consists of only one row, Excel will clear all the cells below the extract range before the database commands start writing records to this range. If there is anything below the extract range, it will be lost. If you define a multiple row extract range, the database commands will write records to it until it is filled and then generate an error. Using multiple row extract ranges is a way to protect valuable data below the extract range.

To define the extract range, select the cells and choose the Set Extract command on the Data menu.

Using Database Commands

Three commands on the Data menu use the database, criteria, and extract ranges you define for your database:

- The Find command locates records that match the criteria.
- The Extract command copies the records that match the criteria to the extract range.
- The Delete command deletes records that match the criteria from the database.

These commands use the criteria in the cells you specified with the Set Criteria command.

After you set up the database, criteria, and extract ranges, you can execute the command you want to use. Most often, you will use the Find command. When you select the Find command, the scroll bar on your worksheet changes. Instead of moving up or down one row when you click on it, it scrolls to the next record that matches the criteria. Use the arrows on the scroll bars to move forward or backward in the database.

Using a Data Form

The simplest way to access an Excel database is with the Form command on the Data menu. Using the field names in the first row of the database range, Excel constructs a data form containing those fields.

The data form includes command buttons to add records, delete records, create a criteria, and search for records matching that criteria. The criteria created on the data form is unrelated to the criteria defined with the Set Criteria command. You can create a custom form for the database if you don't like the one Excel generated. (See Chapter 9 of the *Microsoft Excel User's Guide* for information about creating and using custom forms.)

Using Database Functions

The database statistical functions (listed in Table 1.11) perform statistical calculations on the records that match the criteria. They are identical to the normal statistical functions, except that they are applied only to those records in the range that match the criteria, rather than the whole range. Thus, for example, you can calculate averages or variances of data that has a particular characteristic.

Each of the database functions has three arguments: *database*, *criteria*, and *field*. The *database* argument is a reference to the records of your database. If you use the name Database, you will get the range defined with the Set Database command. Using this range with these functions is not required; any valid cell reference is allowed, as long as it has a top row with field names. The *criteria* argument is a reference to a criterion range. If you use the word Criteria, you get the range defined with the Set Criteria command. The *field* argument is the field in the database to apply the statistical function to. It can be either the text of the field name from the first row of the database, or the number of the column in the database where the first column is 1, the second is 2, and so on.

Prerace Dehydration in Racing Greyhounds   Julie, who has been proofreading this text for me, wanted to know where the biological examples were. I had lots of hard science and engineering examples, but no biology. Being a veterinarian, she is more interested in dogs and cats than in wires and computers. Not wanting to leave out any relevant science (and to keep peace in the house), I asked her to find a good problem for demonstrating database management. So she called a friend of hers, Linda Blythe, DVM, Ph.D., at the college of Veterinary Medicine at Oregon State University in Corvallis, Oregon. A week later, a box arrived containing data from 2552 racing forms.

Dr. Blythe and her coworker Dr. Donald Hansen, were examining the prerace weight loss in racing greyhounds. All the dogs are brought to the track before the racing begins and put in an air-conditioned room known as the "ginny pit." There they wait until the start of their respective races. During their interval in the ginny pit, some dogs lose up to several percent of their weight in body fluid. This is all due to drooling and panting (the dogs are trained not to urinate or defecate in their cages).

The dogs are weighed when they are brought into the room, and again just before their race, to ensure that the weight loss has not been excessive. If they have lost more than three pounds, they must be examined by a veterinarian before they can race. Loss of an excessive amount of fluids can cause acid/base disturbances that can leave a greyhound with a decreased capacity to handle the hydrogen ions produced during the physical activity of a race.

This weight loss is perceived to be a serious problem for some racing greyhounds, so Drs. Blythe and Hansen studied the effect of weight loss on racing performance. As data, they used the racing forms filled out for each dog at each race. The data on these forms includes the dog's age, sex, weight before and after being in the ginny pit, race number, race class, post position, and finish position.

Dr. Blythe sent me the data on 489 dogs in 2552 races, which was far more than I needed for this example. Table 5.2 contains the data for 15 dogs in 100 races. If you don't want to type in all those records, you can still try the database commands by typing only 10 or 20 records. As you would expect, the results will be different. Better yet, use the data from one of your own projects to experiment with the database commands.

TABLE 5.2: Prerace Dehydration in Racing Dogs: Weight Loss/Performance Data

Dog	Sex*	Age (mon.)	Race No.	Initial Weight (lb.)	Post Weight (lb.)	Post Position	Finish Position	Race Class**	Weight Loss
1	0	58	9	70.5	69.5	8	8	1	1.42%
1	0	58	7	70.5	69.5	9	2	6	1.42%
1	0	58	6	71	70	5	4	6	1.41%
1	0	58	2	72	71.5	1	1	2	0.69%
1	0	58	6	72	71	7	2	2	1.39%
1	0	58	8	72.5	72	5	1	3	0.69%
2	0	29	12	68	67.5	2	5	1	0.74%
2	0	29	9	67	67	2	6	1	0.00%
2	0	29	9	67.5	66.5	6	1	1	1.48%
2	0	29	6	68.5	68	2	6	1	0.73%
2	0	29	6	69	68.5	7	5	1	0.72%
2	0	29	2	69	68.5	4	1	2	0.72%
2	0	29	6	68.5	68	5	5	2	0.73%
3	1	40	12	64	62.5	3	6	1	2.34%
3	1	40	2	64	63	4	9	1	1.56%
3	1	40	6	64	63.5	1	3	1	0.78%
3	1	40	4	64.5	63.5	5	6	1	1.55%
3	1	40	12	65	63	2	2	1	3.08%
3	1	40	2	65	64	5	9	1	1.54%
3	1	40	2	64.5	64	2	1	2	0.78%
4	0	23	12	76	75.5	4	8	1	0.66%
4	0	23	2	76.5	76	9	3	1	0.65%
4	0	23	6	76.5	75.5	8	1	1	1.31%
4	0	23	6	76.5	75.5	9	5	7	1.31%
4	0	23	9	77	76	8	4	1	1.30%
4	0	23	6	77	76	8	2	1	1.30%
4	0	23	9	77	76	1	6	1	1.30%
5	0	24	12	71.5	70.5	5	3	1	1.40%
5	0	24	2	71.5	71	5	2	1	0.70%
5	0	24	9	71	70.5	3	1	7	0.70%

TABLE 5.2: Prerace Dehydration in Racing Dogs: Weight Loss/Performance Data (continued)

Dog	Sex*	Age (mon.)	Race No.	Initial Weight (lb.)	Post Weight (lb.)	Post Position	Finish Position	Race Class**	Weight Loss
5	0	24	6	71.5	71	6	2	7	0.70%
5	0	24	9	71	70	7	2	1	1.41%
5	0	24	9	72	71.5	4	4	1	0.69%
5	0	24	9	71.5	71	8	1	1	0.70%
6	1	47	12	59	58	6	7	1	1.69%
6	1	47	6	58	57.5	2	3	1	0.86%
6	1	47	9	58.5	58	1	4	7	0.85%
6	1	47	6	59	58.5	4	4	7	0.85%
6	1	47	9	58.5	58	1	3	1	0.85%
6	1	47	9	58.5	57.5	6	2	1	1.71%
6	1	47	9	58	57	4	1	1	1.72%
7	0	34	12	72	71.5	7	2	1	0.69%
7	0	34	6	71.5	71	5	9	1	0.70%
7	0	34	9	71.5	71.5	2	3	7	0.00%
7	0	34	6	72	71.5	2	1	7	0.69%
7	0	34	9	72.5	71.5	3	1	1	1.38%
7	0	34	9	71.5	71	8	3	1	0.70%
7	0	34	9	71.5	71	2	5	1	0.70%
8	0	23	12	71.5	71	8	4	1	0.70%
8	0	23	9	72	71.5	8	2	1	0.69%
8	0	23	9	71.5	71	1	9	1	0.70%
8	0	23	11	72	71.5	1	1	2	0.69%
8	0	23	8	72	71.5	8	6	2	0.69%
8	0	23	2	72.5	72	2	4	2	0.69%
8	0	23	2	72	72	9	3	2	0.00%
8	0	23	9	72	71.5	4	6	1	0.69%
9	0	36	12	63.5	62.5	9	1	1	1.57%
9	0	36	2	63.5	63	3	1	1	0.79%
9	0	36	2	63.5	63.5	1	1	2	0.00%
9	0	36	12	64	62.5	9	2	1	2.34%

TABLE 5.2: Prerace Dehydration in Racing Dogs: Weight Loss/Performance Data (continued)

Dog	Sex*	Age (mon.)	Race No.	Initial Weight (lb.)	Post Weight (lb.)	Post Position	Finish Position	Race Class**	Weight Loss
9	0	36	12	63	62.5	1	4	1	0.79%
9	0	36	9	63.5	63	5	7	1	0.79%
9	0	36	12	64	63	8	3	1	1.56%
9	0	36	9	63	63	1	9	1	0.00%
10	0	26	11	66	65	1	6	3	1.52%
10	0	26	8	66	65.5	6	9	3	0.76%
10	0	26	5	66	65.5	7	9	3	0.76%
10	0	26	8	66.5	65	6	2	3	2.26%
10	0	26	6	66.5	65.5	3	6	7	1.50%
10	0	26	9	66	64	9	8	7	3.03%
10	0	26	12	67	66	6	3	2	1.49%
11	1	21	11	53.5	52.5	2	1	3	1.87%
11	1	21	5	53	52	1	6	3	1.89%
11	1	21	1	53.5	53	1	4	3	0.93%
11	1	21	1	53.5	53	5	2	3	0.93%
11	1	21	8	53.5	52.5	2	4	3	1.87%
11	1	21	10	53.5	53	2	3	3	0.93%
11	1	21	11	54	53.5	3	9	3	0.93%
11	1	21	5	54	54	2	1	4	0.00%
12	0	28	11	69	68.5	3	4	3	0.72%
12	0	28	8	68	67.5	9	2	3	0.74%
12	0	28	5	69	68.5	5	7	3	0.72%
12	0	28	8	70	69	7	9	3	1.43%
12	0	28	2	68.5	68	2	8	2	0.73%
12	0	28	6	68.5	68	3	8	2	0.73%
12	0	28	12	68	67.5	4	9	2	0.74%
13	1	51	11	62	61.5	4	2	3	0.81%
13	1	51	8	62.5	62	3	6	3	0.80%
13	1	51	7	62	61.5	8	7	6	0.81%
13	1	51	6	62.5	62	4	6	6	0.80%

TABLE 5.2:   Prerace Dehydration in Racing Dogs: Weight Loss/Performance Data (continued)

Dog	Sex*	Age (mon.)	Race No.	Initial Weight (lb.)	Post Weight (lb.)	Post Position	Finish Position	Race Class**	Weight Loss
13	1	51	11	62.5	62	1	4	2	0.80%
13	1	51	12	62.5	62	7	2	2	0.80%
14	1	33	11	52.5	51	5	8	3	2.86%
14	1	33	5	52.5	52	5	9	3	0.95%
14	1	33	8	52	51	7	7	3	1.92%
14	1	33	12	52	51.5	2	2	3	0.96%
14	1	33	12	52	51	4	9	3	1.92%
14	1	33	12	52	51	5	5	2	1.92%
15	0	25	11	64	63	6	5	3	1.56%
15	0	25	5	64	62.5	2	2	3	2.34%

*Sex: 0 = male, 1 = female
** Race class: 1 (fast) through 5 (slow), 6 and 7 are unclassified.
This data is courtesy of Dr. L. Blythe, Oregon State University.

1. Start with a blank worksheet expanded to full size, and change the column widths as follows:

    A = 5   F = 9

    B = 5   G = 6

    C = 5   H = 6

    D = 6   I = 7

    E = 9   J = 6

2. Type **Prerace weight loss in racing dogs** in cell A1.

Create the criterion range, including the range names for the database. While the criterion range can be anywhere on the worksheet, it is simplest to put it directly above the database range.

3. Type **Criterion Range** in cell A3.

4. Make the following entries in cells A4:J4:

A4: **Dog**	B4: **Sex**
C4: **Age**	D4: **Race**
E4: **Init Wt.**	F4: **Post Wt.**
G4: **Post**	H4: **Finish**
I4: **Class**	J4: **Loss**

Create the database range. First come the field names, then the actual data. Do not place blank or dashed lines between the field names and the data.

5. Type **Database Range** in cell A14.

6. Select cells A4:J4. Place the pointer on the border of the selected area, hold down Ctrl (Cmd on the Macintosh), and drag a copy of the field names to cell A15:J15 (in earlier versions of Excel, use the Copy and Paste commands).

Now calculate the percent weight loss.

7. In cell J16, type **=(E16−F16)/E16** and copy it into cells J17:J115.

8. Format cells J16:J115 as 0.00%.

Next type the data into the database and define the database and criteria ranges.

9. In cells A16:I115, type the data in Table 5.2.

10. Select cells A15:J115 and choose the Set Database command on the Data menu.

11. Select cells A4:J5 and choose the Set Criteria command on the Data menu.

12. Turn off the gridlines with the Display command on the Options menu.

Your worksheet should look like Figure 5.10. The two Set commands name the database and criterion ranges as Database and Criteria. To change or remove those

FIGURE 5.10:

Prerace dehydration in racing dogs: initial database setup

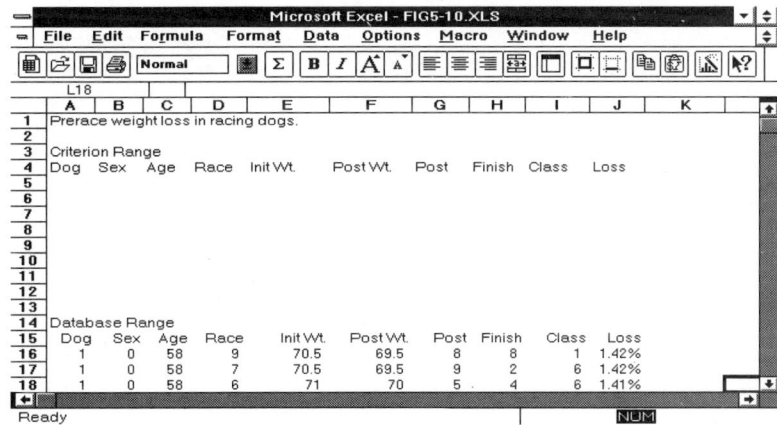

names, either use the Set commands to define another area as the database or criterion range or edit the definitions with the Define Name command on the Formula menu.

Now that you have a database to work with, you can use it to locate some data of interest. Suppose you are interested in finding the records for all winning female dogs. First set the criteria, and then use the database commands to locate the records. The sex of the dogs is coded as 0 for male and 1 for female.

13. Type **1** in cell H5.

14. Type **1** in cell B5.

15. Select the Find command on the Data menu.

The worksheet should now look like Figure 5.11. Note how the interior of the scroll bars has changed, and the selection point has moved to row 35, the first row that satisfies the criteria. Pressing the up or down arrow keys moves to the next or previous matching record, as does clicking above or below the scroll box (the square that moves up and down on the scroll bar).

To extract the records into a table rather than just view them, create an extract range and use the Extract command. Place the extract range out of the way so the extraction won't overwrite any important cells. Assume you want a table of only age and weight loss for the winning female dogs.

FIGURE 5.11:
Prerace dehydration in racing dogs: finding records that match the criteria

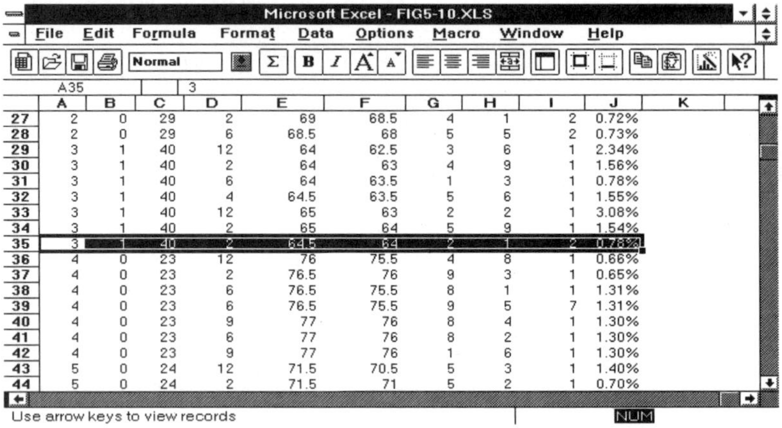
Microsoft Excel - FIG5-10.XLS
File Edit Formula Format Data Options Macro Window Help
Normal
A35 3

	A	B	C	D	E	F	G	H	I	J	K
27	2	0	29	2	69	68.5	4	1	2	0.72%	
28	2	0	29	6	68.5	68	5	5	2	0.73%	
29	3	1	40	12	64	62.5	3	6	1	2.34%	
30	3	1	40	2	64	63	4	9	1	1.56%	
31	3	1	40	6	64	63.5	1	3	1	0.78%	
32	3	1	40	4	64.5	63.5	5	6	1	1.55%	
33	3	1	40	12	65	63	2	2	1	3.08%	
34	3	1	40	2	65	64	5	9	1	1.54%	
35	3	1	40	2	64.5	64	2	1	2	0.78%	
36	4	0	23	12	76	75.5	4	8	1	0.66%	
37	4	0	23	2	76.5	76	9	3	1	0.65%	
38	4	0	23	6	76.5	75.5	8	1	1	1.31%	
39	4	0	23	6	76.5	75.5	9	5	7	1.31%	
40	4	0	23	9	77	76	8	4	1	1.30%	
41	4	0	23	6	77	76	8	2	1	1.30%	
42	4	0	23	9	77	76	1	6	1	1.30%	
43	5	0	24	12	71.5	70.5	5	3	1	1.40%	
44	5	0	24	2	71.5	71	5	2	1	0.70%	

Use arrow keys to view records NUM

16. Select the Exit Find command on the Data menu.

17. Type **Extract range** in cell L3, **Age** in cell L4, and **Loss** in cell M4.

18. Select cells L4:M4 and choose the Set Extract command on the Data menu.

19. Choose the Extract command on the Data menu. Click on OK in the dialog box.

The extract range, shown in Figure 5.12, contains only the records that match the criteria and only those fields included in the extract range heading.

Another way to search and maintain the database is with the Form command.

20. Choose the Form command on the Data menu.

You should see the data form shown in Figure 5.13. Each independent field in the database is represented by a text box on the form. The scroll bar down the center allows you to select any record in the database to be displayed. Changing any value on the form changes the corresponding value in the database, except for the last field, which is a calculated value. The New and Delete buttons allow you to add or delete records from the database without redefining the database range after making changes. The Restore button restores a record to the values it had before you made changes, as long as you have not moved to another cell. However, Restore cannot recover a deleted record.

FIGURE 5.12:

Prerace dehydration in racing dogs: extracting matching records to the extract range

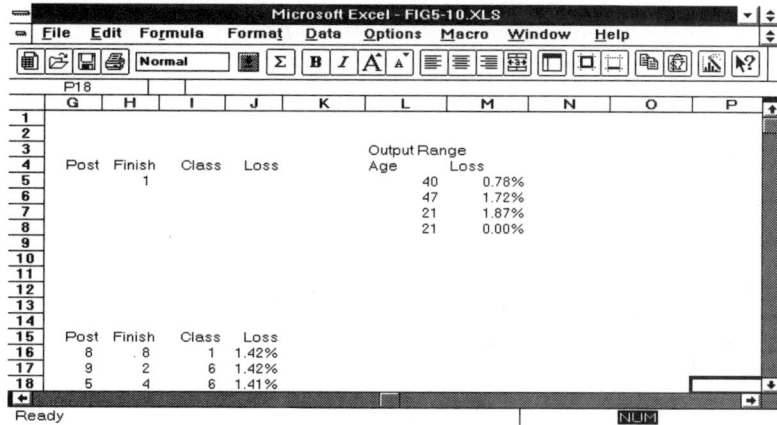

FIGURE 5.13:

Prerace dehydration in racing dogs: the data form

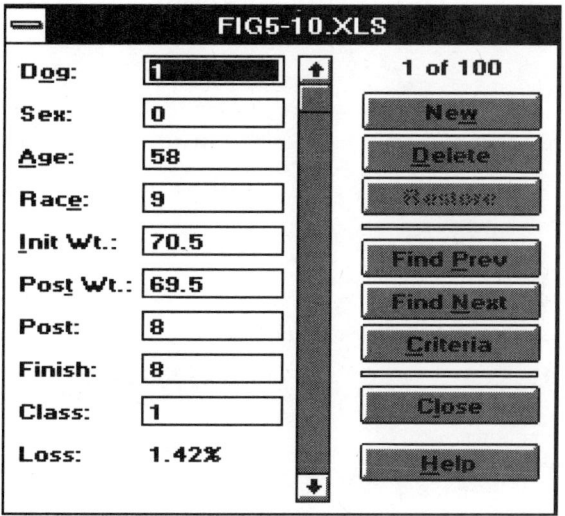

To set the search criteria, click on the Criteria button and type the criteria on the form. The criteria used here is unrelated to the criteria set with the Set Criteria command. To set the same criteria as was set in the last example, place a 1 in the Sex box and a 1 in the Finish box, as shown in Figure 5.14. Click on the Form button to return to the form. Click on the Find Next button to find the first occurrence of a matching record, as shown in Figure 5.15. The Find Next and Find Prev buttons move from one matching value to the next.

21. When you are finished with the data form, click on the Close button.

FIGURE 5.14:

Prerace dehydration in racing dogs: setting criteria with the data form

FIGURE 5.15:

Prerace dehydration in racing dogs: searching for matching records with the data form

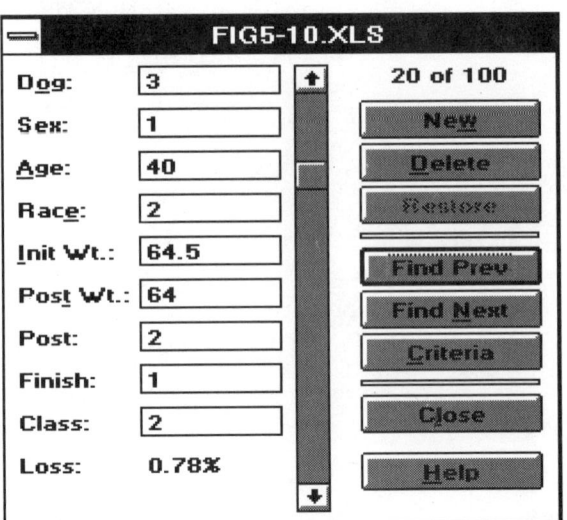

Suppose you want to know the fraction of male and female dogs in the races. You could search for each record and manually count them, but the database functions provide a better way. You could use the DCOUNT function to count the number of males and count the number of females, and then divide the numbers. However, since the males are marked with a 0, and the females with a 1, all you need to do is to average the Sex column of the database.

22. Clear the values from the criterion range in cells A5:J5.

23. In cell E10, type the formula

    =DAVERAGE(Database,2,Criteria)

24. Format cell E10 as 0.00%.

As soon as the worksheet recalculates, you will see the figure 34.00% (35.00% if you used only the first 20 records), as shown in Figure 5.16. This indicates that 34 percent of the dogs are female. Note that an empty criterion range matches the whole database.

Now see how the female dogs are doing at the finish line. Find the percentage of the dogs in the first three places that are female.

25. Type **=H16<4** in cell H5.

FIGURE 5.16:

Prerace dehydration in racing dogs: using the database statistical functions

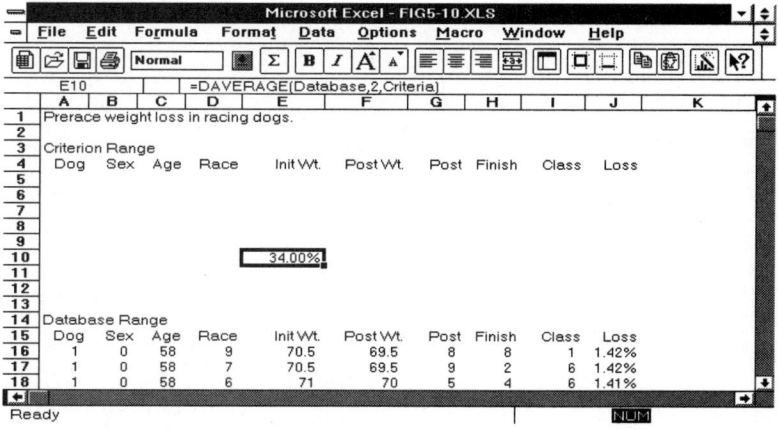

Cell E10 now contains 30.43% (33.33% for 20 records). You have limited the records being averaged to those with dogs in the first three places. You see that the percentage of winning females has decreased slightly. The reference to cell H16 is to establish which field in the database to apply the criteria to and must be a cell in the second row of the database range.

Since this study is about weight loss, look at those dogs that win and that have a high weight loss (greater than 2.5 percent of their body weight).

26. Type **=J16>0.025** in cell J5.

The percentage in cell E10 changes to 100 (this value is the same for 20 records). This figure indicates that all the dogs in the first three places that have high fluid loss are females.

You could continue changing the restrictions in the criterion range and see what the results are. You could also count cells that match the criterion with the DCOUNT function, find the minima or maxima with DMIN and DMAX, calculate the standard deviation and variance with DSTDEV and DVAR, or add the values with the DSUM command. Additionally, you can create tables of values using these functions. Remember, the criterion range does not need to be the one you defined with the Set Criteria command, and it does not need to contain all the field names, only those that you want to search.

Sorting Data

The Sort command on the Data menu will sort any set of data and text records. Excel can sort data in ascending or descending order, according to a primary and a secondary key. You can sort many columns of data according to the values in a single column.

As an example, sort the racing dogs database range according to finishing position and weight loss.

1. Select all of the database range but the field headings, cells A16:J115.

2. Choose the Sort command on the Data menu.

3. Click in the 1st Key box, then on cell H16, then on Ascending.

4. Click in the 2nd Key box, then on cell J16, then on Descending.

5. Click on OK.

Your worksheet database should now look like Figure 5.17. All the records are sorted according to the winning position and the weight loss.

Summary

Experimental data is an important resource of scientists and engineers. Excel provides methods for managing that resource. In this chapter, you investigated how to enter data into the worksheet and how to store and retrieve it after it's in Excel. You also saw how to define and use a database to analyze experimental data.

For More Information

Spark Gaps

CRC, *Handbook of Chemistry and Physics*, 51st ed. (Cleveland, Ohio: Chemical Rubber Co., 1971), p. E61.

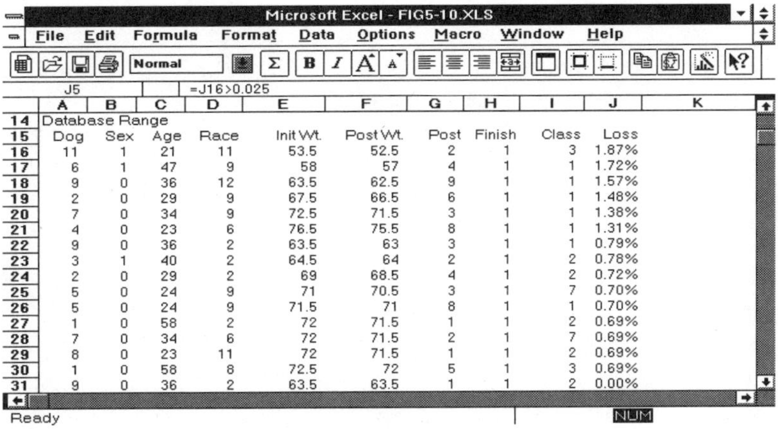

FIGURE 5.17:

Prerace dehydration in racing dogs: sorted database records

	A	B	C	D	E	F	G	H	I	J	K
14	Database Range										
15	Dog	Sex	Age	Race	Init Wt.	Post Wt.	Post	Finish	Class	Loss	
16	11	1	21	11	53.5	52.5	2	1	3	1.87%	
17	6	1	47	9	58	57	4	1	1	1.72%	
18	9	0	36	12	63.5	62.5	9	1	1	1.57%	
19	2	0	29	9	67.5	66.5	6	1	1	1.48%	
20	7	0	34	9	72.5	71.5	3	1	1	1.38%	
21	4	0	23	6	76.5	75.5	8	1	1	1.31%	
22	9	0	36	2	63.5	63	3	1	1	0.79%	
23	3	1	40	2	64.5	64	2	1	2	0.78%	
24	2	0	29	2	69	68.5	4	1	2	0.72%	
25	5	0	24	9	71	70.5	3	1	7	0.70%	
26	5	0	24	9	71.5	71	8	1	1	0.70%	
27	1	0	58	2	72	71.5	1	1	2	0.69%	
28	7	0	34	6	72	71.5	2	1	7	0.69%	
29	8	0	23	11	72	71.5	1	1	2	0.69%	
30	1	0	58	8	72.5	72	5	1	3	0.69%	
31	9	0	36	2	63.5	63.5	1	1	2	0.00%	

Elementary Particles

D. Haliday and R. Resnick, *Physics* (New York: Wiley, 1967), pp. 551-552.

Prerace Dehydration in Racing Greyhounds

L.L. Blythe and D. E. Hansen, "Factors Affecting Prerace Dehydration and Performance of Racing Greyhounds," *J. Am. Vet. Med. Assoc. 189*, 12 (Dec. 15, 1986): 1572-1574.

Problems

1. Type the ASCII file shown in Figure 5.2. Read it into a worksheet and parse it with the Parse command on the Data menu.

2. Create a text file containing the following 8 rows of comma-delimited numbers.

   23.7,569.82,19.2

   1.882,27.9,26

   19.3,239,4

   95.76,9,23

   115.98,23.7,23.8

   19.220,19876.3, 2

   27.886,14.3,67.5

   23.9,14.5,14.4

   Read this file into a worksheet and parse it into separate cells using the Open command on the File menu.

3. Create a database of journal articles you are using. Store the author's name, article name, citation, and keywords in four separate fields. Create a criterion range and try extracting articles according to specific keywords and authors.

4. Using the journal article database created in problem 4, create a custom form to view and search the database for articles. A custom database form is created in the same manner as a custom dialog box (see Chapter 4).

5. Write a macro that scrolls down a database until it finds a specific string or word anywhere in a field. Each time you execute the macro, it should scroll down to the next record containing the string. Hint: Move down one cell and test its contents for the string with FIND. Stop when you reach the bottom of the database.

6. Use the data file from problem 3 and create a macro to read this file and parse it into three columns of numbers. Do not use the Open command this time, but write a macro that uses FOPEN to open the file, FREADLINE to read a line of text, FIND to locate the commas, and MID to extract the characters between them.

7. Input the greyhound database (Table 5.2) and compare the average weight loss for female dogs with that for male dogs. Compare the average weight loss for dogs in the first three finish positions.

8. Using the database created in problem 8, copy the records of all female dogs into an extract range. Sort the copied data first by finish position and then by weight loss.

9. Using the database created in problem 8, compare the variance in the weight loss for male and female dogs, and then for dogs in the first three finish positions.

CHAPTER
SIX

Curve Fitting

6

Fitting an analytical equation to a set of data points is a common task of scientists and engineers. For scientists, being able to fit a theoretical equation to some experimental data often vindicates a theory. Engineers are often required to fit instrument calibration data to an analytical equation so that they can convert the output of the instrument to the physical parameter being measured.

Excel provides three ways to do curve fitting. You can fit most equations to data with the built-in linear regression commands. You can use linear regression to fit nonlinear data by transforming the data suitably before fitting it. You can fit more complex equations by manually adjusting the coefficients of the equation until the residual error (the sum of the squares of the differences between the data and the curve) is minimized, or the correlation coefficient is maximized. Finally, for data that cannot be fit to any reasonable curve, you can use table lookup functions and interpolation to supply values.

Using the Built-In Functions

Excel has the built-in curve-fitting capability known as multiple linear regression. With this capability, you can fit data to either a simple line or a complex polynomial. You can accomplish most curve-fitting tasks with Excel's linear-regression capabilities.

Regression Calculations

When you fit a curve to some data points using regression, you are minimizing the residual square error between the data points and the curve (least-squares analysis). The residual square error (E) is found with the following equation:

$$E = \sum_{i=1}^{n} \left(y(x_i) - y_i \right)^2$$

where $y(x_i)$ is the curve being fit, n is the number of data points, and x_i and y_i are the data points the curve is being fit to.

Excel uses multiple linear regression, so it assumes that the curve $y(x_i)$ is of the form

$$y\left(x_{1,i}, x_{2,i}, \ldots\right) = A + Bx_{1,i} + Cx_{2,i} + \ldots$$

where A, B, and C are the coefficients of the equation that need to be adjusted to make the curve fit the data. This is done by inserting the function for $y(x_{1,i}, x_{2,i}, \ldots)$ into the equation for the residual error, and then setting the derivative of that equation with respect to each of the coefficients equal to zero. This results in one equation for each of the coefficients in terms of the other coefficients and the data points, which are then solved for the coefficients. Excel's built-in regression functions take care of all of the multiple linear-regression calculations for you.

Along with the coefficients of the regression equation, Excel also calculates some statistics about the curve fit:

- Standard error of the y estimate ($S_y.x$)
- Correlation index (coefficient of determination) (r^2)
- Standard errors of the coefficients (S_A, S_B, $\ldots$)
- F statistic
- Number of degrees of freedom
- Sum of the squares of the regression and of the residuals

Standard Error of the y Estimate

The standard error of the y estimate is an estimate of the error in a single value of y calculated with the equation. This estimate is used, in conjunction with the Student's t test, to calculate the confidence limits of the calculated curve. The confidence limit is a band about the calculated curve that, with some level of confidence (say 95 percent), contains the true curve. The standard error of the y estimate is calculated with this equation:

$$S_{y.x} = \sqrt{\frac{\sum_{i=1}^{n}(y_i - y(x_i))^2}{p}}$$

where p is the number of degrees of freedom ($p = n - 2$ for a simple linear curve).

Correlation Index

The correlation index, or coefficient of determination, is equal to the square of the correlation coefficient (r) and is a measure of how well the curve fits the data points.

It has a range of 0 to 1, with 1 indicating a perfect fit to the data points. A good curve fit will have a correlation index with a value greater than 0.9. It is calculated with this equation:

$$r^2 = 1 - \frac{\sum\limits_{i=1}^{n}\left(y_i - y(x_i)\right)^2}{\sum\limits_{i=1}^{n}\left(y_i - \langle y_i \rangle\right)^2}$$

where

$$\langle y_i \rangle = \frac{\sum\limits_{i=1}^{n} y_i}{n}$$

is the average of the y data.

Standard Errors of the Coefficients

The standard errors in the coefficients are measures of the errors in each of the regression coefficients. The standard error in the first coefficient (S_A) is calculated using the standard error of the y estimate:

$$S_A = \sqrt{\frac{1}{n} + \frac{\langle x \rangle^2}{\sum\limits_{i=1}^{n}\left(x_i - \langle x \rangle\right)^2}}\, S_{y \cdot x}$$

where

$$\langle x \rangle = \frac{\sum\limits_{i=1}^{n} x_i}{n}$$

The main use of the standard errors of the coefficients is to test a coefficient to see if it is statistically zero. Since the coefficients all multiply linear x terms, if one is zero, there is no correlation between that x term and the y data. To test a coefficient, get the appropriate Student's t value for the required confidence interval (1-α) and degrees of freedom (p), and calculate

$$|B| > t_{\frac{\alpha}{2},p} S_B$$

If this equation is true, the coefficient is significant and the values of y depend on the values of x that are multiplied by the coefficient. If this equation is false, the y values do not depend on those x values, and 0 should be used for the coefficient. The rest of the coefficients are handled in a similar manner. A good engineering statistics book will give you a lot more information about how to use these statistics and will include a table of Student's t values.

In general, if the absolute value of the coefficient is an order of magnitude larger than the standard error of the coefficient, you can be sure that it is significant. If you have at least four degrees of freedom (for example, six data points for a linear fit) the 95 percent confidence interval Student's t value is only about 2.1 and decreases for more degrees of freedom. Therefore, a good rule of thumb is if the absolute value of the coefficient is greater than 2.5 times the standard error of that coefficient, it is significant. If it is smaller than that, you will need to look up the correct Student's t value in a statistics book and insert it in the last equation to know for sure if the coefficient is significant.

F Statistic

The F statistic is used with a table of F values to determine if the data really follows the curve, or if the apparent fit is due only to random fluctuations in the data. As with the Student's t test, to use the F statistic, you need a table of F values from a book of math tables or statistics. From the number of degrees of freedom and the confidence limit (say 95 percent), you get an F value from the table and compare it to the calculated F value. As long as the calculated F value is larger than the F value from the table, the fit is due to a real correlation, not chance.

The F table requires two degree-of-freedom values in addition to the confidence limit. The first, n_{f1}, is equal to the number of coefficients in the regression equation minus one. The second, p, is the standard number of degrees of freedom and is equal to the number of data sets minus the number of coefficients in the equation being fit to the data. The value p is the degree-of-freedom value returned by the

LINEST function and is the one used for the Student's t test.

Number of Degrees of Freedom

The number of degrees of freedom, p, is equal to the number of data points minus the number of regression coefficients. The equation of a line has two coefficients: the slope and the constant or y-offset term. If you have ten data points, the number of degrees of freedom would be 8 ($=10 - 2$). The number of degrees of freedom is needed with many statistical tables to calculate confidence limits.

Sum of the Squares of Regression and Residuals

The two sum-square statistics are a measure of the error still remaining in a curve fit. The regression sum-square is equal to the sum of the squared differences between the y-data values and the average of the y-data values:

$$\sum_{i=1}^{n}\left(y_i - \langle y\rangle\right)^2$$

Thus, it is a measure of the scatter of the data about the average.

The sum-square of the residuals is the sum of the squared differences between the original y-data values and the corresponding calculated y values on the curve:

$$\sum_{i=1}^{n}\left(y_i - y(x_i)\right)^2$$

Thus, it is a measure of the scatter of the y data about the regression line. When you divide these values by the number of degrees of freedom, you get the variance of the data about the average and the variance about the regression line. Take the square root of the variance, and you get the standard deviation of the data about the average and the standard deviation of the data about the regression line.

Linear Regression Calculations

Linear regression analysis is performed with Excel's LINEST, LOGEST, TREND, and GROWTH functions. The LINEST function performs straightforward linear regression on a set of data points. LOGEST is a variation of linear regression that fits the following equation to the data:

$$y = A(B^{x_1})(C^{x_2})\cdots$$

The LINEST and LOGEST functions return the coefficients of the formulas. The TREND and GROWTH functions return the curve that was fit to the data. All four functions return arrays of data rather than single values. You must insert them into blocks of cells, or use the INDEX function to extract a single element from the array. Inserting a function into a block of cells is described in Chapter 1. When you have entered an array function into a group of cells, you cannot change any single cell in that group. You must change the whole group, or you must delete the whole group and then make the changes.

The LINEST and LOGEST functions have the following syntax:

LINEST*(y-array,x-array,const,statistics)*
LOGEST*(y-array,x-array,const,statistics)*

where *y-array* is a reference to the *y*-data points, *x-array* is a reference to one or more sets of *x*-data points, *const* is a logical value controlling the constant term, and *statistics* is a logical value specifying whether to return the statistical values or not.

If the *x-array* term is omitted, the set of numbers {1, 2, 3,…} is used. If the *const* term is True or omitted, the constant term in the curve fit (*A*) is calculated normally. If *const* is False, the constant term is forced to be 0 for LINEST or 1 for LOGEST. If the *statistics* term is true, a table of eight or more statistical values is returned with the coefficients of the equation.

Thermal Conductivity   In Chapter 2, you calculated the temperature dependence of the thermal conductivity of silicon from an equation. Silicon is a well-known semiconductor, so an equation for the thermal conductivity is easy to find in the literature. Gallium arsenide (GaAs), on the other hand, is not as well known, so you must fit the experimental data to some curve.

Table 6.1 lists some experimental data for the temperature dependence of the thermal conductivity of heavily doped, p-type gallium arsenide. First try a simple linear fit of the data. The temperature and thermal conductivity values for the worksheet are listed in Table 6.1.

TABLE 6.1: Thermal Conductivity of Heavily Doped Gallium Arsenide (GaAs) versus Temperature

T(K)	K (W/cm-K)
250	0.445
300	0.362
350	0.302
400	0.256
450	0.223
500	0.197
550	0.176
600	0.158
650	0.144
700	0.132
750	0.121
800	0.112
850	0.103

1. Start with a new worksheet expanded to full size.

2. Set column D to 2 characters wide and column H to 18 characters wide.

3. Type **Thermal conductivity of GaAs; Linear Curve Fit** in cell A1.

4. In cells A3: B4, type and center the following entries:

   A3: **T**   B3: **K**

   A4: **(K)**   B4: **(W/cm-K)**

5. In cells A5:A17, type the temperature values in Table 6.1.

6. In cells B5:B17, type the thermal conductivity values in Table 6.1.

Set up a formula to calculate the y estimates of the linear fit.

7. In cell C3, type **K** and center it.

8. In cell C4, type **Est.** and center it.

9. Name cells F7 and G7 as **B** and **A**, respectively.

10. In cell C5, type **=B*A5+A** and copy it to cells C6:C17.

11. Format cells C5:C17 as 0.000.

Set up a location for the table of regression coefficients and statistics. The full regression table is five rows high and one column wide for each regression coefficient. For a simple linear curve fit, the table is two columns wide.

12. Make the following entries in columns E, F, G, and H:

E5: **Regression Table**	F6: **B**	G6: **A**	H7: **Coeffs**
E9: **r^2**	F12: **Reg.**	G12: **Residual**	H8: **Std Err of Coeffs**
E10: **F**			H9: **Std Err of Y est.**
E11: **Sum Sq**.			H10: **Degrees of Freedom**

13. Outline the following cells:

E5:F5	F6
E6:H6	G6
E7:H11	F12
E12:H12	G12
F7:G11	

Now calculate the coefficients.

14. Select cells F7:G11 and type this formula:

=LINEST(B5:B17,A5:A17,TRUE,TRUE)

15. Press Ctrl-Shift-Enter (Cmd-Enter on the Macintosh) to insert the formula in all the cells as an array.

16. Turn off the gridlines with the Display command on the Options menu.

The worksheet should now look like Figure 6.1. Compare the linear fit with the experimental data. You can see that you have fit the trend of the data, but the individual points do not fit very well. Checking r^2, you see that it has a value of 0.875.

FIGURE 6.1:

Thermal conductivity of GaAs:
a linear curve fit

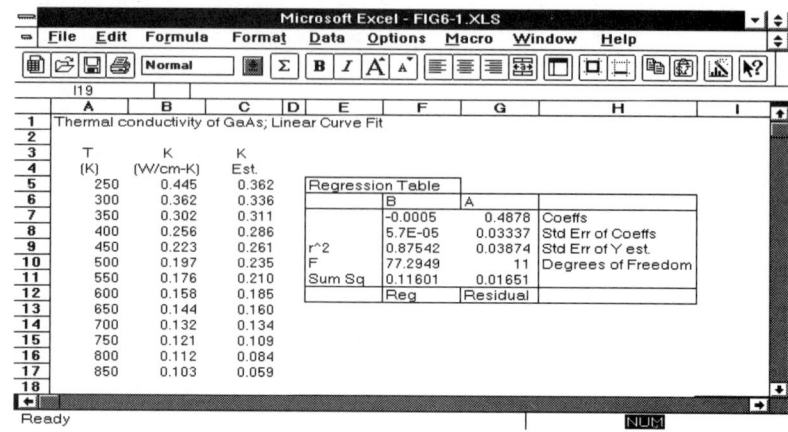

Figure 6.2 is a plot of the experimental data and the linear curve fit (you should be able to create this chart on your own). The plot confirms that the data does not fit very well.

Since GaAs and silicon are both semiconductors, try fitting the equation for silicon to the data for GaAs. The thermal conductivity of silicon fits the following simple equation:

$$K = \frac{K_0}{(T - T_0)}$$

FIGURE 6.2:

Results of fitting the thermal
conductivity of GaAs with a line

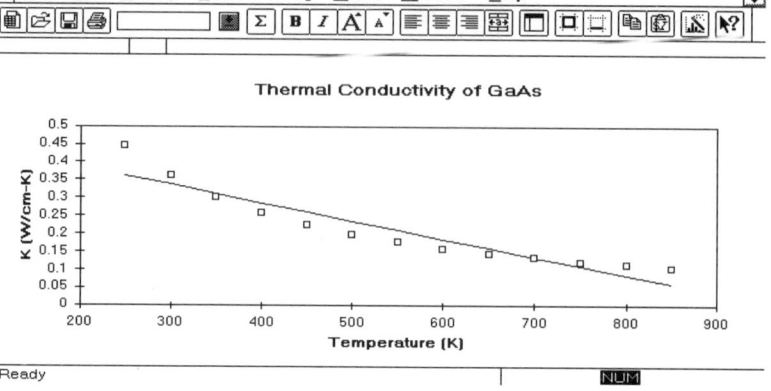

where K_0 and T_0 are constants to be determined. However, this equation cannot be used in a linear regression program. But solving it for the temperature:

$$T = \left(\frac{1}{K}\right)K_0 + T_0$$

yields an equation for T that is linear in the variable $1/K$, rather than a nonlinear equation for K in the variable T. You can easily rearrange the worksheet to calculate $1/K$ and use it as the x-range and T as the y-range.

1. Use the worksheet from the last example as a starting point. Save it with a different name first if you want to keep it.

2. Click on the heading of column C to select the whole column and choose the Insert command on the Edit menu to insert a new column.

3. Change the widths of columns A through D to 7 characters.

4. Type **Thermal conductivity of GaAs; Linear regression of a formula** in cell A1.

5. Type **1/K** in cell C3.

6. In cell C5, type **=1/B5** and copy it to cells C6:C17.

Put in the new estimator formula for K.

7. Type **K0** in cell G6 and **T0** in cell H6.

8. Select cells G6:H7, choose the Create Names command on the Formula menu, be sure Top Row is selected, and click on OK. This names cells G7 and H7 as K0 and T0. Use the Define Name command to delete the definitions for A and B.

9. In cell D5, type **=K0/(A5-T0)** and copy it to cells D6:D17.

Now calculate the regression.

10. Select cells G7:H11 and edit the formula to read

    =LINEST(A5:A17,C5:C17,TRUE,TRUE)

11. Press Ctrl-Shift-Enter (Cmd-Enter on the Macintosh).

The worksheet should now look like Figure 6.3. Note that the value of r^2 has improved tremendously; it is now 0.998, indicative of a good fit to the data points. Figure 6.4 shows that the regression line follows the data much better than the linear curve.

FIGURE 6.3:

Thermal conductivity of GaAs: fitting a nonlinear equation

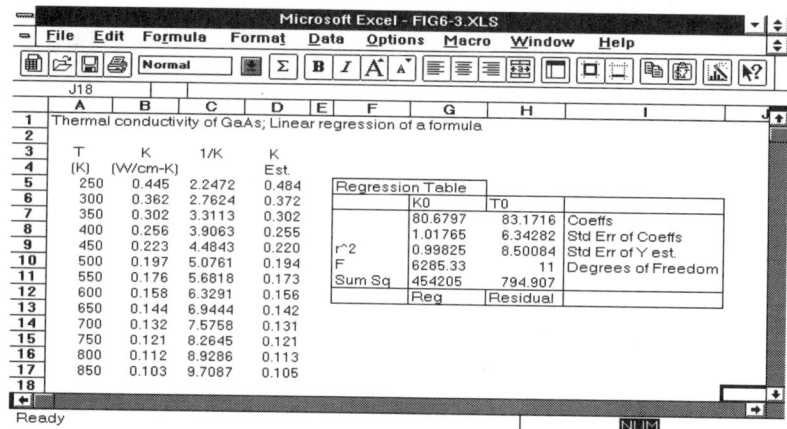

FIGURE 6.4:

Comparison of the experimental data and the nonlinear curve fit

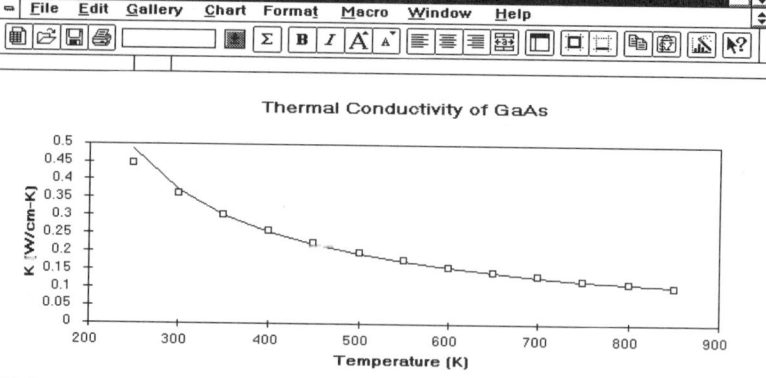

Note that you have fit a nonlinear curve with a linear curve fitting program. Something to keep in mind when you fit a nonlinear equation by transforming it is that what you calculate is the best fit to the transformed equation, not the original one. In most cases, this won't make much difference, but with exponential and logarithmic functions, you may find that the data at one end of the curve comes closer to the curve than the data at the other end.

Polynomial Regression Calculations

Although Excel's data regression functions are not explicitly set up to do polynomial regression, you can perform it easily. Polynomial regression fits data with a line of the form

$$y = A + Bx + Cx^2 + \cdots$$

You can fit this equation with a multiple linear regression program by letting

$$x_{1,i} = x_i$$
$$x_{2,i} = x_i^2$$
$$x_{3,i} = x_i^3$$
$$\vdots$$

Fit the thermal conductivity data again, but this time using a third-order (up to x^3) polynomial equation.

1. Use the worksheet from the previous example as a starting point. Save it with a different name if you want to keep it.

2. Type **Thermal conductivity of GaAs; Polynomial regression** in cell A1.

3. Select column C and choose the Delete command on the Edit menu.

4. Select columns B and C and choose the Insert command on the Edit menu.

5. Type **T^2** in cell B3, and **T^3** in cell C3.

6. In cell B5, type **=A5^2** and copy it to cells B6:B17.

7. In cell C5, type **=A5^3** and copy it to cells C6:C17.

8. Format cells B5:C17 as 0.00E+00.

Put in the new estimator equation for K. Note that a C with an underscore (C_) is used for the C coefficient because C is a reserved word. The cells will all show the #REF! error value because you have not defined the names for the coefficients yet.

9. In cell E5, type **=A+B*A5+C_*B5+D*C5** and copy it into cells E6:E17.

Now move the table out of the way to make room for the regression results, and then enlarge the regression table.

10. Select A3:E17 and drag it by its outline to A14:E28.

11. Select G5:J12 and drag it to B4:E11.

12. Select E5:E11 and drag it to G5:G11.

13. Widen columns F and G to 7 and 20 characters, respectively.

14. Type **D** in cell C5, **C** in cell D5, **B** in cell E5, and **A** in cell F5.

15. Outline cells E5, F5, E11:F11, F11, and G6:G10.

16. Select cells D6:D10 and choose the Border command on the Format menu. Click on the Right box to remove the check, and then click on OK.

17. Select cells C5:F6 and choose the Create Names command on the Formula menu. Click on OK. Note that cell D6 is defined as C_, not C.

Now you can perform the regression.

18. Select cells C6:F10 and type the formula

       =LINEST(D16:D28, A16:C28,TRUE,TRUE)

19. Press Ctrl-Shift-Enter (Cmd-Enter on the Macintosh).

The worksheet should now look like that in Figure 6.5. Again, r^2 indicates that the curve is a good fit to the data, as you can see by the graph in Figure 6.6.

You could try using a higher order curve to get a better fit of the data, but with polynomial regression, the curve will often oscillate if the order is too high. In this case, even though the curve hits all the data points, it is usually not a good predictor for points between the data points. You should always plot the results of regression to make sure that the curve you have calculated is what you expect.

FIGURE 6.5:

Thermal conductivity of GaAs: polynomial regression curve fit

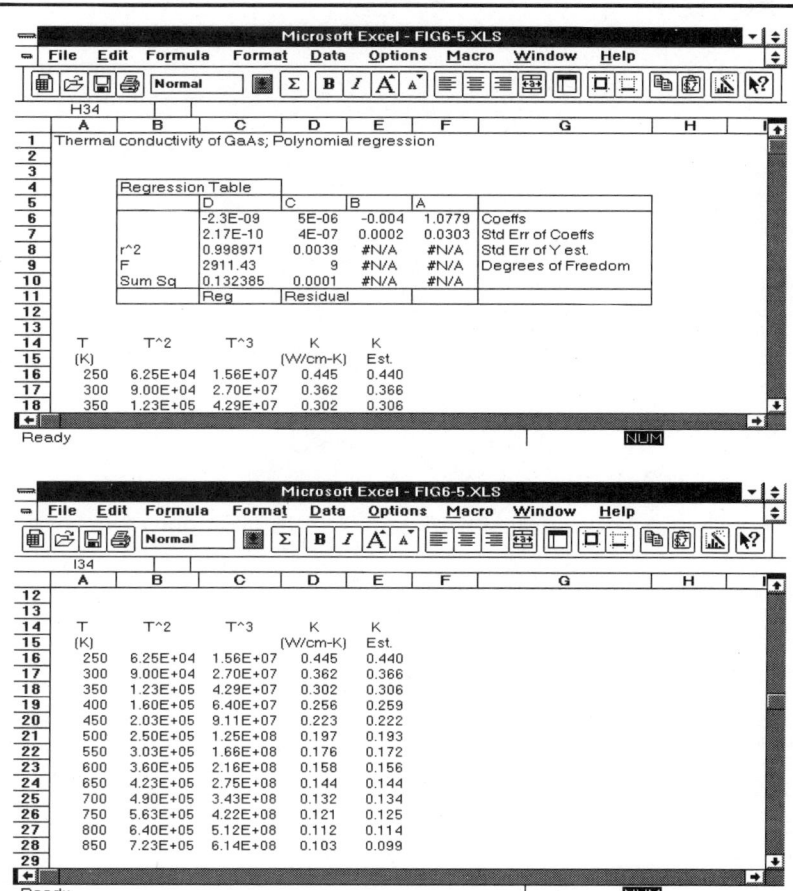

Checking the Statistics

Check the statistics for the curve fit you just performed. First check the coefficients of the regression (A, B, C, and D) with a 95 percent confidence interval:

$$\alpha = (1 - 0.95) = 0.05$$

$$\alpha/2 = 0.025$$

$$p = 9 \text{ (from the worksheet)}$$

FIGURE 6.6:

Plotted curve fit to the thermal conductivity of GaAs

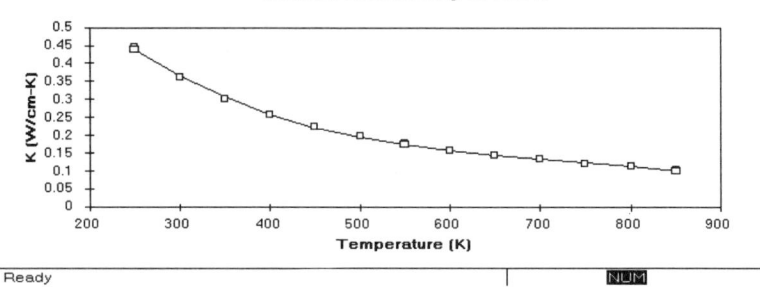

Thermal Conductivity of GaAs

$t_{a/2,p} = t_{0.025,9} = 2.262$ (from a table of Student's t values)

$S_A = 0.0303$ (from the worksheet)

$t_{0.025,9}S_A = 2.262 \times 0.0303 = 0.0685$

This is much smaller than A, so A is significant. The same analysis is applied to the other coefficients.

Next check to see if the data really correlates with the curve or if the apparent correlation is the result of a random process. The F-value from a table of F-values for $p = 9$ and $n_t = 3$ is 3.86, which is much smaller than the calculated F-value of 2911, so the correlation between the data and the curve is significant and not a random event.

Working with Complex Functions

If a function cannot be linearized into the form required for linear regression, you cannot use the built-in functions to determine the best fit of an equation to the data. For example, an exponential function, $y = Ae^{Bx}$, can be linearized by taking the natural logarithm of it, $Ln(y) = Ln(A) + Bx$, and identifying $Ln(A)$ and B as the regression coefficients rather than the A and B of the original equation. On the other hand, a double exponential function, $y = Ae^{Bx} + Ce^{Dx}$, cannot be linearized unless you know B and D.

As mentioned earlier in the chapter, although the calculated coefficients for the linearized equation are the best fit (least square) for that equation, they are usually not the best fit for the original function. For example, regression on the linearized version of the single exponential equation above will calculate the best values of Ln(A) and B for the logarithmic equation. They will not necessarily be the best values of A and B for the exponential equation, but they will be close.

Making Manual Adjustments

To fit equations that cannot be fit with regression analysis, you must sequentially adjust the coefficients to find the maximum of r^2, which corresponds to the minimum in the residual square error. You increase or decrease a coefficient until you find the maximum of r^2. You then adjust the next coefficient to find the maximum, and so on, until you have adjusted all the coefficients. Then start with the first one again to see if changing any of the other coefficients changed the location of the maximum for this coefficient. Continue adjusting the coefficients until you find the values that simultaneously give the maximum value of the correlation coefficient, at which point you are finished.

Occasionally, changing one coefficient changes the maximum of another, but changing the other moves the maximum of the first back again. Your adjustment algorithm just oscillates back and forth between these two coefficients and never converges. Try adjusting the values by a smaller amount and see if it will converge. If that does not work, you must use your scientific judgment and knowledge of the equation being fit to determine the best values. Bear in mind that there may be two maxima.

Electron Ionization Cross Sections   Table 6.2 lists the total cross sections for electron impact ionization of helium versus electron energies between 150 eV and 1 KeV. A cross section is an effective area for an atom that is used to determine the probability that a collision takes place between an electron and the atom. If you imagine atoms as a bunch of small targets that a beam of electrons is trying to hit, the cross section is the area of the target. The larger the cross section, the easier it is to hit the atom with an electron and the higher the probability that an ionization will occur.

TABLE 6.2: Experimental Total Ionization Cross Section versus Energy for Helium

Electron Energy (eV)	Cross Section (πa_{02})*
150	0.419
175	0.408
200	0.394
250	0.365
300	0.337
350	0.313
400	0.292
450	0.272
500	0.255
550	0.240
600	0.227
650	0.216
700	0.205
750	0.194
800	0.187
850	0.178
900	0.171
950	0.165
1000	0.160

$*\pi a_0^2 = \pi(5.29 \times 10^{-11})^2 \, m^2 = 8.79 \times 10^{-21} m^2$

From previous experience, I know that the cross section looks like a decreasing exponential in this energy range. Therefore, fit it with an equation of the following form:

$$S(E) = A\left(1 - e^{-B/E}\right)$$

where S is the cross section in units (πa_0^2), E is the electron energy in eV, and A and B are the coefficients to be determined.

1. Start with a new worksheet expanded to full size.

2. Type **Electron Ionization Cross Section in Helium** in cell A1.

3. Make the following entries in cells A3:E3 (enter the π by holding down Alt and typing 227 on the numeric keypad):

   A3: **E (eV)**   B3: S (π**a0^2**)

   C3: **S Est.**   D3: **(y-yx)^2**

   E3: **(y-<y>)^2**

4. In cells A4:B22, type the data in Table 6.2.

Create a table of the coefficients to be determined.

5. Make the following entries in cells F3:G4:

   F3: **A**   G3: **0.5**

   F4: **B**   G4: **500**

6. Name cells as follows:

   G3: **A**   H6: **AVEY**

   G4: **B**   H7: **FREE**

Put in the equation being fit to calculate the estimated values of y. The next two columns calculate the sum of squares about the curve and the sum of squares about the average, which are needed to calculate the standard error of the y estimate and r^2. Note that Excel has built-in functions for calculating the standard error of the y estimate and r^2, but the formulas used are only valid for linear curve fits. The formulas used here are for any equation.

7. In cell C4, type the formula

   =A*(1−EXP(−B/A4))

   and copy it to cells C5:C22.

8. In cell D4, type the formula

   =(B4−C4)^2

   and copy it to cells D5:D22.

9. In cell E4, type the formula

   =(B4−AVEY)^2

and copy it to cells E5:E22.

Create a table of the curve-fit statistics.

10. Type **Average of y <y>** in cell F6.

11. In cell H6, type the formula

    =AVERAGE(B4:B22)

12. Type **Deg. of Freedom** in cell F7.

13. In cell H7, type the formula

    =COUNT(B4:B22)−2

14. Type **Std. err of Y est** in cell F8.

15. In cell H8, type the formula

    =SQRT(SUM(D4:D22)/FREE)

16. Type **r^2** in cell F9.

17. In cell H9, type the formula

    =1−SUM(D4:D22)/SUM(E4:E22)

18. Format cells B4:C22 as 0.000.

19. Format cells D4:E22 as 0.00E+00.

The worksheet should now look like Figure 6.7. To use it, pick some reasonable starting values for A and B (say 0.5 and 500) and put them in the table (in cells G3 and G4). Add 0.1 to A and then subtract 0.1 from A and see which increases the value of r^2. Continue adding or subtracting 0.1 from A until you find the value that maximizes r^2. Now adjust B, adding and subtracting 100 from it until you maximize r^2 again. Go back to A and see if the maximum of r^2 has moved. Readjust A if it has changed. Continue adjusting A and B until you find the values that maximize r^2 for both of them.

FIGURE 6.7:

Electron ionization cross section in helium: manual curve fit

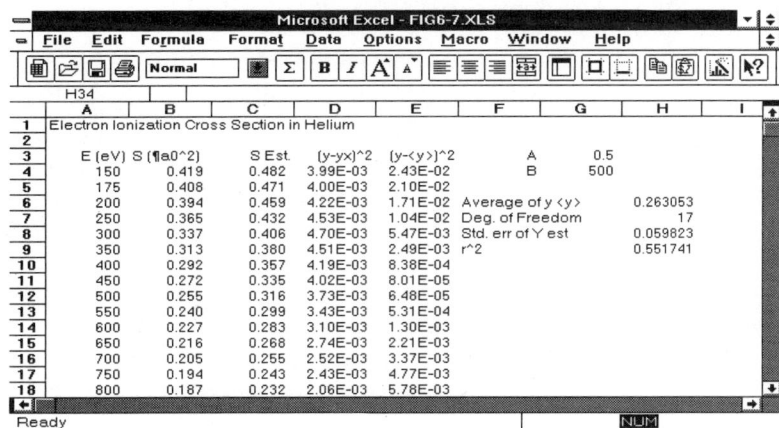

Next decrease the amount that you add to A and B by a power of ten. Add and subtract 0.01 from A and 10 from B until you maximize r^2 again. Decrease the amount that you change A and B by another power of 10 (0.001 and 1) and do it again. When you find the maximum value of r^2 this time, you will have three-place accuracy in the coefficients (A = 0.443, B = 434, r^2 = 0.999582). As you can see from Figure 6.8, the equation is a good fit to the data.

FIGURE 6.8:

Plotted curve fit to the electron ionization cross section in helium

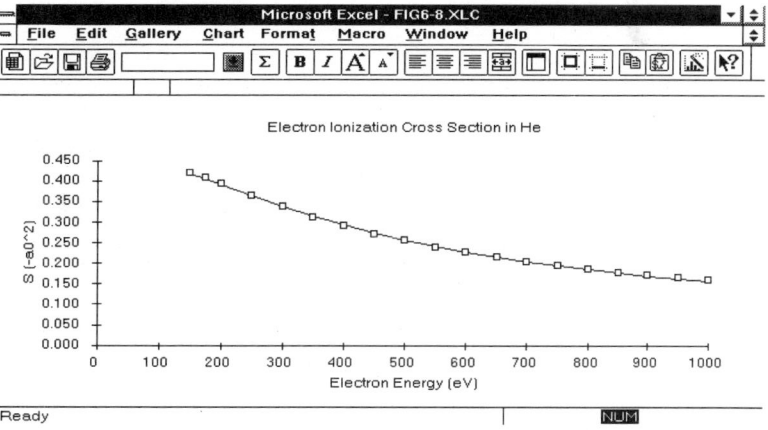

Making Automatic Adjustments

In the last example, you manually adjusted the coefficients of the equation being fit to the data until r^2 was maximized. Manual adjustments are sometimes necessary when the equation is extremely nonlinear or does strange things near the solution. Equations with local minima and maxima fall into this category. You need to make changes intuitively to find the true or best solution. However, in most cases, a mechanical approach can be applied to find the solution.

Excel 4.0 includes the Solver add-in program, which can be used to automatically maximize r^2 and find the best fit to a data set. The Solver is designed to intelligently adjust some values until a criterion is met. If you have an earlier version of Excel, you can write a macro to do the same task.

Using the Solver

The worksheet setup for using the Solver is identical to the setup for the previous example. The Solver add-in effectively takes your place, inserting the values of A and B and watching how r^2 changes. In addition, you can use array formulas to calculate the standard error of the y coefficient and r^2. You could have used these array formulas in the previous example, but they are not as easy to understand. First replace the formulas in the columns with array formulas.

1. Start with the worksheet from the previous example.

2. Select columns D and E and clear their contents with the Clear command on the Edit menu.

3. In cell H8, type the formula

    =SQRT(SUM((B4:B22−C4:C22)^2)/FREE)

4. Press Ctrl-Shift-Enter (Cmd-Enter on the Macintosh).

5. In cell H9, type the formula

    =1-SUM((B4:B22−C4:C22)^2)/SUM((B4:B22−AVEY)^2)

6. Press Ctrl-Shift-Enter (Cmd-Enter on the Macintosh).

7. Name cell H9 as **rsq**.

These two array formulas completely replace the two columns of calculations on the previous version of this worksheet. By replacing cell references in the formulas with array references and entering the formula with Ctrl-Shift pressed, you have compressed two columns of calculations into two cells.

In an array formula, Excel matches the first cell in each array reference and calculates a result. It then does this for the next set of values, and so on, until it reaches the end of the array references. For example, in cell H8, Excel subtracts the values in cells C4:C22 from the values in cells B4:B22. The result is a list of 19 numbers, which is passed to the SUM function. The SUM function adds the list, the result is divided by the value of FREE, and then the square root is taken. If you had pressed Enter instead of Ctrl-Shift-Enter, the formula would have been applied to only cells B8 and C8 (the array elements in the same row as the formula).

Now use the Solver to find the solution.

8. Set the values of A and B in cells G3 and G4 to 0.5 and 500.

9. Choose the Solver command on the Formula menu. The Solver Parameters dialog box appears.

10. In the dialog box, type **rsq** in the Set Cell box, click on the Max button for the Equal To option, and type **A, B** in the By Changing Cells box. Your dialog box should look like Figure 6.9.

FIGURE 6.9:

Using the Solver with the electron ionization cross section worksheet

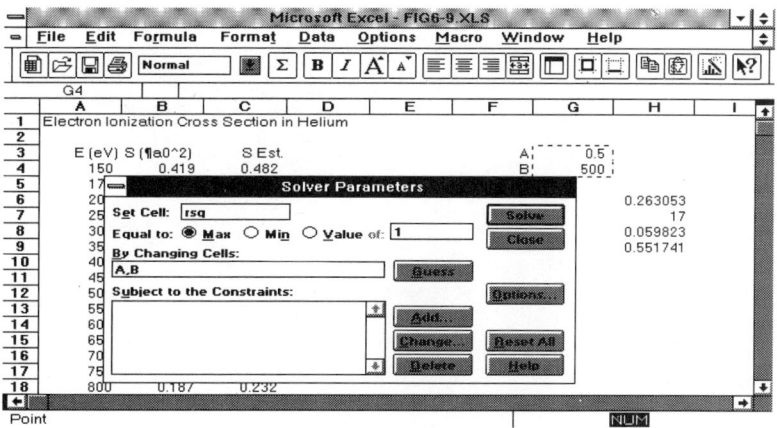

You have set up the Solver to try to maximize the value of rsq by adjusting the values of A and B. Now run the Solver to find the solution.

11. Click on the Solve button and wait for the Solver to find the solution.

While the Solver is working, it displays the values of rsq at the bottom of the screen so you can see what is going on. When the Solver finds a solution, it displays the dialog box shown in Figure 6.10. You can choose to keep the solution or restore the original values. You can also print one of the reports listed in the Reports box. If you are using the Scenario Manager, you can save the solution as a scenario with the Save Scenario button. See the *Microsoft Excel User's Guide* for more information.

12. Click on OK in the Solver dialog box.

You see the final result, as shown in Figure 6.11. The result is slightly different from that found with the manual method, because we stopped at three places of accuracy with the manual method. Some local maxima that can fool you (and the Solver) are also in the area of the solution. After the Solver is finished, you might want to explore the area near the solution by changing A and B to see if there is another solution with a larger value of r^2.

FIGURE 6.10:

The Solver dialog box after finding the solution

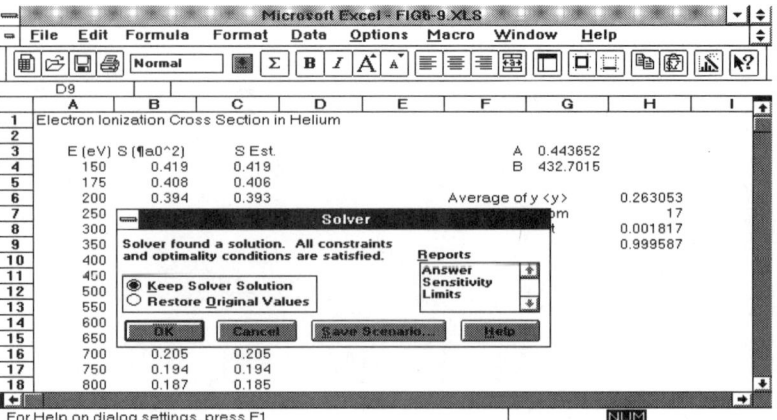

FIGURE 6.11:

The worksheet after the Solver adjusted the coefficients

Using a Macro for Automatic Adjustments

As mentioned previously, if you don't have the Solver, you need to write a macro to do the job. The macro shown in Figure 6.12 adjusts A and B up and down looking for an increase in the value of r^2.

The macro first initializes some values and copies the starting values of A and B from the worksheet. The next block of code increases the value of A by DA and checks to see if r^2 increased. If it did, the macro saves the value of r^2, sets the flag TST, and goes on to the next block of code, starting in B30. If it didn't, A is reduced by 2*DA and r^2 is checked again. If it increased, r^2 is saved, the TST flag is set, and the macro continues with the next block; otherwise, A is restored to its previous value. The next block of code starting in B30 does the same for B.

After both A and B have been adjusted, the macro, in B49, checks the flag TST. If TST is 1, then A or B has been changed, and the adjustments need to be done again, so the macro jumps back to B10. If neither has been changed, the macro reduces the value of DA and DB, checks to see if the stopping value has been reached, and then jumps back to B10. If the stopping value has been reached, the macro quits.

To use the macro, type it in as shown in Figure 6.12. Name the cells in column B with the names in column A. Name cell B1 as AutoAdjuster, and make it a command macro.

FIGURE 6.12:

The AutoAdjustment macro to solve the curve fit on the electron ionization worksheet

```
                       Column
                       B                              C
Row  A
1          AutoAdjuster
2          =SET.VALUE( RSQMAX,0)              Zero RSQMAX
3          =SET.VALUE(A,GET.CELL(5,!a))       Get the starting
                                              values of A and B
4          =SET.VALUE(B,GET.CELL(5,!B))       from the worksheet
5          =SET.VALUE(DA,A/5)                 Initialize DA, DB,
                                              DAA, and DBB
6          =SET.VALUE(DB,B/5)
7          =SET.VALUE(DAA,DA/10)
8          =SET.VALUE(DBB,DB/10)
9          =SET.VALUE(STOP,DA*0.0001)         Set the stopping
                                              value
10         =SET.VALUE(TST,0)                  Top of the loop,
                                              zero TST
11         =SET.VALUE(A,A+DA)                 Increase A
12         =FORMULA(A,!a)                     Copy A to the
                                              worksheet
13         =SET.VALUE(RSQ,GET.CELL(5,!rsq))   Get the new r^2 from
                                              the worksheet
14         =IF(RSQ>RSQMAX)                    See if r^2 increased
15         =SET.VALUE(RSQMAX,RSQ)             If it did, save it
                                              and set TST
16         =SET.VALUE(TST,1)
17         =ELSE()
18         =SET.VALUE(A,A-2*DA)               If it didn't, reduce
                                              A
19         =FORMULA(A,!a)                     Copy it to the
                                              worksheet
20         =SET.VALUE(RSQ,GET.CELL(5,!rsq))   Get the new r^2 from
                                              the worksheet
21         =IF(RSQ>RSQMAX)                    See if it increased
22         =SET.VALUE(RSQMAX,RSQ)             If it did, save it
                                              and set TST
23         =SET.VALUE(TST,1)
24         =ELSE()
25         =SET.VALUE(A,A+DA)                 If it didn't, reset
                                              A
26         =FORMULA(A,!a)                     Copy A to the
                                              worksheet
27         =SET.VALUE(RSQ,GET.CELL(5,!rsq))   Get r^2 from the
                                              worksheet
28         =END.IF()
29         =END.IF()
30         =SET.VALUE(B,B+DB)                 Increase B
31         =FORMULA(B,!B)                     Copy B to the
                                              worksheet
32         =SET.VALUE(RSQ,GET.CELL(5,!rsq))   Get the new r^2 from
                                              the worksheet
33         =IF(RSQ>RSQMAX)                    See if r^2 increased
34         =SET.VALUE(RSQMAX,RSQ)             If it did, save it
                                              and set TST
35         =SET.VALUE(TST,1)
36         =ELSE()
37         =SET.VALUE(B,B-2*DB)               If it didn't, reduce
                                              B
38         =FORMULA(B,!B)                     Copy B to the
                                              worksheet
39         =SET.VALUE(RSQ,GET.CELL(5,!rsq))   Get the new r^2 from
                                              the worksheet
40         =IF(RSQ>RSQMAX)                    See if it increased
41         =SET.VALUE(RSQMAX,RSQ)             If it did, save it
                                              and set TST
```

FIGURE 6.12:

The AutoAdjustment macro to solve the curve fit on the electron ionization worksheet (continued)

Row	A	Column B	C
42		=SET.VALUE(TST,1)	
43		=ELSE()	
44		=SET.VALUE(B,B+DB)	If it didn't, reset B
45		=FORMULA(B,!B)	Copy B to the worksheet
46		=SET.VALUE(RSQ,GET.CELL(5,!rsq))	Get r^2 from the worksheet
47		=END.IF()	
48		=END.IF()	
49		=IF(TST=1)	See if A or B was adjusted
50		=GOTO(top)	If one was, then do it again
51		=END.IF()	
52		=SET.VALUE(DA,DAA)	If it wasn't, then reduce DA and DB
53		=SET.VALUE(DB,DBB)	
54		=SET.VALUE(DAA,DA/10)	
55		=SET.VALUE(DBB,DB/10)	
56		=IF(DA>STOP)	See if you have passed the stop value
57		=GOTO(top)	If not, then continue
58		=END.IF()	
59		=RETURN()	Otherwise end
60			
61	A	0.44362	Local copies of A and B
62	B	432.76	
63	DA	0.000001	Amount to change A and B at a step
64	DB	0.001	
65	DAA	0.0000001	Amount to change DAA and DBB
66	DBB	0.0001	for a new step
67	RSQMAX	0.99958	Max value of r^2
68	TST	0	Flag for A,B changed
69	STOP	0.000001	Stopping value for DA
70	RSQ	0.999586513200457	Local copy of RSQ

Open the worksheet shown in Figure 6.11 and set the starting values for A and B (0.5 and 500). Execute the macro by choosing the Run command on the Macro menu, clicking on AutoAdjuster, and clicking on OK. You can watch the macro search for the solution.

Table Lookup and Interpolation

Often, you will have data that cannot be fit with any simple or moderately complex equation. In this case, the best method is to use a data table and a table lookup function. A table lookup function finds and interpolates values in the table for a particular value of x. Essentially, you are fitting a simple curve to a few of the data points in the neighborhood of the point that you are interested in rather than fitting a complicated curve to the whole data set.

Table lookup is accomplished with Excel's HLOOKUP, VLOOKUP, MATCH, and FASTMATCH functions. The HLOOKUP and VLOOKUP functions search for a value in one column of a table and return the value from another column on the same row. The MATCH and FASTMATCH functions search for a value in a table and return the position of the cell that contains that value.

The interpolation method can be coded as a macro or with cell formulas. The differences in the various interpolation methods are in the equation used to estimate the value of the function between two known data points. The simplest, and most common, is linear interpolation. Actually, the simplest method is to use the table lookup functions and accept the value returned rather than interpolating between values in the table. In many cases, this may be sufficient and will save you a lot of work. Also common are quadratic and cubic curves, which are fit to three or four data points. More complicated functions are splines and Chebyshev polynomials. Consult an applied numerical analysis text for more information about these functions.

Using Linear Interpolation

Linear interpolation consists of simply connecting the two data points on either side of the value being interpolated with a straight line. If the data points are not far apart, linear interpolation works very well. It is also simple to implement compared with higher order interpolations.

The interpolation formula in Lagrangian form for linear interpolation is

$$y = \frac{(x - x_2)}{(x_1 - x_2)} y_1 + \frac{(x - x_1)}{(x_2 - x_1)} y_2$$

where x_1, x_2, y_1, and y_2 are the data points from the table and x, the value being interpolated, is between x_1 and x_2.

Steam Tables   Steam tables are tables of temperature; pressure; density; enthalpy; and entropy of saturated steam and water, superheated steam, and compressed water. Saturated steam and water is a mixture of steam and water at a temperature and pressure where they both coexist in equilibrium. The saturation line on a graph of temperature and pressure divides the graph into all water and all steam regions, as shown in Figure 6.13. Superheated steam data points are those pressure and temperature points above the saturation line in the direction of increasing temperature. Compressed water data points are those pressure and temperature points above the saturation line in the direction of increasing pressure.

Steam tables are used by engineers who design and operate energy transportation and conversion equipment that employs steam as the working fluid. This equipment includes steam engines, steam turbines, steam and hot water heating systems, and nuclear reactors. Steam tables are also used by scientists who need to know the properties of hot, pressurized water and steam.

For example, in a pressurized water reactor (PWR), if the pressure decreases to the saturation line, the water flashes into steam. The temperature and pressure in the reactor then move along the saturation line until either the pressure is increased to

FIGURE 6.13:

Pressure/temperature saturation line of a steam-water mixture (above the line is all water, below is all steam; only on the saturation line can steam and water coexist)

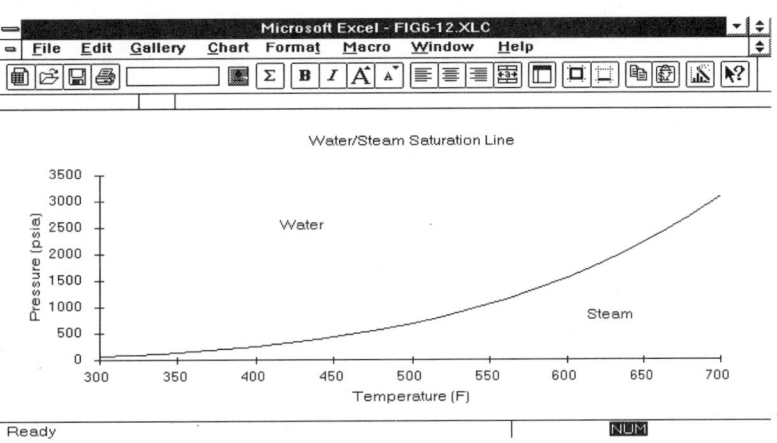

the point that the water stops boiling into steam, or all the water is boiled away (not a good thing). Luckily, this is a self-quenching process. As the pressure decreases, the enthalpy (the heat-carrying capacity) also decreases which, in a reactor (or any boiler for that matter), causes the water temperature to increase, because the heat flow from the heat-generation region has been decreased. Increasing the temperature increases the pressure and quenches the process.

In any event, it is not a good idea to let your cooling water boil away inside a reactor, so reactor engineers and operators need to know where this saturation line is so that they can design and operate the reactor with an adequate safety margin. A representative PWR operates at around 600 °F and 2250 psi, well away from the saturation line.

In the next example, you will build a worksheet that calculates the saturated pressure for a given temperature. The worksheet uses a table lookup function and linear interpolation to calculate the pressure. Table 6.3 contains the data for the steam table.

TABLE 6.3: Pressure and Temperature Saturation Line for a Water and Steam Mixture

Temperature (F)	Pressure (psia)*
300	67
320	90
340	118
360	153
380	196
400	247
420	309
440	382
460	467
480	566
500	681
520	812
540	963

TABLE 6.3:   Pressure and Temperature Saturation Line for a Water and Steam Mixture (continued)

Temperature (F)	Pressure (psia)*
560	1133
580	1326
600	1543
620	1787
640	2060
660	2366
680	2709
700	3094

*psia = pounds per square inch absolute

1. Start with a new worksheet expanded to full size.

2. Type **Steam table: Saturated steam/water: Linear Interpolation** in cell A1.

3. Type the following entries in cells A3:B4:

   A3: **Temp.**   B3: Press.
   A4: **(F)**   B4: **(psia)**

Now type in the temperature and pressure data.

4. In cells A5:A25, type **300** to **700** in steps of 20.

5. In cells B5:B25, type the pressure data in Table 6.3.

6. Name cells A5:A25 as **Temperature** and cells B5:B25 as **Pressure**.

Next create a table to do the linear interpolation.

7. Type **Linear Interpolation** in cell E3.

8. Type **Temperature** in cell D4, and **Output Pressure** in cell F4.

9. Make the following entries in cells D5:H5:

D5: **Input**   E5: **Index**

F5: **Calc.**   G5: **'True**

H5: **Error**

Use some random temperature values for input to the linear interpolation. Put the true values of the pressure in column G so that you can compare them with the interpolated values.

10. Make the following entries in cells D6:D11:

D6: **510**   D9: **622**

D7: **520**   D10: **538**

D8: **302**   D11: **456**

The table lookup and interpolation equations are too large to fit in one cell, so put the table lookup function in one cell and the interpolation function in the next. For each temperature value, the MATCH function returns the index of the row that contains the largest temperature that is less than or equal to the lookup value. Note that the temperature values must be sorted for MATCH to work. Use this index with the INDEX function to access the pressure and temperature values needed for the linear interpolation function in column F.

11. In cell E6, type the formula

=MATCH(D6,Temperature)

and copy it into cells E7:E11.

12. In cells F6, type the formula

=(D6−INDEX(Temperature,E6+1))*INDEX(Pressure,E6)/
(INDEX(Temperature,E6)−INDEX(Temperature,E6+1))+
(D6−INDEX(Temperature,E6))*INDEX(Pressure,E6+1)/
(INDEX(Temperature,E6+1)−INDEX(Temperature,E6))

and copy it into cells F7:F11.

13. In cells G6:G11, make the following entries:

G6: **744.5**	G9: **1812.8**
G7: **812**	G10: **946.9**
G8: **69**	G11: **448.7**

Calculate the error in the interpolated values.

14. In cells H6:H11, type the formula

=(G6−F6)/G6

15. Format cells H6:H11 as 0.000%.

Your worksheet should now look like Figure 6.14. Note that for the six random test values, the maximum error is only about ½ of a percent.

For a smooth function like this, linear interpolation works quite well. But be aware that the derivative of linearly interpolated functions is not continuous; it has sharp changes at each data point in the table. In most cases, this is not a problem. However, I have encountered a case where the discontinuity caused obvious structure in the output of a simulation code that used a table lookup function to create the input. Until I tracked it down, we thought that we had found some new physical process. If you need something with a continuous derivative, a spline curve would be more appropriate (and harder to implement, of course).

FIGURE 6.14:

Steam table, steam/water saturation line: using the table lookup function and linear interpolation

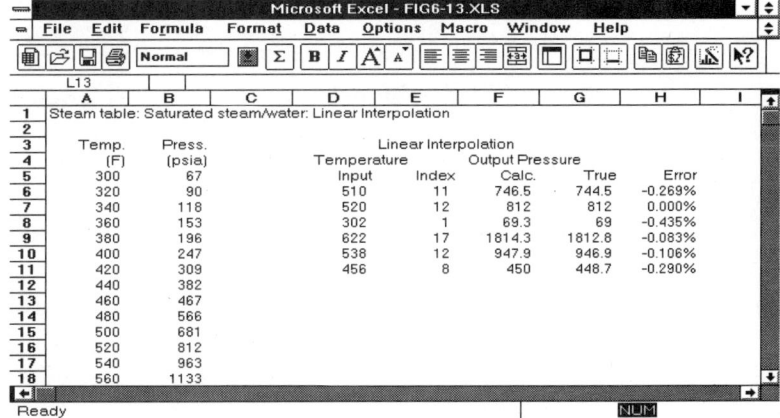

Cubic Interpolation

After linear interpolation comes quadratic, then cubic interpolation. Cubic interpolation is more accurate than quadratic interpolation, not only because it uses a higher order curve, but more important, because it is more symmetric about the range being interpolated. Cubic interpolation fits a third-order curve to four data points in a row, with the interpolation being between the center two points. The interpolation equation, in Lagrangian form, is

$$y = \frac{(x-x_2)(x-x_3)(x-x_4)}{(x_1-x_2)(x_1-x_3)(x_1-x_4)}y_1 + \frac{(x-x_1)(x-x_3)(x-x_4)}{(x_2-x_1)(x_2-x_3)(x_2-x_4)}y_2$$
$$+ \frac{(x-x_1)(x-x_2)(x-x_4)}{(x_3-x_1)(x_3-x_2)(x_3-x_4)}y_3 + \frac{(x-x_1)(x-x_2)(x-x_3)}{(x_4-x_1)(x_4-x_2)(x_4-x_3)}y_4$$

where x_1, x_2, x_3, x_4, y_1, y_2, y_3, and y_4 are consecutive x and y values from the table. The value being interpolated, x, should lie between x_2 and x_3 to get the best value for y.

So that you can compare cubic interpolation to linear interpolation, put a cubic interpolation table on the same worksheet as the linear interpolation. Since the cubic interpolation formula is somewhat more complicated than the linear formula, create a macro to calculate it instead of placing it on the worksheet. Also, the cubic interpolation formula can be implemented with a short FOR/NEXT loop in a macro. First make an interpolation table with the same test values as the linear interpolation table.

1. Start with a copy of the worksheet from the previous example.

2. Type **Steam table: Saturated steam/water: Linear & Cubic Interpolation** in cell A1.

3. Type **Cubic Interpolation** in cell E12.

4. Select cells D6:D11 and copy them to cells D13:D18.

5. Select cells G6:H11 and copy them to cells G13:H18.

6. In cell F13, type the formula

='FIG6-15.XLM'!Cubic_Interpolation(Temperature,Pressure,D13)

and copy it to cells F14:F18.

7. Open a new macro sheet and save it as **FIG6-15.XLM**.

8. Type the macro shown in Figure 6.15.

9. Name the cells in column B with the names in column A.

10. Use the Define Name command on the Formula menu to name cell B1 as **Cubic_Interpolation**, click on the Function Macro button, and then click on OK.

The worksheet should now look like Figure 6.16, with the function macro in Figure 6.15. The formula in step 6 above is an external reference to the function macro named Cubic_Interpolation on the FIG6-15.XLM macro sheet. The macro has three arguments: the Temperature array, the Pressure array, and the temperature point to interpolate.

Note that the error has decreased by an order of magnitude over the linear interpolation value. This decrease may not seem so important, since the linear interpolation did well on this curve. On more nonlinear curves, the increase in accuracy may

FIGURE 6.15:

Cubic interpolation macro function

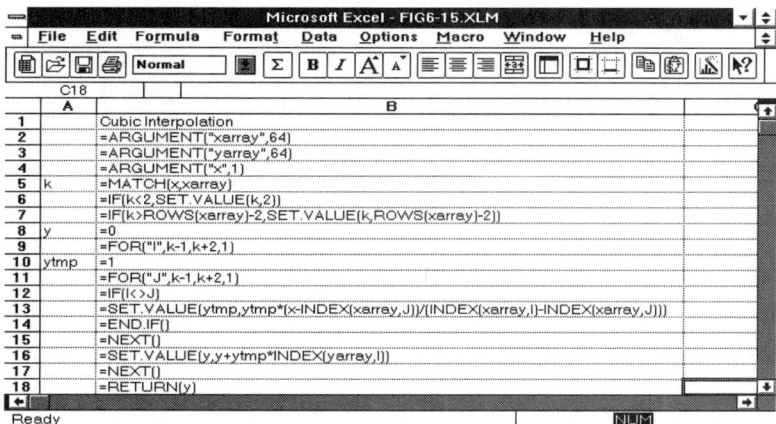

FIGURE 6.16:

Linear and cubic interpolation of the steam-water saturation line

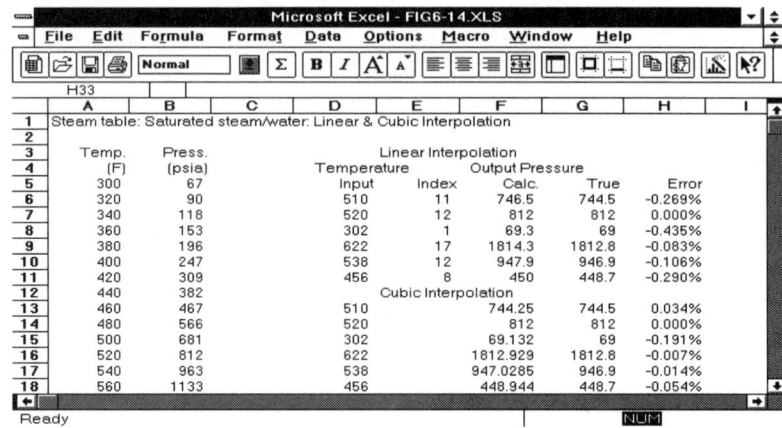

be needed. Also, the discontinuity in the derivative at the data points will be much less with this type of interpolation.

Summary

In this chapter, you saw how to fit curves to data points. The simplest methods to use are Excel's linear regression functions LINEST and LOGEST, which perform multiple linear regression. By suitably transforming your equations, you can fit many nonlinear equations with these functions. In addition, the LINEST function can be used to perform polynomial regression to fit a data set with a polynomial. For more complicated equations, you used a steepest descents algorithm to find the coefficients for a nonlinear equation. You then automated that algorithm with the Solver and a macro program.

When it is difficult or unreasonable to fit experimental data with a known function, you can use table lookup and interpolation functions. You developed a simple interpolation function in the worksheet, and a more complicated one as a macro function.

For More Information

Statistical Methods and t Tests

C. Lipson and N. J. Sheth, *Statistical Design and Analysis of Engineering Experiments* (New York: McGraw-Hill, 1973).

R. M. Bethea, B. S. Duran, and T. L. Boullion, *Statistical Methods for Scientists and Engineers* (New York: Marcel Dekker, 1975).

Thermal Conductivity in Gallium Arsenide

Maycock, "Thermal Conductivity of Silicon, Germanium, III-V Compounds and III-V Alloys," *Solid State Electronics 10* (1967): 161-168.

Electron Ionization Cross Sections

D. Rapp and P. Englander-Golden, "Total Cross Sections for Ionization and Attachment in Gases by Electron Impact: I. Positive Ionization," *J. Chem. Physics 43*, 5 (Sept. 1, 1965): 1464-1479.

Curve-Fitting Functions and Methods

C. Gerald, *Applied Numerical Analysis* (Reading, Mass.: Addison-Wesley, 1978).

W. H. Press, et al., *Numerical Recipes: The Art of Scientific Computing* (Cambridge, Eng.: Cambridge University Press, 1986).

Steam Tables

C. A. Meyer, *Thermodynamic and Transport Properties of Steam* (New York: American Society of Mechanical Engineers, 1967).

Problems

1. The temperature dependence of the band gap in silicon is shown in the following table.

Temperature (K)	Band Gap (eV)	Temperature (K)	Band Gap (eV)
0	1.16	400	1.09
50	1.16	450	1.07
100	1.15	500	1.05
150	1.15	550	1.03
200	1.14	600	1.01
250	1.13	650	0.99
300	1.12	700	0.97
350	1.10	750	0.95
		800	0.92

Using linear regression, find the line that best fits this data and plot the data and the regression results.

2. Fit the data in problem 1 using a second-order polynomial regression and plot the results.

3. The temperature dependence of the band gap of silicon follows the equation

$$E_g = E_{g0} - \frac{AT^2}{(T+B)}$$

Where E_g is the energy gap; T is the temperature in Kelvin; and E_{g0}, A, and B are constants to be determined. This equation can be rewritten as a polynomial

$$\left[\frac{1}{E_{g0} - E_g}\right] = \frac{A}{B}\left[\frac{T}{E_{g0} - E_g}\right]^2 - \frac{1}{B}\left[\frac{T}{E_{g0} - E_g}\right]$$

E_{g0} is equal to the value of E_g at $T = 0$. Solve for the coefficients of this equation using polynomial regression. The solution will yield A/B and $1/B$, from which you can easily determine A and B. Plot the results.

4. Use the manual and automatic methods of coefficient adjusting to fit the data in problem 1 to the first equation in problem 3. Plot the results.

5. Do the manual adjustments example in the book (Figure 6.7). For integer values of B from 430 to 438, maximize the value of r^2 by adjusting the value of A. Plot the values of r^2 versus the values of B. The three local maxima in that plot confuse the automatic search routine in Figure 6.10, which finds one, but not necessarily the largest of them.

6. Use the data in problem 1 as a lookup table. Write a linear lookup function to interpolate the values of E_g for given values of T.

7. Complete problem 6 using cubic interpolation.

8. Fit a line to the steam table values of pressure versus temperature in Table 6.3. Calculate and plot the residual error (the difference between the regression curve and the data value) at each point.

9. Fit the steam table values of pressure versus temperature in Table 6.3 using polynomial regression. Try different orders of the regression and plot the results. Calculate and plot the residual error.

10. Use linear interpolation to calculate the value of the electron ionization cross section given in Table 6.2 for electrons with an energy of 524 eV.

11. Complete problem 10 using cubic interpolation.

CHAPTER
SEVEN

Summing Series

7

Many important functions of science and engineering are available only as series formulas. Differential equations without closed-form analytic solutions often have solutions in the form of a series. Bessel functions, Legendre polynomials, and Laguerre polynomials are examples of series solutions of differential equations.

With Excel, you can calculate the value of a series formula in two ways. One way is to calculate the series term by term in the cells of the worksheet and then add them up. The other, more powerful, method is to write a macro function to calculate the series for any number of terms.

Summing a Series in the Worksheet

The simplest method you can use to sum a series is to calculate the terms in consecutive cells, and then add them up. This method can use a lot of worksheet real estate if many terms are required; however, being able to see the values of all the terms gives you a better feel for when the series has converged, and you may understand the result better.

Excel's built-in series summing function, SERIESSUM, is limited to a series of the following form:

$$ssum = a_1 x^n + a_2 x^{(n+m)} + a_3 x^{(n+2m)} + \cdots$$

To use this function, you must supply an array that contains all the coefficients. If you need to create an array with all the coefficients, you might as well include the powers of x there as well, and not use the SERIESSUM function at all.

For most series, you can find a recursion relation for calculating a term using the previous term. Using a recursion relation will usually reduce the number of calculations you need to perform significantly, especially when a series involves factorials.

Bessel Functions   A Bessel function ($J_n(x)$) is the solution to Bessel's differential equation:

$$x^2 \frac{d^2 y}{dx^2} + x \frac{dy}{dx} + \left(x^2 - n^2\right)y = 0$$

with $y = J''(x)$. Bessel's equation is encountered in many physical problems. For example, the solution of the wave equation in cylindrical coordinates results in Bessel's equation. Bessel functions are also solutions of a class of definite integrals:

$$J_n(x) = \frac{1}{\pi} \int_0^\pi \cos(nv - x\sin(v))dv$$

Although Bessel functions are defined for any value of n, most values of n are integers. A series solution exists for Bessel functions with integer values of n:

$$J_n(x) = \sum_{s=0}^\infty \frac{(-1)^s}{s!(n+s)!} \left(\frac{x}{2}\right)^{n+2s} = \sum_{s=0}^\infty G_s(n, x)$$

For noninteger values of n, a gamma function ($\Gamma(n + s + 1)$) must be substituted for the factorial $(n + s)!$.

You can find the recursion relation for the terms ($Gs(n,x)$) of the series by inspection:

$$G_s(n, x) = G_{s-1}(n, x) \frac{(-1)}{s(n+s)} \left(\frac{x}{2}\right)^2$$

$$G_0 = \frac{x^n}{2^n n!}$$

Using this recursion relation, you only need to calculate the factorial for the first term (G_0). You can then calculate the rest of the terms in the series without calculating another factorial. Each term is created from the previous term by multiplying by the recursion factor above.

In the next example, you will calculate values of the Bessel function with integral values of n. You need to sum only the first ten terms to get less than one percent error for values of x up to about seven or eight. Additionally, Excel has an add-in function, BESSELJ, which also calculates the value of Bessel functions. Use it to check the accuracy of your calculations.

1. Start with a new worksheet expanded to full size.

2. Set the width of column A to 14.

3. Type **Bessel Function; Worksheet method** in cell A1.

Now put in *n*, *n!*, and *x*.

4. In cells A4, B2, and B3, type the labels **x**, **n**, and **n!**, respectively, and right-justify them.

5. Name cell C2 as **N**, C3 as **NF**, and B4 as **X**.

6. Type **=FACT(N)** in cell C3.

Insert the BESSELJ add-in function. Enter a summation formula to add up all the terms.

7. In cell A5, type **BESSELJ(X,N)** and right-justify it.

8. In cell B5, type the formula

   =BESSELJ(XN)

9. In cell A6, type **Jn(x)** and right-justify it.

10. Type **=SUM(B8:B18)** in cell B6.

Calculate the first ten terms of the series for the values of the summation variable *s*. In cell B8, insert the value of the zero-order term. In cells B9:B18, use the recursion relation to calculate the different terms.

11. In cell A7, type **s** and right-justify it.

12. In cell B7, type **Terms** and right-justify it.

13. In cell B8, type the formula

   =B4^N/(2^N*NF)

14. In cell B9, type the formula

   =B8*(−1)*X^2/(4*$A9*(N+$A9))

   and copy it to cells B10:B18.

15. In cell A8, type **0**, and in cell A9, type **1**.

16. Select cells A8:A9, grab the fill handle, and drag it down to cell A18 to create the ten *s* values.

17. Format cells B8:B18 as 0.00E+00.

To use the worksheet, put the value of *x* (0.5, for example), up to a maximum of 8, in cell B4, and the value for *n* (1, for example) in cell C3. When the worksheet is updated, the value of the Bessel function will be in cells B5 and B6. Note that the size of the terms decreases rapidly, indicating rapid convergence of the series. Your worksheet should now look like Figure 7.1.

FIGURE 7.1:

Bessel function using the worksheet method

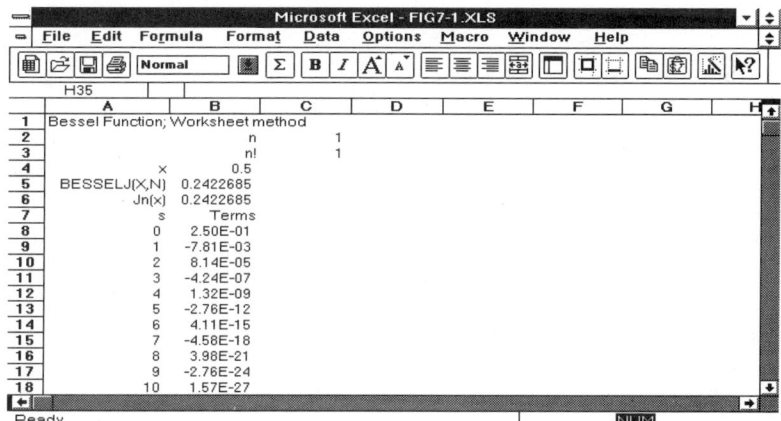

Using this format, you can calculate the Bessel function for a whole set of *x* values. Note that the appropriate parts of the cell references have been made absolute, so that the formulas in cells B8:B18 can be copied into the cells to their right and still reference the correct cells.

18. Copy cells B4:B18 into C4:AB18.

19. In cell B4, type **0**, and in cell C4, type **0.3**.

20. Select cells B4:C4, grab the fill handle, and drag it to cell AB4.

21. Name cells B4:AB4 as **x**.

Your worksheet should now look like Figure 7.2. Here you have calculated the Bessel function for $n = 1$ and for a series of x values up to about eight. Figure 7.3 is a plot of those values. If you want to calculate the Bessel function for larger values of x or increase the accuracy for the current values of x, you must increase the number of terms in the series.

FIGURE 7.2:

Bessel function for multiple values of x

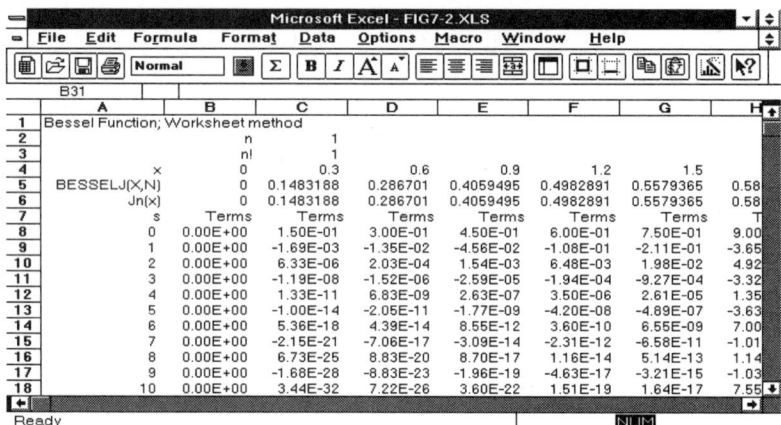

FIGURE 7.3:

Bessel function $J_1(x)$

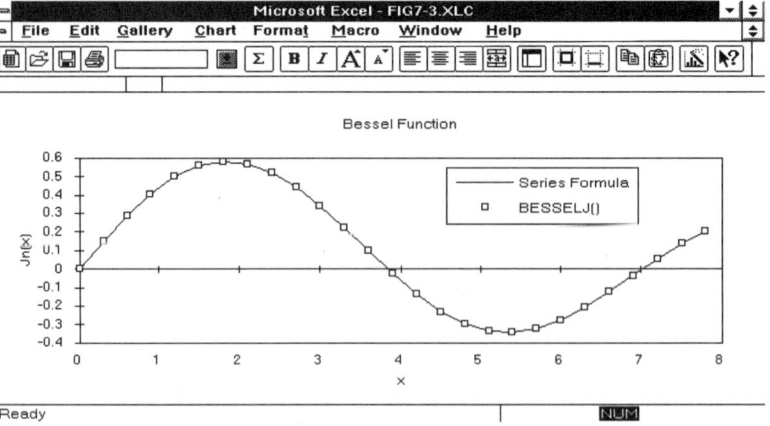

Using a Macro to Sum Series

You can also write an Excel macro program to calculate the value of a series summation. The algorithm is much the same as you would use to calculate the series summation with a high-level language such as BASIC or Fortran.

Legendre Polynomials   Legendre polynomials ($Pn(x)$) are often encountered in central-force problems (such as electromagnetics) defined in spherical coordinates. For example, an electric dipole consists of two charges of magnitude $+q$ and $-q$, located at $+a$ and $-a$ in a spherical coordinate system. The potential (ϕ) due to this dipole at large distances ($r \gg a$) from the dipole is described with a Legendre polynomial:

$$\Phi = \frac{2aq}{4\pi\varepsilon} \frac{P_1(\cos(\theta))}{r^2}$$

where ε is the free space dielectric constant, and r and θ are the coordinates in a spherical polar coordinate system.

Legendre polynomials are solutions of the differential equation:

$$\left(1-x^2\right)\frac{d^2y}{dx^2} - 2x\frac{d^2y}{dx^2} + n(n+1)y = 0$$

with $y = P_n(x)$. The series representation of the Legendre polynomials is:

$$P_n(x) = \sum_{s=0}^{n/2} \frac{(-1)^s (2n-2s)!}{2^n s!(n-s)!(n-2)!} x^{n-2s}$$

which has a finite number of terms in the summation.

In the following example, you will create a macro function to calculate the series formula above. You will also calculate the factorials for each term explicitly, rather than using a term recursion relation.

1. Start with a new macro sheet expanded to full size.

2. Change the width of column A to 4 and column B to 14.

3. Type **Legendre Polynomial** in cell B1.

4. Type **Legendre** in cell A2.

5. Type **=ARGUMENT("N",1)** in cell B2.

6. Type **=ARGUMENT("X",1)** in cell B3.

7. Type **sersum** in cell A4.

8. Type **=0** in cell B4.

9. Type **=FOR("s",0,N/2)** in cell B5.

10. In cell B6, type the formula

    =SET.VALUE(sersum,sersum+X^(N−2∗s)∗(−1)^s∗
    FACT(2∗N−2∗s)/(2^N∗FACT(s)∗FACT(N−s)∗FACT(N−2∗s)))

11. Type **=NEXT()** in cell B7.

12. Type **=RETURN(sersum)** in cell B8.

13. Use the Define Name command on the Formula menu to name cell B4 as **sersum**.

14. Use the Define Name command on the Formula menu to name cell B2 as **Legendre** and set its type as Function.

15. Save the macro sheet as **FIG7-4.XLM**.

This completes the macro sheet, which should look like Figure 7.4. The formulas in cells B2 and B3 define the arguments the function expects to receive from a calling

FIGURE 7.4:

Legendre polynomial macro function

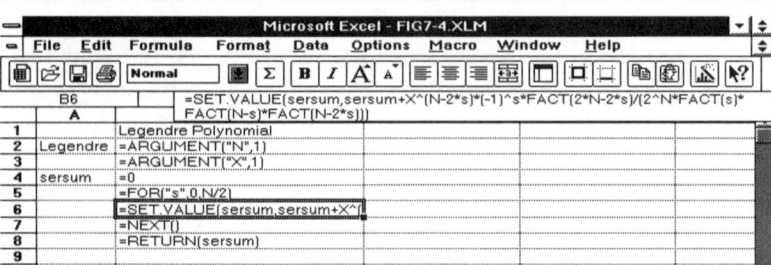

cell. Cell B4 is named sersum, and is a summing variable to hold the current sum while you calculate the next term. Cell B5 is the start of a loop. One term is calculated and added to the series each time the loop executes. The formula in cell B6 calculates a term of the polynomial and adds it to the summing variable. Cell B7 is the bottom of the loop, and cell B8 ends the macro and returns the value of sersum to the calling cell.

In this case, the series has a finite number of terms, with a fixed upper limit of $n/2$. Thus, you know how many terms to calculate to get the correct value. For a series with an infinite number of terms, you must decide when to stop adding terms. You can pick some fixed number of terms that produces accurate results over the range of arguments you are interested in, such as you did with the Bessel function. Alternatively, you can put some logic in the macro program to watch the size of each term as it is added and to stop calculating when it gets insignificant. Add an IF function to check the value of each term as it is added to the series, and a BREAK function to terminate the loop.

Now create a worksheet to call the macro in the macro sheet for several values of n and x. As a comparison, here are the analytical solutions for the first six Legendre polynomials:

$$P0(x) = 1$$
$$P1(x) = x$$
$$P2(x) = (1/2)(3x2 - 1)$$
$$P3(x) = (1/2)(5x3 - 3x)$$
$$P4(x) = (1/8)(35x4 - 30x2 + 3)$$
$$P5(x) = (1/8)(63x5 - 70x3 + 15x)$$

Calculate these solutions as well and compare them with the results from the macro.

First put in some values of x and n to calculate.

16. Choose the New command on the File menu and create a new worksheet.

17. Type **Legendre Polynomials: Macro Function** in cell A1.

18. Type **n** in cell A3.

19. In cells B3:G3, type the integers **0** through **5**.

20. Name cells B3:G3 as **N**.

21. Type **x** in cell A4.

22. In cell B4, type **0.3** and copy it to cells C4:G4.

23. Name cells B4:G4 as **X**.

Next put in the calls to the macro function. Each call must include the worksheet name as well as the name of the macro function and its arguments. The simplest way to ensure that you do it right is to use the Paste Function command on the Formula menu and select the function in the User Defined section of the dialog box. After the macro function solution, put in the analytic solutions shown earlier.

24. Type **Pn(x)** in cell A5.

25. In cell B5, type (or insert with the Paste Function command)

> **='FIG7-4.XLM'!Legendre(n,x)**

and copy it to cells C5:G5.

26. Type **Analytic** in cell A6.

27. Make the following entries in cells B6:G6:

B6: **1**	C6: **=X**
D6: **=0.5*(3*x^2−1)**	E6: **=0.5*(5*x^3−3*x)**
F6: **=0.125*(35*x^4−30*x^2+3)**	G6 **=0.125*(63*x^5−70*x^3+15*x)**

As you can see in Figure 7.5, the analytic values and macro function values match. Create a table of values as shown at the bottom of the figure and plot the results. First put in a range of x values.

28. Type **0** in cell A8 and **0.3** in cell A9.

29. Select cells A8:A9, grab the fill handle, and drag it to cell A30.

Change the first x value to a small number other than 0, because the function is not defined at $x = 0$. Place the macro function in the body of the table.

30. Change cell A8 to **0.001**.

31. Type **='FIG7-4.XLM'!Legendre(n,$A8)** in cell B8.

FIGURE 7.5:
Legendre polynomials calculated with a macro program

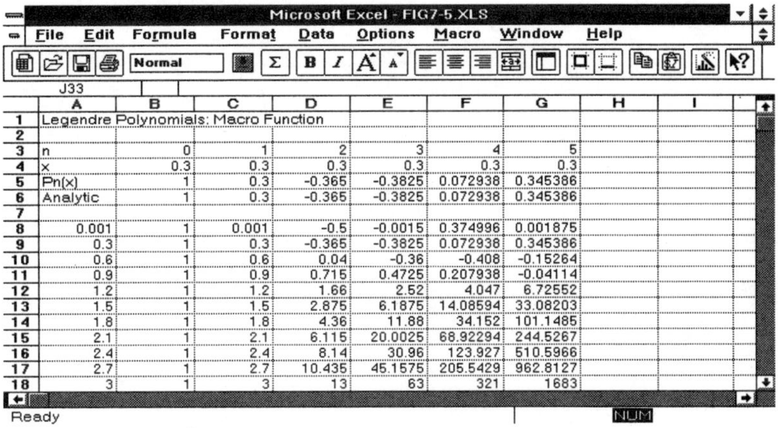

	A	B	C	D	E	F	G	H	I
1	Legendre Polynomials: Macro Function								
2									
3	n	0	1	2	3	4	5		
4	x	0.3	0.3	0.3	0.3	0.3	0.3		
5	Pn(x)	1	0.3	-0.365	-0.3825	0.072938	0.345386		
6	Analytic	1	0.3	-0.365	-0.3825	0.072938	0.345386		
7									
8	0.001	1	0.001	-0.5	-0.0015	0.374996	0.001875		
9	0.3	1	0.3	-0.365	-0.3825	0.072938	0.345386		
10	0.6	1	0.6	0.04	-0.36	-0.408	-0.15264		
11	0.9	1	0.9	0.715	0.4725	0.207938	-0.04114		
12	1.2	1	1.2	1.66	2.52	4.047	6.72552		
13	1.5	1	1.5	2.875	6.1875	14.08594	33.08203		
14	1.8	1	1.8	4.36	11.88	34.152	101.1485		
15	2.1	1	2.1	6.115	20.0025	68.92294	244.5267		
16	2.4	1	2.4	8.14	30.96	123.927	510.5966		
17	2.7	1	2.7	10.435	45.1575	205.5429	962.8127		
18	3	1	3	13	63	321	1683		

32. Copy cell B8 into cells B8:G30 by first copying it down column B to B30, then copying column B to columns C through G.

33. Select cells A8:G30 and choose the Copy command on the Edit menu.

34. Choose the New command on the File menu and create a new chart.

35. Choose the Paste Special command on the Edit menu, click on Columns, Categories (X Labels) in First Column. Then click on OK.

36. Select the XY (Scatter) chart type on the Gallery menu and select chart type number 2.

37. Add labels and a legend to the chart, as shown in Figure 7.6. Remember, the text in the legend is inserted into each of the series functions. Select each series on the chart, and insert text in quotation marks for the legend as the first argument of the series function in the formula bar. Alternatively, you can use the Edit Series command on the Chart menu to select the series and insert its name.

Summary

In this chapter, you investigated two methods for summing a series with a worksheet. The simplest is to calculate the series term by term in the cells of the

FIGURE 7.6:

The first six orders of the
Legendre polynomials

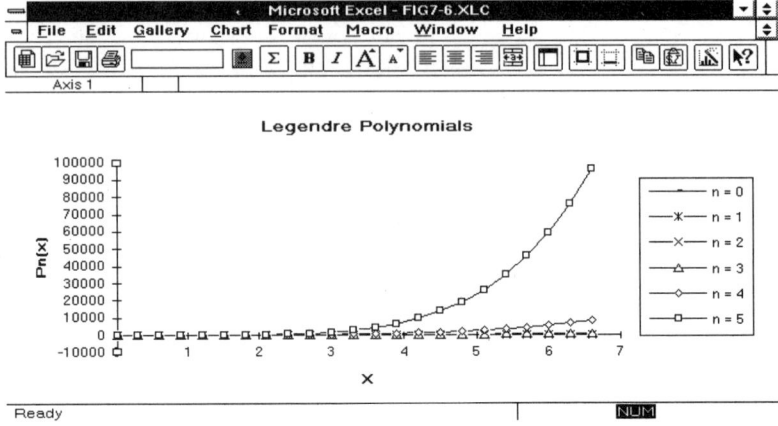

worksheet and to add them up. The other method is to write a macro function to calculate the series for any number of terms. A macro function doesn't use much worksheet area, and you can increase the number of terms calculated by simply changing a number.

For More Information

Bessel Functions and Legendre Polynomials

G. Arfken, *Mathematical Methods for Physicists* (Orlando, Fla.: Academic Press, 1970), pp. 438, 537.

Problems

1. A square wave can be described by the Fourier series

$$f(x) = \frac{4}{\pi} \sum_{n=1,3,5,\dots} \frac{1}{n} \sin\left(\frac{n\pi x}{L}\right)$$

where L is the half period of the square wave. Sum the series using the spreadsheet method and plot it for values of x where $0 \le x \le 2L$ and $L = 1$. Use enough values of x to accurately represent the square wave.

2. A saw-toothed function can be represented by the Fourier series

$$f(x) = \frac{2}{\pi} \sum_{n=1}^{\infty} \frac{(-1)^{n+1}}{n} \sin\left(\frac{n\pi x}{L}\right)$$

Create a macro function and a worksheet to calculate $f(x)$ for a range of values of x where $0 \le x \le 2L$ and $L = 3$. Plot the function.

3. The natural logarithm can be calculated using the series representation for values of x between 0 and 2

$$\ln(1 + x) = \sum_{n=1}^{\infty} \frac{(-1)^{n+1} x^n}{n}$$

Use the worksheet method to sum this series and calculate the value of $\ln(1.7)$.

4. Calculate the cosine of 2.85 radians using this series formula and the worksheet method:

$$\cos(x) = \sum_{n=0}^{\infty} \frac{x^{2n}(-1)^n}{2n!}$$

Compare the result to the value of =COS(2.85) found with the cosine function.

5. The arccosine is calculated by the series

$$\arccos(x) = \frac{\pi}{2} - \left(x - \frac{1}{2 \cdot 3} x^3 + \frac{1 \cdot 3}{2 \cdot 4 \cdot 5} x^5 + \frac{1 \cdot 3 \cdot 5}{2 \cdot 4 \cdot 6 \cdot 7} x^7 + \dots \right)$$

Write a macro function to calculate the arccosine and calculate the arccosine of 0.85 with it.

6. The following Fourier series produces a positive square pulse at $x = L/4$ of width c, and a negative square pulse at $x = 7L/4$ of width c:

$$f(x) = \frac{4}{\pi} \sum_{n=1}^{\infty} \frac{1}{n} \sin\left(\frac{n\pi}{4}\right) \sin\left(\frac{n\pi c}{2L}\right) \sin\left(\frac{n\pi x}{L}\right)$$

Let $L = 2$ and $c = 0.25$. Calculate and plot $f(x)$ for $0 \le x \le 2L$.

7. The Chebyshev polynomials $T_n(x)$ and $U_n(x)$ are defined by the series

$$T_n(x) = x^n - \binom{n}{2} x^{n-2}\left(1 - x^2\right) + \binom{n}{4} x^{n-4}\left(1 - x^2\right)^2 - \binom{n}{6} x^{n-6}\left(1 - x^2\right)^3 + \ldots$$

$$U_n(x) = \binom{n+1}{1} x^n - \binom{n+1}{3} x^{n-2}\left(1 - x^2\right) + \binom{n-1}{5} x^{n-4}\left(1 - x^2\right)^2 + \ldots$$

where

$$\binom{p}{n} = \frac{p(p-1)(p-2)\ldots(p-n+1)}{1 \cdot 2 \cdot 3 \ldots n} = \frac{p!}{(p-n)!n!}, \quad P > N-1$$

$$\binom{p}{n} = 0, \quad P < N$$

Calculate $T_3(5)$ and $U_3(5)$ and compare the results to the exact results calculated by

$$T_3(x) = 4x^3 - 3x, \qquad U_3(x) = 8x^3 - 4x$$

8. The Hermite polynomials $H_n(x)$ are defined by

$$H_n(x) = 2^n x^n - 2^{n-1}\binom{n}{2} x^{n-2} + 2^{n-2}1 \cdot 3\binom{n}{4} x^{n-4} - 2^{n-3}1 \cdot 3 \cdot 5\binom{n}{6} x^{n-6} + \ldots$$

Calculate $H_4(7)$ and compare the result to the exact results calculated by

$$H_4(x) = 16x^4 - 48x^2 + 12$$

9. The Laguerre polynomials $L^a_n(x)$ are defined by

$$L^a_n(x) = \sum_{m=0}^{n} (-1)^m \binom{n+a}{n-m} \frac{x^m}{m!}$$

Calculate $L^0_2(2.3)$.

10. The Bernoulli polynomials $B_n(x)$ for $0 < x < 1$ are defined by

$$B_{2n}(x) = \frac{(-1)^{n-1} 2(2n)!}{(2\pi)^{2n}} \sum_{k=1}^{\infty} \frac{\cos(2k\pi x)}{k^{2n}}$$

Calculate $B_4(13)$ and compare the result with the exact result calculated by

$$B_4(x) = x^4 - 2x^3 + x^2 - 1/30$$

CHAPTER
EIGHT

Performing Differentiation and Integration

8

Differentiation and integration are usually performed on analytical equations. However, if a function exists only as a set of discrete data points, you must use numerical differencing and integration techniques to calculate the derivative and integral.

You can use Excel to calculate numerical derivatives of data and functions and to numerically integrate data and functions. These techniques are usually applied with a short computer program, but they can easily be applied to data in a worksheet. In a worksheet, you can also see the intermediate results, which can often be enlightening (or scary).

Calculating Numerical Derivatives

Differentiation of discrete data (or functions that are troublesome to work out) can be done with difference formulas. Central difference formulas are the most accurate and the most popular. Forward and backward differences are used in special situations.

Types of Difference Formulas

Forward, backward, and central differences predict the derivative at a point based on different sets of data. Forward differences use the data points that come after the point in question to predict the derivative at that point. Backward differences are the same, except that they use the points that come before the point in question. Central differences use an equal number of data points before and after the point in question; thus, they give a more balanced prediction of the derivative for relatively continuous data.

Forward and backward differences are useful at the boundaries of a data set where a central difference is impossible to calculate. Forward and backward differences are also often more accurate in data that has sharp changes, because they reduce the effect of the change on the derivative for points near the change. You would use backward differences as you approach a sharp change and forward differences after you have passed it.

The equation for the first derivative is the same for forward, backward, and central differences. The difference between them is the value of x at which they are predicting the derivative. For example, the first derivative is approximated with this equation:

$$\frac{dy}{dx} = \frac{y_2 - y_1}{h}$$

where $h = x_2 - x_1$ is the separation between the data points, and (x_1, y_1) and (x_2, y_2) are consecutive pairs of x-y data. The type of difference calculated depends on which value is being approximated:

- If this equation is an approximation for the derivative at x_2, it is a backward difference.

- If it is an approximation for the derivative at x_1, it is a forward difference.

- If it is an approximation for the derivative at the center of the interval between x_1 and x_2, it is a central difference.

The following are the difference formulas for the first few derivatives and the order $(O(h^n))$ of the error associated with them. The formulas all calculate the derivative at the point x_0. The forward difference formulas can be changed to backward differences by changing the point at which the derivative is calculated to the opposite side of the formula. The order of the error is the power (n) of the separation between the data points (h) to which the error is proportional. Use this order to check the relative accuracy of the formulas. The higher the power of h, the more accurate the formula.

Derivative at x_0	Error	Difference Type
$\dfrac{dy}{dx} = \dfrac{y_1 - y_0}{h}$	$O(h)$	Forward, backward at x_1@X_CAPTION
$\dfrac{dy}{dx} = \dfrac{y_1 - y_{-1}}{h}$	$O(h^2)$	Central
$\dfrac{d^2y}{dx^2} = \dfrac{y_2 - 2y_1 + y_0}{h^2}$	$O(h)$	Forward, backward at x_2
$\dfrac{d^2y}{dx^2} = \dfrac{y_1 - 2y_0 + y_{-1}}{h^2}$	$O(h^2)$	Central

Derivative at x_0	Error	Difference Type
$\dfrac{d^3y}{dx^3} = \dfrac{y_3 - 3y_2 + 3y_1 - y_0}{h^3}$	$O(h)$	Forward, backward at x_3
$\dfrac{d^3y}{dx^3} = \dfrac{y_2 - 2y_1 + 2y_{-1} - y_{-2}}{2h^3}$	$O(h^2)$	Central

Errors in Difference Formulas

Difference formulas can have truncation and round-off errors. The order of the error shown with the equations above is for truncation error. Truncation error results from predicting the derivative with a few discrete data points rather than a continuous function. Since truncation error is proportional to the separation of the data points (h), it would seem that if you decreased h you would decrease the error. However, this is true only to the point where round-off error becomes significant.

Round-off error results from the fact that a computer stores numbers with a fixed number of digits. When two nearly equal numbers are subtracted, the difference can be quite small. Divide this difference into one of the original numbers and see how many digits are to the left of the decimal. If the number of digits is comparable to the number of digits in the computer's numbers, the difference will be meaningless. For example, if two numbers with values near 1 are subtracted, and the difference is on the order of 1×10^{-14} on a machine with 14 digits of accuracy, the difference is meaningless. Thus, round-off error increases with decreasing h. This means that you need to consider the trade-off between decreasing h to reduce truncation error and increasing h to reduce round-off error. Some optimum, nonzero value of h will minimize the total error.

Using Difference Formulas in a Worksheet

The difference formulas shown above are relatively simple, so the best way to apply them to the data is in the worksheet, rather than with a macro. In the worksheet, you can keep an eye on the scatter in the differences to see if the truncation error is growing.

Free Fall   A classic experiment in college freshman physics is on uniformly accelerated motion in free fall. It is performed by dropping a metal weight along a strip of waxed paper. High-voltage alternating current is applied across the weight and a wire behind the paper. Every half cycle of the power supply, a spark is generated between the weight and the wire. The spark burns a small hole in the paper, marking the position of the weight as it falls. Knowing the frequency of the power supply and the distance between the holes in the paper, you can calculate the velocity and acceleration of the weight.

The following data is from a free-fall experiment. The sparks were generated at a rate of 60 per second, making the holes in the paper 1/60 of a second apart. To calculate the velocity, you need to find the first derivative of this data. To find the acceleration due to gravity, you need the second derivative, which should be a constant.

The values represent distance of the holes from an arbitrary starting point (in centimeters):

0.00	13.05	31.30
1.55	16.15	35.75
3.25	19.50	40.55
5.30	23.15	45.55
7.55	27.05	50.80
10.20		

Enter some titles and the time between sparks that generated the holes in the paper.

1. Start with a new worksheet expanded to full size.

2. Type **Free Fall** in cell A1.

3. In cell C1, type **DT =** and right-justify it.

4. Type **=1/60** in cell D1.

5. Name cell D1 as **DT**.

6. Type **sec.** in cell E1.

Label the column headings.

7. In cells A3:D3, type the labels **t**, **x**, **dx/dt**, and **d2x/dt2** and right-justify them.

8. In cells A4:D4, type the labels **(s)**, **(cm)**, **(cm/s)**, and **(cm/s^2)** and right-justify them.

Calculate the time in column A. Note that zero time in this table does not imply zero velocity at the first data point. In the experiment, I skipped the first few data points because they were not clear enough to read accurately. Put the free-fall data shown above in column B.

9. Type **0** in cell A5.

10. In cell A6, type **=A5+DT** and copy it to cells A7:A20.

11. In cells B5:B20, type the free-fall data listed above.

In column C, calculate the first derivative of the data using a central difference centered on the interval between two points. In column D, calculate the second derivative using a central difference centered on each point. Average the acceleration found in column D.

12. In cell C5, type **=(B6-B5)/DT** and copy it to cells C6:C19.

13. In cell D5, type **=(B7-2*B6+B5)/($DT^2)** and copy it to cells D6:D18.

14. In cell C2, type **Ave. =** and right-justify it.

15. Type **=AVERAGE(D5:D18)** in cell D2.

16. Type **cm/s^2** in cell E2.

17. Format cells B5:D20 and D2 as 0.00, and cells A5:A20 as 0.0000.

18. Choose the Display command on the Options menu and turn off the worksheet gridlines.

Your worksheet should now look like Figure 8.1, without the regression output in cells F5:G15, which will be discussed in a moment. Column C contains the velocity of the weight, which is graphed in Figure 8.2. As expected, this is uniformly accelerated motion, with a relatively smooth curve.

FIGURE 8.1:

Uniformly accelerated motion: numerical differentiation

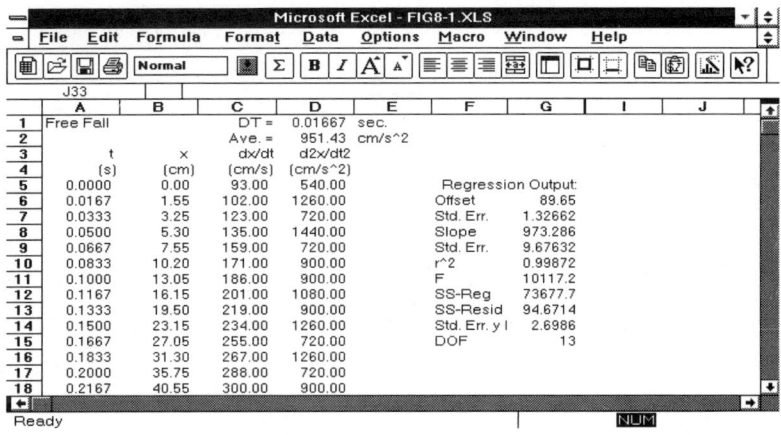

FIGURE 8.2:

Uniformly accelerated motion: velocity of the free-falling object

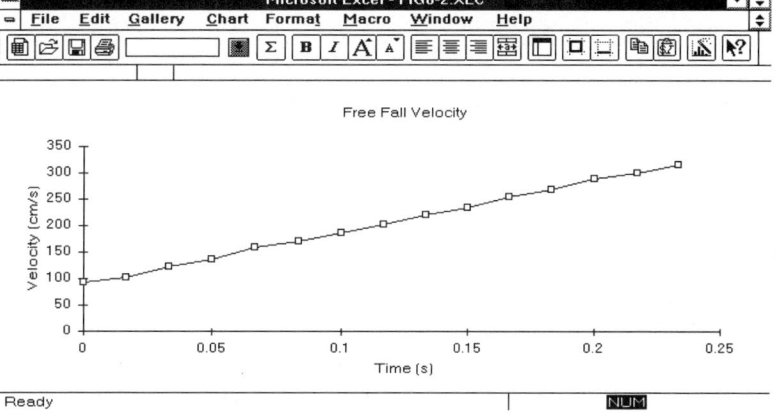

Since the object is freely falling, the acceleration in column D should be a constant and equal to the acceleration due to gravity (980 cm/s^2). As you can see in the worksheet and in the chart in Figure 8.3, there is a tremendous amount of scatter in the data, although the average gives a reasonable value (951.43 cm/s^2).

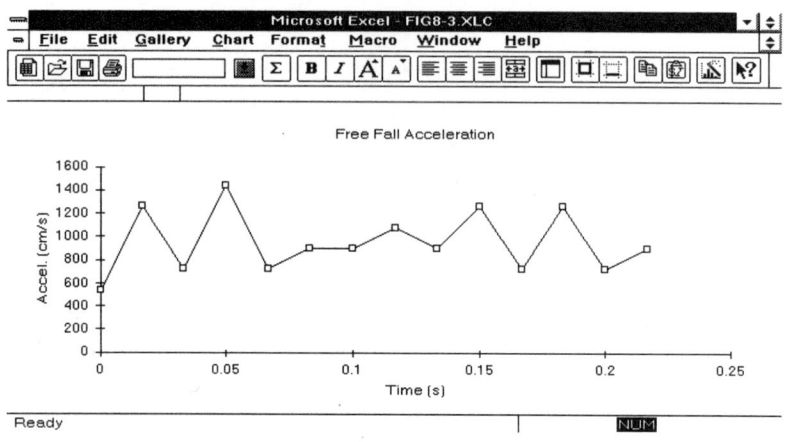

In the acceleration calculation, the random experimental error is magnified each time you take the derivative. You are taking the difference of data that contains random error. When you subtract two numbers of similar size, the result is smaller than the original numbers. The magnitude of the error is not reduced by the subtraction because it is random. The result is that you have the same magnitude of error in smaller numbers, which makes the percent error increase with each subtraction. To find the second derivative, you subtract the differences, and this increases the relative magnitude of the error even more.

Experimental data must often be smoothed before a reasonable approximation of the derivative can be calculated. A good way to smooth the data is to fit a known curve to the data and to take the derivative of that curve. But be careful not to smooth out any important details. You know that this should be uniformly accelerated motion, and the velocity data shows that, so fit a line to the velocity data. The slope of that line is equal to the derivative of the velocity, or the acceleration.

19. Type **Regression Output** in cell F5.

20. Select cells G8:H12, and type the formula

    =LINEST(C5:C19,A5:A19,TRUE,TRUE)

21. This is an array formula, so enter it into the whole range by pressing Ctrl-Shift-Enter (Cmd-Enter on the Macintosh) when you are finished typing.

Add some labels on the regression output and put in range references to move parts of the regression output to a more readable position. You cannot simply move the values, because they are part of a table, and you cannot change or move a part of a table. Hide column H after you have displayed the regression output in column G.

22. Type **Offset** in cell F6.

23. Type **=H8** in cell G6.

24. Type **Std. Err.** in cell F7.

25. Type **=H9** in cell G7.

26. Type **Slope** in cell F8.

27. Type **Std. Err.** in cell F9.

28. Type **r^2** in cell F10.

29. Type **F** in cell F11.

30. Type **SS-Reg** in cell F12.

31. Type **SS-Resid** in cell F13.

32. Type **=H12** in cell G13.

33. Type **Std. Err. y Est.** in cell F14.

34. Type **=H10** in cell G14.

35. Type **DOF** in cell F15.

36. Type **=H11** in cell G15.

37. Change the width of column H to 0 to hide it.

38. Save the worksheet.

The slope of the line through the velocity data (973 cm/s^2) is in cell G8, and it is quite close to the correct value of 980 cm/s^2.

Integrating Data

Integrating discrete data involves fitting a function that approximates the real function and whose integral is known to the intervals between the data points. Then you just add each of these subintegrals to get the total integral of the curve.

Types of Integration Formulas

The most common integral formulas for discrete data are the rectangle rule, the trapezoid rule, Romberg integration, Simpson's rules, and Gaussian quadratures. Each of these formulas is more accurate than the last, because it puts a more complicated curve through the data to approximate the function between the data points.

Rectangle Rule

The rectangle rule fills the space between two data points with a rectangle whose height is equal to the value of the function at one of the data points, and whose width is equal to the width of the interval. This would seem like a terrible approximation, but it works quite well. It is also very simple to implement, because you only need to multiply each data value by the separation of the data values and then add them together. This rule is stated as follows:

$$I = \sum_{i=1}^{n-1} y_i \left(x_{i+1} - x_i \right)$$

where I is the value of the integral.

Trapezoid Rule

The trapezoid rule puts a line between the two data points. The area of the trapezoid formed is equal to the average of the two data values multiplied by their separation:

$$I = \sum_{i=1}^{n-1} \frac{\left(y_i + y_{i+1} \right)}{2} \left(x_{i+1} - x_i \right)$$

Romberg Integration

The trapezoid rule can be improved by using Romberg integration, which combines two estimates of the integral to get a more accurate estimate of the integral. The first integral uses every value, and the second uses every other value:

$$I_1 = \sum_{i=1}^{n-1} \frac{(y_i + y_{i+1})}{2}(x_{i+1} - x_i)$$

$$I_2 = \sum_{i=1,3,5,\cdots}^{n-2} \frac{(y_i + y_{i+2})}{2}(x_{i+2} - x_i)$$

$$I = I_1 + \tfrac{1}{3}(I_1 - I_2)$$

Simpson's Rules

Simpson's 1/3 rule puts a quadratic (piece of a parabola) equation through three data values and then calculates the area. Simpson's 3/8 rule puts a cubic equation through four data values. Note that Simpson's rules require equally spaced data points.

$$I = \sum_{i=1,3,5,\cdots}^{n-2} \tfrac{1}{3}(y_i + 4y_{i+1} + y_{i+2})h$$

$$I = \sum_{i=1,4,7,\cdots}^{n-3} \tfrac{3}{8}(y_i + 3y_{i+1} + 3y_{i+2} + y_{i+3})h$$

where h is the constant separation between data points.

Gaussian Quadratures

If you are integrating a formula rather than a set of data points, you can use Gaussian quadratures. This is an integration formula where the value of an integral is found by adding the value of the function at a few specific points. The number of points needed is determined by the order of the curve that you want to be fit between the limits. Up to a third-order curve can be calculated with only two values of the function.

$$\int_{-1}^{+1} f(t)dt = f(-0.5773) + f(0.5773)$$

To use the formula, with a specific function and specific limits of integration, you must change variables to put your integral into the form above. (See the references for higher order formulas at the end of this chapter.)

Improper Integrals

Often, you must integrate functions where one or both of the limits are infinite, or that become undefined somewhere between the limits. For example, many of the special functions of physics and engineering (gamma function, error function, and so on) are defined with integrals that have infinity as one of the limits. You can handle these problems in several ways.

The simplest method is to transform the variables of the function so that the function no longer has an infinite upper limit. For example, consider the following function:

$$I = \int_0^\infty x^2 e^{-x} dx$$

Break it into two integrals:

$$I = \int_0^1 x^2 e^{-x} dx + \int_1^\infty x^2 e^{-x} dx$$

Then transform the variables in the second integral with $y = 1/x$:

$$I = \int_0^1 x^2 e^{-x} dx + \int_0^1 \frac{e^{-1/y}}{y^4} dy$$

Now you have two integrals with rational limits. The value of the function at the lower limit is indeterminate $(0/0)$, but the limit is zero, so this will not be a problem.

Many calculations with infinite limits converge rapidly to zero as the argument of the function increases towards infinity. Actually, they must converge rapidly for the value of the function to be finite. In this case, you can continue integrating the function until the value of the term to be added is much smaller than the value of the integral, and then truncate the integration at that point.

The function in the second integral in the equation above is indeterminate at the lower limit. You may happen to know that the limit of the function at this value is zero, so you could use that fact to evaluate the integral. If you did not know the value of the function at the limit, or if it is infinite as in

$$I = \int_0^1 \frac{dx}{\sqrt{x}}$$

you need to add a small number ε to the lower limit and then perform the integral. You then reduce the size of ε until the value of the integral converges (assuming it does converge). Note that this is exactly how you would solve the integral analytically.

Using Integration Methods in a Worksheet

Worksheet integration methods are relatively straightforward. Each cell calculates the value of the integral between two of the data points. A final cell then adds them up.

Gamma Function   A gamma function is one of the special functions of science and engineering. It arises occasionally in physical problems, such as the normalization of the Coulomb wave functions and the computation of probabilities in statistical mechanics. You encountered it in the last chapter as part of the series representation of the Bessel function ($J_n(x)$) for cases when n is not an integer. When n is an integer, the gamma function is equal to the factorial function:

$$\Gamma(n+1) = n!$$

The gamma function is defined with the following integral:

$$\Gamma(x) = \int_0^\infty e^{-t} t^{x-1} dt$$

which has no analytic solution. The gamma function is generally listed in a table for various values of x. Figure 8.4 is a plot of the integrand of the gamma function integral. Note that it goes to zero rapidly, so you can truncate the integral at a t value of about 10, and have better than three-place accuracy.

FIGURE 8.4:

A plot of the integrand of the gamma function integral for $x = 1.5$

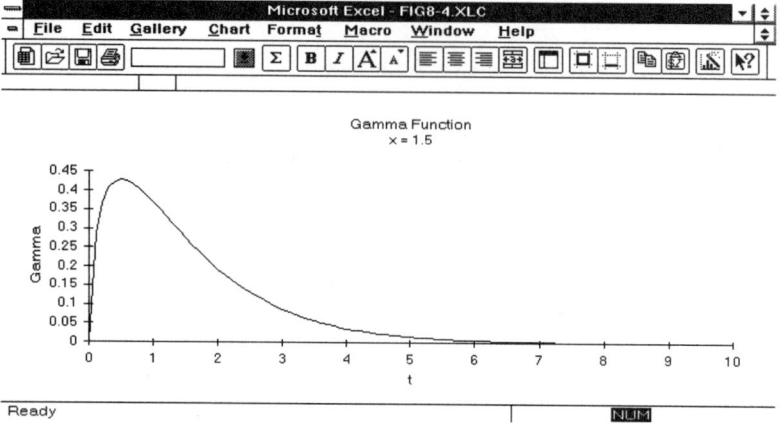

In the next example, you will calculate the gamma function by numerically performing the integration above. You will use all the integration methods discussed so far. The value of the gamma function at $x = 1.5$ is equal to $\pi/2$. Use that value of x so that you can compare the integration results with the correct result.

1. Start with a new worksheet expanded to full size.

2. Change the width of column A to 11.

3. Type **Gamma Function** in cell A1.

Insert and name the value to calculate for (x) and the grid spacing (DT.)

4. In cell C1, type **x =** and right-justify it.

5. Type **1.5** in cell D1.

6. Name cell D1 as X.

7. In cell E1, type **=dt** and right-justify it.

8. Type **0.1** in cell F1.

9. Name cell F1 as **DT**.

10. In cells B3:G3, type the labels **'True, Rect., Trap.,Trap.2, Romberg,** and **Sim.1/3** and center them.

Add the contents of each column to get the total integral for each method. Calculate the error in each method by comparing the calculated integral to the correct value in cell B4. Cell F4 contains the Romberg formula to combine the two trapezoid rule integrals.

11. Type **Integral =** in cell A4 and right-justify it.

12. Type **=SQRT(PI( ))/2** in cell B4.

13. In cell C4, type **=SUM(C8:C102)** and copy it to cells D4:E4.

14. Type **=D4+(D4-E4)/3** in cell F4.

15. Type **=SUM(G8:G102)** in cell G4.

16. Type **Error =** in cell A5 and right-justify it.

17. In cell C5, type **=(C4−$B$4)/$B$4** and copy it to cells D5:G5.

In column B, calculate values of the function for each of the 96 values of t in column A.

18. In cell A7, type **t** and right-justify it.

19. In cell B7, type **f(x,t)** and right-justify it.

20. Type **0** in cell A8.

21. In cell A9, type **=A8+DT** and copy it to cells A10:A103.

22. Format cells A8:A103 as 0.000.

23. In cell B8, type **=EXP(−A8)*A8^(X−1)** and copy it to cells B9:B103.

Calculate the rectangle rule.

24. In cell C8, type **=B8*DT** and copy it to cells C9:C103.

Calculate the trapezoid rule twice, once with single spacing and once with double. The second evaluation of the trapezoid rule is needed to calculate the Romberg formula in cell F4. Note that the second evaluation of the trapezoid rule uses every other data point, so you zero every other formula in column E so that you do not count them twice.

25. In cell D8, type **=DT*(B8+B9)/2** and copy it to cells D9:D103.

26. In cell E8, type **=DT*(B8+B10)** and copy it to cells E9:E103.

27. In alternate rows in column E (E9, E11, E13, …, E103), replace the formula with **0**.

Calculate Simpson's 1/3 rule. As before, zero out every other value of the formula in column G.

28. In cell G8, type **=DT*(B8+4*B9+B10)/3** and copy it to cells G9:G103.

29. In alternate rows in column G (G9, G11, G13, …, G103), replace the formula with **0**.

30. Use the Display command on the Options menu to turn off the gridlines.

31. Save the worksheet.

Your worksheet should now look like Figure 8.5. The value calculated with the rectangle rule and the trapezoid rule are about the same. The Romberg integration decreased the error in the trapezoid rule by about 50 percent, to a value near that calculated with Simpson's rule. In each of these calculations, the range was covered by 96 equally spaced grid points.

You did not use the Gaussian quadratures formula in this worksheet because it is more accurate and needs fewer grid points. You will calculate it using only 15 grid points instead of 96. Actually, you will be using 43 grid points, because third-order

FIGURE 8.5:

Gamma function: calculation of an integral using the rectangle rule, trapezoid rule, Romberg integration, and Simpson's 1/3 rule

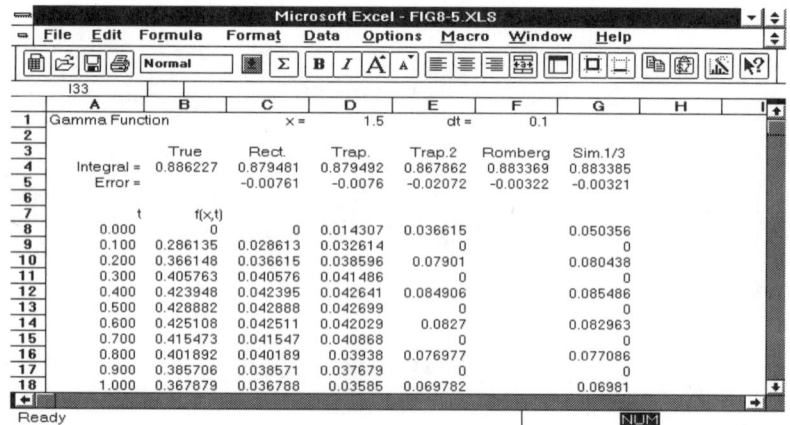

Gaussian quadratures calculate two more grid points in each interval. The layout of this worksheet is the same as the previous one. As a comparison, calculate the trapezoid rule using the same grid points.

To use Gaussian quadrature, you first must change variables to make the limits of integration −1 to 1. Do this with the following substitution:

$$t = \frac{(b-a)y + b + a}{2}$$

where a is the lower limit and b is the upper limit. Inserting this into the integral for the gamma function above gives:

$$\Gamma(x) = \int_0^\infty e^{-t} t^{x-1} dt$$

$$= \frac{(b-a)}{2} \int_{-1}^{+1} e^{-((b-a)y+b+a)/2} \left(\frac{(b-a)y + b + a}{2} \right)^{x-1} dy$$

In this case, you are calculating an integral between each pair of grid points, so the upper and lower limits of integration are equal to the values of t at those grid points. Note that this method can only be used for cases where an explicit function is known, not for experimental data.

Much of the next worksheet is the same as the previous example. The following steps start with a new worksheet, but you can save yourself some work by editing a copy instead of starting from scratch.

1. Start with a new worksheet (or a copy of the previous worksheet) expanded to full size.

2. Change the width of column A to 11.

3. Type **Gamma Function** in cell A1.

4. In cell C1, type **x=** and right-justify it.

5. Type **1.5** in cell D1.

6. Name cell D1 as **X**.

7. In cell A4, type **Integral =** and right-justify it.

8. Type **Error =** in cell A5 and right-justify it.

Enter the grid to use for the integration. Use a nonlinear grid to put a few more grid points at the beginning where the function changes rapidly and fewer later where it does not.

9. In cell A7, type **t** and right-justify it.

10. Type the following values in cells A8:A22:

A8: **0**	A13: **1**	A18: **6**
A9: **0.2**	A14: **2**	A19: **7**
A10: **0.4**	A15: **3**	A20: **8**
A11: **0.6**	A16: **4**	A21: **9**
A12: **0.8**	A17: **5**	A22: **10**

11. Format cells A8:A22 as 0.000.

As before, insert the correct value for a comparison.

12. In cell B3, type **'True** and center it.

13. Type **=SQRT(PI( ))/2** in cell B4.

Calculate the values of the function in cells B8:B22. This calculation is not used by the Gaussian quadratures formula, but it is included here to see when to truncate the integration. It is used by the trapezoid rule in cells D8:D21, which is calculated for comparison.

14. In cell B7, type **f(x,t)** and right-justify it.

15. In cell B8, type **=EXP(−A8)*A8^(x−1)** and copy it to cells B9:B22.

Calculate the Gaussian quadratures formula for each pair of data points and then add these cells together in cell C4. Cells C8:C21 calculate the quadratures formula developed for the gamma function.

16. In cell C3, type **Gaussian** and center it.

17. Type **=SUM(C8:C21)** in cell C4.

18. Type **=(C4-$B$4)/$B$4** in cell C5.

19. In cell C8, type the formula

=((A9−A8)/2)*(EXP(−((A9−A8)*(−1/SQRT(3))+A9+A8)/2)*(((A9−A8)*
(−1/SQRT(3))+A9+A8)/2)^(X−1)+EXP(−((A9−A8)*(1/SQRT(3))
+A9+A8)/2)*(((A9−A8)*(1/SQRT(3))+A9+A8)/2)^(X−1))

and copy it to cells C9:C21.

Calculate the trapezoid rule integration for comparison.

20. In cell D3, type **Trap.** and center it.

21. Type **=SUM(D8:D21)** in cell D4.

22. Type **=(D4-$B$4)/$B$4** in cell D5.

23. In cell D8, type **=(A9−A8)*(B9+B8)/2** and copy it to cells D9:D21.

24. Use the Display command on the Options menu to turn off the gridlines.

25. Save the worksheet.

Your worksheet should now look like Figure 8.6. Note that the Gaussian quadratures integration has only about one-fifth the error of the trapezoid rule integration.

Implementing Integration Formulas as Macro Functions

As you might expect, all the integration formulas can be implemented as macro functions. The equations are the same. You just use a FOR loop to calculate the parts

FIGURE 8.6:

Gamma function: integral formula solved with Gaussian quadratures

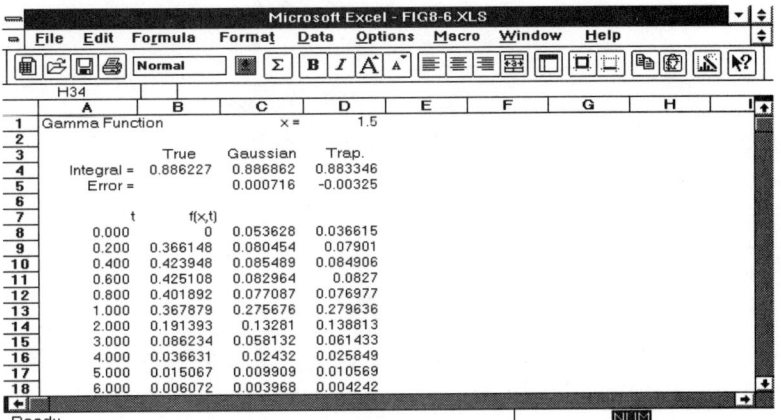

of the integral and add them together, rather than calculating them in separate cells and then combining them with the SUM function.

The macro program is much more flexible than the worksheet for integration of functions. You can change the limits or the step width by simply changing a variable. You don't need to add or delete cells. On the other hand, if you are integrating experimental data, the limits and the step width are fixed, and the data is already in cells, so the worksheet methods are the simplest to implement.

A Macro Function to Calculate the Gamma Function   The macro program you will create in the next example calculates the gamma function using the trapezoid rule.

1. Start with a new macro sheet expanded to full size.

2. Type **Gamma Function** in cell B1.

3. Type **Gamma** in cell A2.

Define the argument of the function as a number, then define and initialize some variables for use in the function. The summing variable is *sum*, which stores the value of the function while it is being calculated. The integration variable is *t*. The three variables *tstart*, *tend*, and *dt* define the starting, ending, and step values for the loop. The smaller the value of *dt*, the more accurate the integration, but the longer it takes to calculate.

4. Type **=ARGUMENT("x",1)** in cell B2.

5. Make the following entries in cells A3:B7:

    A3: **sum**   B3: **=0**

    A4: **t**   B4: **=0**

    A5: **dt**   B5: **=0.01**

    A6: **tstart**   B6: **=0**

    A7: **tend**   B7: **=20**

The loop starts here, it ranges from *tstart* to one step before *tend* with a step *dt*. Since each step ranges from *t* to *t* + *dt*, you must subtract *dt* from the upper limit to make it come out right. To apply the trapezoid rule, calculate the area of the trapezoid between *t* and *t* + *dt*: calculate the value of *y* at *t* (*yone*) and at *t* + *dt* (*ytwo*), average the two values of *y*, and multiply by *dt*. Add this new term to the value of the integral stored in *sum*.

6. Type **=FOR("t",tstart,tend−dt,dt)** in cell B8.

7. Type the following entries in cells A9:B11.

> A9: **yone**   B9:**=EXP(−t)*t^(x−1)**
>
> A10: **ytwo**   B10: **=EXP(−(t+dt))*(t+dt)^(x−1)**
>
> A11: **fact**   B11: **=dt*(yone+ytwo)/2**

8. Type **=SET.VALUE(sum,sum+fact)** in cell B12.

The next instruction is an IF function that breaks the loop when the term being added to the integral is less than 10^{-9} times the value of the integral. The loop is set up to calculate many more terms than are necessary, so use the IF function with the BREAK function when the integral is sufficiently converged. If something goes wrong and the formula does not converge, the loop ends and an error value is returned.

9. Type the following entries in cells B13:B16:

> B13: **=IF(fact/sum<1.0E−9,BREAK( ))**
>
> B14: **=NEXT( )**
>
> B15: **=IF(t>=tend,SET.VALUE(sum,#VALUE!))**
>
> B16: **=RETURN(sum)**

10. Select cells A3:B11, choose the Create Names command on the Formula menu, make sure Left Column is selected, and then click on OK to name the cells in column B with the names in column A.

11. Select cell B2, choose the Define Name command on the Formula menu, type **Gamma** for the name, click on Function, and then click on OK.

12. Widen column B to 12.

13. Save the macro sheet as **FIG8-7.XLM**.

The macro sheet should now look like that in Figure 8.7. To use the new function, open a new worksheet and call the function with a value. Use 1.5 again for the argument so that you can check the accuracy of the result. Call the function with an external reference to the macro function. You can use the Paste Function command on the Formula menu to ensure that you get the syntax right.

FIGURE 8.7:

Gamma function macro

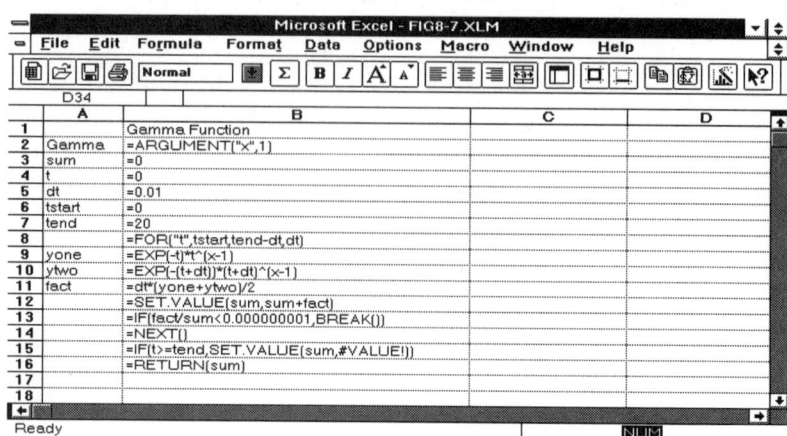

14. Open a new worksheet and expand it to full size.

15. Type **Gamma Function; Macro Function** in cell A1.

16. Make the following entries in cells A4:B7:

A4: **x**	B4: **1.5**
A5: **Gamma(x)**	B5: =**'FIG8-7.XLM'!Gamma(x)**
A6: **True Value**	B6: =**SQRT(PI( ))/2**
A7: **Error**	B7: =**(B6−B5)/B6**

17. Save the worksheet.

After several seconds, the worksheet should look like Figure 8.8. The error using this macro function is only 0.02 percent. The accuracy can be increased even more by making the cutoff value smaller in cell B13 and tend larger in cell B7 on the macro sheet. The trade-off is a slower calculation time, but that may be acceptable, depending on your situation.

FIGURE 8.8:

Using the gamma function macro function in a worksheet

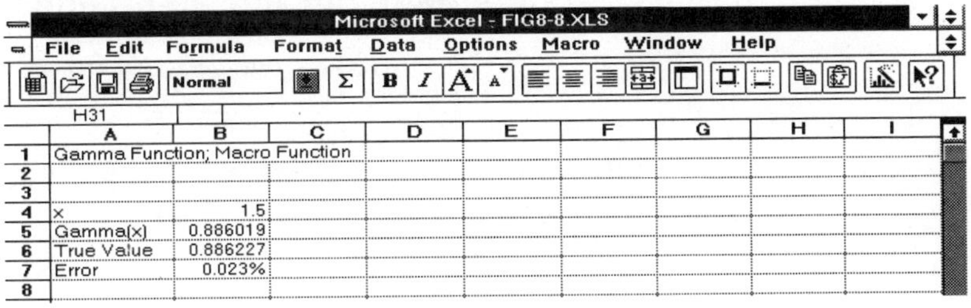

Summary

In this chapter, you calculated numerical derivatives of data and functions. In particular, you looked at worksheet methods to calculate forward, backward, and central differences of worksheet data. You encountered some of the problems in calculating numerical derivatives, namely, truncation, round-off, and error growth due to differencing.

You also numerically integrated functions and data on the worksheet and with a macro function. You implemented several of the standard numerical integration methods that are normally applied with a high-level computer language. These methods include the rectangle rule, the trapezoid rule, Romberg integration, Simpson's rules, and Gaussian quadratures.

If you are interested in the mathematical background of these methods, or in other methods and examples, refer to a book on numerical methods. Most differentiation and integration methods can be adapted to the worksheet format with little difficulty.

For More Information

Science and Engineering Special Functions

G. Arfken, *Mathematical Methods for Physicists* (Orlando, Fla. Academic Press, 1970).

Numerical Differentiation and Integration

C. Gerald, *Applied Numerical Analysis*, 2nd ed. (Reading, Mass.: Addison-Wesley, 1978).

W. H. Press, et al., *Numerical Recipes: The Art of Scientific Computing* (Cambridge, Eng.: Cambridge University Press, 1986).

Problems

1. A simulation of free-fall on the moon created the following list of numbers describing the position of an object every 1/60 of a second. The object is dropped from rest. Using central differences, calculate the velocity and acceleration of the object at each time point.

Point	Position (cm)	Point	Position (cm)
1	0	6	0.578
2	0.023	7	0.833
3	0.093	8	1.134
4	0.208	9	1.481
5	0.370	10	1.874
		11	2.314

2. Using the following table of x and y data points, calculate and plot the first and second derivatives of y with respect to x. Compare the numerically integrated values with the analytic solutions $y' = 6x + 12x^2$ and $y'' = 6 + 24x$. (The difference is caused by approximating a continuous curve with a discrete set of points.)

x	y	x	y	x	y
0.0	2.00	3.5	210.25	7.0	1521.00
0.5	3.25	4.0	306.00	7.5	1858.25
1.0	9.00	4.5	427.25	8.0	2242.00
1.5	22.25	5.0	577.00	8.5	2675.25
2.0	46.00	5.5	758.25	9.0	3161.00

x	y	x	y	x	y
2.5	83.25	6.0	974.00	9.5	3702.25
3.0	137.00	6.5	1227.25	10.0	4302.00

3. Amp ' lere's law is used to calculate the current (I) in a wire by integrating the magnetic field (B) over a closed loop that surrounds the wire. A wire carrying current has its magnetic field measured at several points along the edge of a square centered on the wire. The following are the magnetic field values from the center of one edge to the corner. Because the problem is symmetric, integrals along the eight other half-sides of the square are identical, and the total current is eight times the integral along the one half-edge. Calculate the current in the wire by integrating Amp ' lere's law using the spreadsheet form of the rectangle rule, trapezoid rule, Romberg integration, and Simpson's 1/3 rule. Amp ' lere's law is

$$I = \frac{8}{\mu_0} \int_0^5 B(y)dy$$

$$\mu_0 = 1.26 \times 10^{-6} \quad \textbf{H / m}$$

y (m)	B(y) web/m^2	y (m)	B(y) web/m^2
0.0	1.20×10^{-5}	3.0	8.85×10^{-6}
0.5	1.19×10^{-5}	3.5	8.08×10^{-6}
1.0	1.16×10^{-5}	4.0	7.34×10^{-6}
1.5	1.10×10^{-5}	4.5	6.65×10^{-6}
2.0	1.04×10^{-5}	5.0	6.02×10^{-6}
2.5	9.63×10^{-6}		

4. The sine integral is a special function defined by

$$\text{Si}(x) = -\int_x^\infty \frac{\sin(t)}{t} dt = -\frac{\pi}{2} + \int_0^x \frac{\sin(t)}{t} dt$$

For $x = 0.5$, calculate Si(x) using the rectangle and trapezoid rules using worksheet methods.

5. The exponential integral is a special function defined by

$$\text{Ei}(x) = -\int_{-x}^{\infty} \frac{e^{-t}}{t}\,dt \qquad\qquad x < 0$$

$$= -\lim_{\varepsilon \to 0}\left[\int_{-x}^{-\varepsilon} \frac{e^{-t}}{t}\,dt + \int_{\varepsilon}^{\infty} \frac{e^{-t}}{t}\,dt\right] \qquad x > 0$$

For $x = -3$, calculate $\text{Ei}(x)$ using the trapezoid rule in a macro.

6. Complete problem 4 using Gaussian quadratures.

7. Complete problem 5 using Simpson's rule in a macro.

8. An integral formula for a Bessel function with integer values of n is

$$J_n(z) = \frac{1}{\pi}\int_0^{\pi} \cos(n\theta - z\sin(\theta))\,d\theta$$

Calculate $J_n(z)$ for $n = 1$ and $z = 0.5$ using worksheet methods and the trapezoid rule.

9. Complete problem 8 using Simpson's rule in a macro.

10. Complete problem 8 using Gaussian quadratures in a macro. Compare the result to that in Figure 7.2.

CHAPTER

NINE

Solving Nonlinear Equations

Solving a nonlinear equation is often a frustrating experience. An equation that looks simple can defy solution by any analytical means. Except for polynomials up to order 4, and the simplest transcendental equations (those involving trigonometric or exponential functions), most nonlinear equations cannot be solved analytically. In fact, the solutions of polynomials of orders 3 and 4 are so unwieldy that they are seldom used.

The numerical methods for solving nonlinear equations are all based on guessing a solution and systematically refining that guess. You insert a guess into the equation, and use the result to try to improve the guess. You then repeat this process until you find a root of sufficient accuracy. Or the method diverges, and you give up and go home for the night, to try again the next morning.

Using the Successive Approximations Method

Although there are a number of simple methods for finding the roots of nonlinear equations, the one most adaptable to a worksheet is known as *successive approximations*. To perform successive approximations, you first rewrite the equation in the following form:

$$x = f(x)$$

Any of the several ways to rewrite your original equation are valid for this method, although some may not converge to a solution.

Once you have rewritten the equation, make an initial guess of the value of x. While any value of x may do, the closer your initial guess is to the solution, the faster the problem will converge. Note that for problems with multiple solutions, the initial guess of the value of x determines which solution you get. To get the other solutions, you use different initial guesses.

Insert the initial value of x into $f(x)$ and calculate a new value of x. This is the new guess of the value of x, which you reinsert into $f(x)$. Continue calculating new values of x in this manner, until the value of x converges.

$$x_0 = \text{initial guess}$$

$$x_1 = f(x_0)$$
$$x_2 = f(x_1)$$

.
.
.

$$x_n = f(x_{n-1})$$

Figure 9.1 shows the progress of a solution using this method.

Not all converted functions converge to a root. In order for the function to converge to a root of the original equation, the absolute value of the slope of $f(x)$ must be less than 1:

$$|f'(x)| < 1$$

You could write the derivatives of your functions and test them with the condition above, but it is usually faster to rewrite your equation in the simplest way and try it. If it does not converge, then rewrite it a different way.

Cos(x) = x Here is a simple, nonlinear, transcendental equation:

$$\text{Cos}(x) - x = 0$$

FIGURE 9.1:

Progress of the solution using successive approximations

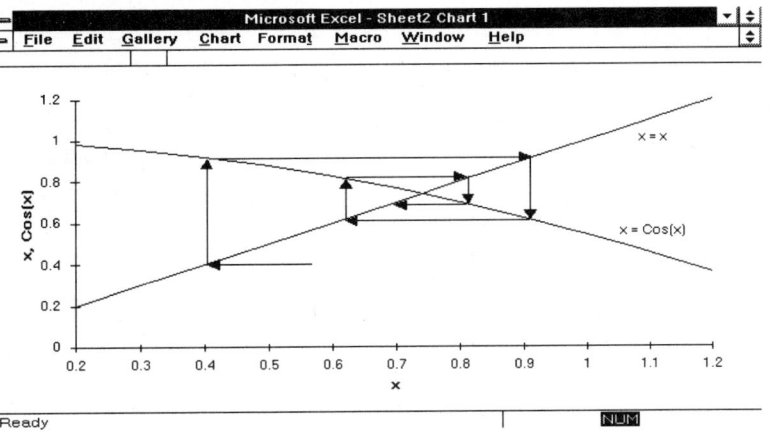

315

which can quickly be rewritten into the required form:

$$x = \text{Cos}(x)$$

In this next example, you will use the worksheet's iteration capability to solve this equation by successive approximations. To implement this method, turn off the worksheet's automatic recalculation and enter formulas with circular references.

Normally, the worksheet calculates cells in natural recalculation order. In natural recalculation order, a cell's precedents (those cells that a cell depends on) are calculated before a cell is calculated. This order is applied to all cells in a worksheet, until all the cells have been calculated. If you change the value of a cell, all cells that depend on that cell, both directly and indirectly, are recalculated. A circular reference occurs when a cell depends on itself, either directly or indirectly through the formulas in other cells. The natural recalculation order cannot calculate a circular reference, because a cell's precedents can never be calculated (it must calculate itself before it can calculate itself).

When you turn on iteration, the worksheet calculates every cell that does not contain a circular reference. It then calculates all the cells that contain circular references one or more times, depending on the settings in the Calculation dialog box. The cells containing circular references are simply calculated, using the current values of the arguments, without trying to calculate all precedents first. After the cells are recalculated the number of times specified in the Calculation dialog box, the recalculation stops. When you press the Calc key (F9 or Ctrl-=; Cmd-= on the Macintosh), all the cells are recalculated again. You will use this capability to successively calculate a formula, and then insert the value of that calculation back into the formula.

In this example, you will set the number of iterations to 1, so that you can watch the values change as the worksheet recalculates. In your own work, you will probably use a higher number to find a solution more quickly.

1. Start with a new worksheet expanded to full size.

2. Choose the Calculation command on the Options menu.

3. Click on Iteration and set Maximum Iterations to **1**.

4. Click on Manual Calculation and click on OK.

5. Change the width of column A to 16.

6. In cell A1, type

   = Cos(x); Successive approximations

Create a table with the initialization value and the initialization flag. The initialization flag forces the worksheet into a predetermined initial state.

7. In cell A3, type **Initial Value** and right-justify it.

8. Type **0** in cell B3.

9. In cell A4, type **Init Flag** and right-justify it.

10. Type **1** in cell B4.

11. Name cells B3 and B4 as **INIT_VALUE** and **INIT**.

In cell B6, test the value of INIT to see if it is 0. If INIT is 0, set x equal to the initialization value; otherwise, set it equal to the cosine of x in cell B7. In cell B7, calculate the cosine of the value in cell B6, creating a circular reference.

12. In cell A6, type **x** and right-justify it.

13. In cell B6, type

    IF(INIT=0,INIT_VALUE,B7)

14. In cell A7, type **Cos(x)** and right-justify it.

15. Type **=COS(B6)** in cell B7.

Calculate the difference between x and $\cos(x)$, to help to determine when the calculation is sufficiently converged.

16. In cell A9, type **Difference** and right-justify it.

17. Type **=B7−B6** in cell B9.

18. Format cell B9 as 0.0E+000.

Set up a second circular reference to count the number of iterations.

19. In cell A11, type **Iteration** and right-justify it.

20. In cell B11, type

    =IF(INIT=0,0,B12+1)

21. Type **=B11** in cell B12.

22. Turn off the gridlines with the Display command on the Options menu.

23. Save the worksheet.

24. To perform the calculation, set the value of the initialization flag in cell B4 to 0 and press F9, the Calc key, to initialize the problem.

25. Change the value of the initialization flag to **1** and press F9 again.

Each time you press F9, the calculation is iterated one time, calculating the next value of x.

26. Continue pressing F9 until the value of x converges to sufficient accuracy.

You can test the accuracy by comparing the value of x with the value of the difference between x and f(x) in cell B9. The worksheet should now look like Figure 9.2, with the converged value of x in cells B7 and B8.

If this calculation had not converged, then you would rewrite the equation in the equivalent form (arccosine):

$$x = \text{Cos}^{-1}(x)$$

and try again.

FIGURE 9.2:

Successive approximations method to find the root of the equation Cos(x) = x

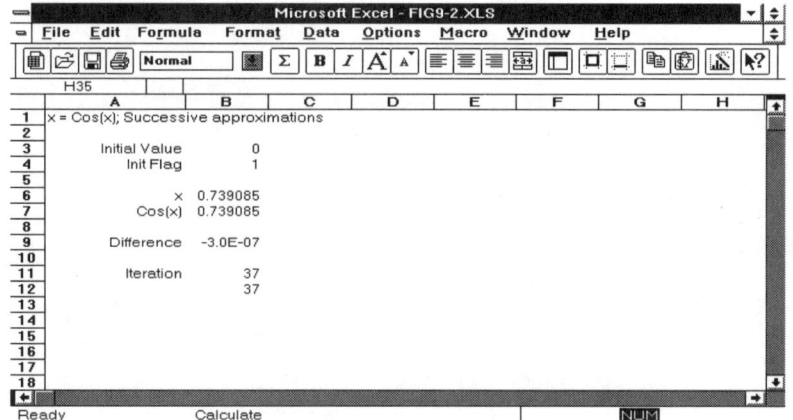

Excel can watch the change in your values for you and stop automatically when values of sufficient accuracy are achieved. To see how this works, change the current example to use Excel's stopping criteria, instead of watching the change in the last term. Begin by clearing cells B9:B12, since these values never converge, but are different every iteration. Next set the iteration and stopping criteria in the Calculation dialog box.

27. Delete the contents of cells B9:B12.

28. Choose the Calculation command on the Options menu.

29. In the Calculation dialog box, change Maximum Iterations to **100**, Maximum Change to **1.0E-7**, and Calculation to Automatic. Then click on OK.

Initialize the calculation by placing a 0 in cell B4, and letting the worksheet recalculate. Place a 1 in cell B4, and the worksheet recalculates until the maximum change in any cell is less than 1.0×10^{-7}.

Using the Under Relaxation Method

In some situations, a function is so nonlinear that the successive approximations method will not converge. Extreme nonlinearity is often caused by inflection points in the curve near the root. These points cause the value of x_i to change too much at each iteration and prevent the calculation from converging. You can correct for this problem by decreasing the change in xi between steps by a fractional amount (c). This is known as under relaxation. The iteration of successive values of x proceeds as

$$x_0 = \text{Initial guess}$$
$$x_1 = x_0 + c\,\Delta x_0$$
$$x_2 = x_1 + c\,\Delta x_1$$
$$.$$
$$.$$
$$.$$
$$x_n = x_n{-}1 + c\,\Delta x_{n-1}$$

where $\Delta x_n = f(x_n) - x_n$ is the change in x in an iteration, and c is the relaxation factor $(0 < c < 1)$. Using a value of $c = 1$ is equivalent to using the successive approximations method. Using values of c that are greater than 1 is known as over relaxation. Over relaxation is used to speed the convergence of slowly converging problems. Inserting the value for Δx_n into the equation for x_n gives

$$x_n = c\,f(x_n-1) + (1-c)x_{n-1}$$

which is the iteration equation to use in the calculation.

Electron Temperature in GaAs　The electron temperature in gallium arsenide (GaAs) due to acceleration by an electric field has been calculated by solving the conservation equations for energy and momentum. This solution is complicated by the fact that GaAs has two conduction bands with different mobilities (that is, electrons move faster in one band than in the other). The result is

$$Te = T + \left(\frac{2}{3}\right)\frac{\tau q E^2 \mu}{k}\left(1 + R\,e^{-\varepsilon/(kTe)}\right)^{-1}$$

where

Te	Electron temperature
T	Ambient temperature (300 K)
τ	Lifetime for relaxation of energy from the electrons to the crystal lattice (10^{-12} s)
q	Electron charge (1.6×10^{-19} coulomb)
E	Electric field
k	Planck's constant (1.38×10^{-23} J/K)
μ	Electron mobility in the lower electron conduction band (0.85 m^2/V-s)
ε	Energy difference between the upper and lower conduction bands (0.31 eV)
R	Splitting factor for splitting of electrons between the upper and lower conduction bands (94.1)

This equation is already in the form for the successive approximations method, so try that method for values of the electric field between 10^2 and 10^8 V/m.

1. Start with a new worksheet expanded to full size.

2. Choose the Calculation command on the Options menu.

3. In the Calculation dialog box, click on Iteration and set the Maximum Iterations to **1**. Click on Manual Calculation and click on OK.

4. Set the width of column C to 10.

5. In cell A1, type **Electron temperature in GaAs; Successive approximations**.

Create a table of the coefficients of the equation.

6. Type the following entries in cells A3:F5:

A3:	B3:	C3: **J**	D3: **K**	E3:	F3:
DELT_E	**=0.31*Q**			**1.38E-23**	**J/K**
A4: **TAU**	B4:	C4: **s**	D4: **Q**	E4:	F4:
	1.0E-12			**1.6E-19**	**Coul**
A5: **U**	B5: **0.85**	C5:	D5: **T**	E5: **300**	F5: **K**
		m^2/V-s			

7. Right-justify cells A3:A5 and D3:D5.

8. In cell D6, type **R** and right-justify it.

9. Type **94.1** in cell E6.

10. Select cells A3:B5, choose the Create Names command on the Formula menu, make sure the Left Column check box is checked, and click on OK.

11. Select cells D3:E6, choose the Create Names command on the Formula menu, make sure the Left Column check box is checked, and click on OK. Note that cell E6 is named R _.

Next create a table of the initial value and the initialization flag.

12. In cell A7, type **Initial value**.

13. Type **300** in cell C7.

14. In cell A8, type **Init Flag**.

15. Type **1** in cell C8.

16. Name cells C7 and C8 as **INIT_VALUE** and **INIT**.

Now type the list of electric field values to solve the equation for.

17. Make the following entries in cells E9:E17:

E9: **E**	E12: **1E3**	E15: **1E6**
E10: **(V/m)**	E13: **1E4**	E16: **1E7**
E11: **1E2**	E14: **1E5**	E17: **1E8**

18. Center the contents of cells E9 and E10.

In column F, test the initialization flag. If the worksheet is initializing, use the initial value; otherwise, set it equal to the function in column E. In column G, calculate the function.

19. In cell F9, type **Te** and center it.

20. In cell F10, type **(K)** and center it.

21. In cell F11, type the formula

=IF(INIT=0,INIT_VALUE,G11)

and copy it to cells F12:F17.

22. In cell G9, type **f(Te)** and center it.

23. In cell G10, type **(K)** and center it.

24. In cell G11, type the formula

=T+(2/3)*TAU*Q*E11^2*U/(K*(1+R *EXP(−DELT_E/(K*F11))))

and copy it to cells G12:G17.

25. Format cells E11:E17 as 0.0E+000.

26. Format cells F11:G17 as 0.00E+00.

27. Turn off the gridlines with the Display command on the Options menu.

28. To use this worksheet, set the initialization flag in cell C8 to **0** and press F9 (the Calc key). Set the initialization flag to **1** and press F9.

The worksheet is calculated each time you press the Calc key. The worksheet will now look like Figure 9.3.

After about five iterations, all the functions except the fifth one have converged. At a field of 10^6 V/m, the temperature is alternating between a value of 6.76×10^3 and 4.17×10^2 K. The plot of $f(Te)$ versus Te, in Figure 9.4, shows the cause of the problem. The function has two plateaus that it is alternating between. Notice that the magnitude of the slope of the function is greater than 1 to the left of the intersection, which violates our convergence condition.

To correct this problem, change to the under relaxation method.

FIGURE 9.3:

Electron temperature in GaAs: successive approximations

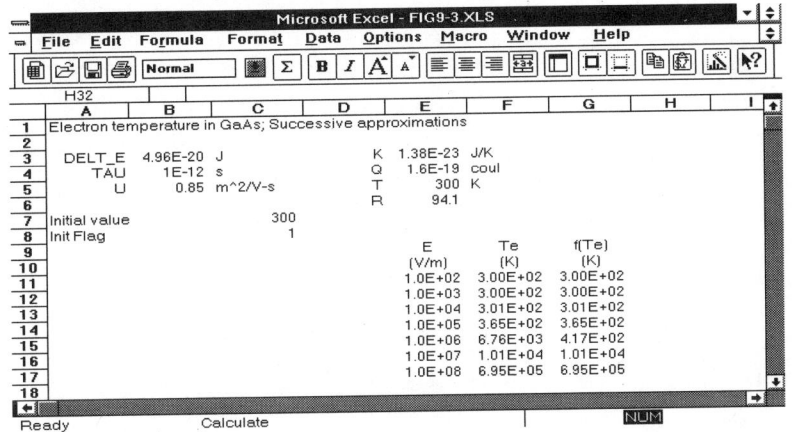

FIGURE 9.4:

Electron temperature in GaAs: plotting $f(Te)$ versus Te at a field of 10^6 V/m to determine the cause of nonconvergence

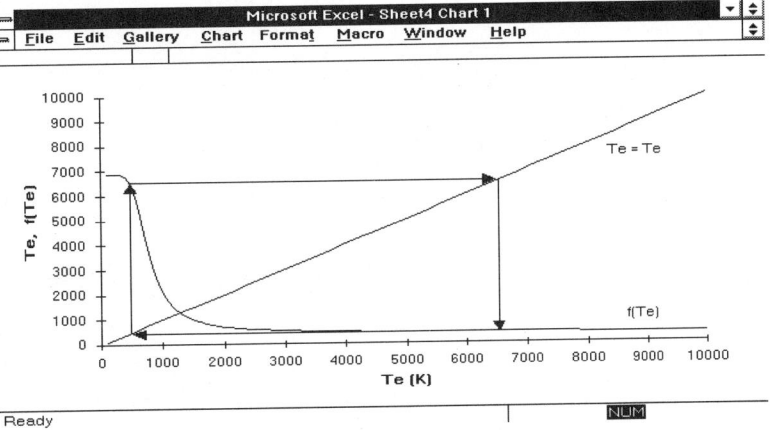

29. Change cell A1 to **Electron temperature in GaAs; Under relaxation**.

Now enter a relaxation factor of 0.5 and calculate the new values of *Te* using the under relaxation equation.

30. In cell A9, type **Relaxation Factor**.

31. Type **0.5** in cell C9.

32. Name cell C9 as **C_** .

33. Change cell G9 to

C*F(Te)+(1−C)*Te

34. Change cells G11:G17 to

=C_*(T+(2/3)*TAU*Q*E11^2*U/(K*(1+R_*
EXP(−DELT_E/(K*F11)))))+(1−C_)*F11

35. Save the worksheet.

Now when you iterate the calculation, it quickly converges for all the values of the electric field, as shown in Figure 9.5.

FIGURE 9.5:

Electron temperature in GaAs: under relaxation method

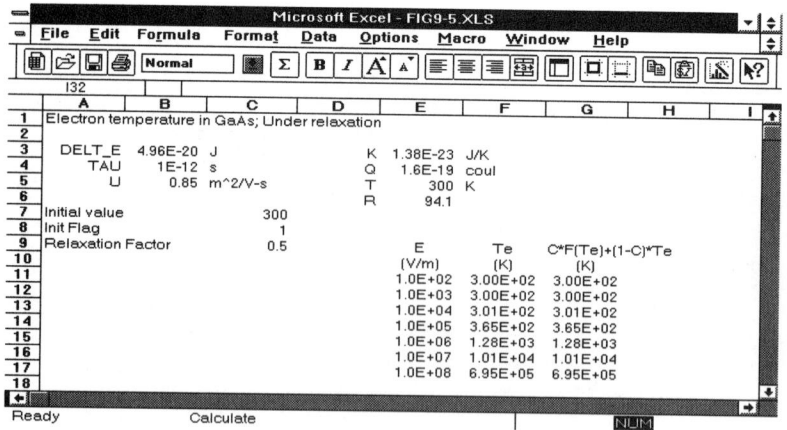

Using Newton's Method

No discussion of the solution of nonlinear equations would be complete without Newton's method. The methods that you have been using all converge linearly to the roots of the equations. Newton's method, on the other hand, converges quadratically, giving a large amount of precision in the solution with fewer iterations of the worksheet. However, to implement Newton's method, you must calculate the derivative of the function, either analytically or numerically.

To use Newton's method, first write your equation as a function equal to 0: $g(x) = 0$ Second, calculate the derivative of the function:

$$g'(x) = \frac{dg(x)}{dx}$$

Finally, calculate the approximations to x with this equation:

$x_0 = $ **initial guess**

$$x_1 = x_0 - \frac{g(x_0)}{g'(x_0)}$$

$$x_2 = x_1 - \frac{g(x_1)}{g'(x_1)}$$

$$\vdots$$

$$x_n = x_{n-1} - \frac{g(x_{n-1})}{g'(x_{n-1})}$$

Taking the derivative of a function is usually straightforward, but it is not always simple. For the electron temperature in GaAs, the function and its derivative are as follows:

$$g(Te) = T - Te + \left(\frac{2}{3}\right)\frac{\tau q E^2 \mu}{k}\left(1 + R e^{-\varepsilon/(kTe)}\right)^{-1}$$

$$g'(Te) = -1 - \left(\frac{2}{3}\right)\frac{\tau q E^2 \mu \varepsilon R e^{-\varepsilon/(kTe)}}{k^2 Te^2}\left(1 + R e^{-\varepsilon/(kTe)}\right)^{-2}$$

Modify the previous example to use Newton's method instead of the under relaxation method.

1. Start with a copy of the previous worksheet.

2. Change cell A1 to **Electron temperature in GaAs; Newton's method**.

3. Clear cells A9:C9.

Now insert Newton's iteration equation, replacing the under relaxation iteration equation.

4. In cell G9, type

   Te-g(Te)/g'(Te)

5. In cell G11, type the formula

   **=F11−(T−F11+(2/3)*TAU*Q*E11^2*U/(K*(1+R_*EXP(−DELT_E/
   (K*F11)))))/(−1−(2/3)*TAU*Q*E11^2*U*DELT_E*R_*EXP(−DELT_E/
   (K*F11))/((K*F11)^ 2*(1+R_*EXP(−DELT_E/(K*F11)))^2))**

   and copy it to cells G12:G17.

6. Save the worksheet.

Your worksheet will now look like Figure 9.6. This worksheet operates in the same way as the earlier examples.

FIGURE 9.6:

Electron temperature in GaAs: Newton's method

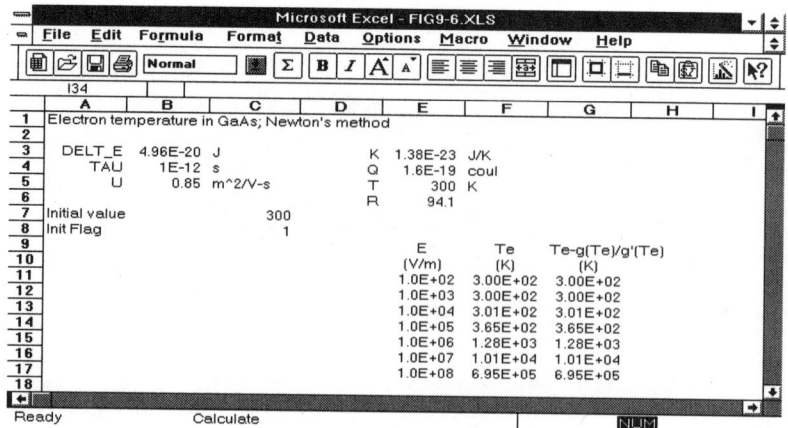

7. Set the value of the initialization flag to **0** and press F9. Reset the initialization flag to **1** and press F9 again. Each time that you press F9, the worksheet is iterated another time.

This method is much faster than the other methods. Under relaxation required 16 iterations of the worksheet to converge the calculations to three-place accuracy. Newton's method required only 4 iterations. The successive approximations method needed 5 iterations to converge all but one equation, and that equation would not converge at all.

Using the Solver

You can use Excel's Solver to control the solution of nonlinear equations. The Solver operates by guessing a trial solution, trying it, and using the result to intelligently select a new trial solution. Since the Solver requires a goal, begin by moving everything to the right side of an equation so that the result is 0 at a solution.

1. Start with a copy of the successive approximations worksheet (Figure 9.3).

2. Select cells A7:C8 and clear them with the Clear command on the Edit menu.

3. Choose the Calculation command on the Options menu. In the dialog box, change the calculation method to Automatic, and turn iteration off by unchecking the Iteration check box.

4. Change cell A1 to **Electron temperature in GaAs; Solver**.

5. Change cell G11 to this formula:

=T+(2/3)*TAU*Q*E11^2*U/(K*(1+R_*EXP(−DELT_E/(K*F11))))−F11

and copy it to cells G12:G17.

Since you have seven separate solutions, you need to create one cell to serve as the goal. First take the absolute value so that positive and negative values don't cancel each other out, then sum all the results. This is the goal, and if it is a zero, the rest of the formulas are also zero, and you have a solution.

6. In cell H11, type this array formula and press Ctrl-Shift-Enter (Cmd-Enter on the Macintosh):

   =SUM(ABS(G11:G17))

7. Choose the Solver command on the Formula menu. In the dialog box, set Set Cell to **H11**, select Equal to Value of 0, and set By Changing Cells to **F11:F17**. Click on Solve and wait for the solution.

Because the Solver might reach its maximum number of trials before the calculations converge, you may need to run the Solver more than once to get a good solution.

8. Save the worksheet.

Your worksheet should look like Figure 9.7. Although the Solver doesn't work as quickly as the other methods, it takes less time to set up a worksheet to use it. To use it again, place the initial guesses in cells F11:F17 and use the Solver command.

FIGURE 9.7:

Electron temperature in GaAs: the Solver method

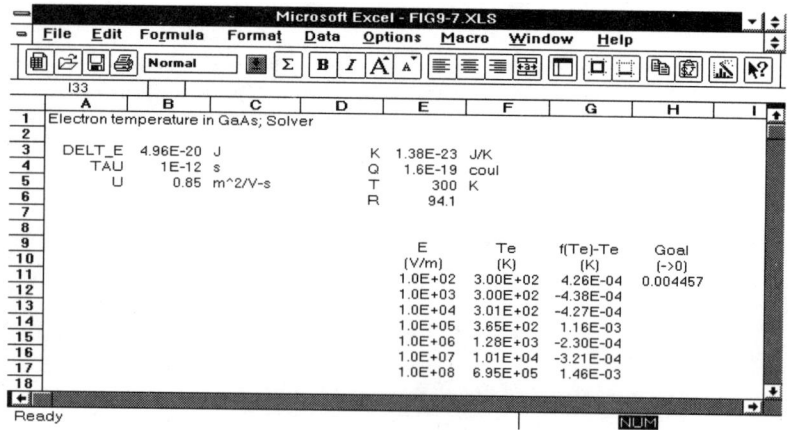

Summary

In this chapter, you examined four different methods for solving nonlinear equations with a worksheet: successive approximations, over and under relaxation, Newton's method, and the Solver. The first two methods will probably solve most of your problems, and Newton's method or the Solver will usually solve the rest. You can use other methods, but the ones covered here are the easiest to implement on a worksheet.

For More Information

Numerical Methods for Solving Nonlinear Equations

C. Gerald, *Applied Numerical Analysis*, 2nd. ed. (Reading, Mass.: Addison-Wesley, 1978).

W. H. Press, B. P. Flannery, S. A. Teukolsky, W. T. Vetterling, *Numerical Recipes; The Art of Scientific Computing* (Cambridge, UK: Cambridge University Press, 1986).

Electron Temperature in GaAs

S. M. Sze, *Physics of Semiconductor Devices*, 2nd. ed. (New York: John Wiley & Sons, 1981), p. 647.

Problems

1. Using the method of successive approximations, solve the following equation for the nontrivial solution for x (that is, a solution other than $x=0$):

$$x = \tan(0.805x) \qquad x \neq 0$$

2. Complete problem 1 using over relaxation and compare the number of iterations of the worksheet needed to achieve the solution with the same degree of accuracy.

3. The forward current density in a Schottky barrier diode is temperature dependent:

$$J = AT^2 e^{\left(\frac{B}{T}\right)}$$

where

$$A = 3.8 \times 10^{-10} \, A/cm^2\text{-}K^2$$
$$B = 1.7 \times 10^3 \, K$$

Find the temperature that gives a current density of $J = 10^{-2} \, A/cm^2$, using successive approximations or under relaxation if necessary.

4. The solution for a simple RC circuit with a resistance (R) and capacitance (C) in series with a battery (V) is:

$$q = CV\left(1 - e^{-\left(\frac{t}{RC}\right)}\right)$$

where q is the charge on the capacitor and t is the time. If $V = 10$ volts and $R = 2000$ ohms, what capacitance is needed to have a charge of $q = 10^{-5}$ coulombs in $t = 4 \times 10^{-3}$ seconds? Use successive approximations and under relaxation to find the answer.

5. The Fermi energy E_f in an n-type semiconductor is calculated by solving this equation:

$$N_c \, e^{-\left(\frac{E_c - E_f}{KT}\right)} = \frac{N_d}{1 + 2e^{\left(\frac{E_f - E_d}{KT}\right)}} + N_v \, e^{\left(\frac{E_v - E_f}{KT}\right)}$$

if

$N_C = 10^{19} \, cm^{-3}$=Density of states in the conduction band

$N_v = 10^{19} \, cm^{-3}$= Density of states in the valance band

$N_d = 10^{16} \, cm^{-3}$= Number of donor states

$E_c = 1.1 \, eV$ = Conduction band energy

$$E_d = 1.05 \text{ eV} = \text{Donor energy level}$$
$$E_v = 0 \text{ eV} = \text{Valance band energy}$$
$$KT = 0.0259 \text{ eV}$$

Find the value of the Fermi energy using successive approximations and under or over relaxation.

6. When designing a photovoltaic energy converter (solar cell) to operate in a maximum power configuration, you must solve the following equation for the optimum operating voltage (V):

$$\left(1 + \frac{eV}{KT}\right) e^{\left(\frac{eV}{KT}\right)} = 1 + \frac{J_s}{J_0}$$

at $T = 300 \text{ K}$ ($KT/e = 0.0259$ volts) and $J_5/J_0 = 2 \times 10^{10}$ (the ratio of the short circuit to the saturation current density). Find the value of the optimum voltage using the Solver.

7. Use Newton's method to find the value of x that is a solution of this equation:

$$3.54 = 2 + 0.3x + 0.07x^2 + 0.004x^3$$

8. Use Newton's method to find the three values of x that are solutions of this equation:

$$27.6 = 14.7x^2 e^{-0.386x}$$

9. Complete problem 4 using Newton's method.

10. Complete problem 6 using Newton's method.

CHAPTER

TEN

Solving Sets of Equations

10

Many problems in science and engineering result in sets of equations that must be solved simultaneously. Numerical solution of partial differential equations; steady-state potentials in electrical networks; and concentration equations for multiple, coupled, and chemical reactions are examples of problems whose solutions involve a set of simultaneous equations. Most of these problems result in sets of linear equations, for which there are several good solution methods. If the equations are nonlinear, relaxation methods will usually work, although they can be difficult to get to converge.

Solving Linear Equations

Most problems that involve simultaneous equations result in sets of linear equations. This is fortunate, in that linear equations are the most straightforward. You can solve most of them with Excel's built-in matrix functions, which can handle inversion and multiplication of up to about 60-by-60-element matrices.

Gauss-Seidel iteration and over/under relaxation methods also work well on a worksheet, and they can be used for linear and nonlinear equations. Gauss-Seidel iteration is the multiequation form of the successive approximations method used on single equations in the previous chapter. As you might expect, the over/under relaxation method is the multiequation analog of the single-equation under relaxation method.

Using Matrix Methods

Matrix solutions of sets of linear equations are the simplest to implement with Excel. First you must write your set of simultaneous equations in matrix format:

$$\mathbf{A}\mathbf{x} = \mathbf{b}$$

where $\mathbf{A}$ is the coefficient matrix, $\mathbf{x}$ is the vector of unknowns, and $\mathbf{b}$ is the result vector. To solve this matrix equation, multiply both sides from the left by the inverse of $\mathbf{A}$:

$$\mathbf{A}^{-1}\mathbf{A}\mathbf{x} = \mathbf{A}^{-1}\mathbf{b}$$

This becomes:

$$x = A^{-1}b$$

and you have the solution. Although this seems simple as an abstract equation, calculating the inverse of a matrix is usually not a trivial matter. Fortunately, Excel has that capability built in, in the MINVERSE function.

Three Equations with Three Variables   As an example, consider this set of linear equations:

$$-8x_1 + x_2 + 2x_3 = 0$$
$$5x_1 + 7x_2 - 3x_3 = 10$$
$$2x_1 + x_2 - 2x_3 = -2$$

The solution is $x_1 = 1$, $x_2 = 2$, and $x_3 = 3$. These can be put in the matrix format:

$$\begin{vmatrix} -8 & 1 & 2 \\ 5 & 7 & -3 \\ 2 & 1 & -2 \end{vmatrix} \begin{vmatrix} x_1 \\ x_2 \\ x_3 \end{vmatrix} = \begin{vmatrix} 0 \\ 10 \\ -2 \end{vmatrix}$$

You can solve this problem easily in a worksheet.

1. Start with a new worksheet expanded to full size.

2. Type **Solving sets of equations; Matrix inversion** in cell A1.

3. Type **Ax = b** in cell B3.

Enter the coefficient matrix **A** and the result vector **b**.

4. In cell A5, type **Input Matrix (A)**.

5. In cells A6:C8, type the contents of matrix A:

Row 1:	−8	1	2
Row 2:	5	7	−3
Row 3:	2	1	−2

6. In cell E5, type **Result Vector (b)**.

7. In cells E6:E8, type the contents of the result vector:

    0 10 −2

Invert matrix **A** and then multiply vector **b** by the inverse of **A**. The MINVERSE function returns an array of values, so the function must be inserted into the whole range as an array.

8. In cell A10, type **Inverse matrix (1/A)**.

9. Select cells A11:C13 and type

    =MINVERSE(A6:C8)

10. Press Ctrl-Shift-Enter (Cmd-Enter on the Macintosh) to insert this formula into the whole selection.

11. In cell E10, type **Solution Vector x = (1/A)b**.

12. Select cells E11:E13 and type

    =MMULT(A11:C13,E6:E8)

13. Press Ctrl-Shift-Enter (Cmd-Enter on the Macintosh) to insert the formula into the whole selection.

14. Save your worksheet if you want to keep a copy.

The worksheet should now look like Figure 10.1, with the solution values 1, 2, and 3, for x_1, x_2, and x_3 in cells E11:E13.

Using Gauss-Seidel Iteration

Gauss-Seidel iteration is a form of the Jacobi method for solving sets of equations. It is similar to the successive approximations method described in the previous chapter. First solve each of the simultaneous equations for one of the variables, which results in one equation for each variable. To decrease the size of the round-off error, try to solve for the variables with the largest coefficients. Pick a set of initial guesses of the values of the variables. Insert them into the equations and calculate a new set of values. Put these values back into the equations and calculate another set. Continue this process until the values converge.

FIGURE 10.1:

Solving simultaneous linear equations with the Excel matrix functions

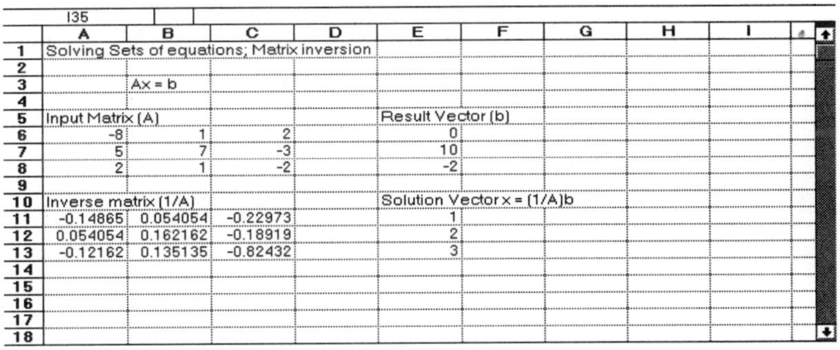

	A	B	C	D	E	F	G	H	I	
1	Solving Sets of equations; Matrix inversion									
2										
3		Ax = b								
4										
5	Input Matrix (A)				Result Vector (b)					
6	-8	1	2		0					
7	5	7	-3		10					
8	2	1	-2		-2					
9										
10	Inverse matrix (1/A)				Solution Vector x = (1/A)b					
11	-0.14865	0.054054	-0.22973		1					
12	0.054054	0.162162	-0.18919		2					
13	-0.12162	0.135135	-0.82432		3					
14										
15										
16										
17										
18										

Calculating all the new values of the variables using only the old values in the equations is Jacobi iteration. However, since the cells are calculated one at a time, some of the new values are available before you finish calculating each of the equations. Using these new values as soon as they are available rather than waiting for the next iteration is known as Gauss-Seidel iteration.

To apply Gauss-Seidel iteration to the problem above, first solve the equations for each of the variables:

$$x_1 = \left(\tfrac{1}{8}\right)\left(x_2 + 2x_3\right)$$
$$x_2 = \left(\tfrac{1}{7}\right)\left(10 - 5x_1 + 3x_3\right)$$
$$x_3 = \left(\tfrac{1}{2}\right)\left(2 + 2x_1 + x_2\right)$$

Create a worksheet to solve these equations using Gauss-Seidel iteration.

1. Start with a new worksheet expanded to full size.

2. Choose the Calculation command on the Options menu and change Calculation to Manual. Click on the Iteration check box, set Maximum Iterations to **1**, and click on OK.

3. Change the width of columns B and C to 11.

4. In cell A1, type **Solving sets of equations: Gauss-Seidel iteration**.

Put in an initialization flag to reset the calculation to a known state. Entering a 0 in cell B3 causes the IF functions in cells B8:B10 to return the initial values in cells A8:A10.

5. In cell A3, type **Init Flag**.

6. Type **0** in cell B3.

7. Name cell B3 as **INIT**.

Put in an initial guess of 0 for the solution.

8. In cell A6, type **Initial**.

9. In cell A7, type **Values**.

10. Type **0** in cells A8:A10.

Enter the three equations. When a worksheet is iterated, cells with circular references are calculated left to right, top down. If you place formulas in column C that use values stored in column B, the values in column B are equated to the value of the formulas before the formulas are calculated, so column B contains the old values. When the formulas in column C are calculated, they will use only the old values in column B for calculating new values. This is Jacobi iteration.

If you reverse that order and put the formulas in column B and store the values in column C, a formula is calculated in column B, and its new value is stored in column C. The next formula in column B can then use that new value, thus the new values are used in the iteration as soon as they are calculated. This is Gauss-Seidel iteration, which is what you want to use.

11. In cell B6, type **Equations**.

12. Type **=(C9+2*C10)/8** in cell B8.

13. Type **=(10−5*C8+3*C10)/7** in cell B9.

14. Type **=(46−5*C8−7*C9)/9** in cell B10.

Reference the equations, creating a circular reference, and do the initialization test.

15. In cell C6, type **Solutions**.

16. In cell C8, type the formula

    =IF(INIT=0,A8,B8)

    and copy it to cells C9:C10.

17. Format cells B8:C10 as 0.000.

18. Save the problem if you want to keep it.

19. To use this worksheet, set the initialization flag to **0** in cell B3 and press F9 or Ctrl-= (Cmd-= on the Macintosh) and let it recalculate. Once the worksheet has initialized, change the initialization flag to **1** and press F9 again. Continue iterating the worksheet by pressing F9 until the values converge.

Your worksheet should look like Figure 10.2.

If you are solving a set of equations that are slow to converge, you do not need to press F9 many times to iterate your equations. Instead, choose the Calculation command on the Options menu and change the Maximum Iterations setting to the desired number of iterations for each time you press F9 or Ctrl-= (Cmd-= on the Macintosh).

Using the Over/Under Relaxation Method

As with single equations, you can often cause a problem to converge more quickly or more stably by adjusting the amount of the correction applied to the values during each iteration. The over/under relaxation method adds only the fraction Cf of the calculated correction to the values during each step. The fraction Cf can be either greater than or less than 1. If Cf equals 1, this method is equivalent to the Jacobi or Gauss-Seidel method.

First calculate a new value for each of the unknowns as you did in the Gauss-Seidel method example. Second, instead of using this value in the next iteration, subtract

FIGURE 10.2:

Solving simultaneous linear equations: Gauss-Seidel iteration

	A	B	C	D	E	F	G	H	I
	H32								
1	Solving sets of equations: Gauss-Seidel iteration								
2									
3	Init Flag	1							
4									
5									
6	Initial	Equations	Solutions						
7	Values								
8	0	1.000	1.000						
9	0	2.000	2.000						
10	0	3.000	3.000						

the old value of each unknown to find the change in the unknown. Third, multiply the change in the unknown by Cf and then add it to the old value of the unknown. This is the value to use in the next iteration.

$$x_1^{n+1} = x_1^n + Cf\left[\left(\tfrac{1}{8}\right)\left(x_2^n + 2x_3^n\right) - x_1^n\right]$$

$$x_2^{n+1} = x_2^n + Cf\left[\left(\tfrac{1}{7}\right)\left(10 - 5x_1^n + 3x_3^n\right) - x_2^n\right]$$

$$x_3^{n+1} = x_3^n + Cf\left[\left(\tfrac{1}{2}\right)\left(2 + 2x_1^n + x_2^n\right) - x_3^n\right]$$

The n and $n+1$ superscripts refer to iterations n and $n+1$.

Create a worksheet that uses the over/under relaxation method. This worksheet has almost the same layout as the previous example, so you can start with that worksheet and save yourself some typing.

1. Start with a new worksheet expanded to full size (or a copy of the previous example).

2. Choose the Calculation command on the Options menu and change Calculation to Manual, check Iteration, set Maximum Iterations to **1**, and click on OK.

3. Change the width of columns B and C to 11.

4. In cell A1, type **Solving sets of equations: Over/Under Relaxation**.

This worksheet has both an initialization flag and a relaxation factor. The initialization flag sets the worksheet to a predefined initial state. The relaxation factor is multiplied by the change in the values to increase or decrease the amount of correction applied at each iteration.

5. In cell A3, type **Init Flag**.

6. Type **0** in cell C3.

7. In cell A4, type **Relaxation factor**.

8. Type **0.5** in cell C4.

9. Name cells C3 and C4 as **INIT** and **Cf**, respectively.

Enter a zero as the initial guess for the solution values. You can put any reasonable values here; but the closer the values are to the solution, the faster the equations will converge.

10. In cell A6, type **Initial**.

11. In cell A7, type **Values**.

12. Type **0** in cells A8:A10.

Put in the relaxation equations. You will recognize the equations from the Gauss-Seidel method, with the added complication of the relaxation factor controlling the amount of the change in each value. Do this by subtracting the old value from the equation, multiplying by *Cf*, and then adding the old value to the result.

13. In cell B6, type **Equations**.

14. Type the following formulas in cells B8:B10:

> B8: =C8+Cf*(((C9+2*C10)/8)-C8)
> B9: =C9+Cf*(((10-5*C8+3*C10)/7)-C9)
> B10: =C10+Cf*(((46-5*C8-7*C9)/9)-C10)

Create the circular references and do the initialization.

15. In cell C6, type **Solutions**.

16. In cell C8, type the formula

> =IF(INIT=0,A8,B8)

and copy it to cells C9:C10.

17. Format cells B8:C10 as 0.000.

18. Save the problem if you want to keep it.

19. To use this worksheet, set the value of the relaxation factor in C4. A value of **0.5** seems to work well for this problem.

Different problems will respond differently to the value of the relaxation factor. Although you can use any value, it is doubtful that you could get the worksheet to converge with a value greater than about 2. Smaller values are generally more stable but do not converge as fast. Usually, you would start with a value of 1 or 1.5 and see if the worksheet is converging. If it is converging, increase the value; otherwise, decrease it. You do not need to reinitialize the worksheet when you change the value of the relaxation factor as long as the calculated solution values are still reasonable. If the solution values have started to diverge, you will need to reinitialize the worksheet to get them back near the true solution.

20. Set the value of the initialization flag in cell C3 to **0** and press F9 or Ctrl-= (Cmd-= on the Macintosh). Change the initialization flag to **1** and press F9 again. Continue pressing F9 until the values converge.

When the worksheet converges, it should look like Figure 10.3. Remember, you do not need to sit at your computer and press F9 many times to iterate your equations. You can increase the number of times the problem is iterated by changing the Maximum Iterations setting in the Calculation dialog box.

FIGURE 10.3:

Solving simultaneous linear equations: over/under relaxation method

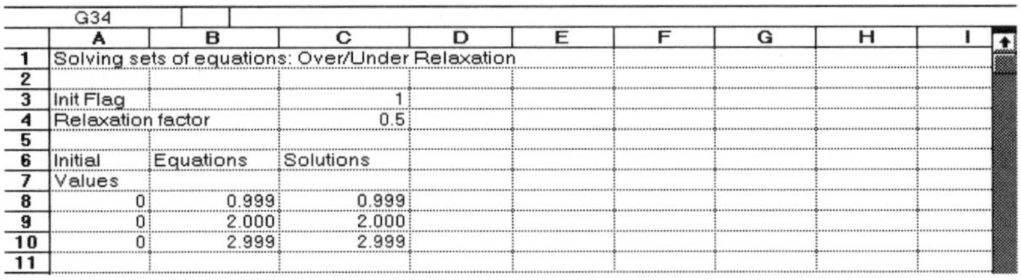

	A	B	C	D	E	F	G	H	I
	G34								
1	Solving sets of equations: Over/Under Relaxation								
2									
3	Init Flag		1						
4	Relaxation factor		0.5						
5									
6	Initial	Equations	Solutions						
7	Values								
8	0	0.999	0.999						
9	0	2.000	2.000						
10	0	2.999	2.999						
11									

Using the Solver with Sets of Equations

If you lay out the worksheet carefully, you can use the Solver with simultaneous linear equations. The Solver can optimize only the value of a single cell, so you must combine the results of all the calculations into one cell. You can combine the results by rewriting all the equations to equal zero when a solution is reached, and then add the absolute values of these solutions. When the sum is zero, you have solved all the equations. The absolute value ensures that the results from two equations don't cancel each other by having equal results of the opposite sign instead of zero. The Solver can adjust several values to optimize the result, so the input values do not require special handling.

Since the layout of the worksheet in this example is similar to the one in the previous example, you can use a copy of it and save yourself some typing.

1. Start with a new worksheet expanded to full size (or a copy of the last worksheet).

2. Change the width of column A to 4.

3. Change the width of columns B and C to 11.

4. In cell A1, type **Solving sets of equations; Solver method**.

Now put in the formulas. These formulas are the same as in the last problem, except that the value on the left side of the equation is subtracted from the right to make the result 0. If all these formulas evaluate to 0, the problem is solved.

5. In cell B6, type **Equations**.

6. In cell B8, type

    =(C9+2*C10)/8−C8

7. In cell B9, type

    =(10−5*C8+3*C10)/7−C9

8. In cell B10, type

    =(2+2*C8+C9)/2−C10

Next insert the initial guess as to the solutions.

9. In cell C6, type **Solutions**.

10. In cell C8, type **1** and copy it to cells C9:C10.

11. Format cells B8:C10 as 0.000.

Sum the absolute values of these solutions to create a single cell for the Solver to optimize. The cell calculates an array formula, so enter it with Ctrl-Shift (Cmd-Enter on the Macintosh).

12. In cell C12, type

    =SUM(ABS(B8:B10))

    and press Ctrl-Shift-Enter (Cmd-Enter on the Macintosh).

Now solve the formulas with the Solver.

13. Choose the Solver command on the Formula menu.

14. Select cell C12 for the Set Cell option (the cell to optimize) and cells C8:C10 as the cells to change, as shown in Figure 10.4. Select the Value option and enter **0** in the Value Of box. Click on Solve to search for a solution.

When the Solver locates a solution to the problem, it displays the answer, as shown in Figure 10.5. If it can't find a solution, it will tell you. If it does not work, try running the Solver again. It may have reached its maximum number of trial solutions and just needs to try a few more. You may also need to try different starting values.

15. Save the problem if you want to keep it.

FIGURE 10.4:

Setting up the Solver to find a solution

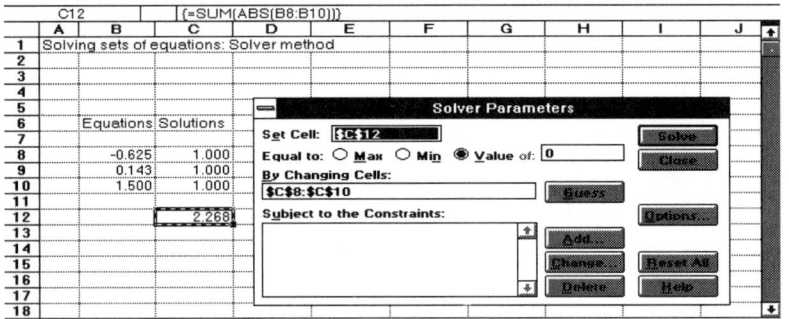

FIGURE 10.5:

A solution found by the Solver

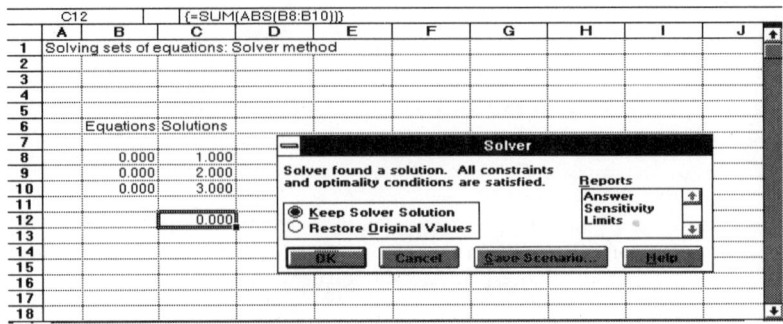

Solving Simultaneous Nonlinear Equations

In some cases, you can use the Gauss-Seidel or Jacobi method to solve multiple, simultaneous, nonlinear equations. However, usually you will need the extra control of the over/under relaxation method to get the equations to converge. The Solver is also useful if the equations can be put into a form where only a single cell needs to be optimized, and the results of the formulas are all of about the same value. If the results vary widely, the formula with the largest value will dominate the solution. You apply these methods in the same way as you use them with linear equations.

Nonlinear equations may have multiple solutions, so the starting value can be important. If the equations are extremely nonlinear, they may not converge if the initial values are too far from the solution. Try changing those values as well as the relaxation factor if you are having trouble getting a solution.

Accuracy and Scaling

An unfortunate consequence of using matrix and iteration methods to solve simultaneous equations is that the accuracy of the solution can depend on the order in which you solve the equations. When you are preparing the equations for numerical solution, you must solve one equation for each variable. For the best results, try to solve each equation for the variable with the largest coefficient (ignore the sign of the coefficient). Ideally, you would end up with one equation solved for each variable, but that is not usually the case. Use your judgment to decide which equation to solve for which variable.

When you are using the matrix methods, the relative size of the values in the coefficient matrix that you are solving is also important. All the values in the coefficient matrix should be about the same order of magnitude. If one equation has coefficients that are several orders of magnitude larger or smaller than any of the others, the accuracy of the solution will be poor. To correct this situation, scale each equation (a row in the matrix) by dividing each of the coefficients by the magnitude of the largest coefficient in that equation. When you are scaling an equation, do not forget to also scale the result (the **b** values on the right sides of the equations).

If your matrix is singular (it has a zero on the diagonal), you will never get a solution. To test for singularity, calculate the determinant of the **A** matrix using the MDETERM function. If the determinant is zero, the matrix is singular. If the determinant is very small, but not zero, it may have a solution, but that solution might be very hard to find. Round-off error may make a matrix appear singular even though it has a small but real determinant. If the determinant is small, check the result very carefully to be sure it is real. If you are having trouble getting a good solution, consult a numerical methods book for more information about matrix methods.

Summary

This chapter reviewed five methods for solving linear and nonlinear sets of simultaneous equations with a worksheet. Excel has the built-in capability to invert and multiply matrices, which can be used to solve most sets of linear equations. The Gauss-Seidel, Jacobi, and over/under relaxation methods are all implemented with the iteration capability of the worksheet. These three methods are applicable to the solution of nonlinear as well as linear equations. Also, the Solver add-in program can often be adapted to solve both linear and nonlinear equations.

For More Information

Numerical Methods for Solving Nonlinear Equations

C. Gerald, *Applied Numerical Analysis*, 2nd. ed. (Reading, Mass.: Addison-Wesley, 1978).

W. H. Press, B. P. Flannery, S. A. Teukolsky, W. T. Vetterling, *Numerical Recipes; The Art of Scientific Computing* (Cambridge, UK: Cambridge University Press, 1986).

Problems

1. Solve the following set of equations for x, y, and z using the matrix functions.

   $4x + 3.9y + 0.27z = 39.6$

   $22x + 14y + 5z = 233.12$

   $5.6x + 4.8y + 2.1z = 69.91$

2. Solve these circuit equations for the circuit in the illustration below for I_1 and I_2 using Gauss-Seidel iteration.

   $V = I_1(R_1 + R_2) + I_2R_1$

   $0 = I_2R_3 - I_1R_2$

   $R_1 = 10$ ohms, $R_2 = 5$ ohms, $R_3 = 10$ ohms, $V = 10$ volts

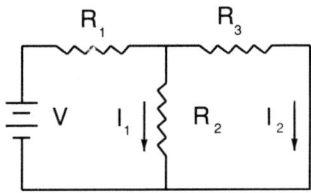

3. Solve the following set of equations for x, y, and z using the matrix functions.

   $x + y - 2z = 10$

   $1.5x + 2y + 2z = 1$

   $2.5x + 4y + 3z = 4$

4. Solve the following set of equations for x, y, z, w, and v using the matrix functions.

   $3x + 7y + 5z + 20w + 4v = 96$

   $x + 2y + 3z + 9w + 10v = 67$

   $5x + y + 16z - 4w + 6v = 124$

   $2x + 2y + z + w + 18v = 73$

   $x + 3y - z + 5w + 2v = 19$

5. Solve the following set of equations for x, y, and z using the over/under relaxation method.

$$x + 3y + z = 17$$
$$4x + 2y + z = 27$$
$$5x + 6y - z = 25$$

6. Balanced bridge circuits (illustrated below) are commonly used in pressure transducers. When pressure is applied to the transducer, resistors R_5 and R_6 change in opposite directions (one increases and one decreases), creating an imbalance in the bridge. This produces an output V_0 at the terminals.

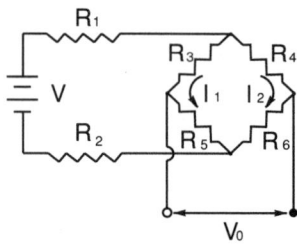

Given that:

$$R_1 = R_2 = 1 \text{ ohm}$$
$$R_3 = R_4 = 100 \text{ ohms}$$
$$R_5 = 1002 \text{ ohms}$$
$$R_6 = 998 \text{ ohms}$$
$$V = 10 \text{ volts}$$

solve the following circuit equations for I_1, I_2, and V_0 using the over/under relaxation method.

$$V = (I_1 + I_2)(R_1 + R_2) + I_1(R_3 + R_5)$$
$$V_0 = I_2R_4 - I_1R_3 \quad V_0 = I_1R_5 - I_2R_6$$

Solve the equations again, letting $R_5 = R_6 = 1000$ ohms (this is the balanced situation). Try different values of R_5 and R_6, always increasing one while decreasing the other.

7. When one particle scatters elastically off of a stationary particle (illustrated below), the initial and final velocities and directions can be calculated using the equations for conservation of momentum and energy.

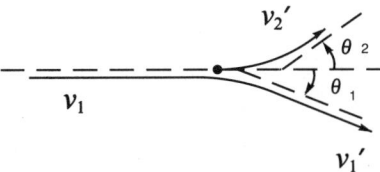

Here, unprimed velocities (v) occur before the collision and primed ones occur after.

$$m_1 v_1 = m_1 v_1' \cos(\theta_1) + m_2 v_2' \cos(\theta_2)$$
$$m_1 v_1' \sin(\theta_1) = m_2 v_2' \sin(\theta_2)$$
$$\tfrac{1}{2} m_1 v_1^2 = \tfrac{1}{2} m_1 v_1'^2 + \tfrac{1}{2} m_2 v_2'^2$$

If particle 1 is a proton ($m_1 = m_p = 1.67 \times 10^{-27}$ Kg) moving at 250 m/s, particle 2 is a helium nucleus ($m_2 = 4m_p$), and particle 1 flies off at an angle (θ_1) of 25 degrees, calculate θ_2, v_1', and v_2' using over/under relaxation.

8. Four different springs are attached end to end and stretched between two walls (illustrated below). The force (F) applied by each spring to the adjacent springs is of the form

$$F = k(x - x_0)$$

k is the spring constant and x_0 is the unstretched length of the spring.

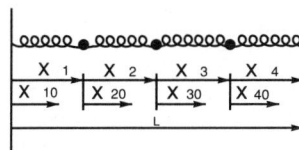

At equilibrium, all the forces are equal, and the system can be described by the following equations.

$$k_1(x_1 - x_{10}) = k_2(x_2 - x_{20})$$
$$k_2(x_2 - x_{20}) = k_3(x_3 - x_{30})$$
$$k_3(x_3 - x_{30}) = k_4(x_4 - x_{40})$$
$$x_1 + x_2 + x_3 + x_4 = L$$

Given that:

$$k_1 = 10\ \text{Nt/m}$$
$$k_2 = 20\ \text{Nt/m}$$
$$k_3 = 30\ \text{Nt/m}$$
$$k_4 = 40\ \text{Nt/m}$$
$$x_{10} = x_{20} = x_{30} = x_{40} = 10\ \text{cm}$$
$$L = 80\ \text{cm}$$

find x_1, x_2, x_3, and x_4 using over/under relaxation.

9. Solve the following nonlinear equations for x and t using over/under relaxation.

$$x = ae^{-\alpha t}$$
$$x = b\sin(\theta t)$$
$$a = b = 2,\ \theta = 4,\ \alpha = 0.5$$

10. Solve the following nonlinear equations for θ, α, and β using over/under relaxation.

$$2\sin(\theta) + 3\cos(\alpha) + 9\cos(\beta) = 7.548$$
$$4\cos(\theta) + 4\cos(\alpha) + 2\sin(\beta) = 6.390$$
$$5\sin(\theta) + \sin(\alpha) + 2\sin(\beta) = 3.587$$

CHAPTER

ELEVEN

Solving Ordinary Differential Equations

11

Most people do not think of using a worksheet to solve differential equations. However, with a worksheet's dynamically linked cells and iterative capability, you can calculate the solutions of many differential equations. Two kinds of ordinary differential equations are readily solved on a worksheet: initial-value problems and boundary-value problems. The differential equations for these types of problems can be the same; the difference is in the boundary conditions available.

Solving Initial-Value Problems

Initial-value problems are those in which the known boundary conditions are all at one boundary of the problem. The goal is to integrate the differential equation from the known boundary to the unknown one. Differential equations with time derivatives are often of this type, where you know the value of the solution now (the known boundary) and need to integrate the differential equation for some time into the future (the unknown boundary). In this section, you will examine four of the most popular methods for solving these types of equations: Taylor series, Euler, modified Euler, and Runge-Kutta.

An Initial-Value, Ordinary Differential Equation   Consider the following first-order ordinary differential equation:

$$\left(1+x^2\right)^{1/2}\frac{du(x)}{dx}+u(x)=x \qquad x>0$$
$$u(0)=0$$

This is an initial-value problem because the boundary condition is known only at one location. Actually, first-order, ordinary differential equations with one variable should have only one boundary condition. If there were more than one boundary condition, the problem would be over-specified and possibly unsolvable. Second- and higher-order differential equations require more boundary conditions in order to be solved.

The problem is to calculate the value of u over the range $x = 0$ to 0.2. For this problem, I know that the analytical solution is

$$u(x) = \frac{1}{2}\left[x - \frac{\ln\left(x + \sqrt{1+x^2}\right)}{\left(x + \sqrt{1+x^2}\right)} \right]$$

which you will use to evaluate the effectiveness of the different solution methods. Figure 11.1 shows this solution over the range $x = 0$ to 0.2.

FIGURE 11.1:

Analytic solution to an initial-value problem

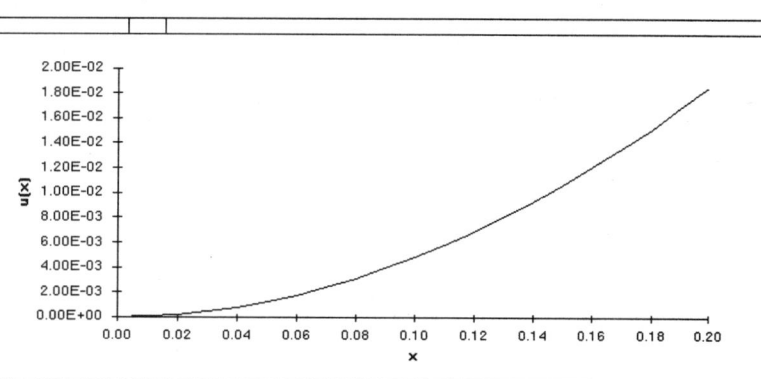

Using the Taylor Series Method

One of the more popular methods of solving an initial-value problem is the Taylor series method. Consider the Taylor series expansion of some function $u(x)$ about the value x_0:

$$u(x) = u(x_0) + \frac{(x - x_0)}{1!}u'(x_0) + \frac{(x - x_0)^2}{2!}u''(x_0)$$
$$+ \frac{(x - x_0)^3}{3!}u'''(x_0) + \frac{(x - x_0)^4}{4!}u''''(x_0) + \cdots$$

using the notation

$$u'(x) = \frac{du}{dx}, \quad u''(x) = \frac{d^2u(x)}{dx^2}, \cdots$$

Let $h = (x - x_0)$, and the equation becomes

$$u(x) = u(x_0) + \frac{h}{1!}u'(x_0) + \frac{h^2}{2!}u''(x_0)$$

$$+ \frac{h^3}{3!}u'''(x_0) + \frac{h^4}{4!}u''''(x_0) + \cdots$$

For $x_0 = 0$, the values of the first two terms of the Taylor series are known. You know the first from the boundary condition and the second from the differential equation. These values are

$$u(0) = 0$$

$$u'(x) = \frac{\left(x - u(x)\right)}{\left(1 + x^2\right)^{1/2}}$$

By successively taking derivatives of the equation for the first derivative, you get equations for the higher-order derivatives:

$$u''(x) = \frac{\left(x - u'(x)\right)}{\left(1 + x^2\right)^{1/2}} - \frac{x\left(x - u(x)\right)}{\left(1 + x^2\right)^{3/2}}$$

$$u'''(x) = -\frac{u''(x)}{\left(1 + x^2\right)^{1/2}} - \frac{2x\left(1 - u'(x)\right) + x - u(x)}{\left(1 + x^2\right)^{3/2}}$$

$$+ \frac{3x^2\left(x - u(x)\right)}{\left(1 + x^2\right)^{5/2}}$$

$$u''''(x) = -\frac{u'''(x)}{\left(1 + x^2\right)^{1/2}} - \frac{3xu''(x) - 3\left(1 - u'(x)\right)}{\left(1 + x^2\right)^{3/2}}$$

$$+ \frac{9x^2\left(1 - u'(x)\right) + 9x\left(x - u(x)\right)}{\left(1 + x^2\right)^{5/2}} + \frac{15x^2\left(x - u(x)\right)}{\left(1 + x^2\right)^{7/2}}$$

from which you get:

$u(0) = 0$

$u'(0) = 0$

$u''(0) = 1$

$u'''(0) = -1$

$u''''(0) = -2$

Insert these into the first five terms of the Taylor expansion, and then truncate the expansion after the fifth term. This creates the approximation function:

$$u(h) = \frac{h^2}{2} - \frac{h^3}{6} - \frac{h^4}{12}$$

which can be used to calculate values of the differential equation for different values of h, as long as h is small.

In this next example, use the Taylor series method to calculate the values of $u(x)$ for $x = 0$ to 0.2.

1. Start with a new worksheet expanded to full size.

2. Change the widths of columns A through D as follows:

    A = 7

    B = 12

    C = 11

    D = 11

3. In cell A1, type **Ordinary Differential Equations; Taylor series method**.

Enter the x range data and calculate the value of the analytic solution to the problem to use as a comparison.

4. In cell A3, type **x** and center it.

5. Type **0** in cell A5.

6. Type **0.01** in cell A6.

7. Select cells A5:A6 and drag the fill handle to cell A25.

8. Format cells A5:A25 as 0.00.

9. In cell B3, type **u(x)** and center it.

10. In cell B4, type **Analytical** and center it.

11. In cell B5, type

    =0.5*(A5−LN(A5+SQRT(1+A5^2))/(A5+SQRT(1+A5^2)))

    and copy it to cells B6:B25.

Use the Taylor series expansion to calculate the solution of the partial differential equation. Compare these values with the correct values in column B.

12. In cell C3, type **u(x)** and center it.

13. In cell C4, type **Taylor** and center it.

14. In cell C5, type

    =A5^2/2−A5^3/6−A5^4/12

    and copy it to cells C6:C25.

15. Format cells B5:C25 as 0.00E+00.

16. In cell D3, type **Error** and center it.

17. In cell D4, type **%** and center it.

18. In cell D6, type **=(B6−C6)/B6** and copy it to cells D7:D25.

19. Format cells D6:D25 as 0.00000%.

20. Save the worksheet if you want to keep it.

The worksheet should now look like Figure 11.2. Note that the solution is extremely accurate for these small values of x. If you try larger values of x (say 0 to 2) the error will be quite large. You must use values of h (x in this case, since $x_0 = 0$) that are less than 1 for this method to be accurate.

Note that for the Taylor series method, h is measured from x_0 and is not the step size that will be used in the rest of these problems. To calculate values of u over longer

FIGURE 11.2:

Solution of an initial-value problem using the Taylor series method

	A	B	C	D	E	F	G	H	
1	Ordinary Differential Equations; Taylor series method								
2									
3	x	u(x)	u(x)	Error					
4		Analytical	Taylor	%					
5	0.00	0.00E+00	0.00E+00						
6	0.01	4.98E-05	4.98E-05	0.00001%					
7	0.02	1.99E-04	1.99E-04	0.00011%					
8	0.03	4.45E-04	4.45E-04	0.00037%					
9	0.04	7.89E-04	7.89E-04	0.00088%					
10	0.05	1.23E-03	1.23E-03	0.00174%					
11	0.06	1.76E-03	1.76E-03	0.00303%					
12	0.07	2.39E-03	2.39E-03	0.00486%					
13	0.08	3.11E-03	3.11E-03	0.00731%					
14	0.09	3.92E-03	3.92E-03	0.01049%					
15	0.10	4.83E-03	4.83E-03	0.01451%					
16	0.11	5.82E-03	5.82E-03	0.01946%					
17	0.12	6.90E-03	6.89E-03	0.02547%					
18	0.13	8.06E-03	8.06E-03	0.03263%					

distances, you must recalculate the values of the derivatives at the end of the current step so that you can take another step beyond that point.

Using the Euler and Modified Euler Methods

One of the major difficulties with the Taylor series method is that you must analytically calculate several derivatives of your equation. Some equations may have simple derivatives, but others, such as the one used in the example, do not. The Euler method eliminates calculating these derivatives by truncating the Taylor series at the first derivative term. To make it work, you must use small steps (h) and recalculate the value of the first derivative at each step:

$$u(x+h) = u(x) + hu'(x)$$

Create a worksheet to calculate the differential equation using the Euler method. You can use the worksheet that you set up for the Taylor series example, because the layouts are similar.

1. Start with a new worksheet expanded to full size (or a copy of the previous worksheet).

2. Change the widths of columns A:F as follows:

   A = 7   B = 12

   C = 11   D = 11

   E = 11   F = 9

3. In cell A1, type **Ordinary Differential Equation; Euler and modified Euler methods**.

Put in the x range of data and calculate the value of the analytic solution to the problem to use as a comparison. These two columns are identical to those from the Taylor series problem, so you can reuse part of that worksheet.

4. In cell A3, type **x** and center it.

5. Type **0** in cell A5.

6. Type **0.01** in cell A6.

7. Select cells A5:A6 and drag the fill handle to cell A25.

8. Format cells A5:A25 as 0.00.

9. In cell B3, type **u(x)** and center it.

10. In cell B4, type **Analytical** and center it.

11. In cell B5, type

$$=0.5*(A5-LN(A5+SQRT(1+A5\wedge2))/(A5+SQRT(1+A5\wedge2)))$$

and copy it to cells B6:B25.

Calculate the solution of the equation using the Euler method.

12. In cell C4, type **Euler** and center it.

13. Type **0** in cell C5.

14. In cell C6, type

$$=C5+(A6-A5)*(A5-C5)/SQRT(1+A5\wedge2)$$

and copy it to cells C7:C25.

15. Format cells B5:C25 as 0.00E+00.

Your worksheet should now look like Figure 11.3. As you can see, this method is not very accurate.

Since you are using the slope (the derivative) at the beginning of a step to determine the value at the end of the step, the method will be in error every time, and the error

FIGURE 11.3:

Solution to the initial-value problem using the Euler method

	A	B	C	D	E	F	G	H	
			H33						
1	Ordinary Differential Equations; Euler and modified Euler methods								
2									
3	x	u(x)							
4		Analytical	Euler						
5	0.00	0.00E+00	0.00E+00						
6	0.01	4.98E-05	0.00E+00						
7	0.02	1.99E-04	1.00E-04						
8	0.03	4.45E-04	2.99E-04						
9	0.04	7.89E-04	5.96E-04						
10	0.05	1.23E-03	9.90E-04						
11	0.06	1.76E-03	1.48E-03						
12	0.07	2.39E-03	2.06E-03						
13	0.08	3.11E-03	2.74E-03						
14	0.09	3.92E-03	3.51E-03						
15	0.10	4.83E-03	4.37E-03						
16	0.11	5.82E-03	5.32E-03						
17	0.12	6.90E-03	6.36E-03						
18	0.13	8.06E-03	7.49E-03						

is additive and grows as you integrate farther. A better way to estimate the value of the next point is to use the average slope over a step:

$$u(x+h) = u(x) + h\frac{(u'(x) + u'(x+h))}{2}$$

The difficulty with this approach is that you do not know the value of the slope at the end of the step. The modified Euler method uses the Euler method to make an initial estimate of the solution. This initial estimate is then used to calculate the value of the slope at the end of the step. Using the average value of the slopes, you can calculate a better value for the solution. You could apply this method again to try to improve the solution, but when you use more than one or two iterations, the error in the method is as large as any increase in accuracy gained by iteration.

Now recalculate the worksheet using the modified Euler method. First calculate the initial prediction of the solution using the Euler method.

16. In cell D3, type **Modified Euler**.

17. Select cells D3:E3 and click on the center across columns tool on the toolbar (the icon looks like an *a* with arrows pointing right and left from it).

18. In cell D4, type **Predicted** and center it.

19. In cell D6, type

=E5+(A6−A5)*(A5−E5)/SQRT(1+A5^2)

and copy it to cells D7:D25.

Use that initial prediction to calculate the average slope and to calculate a corrected value of the solution. Compare that value to the analytic solution.

20. In cell E4, type **Corrected** and center it.

21. Type **0** in cell E5.

22. In cell E6, type

   =E5+((A6−A5)/2)*((A5−E5)/SQRT(1+A5^2)+(A6−C6)/SQRT(1+A6^2))

   and copy it to cells E7:E25.

23. Format cells D5:E25 as 0.00E+00.

24. In cell F3, type **Error** and center it.

25. In cell F4, type **%** and center it.

26. In cell F6, type **=(B6−E6)/B6** and copy it to cells F5:F25.

27. Format cells F6:F25 as 0.00%.

28. Save the problem if you want to keep a copy.

Your worksheet should now look like Figure 11.4. Note that the solution has improved tremendously, with the error staying around ¼ percent. You can use this method to calculate the value of the solution to large values of x, as long as you take small steps to get there.

FIGURE 11.4:

Solution to an initial-value problem using the Euler and modified Euler methods

	A	B	C	D	E	F	G	H
1	Ordinary Differential Equations; Euler and modified Euler methods							
2								
3	x	u(x)		Modified Euler		Error		
4		Analytical	Euler	Predicted	Corrected	%		
5	0.00	0.00E+00	0.00E+00		0.00E+00			
6	0.01	4.98E-05	0.00E+00	0.00E+00	5.00E-05	-0.33%		
7	0.02	1.99E-04	1.00E-04	1.49E-04	1.99E-04	-0.29%		
8	0.03	4.45E-04	2.99E-04	3.97E-04	4.47E-04	-0.27%		
9	0.04	7.89E-04	5.96E-04	7.42E-04	7.91E-04	-0.26%		
10	0.05	1.23E-03	9.90E-04	1.18E-03	1.23E-03	-0.26%		
11	0.06	1.76E-03	1.48E-03	1.72E-03	1.77E-03	-0.25%		
12	0.07	2.39E-03	2.06E-03	2.35E-03	2.40E-03	-0.25%		
13	0.08	3.11E-03	2.74E-03	3.07E-03	3.12E-03	-0.25%		
14	0.09	3.92E-03	3.51E-03	3.89E-03	3.93E-03	-0.25%		
15	0.10	4.83E-03	4.37E-03	4.79E-03	4.84E-03	-0.24%		
16	0.11	5.82E-03	5.32E-03	5.78E-03	5.83E-03	-0.24%		
17	0.12	6.90E-03	6.36E-03	6.87E-03	6.91E-03	-0.24%		
18	0.13	8.06E-03	7.49E-03	8.04E-03	8.08E-03	-0.24%		

Using the Runge-Kutta Method

The current method of choice for most initial-value problems is the fourth-order Runge-Kutta method. This method uses a combination of four estimators of the solution to calculate an accurate value of the solution. Refer to a book on numerical methods if you are interested in the background of this method.

The development of a step with the Runge-Kutta method goes as follows:

$$u(x+h) = u(x) + \tfrac{1}{6}\left(k_1 + 2k_2 + 2k_3 + k_4\right)$$

where

$$k_1 = hu'(x, u(x))$$
$$k_2 = hu'(x + \frac{h}{2}, u(x) + \frac{k_1}{2})$$
$$k_3 = hu'(x + \frac{h}{2}, u(x) + \frac{k_2}{2})$$
$$k_4 = hu'(x + h, u(x) + k_3)$$

Here $u'(x, u(x))$ is the first derivative of $u(x)$ with respect to x, which is a function of x and $u(x)$.

Now recalculate the worksheet using the Runge-Kutta method. This problem uses the same differential equation and setup as the two previous examples.

1. Start with a new worksheet expanded to full size (or a copy of the previous worksheet).

2. Change the widths of columns A through H as follows:

   A = 7   B = 11
   C = 10   D = 10
   E = 10   F = 10
   G = 10   H = 11

3. In cell A1, type **Ordinary Differential Equations; Runge-Kutta method**.

Enter the x range of data and calculate the value of the analytic solution to the problem to use as a comparison. These two columns are identical to those in the Taylor series and the Euler method problems, so you can reuse that part of either of those worksheets.

4. In cell A3, type **x** and center it.

5. Type **0** in cell A5.

6. Type **0.01** in cell A6.

7. Select cells A5:A6 and drag the fill handle to cell A25.

8. Format cells A5:A25 as 0.00.

9. In cell B3, type **u(x)** and center it.

10. In cell B4, type **Analytical** and center it.

11. In cell B5, type

    =0.5*(A5−LN(A5+SQRT(1+A5^2))/(A5+SQRT(1+A5^2)))

    and copy it to cells B6:B25.

Calculate the values of the four estimators. These estimators will be used to advance to the next step.

12. In cell C3, type **k1** and center it.

13. In cell C6, type

    =(A6−A5)*(A5−G5)/SQRT(1+A5^2)

    and copy it to cells C7:C25.

14. In cell D3, type **k2** and center it.

15. In cell D6, type

    =(A6−A5)*((A5+(A6−A5)/2)−(G5+C5/2))/SQRT(1+(A5+(A6−A5)/2)^2)

    and copy it to cells D7:D25.

16. In cell E3, type **k3** and center it.

17. In cell E6, type

    =(A6−A5)*((A5+(A6−A5)/2)−(G5+D5/2))/SQRT(1+(A5+(A6−A5)/2)^2)

and copy it to cells E6:E24.

18. In cell F3, type **k4** and center it.

19. In cell F6, type

    =(A6−A5)*(A6−(G5+E5))/SQRT(1+A6^2)

and copy it to cells F7:F25.

Calculate the solution of the problem by combining the values of the estimators. Compare the solution to the analytic result.

20. In cell G3, type **u(x)** and center it.

21. Type **0** in cell G5.

22. In cell G6, type

    =G5+(1/6)*(C6+2*D6+2*E6+F6)

and copy it to cells G7:G25.

23. Format cells B5:G25 as 0.00E+00.

24. In cell H3, type **Error** and center it.

25. In cell H4, type % and center it.

26. In cell H6, type **=(B6-G6)/B6** and copy it to cells H7:H25.

27. Format cells H6:H25 as 0.0E+00%.

Your worksheet should look like Figure 11.5. Now you see some real improvement in the accuracy of the solution. Although this method takes up five columns of the worksheet, the largest error is -1.3×10^{-6} percent. This is several orders of magnitude better than any of the other methods.

Solving Higher-Order Equations

Boundary-value problems are not always first-order differential equations; often they are second- or third-order equations. To solve these higher-order equations,

FIGURE 11.5:

Solving an initial-value problem using the Runge-Kutta method

	A	B	C	D	E	F	G	H	
								H32	
1	Ordinary Differential Equations; Runge-Kutta method								
2									
3	x	u(x)	k1	k2	k3	k4	u(x)	Error	
4		Analytical						%	
5	0.00	0.00E+00					0.00E+00		
6	0.01	4.98E-05	0.00E+00	5.00E-05	4.97E-05	9.95E-05	4.98E-05	-1.3E-06%	
7	0.02	1.99E-04	9.95E-05	1.49E-04	1.49E-04	1.98E-04	1.99E-04	-6.3E-07%	
8	0.03	4.45E-04	1.98E-04	2.47E-04	2.47E-04	2.95E-04	4.45E-04	-4.2E-07%	
9	0.04	7.89E-04	2.95E-04	3.44E-04	3.44E-04	3.92E-04	7.89E-04	-3.1E-07%	
10	0.05	1.23E-03	3.92E-04	4.40E-04	4.39E-04	4.87E-04	1.23E-03	-2.5E-07%	
11	0.06	1.76E-03	4.87E-04	5.34E-04	5.34E-04	5.81E-04	1.76E-03	-2.1E-07%	
12	0.07	2.39E-03	5.81E-04	6.28E-04	6.28E-04	6.74E-04	2.39E-03	-1.8E-07%	
13	0.08	3.11E-03	6.74E-04	7.21E-04	7.20E-04	7.66E-04	3.11E-03	-1.5E-07%	
14	0.09	3.92E-03	7.66E-04	8.12E-04	8.12E-04	8.57E-04	3.92E-03	-1.4E-07%	
15	0.10	4.83E-03	8.57E-04	9.02E-04	9.02E-04	9.47E-04	4.83E-03	-1.2E-07%	
16	0.11	5.82E-03	9.47E-04	9.92E-04	9.91E-04	1.04E-03	5.82E-03	-1.1E-07%	
17	0.12	6.90E-03	1.04E-03	1.08E-03	1.08E-03	1.12E-03	6.90E-03	-1.0E-07%	
18	0.13	8.06E-03	1.12E-03	1.17E-03	1.17E-03	1.21E-03	8.06E-03	-9.4E-08%	

divide them into two or more simultaneous differential equations by substituting new variables for the derivatives. For example, consider this equation:

$$au'' + bu' + cu + d = 0$$

Make the substitution $y = u'$, and you have two simultaneous first-order differential equations:

$$u' - y = 0$$
$$ay' + by + cu + d = 0$$

To solve these equations, use the methods described earlier for solving a single equation. For each step, calculate the solutions for both equations independently using the single-equation methods. At the end of each step, you have solutions for both equations. Use those solutions to calculate the solutions at the end of the next step.

Solving Boundary-Value Problems

Boundary-value problems make up a second class of ordinary differential equations. While initial-value problems have all the boundary conditions located at one side of the solution space, boundary-value problems have part of the boundary conditions on one side and the rest on the other. Thus, they must satisfy boundary conditions at both boundaries of the problem rather than just one.

Two well-known methods for solving boundary-value problems are the shooting method and the finite-difference method.

Using the Shooting Method

The shooting method solves boundary-value problems using the methods used to solve initial-value problems. You guess values for the unknown boundary conditions at one of the boundaries (side 1) to change the problem into an initial-value problem. Then you integrate the equations from side 1 to the other side (side 2) with, for example, the modified Euler method. When you have completed the solution, compare the boundary values you calculated at side 2 with those required by the boundary conditions. If they are the same, you have solved the problem; otherwise, you need to change your guess at the unknown boundary values on side 1 and integrate the problem again. Thus, you are shooting at the boundary values on side 2 of the solution space by guessing values of the boundary conditions on side 1.

For example, to solve a second-order differential equation, you need two boundary conditions. If this were an initial-value problem, you would be given the value of the solution and its derivative at one of the boundaries. For a typical boundary-value problem, you would be given only the value of the solution at both sides of the solution space. To integrate this solution to the other side of the solution space using the initial-value problem methods, you need an estimate of the derivative of the solution at one boundary as well. Given that value, you could integrate the solution to the other boundary, and then compare the value of your solution with the required value from the boundary condition. If they are the same, you are finished; otherwise, you must try a different estimate of the value of the derivative of the solution. Continue this process until you find the value on the boundary.

Bending of a Uniformly Loaded Beam   If you simply support a beam at both ends, as shown in Figure 11.6, it will sag slightly under its own weight. The amount of that sag can be calculated using this differential equation:

$$\frac{d^2 y}{dx^2} = -\frac{m}{EI}$$

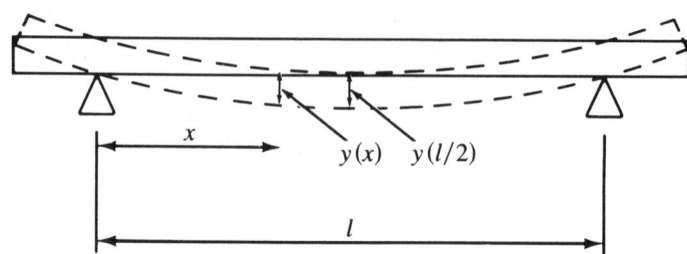

Here, y is the displacement or sag at the point x, I is the moment of inertia, E is the modulus of elasticity (30×10^6 psi for steel), and m is the bending moment. For a beam with a constant cross section, m is equal to

$$m = \frac{w}{2} x(l - x)$$

where w is the weight per unit length and l is the length. Calculate the sag in a 50-foot piece of an 8-WF-67, steel beam, an 8-inch wide-flange section (a wide I-beam) that weighs 67 pounds per foot. For the orientation with the flange horizontal, the moment of inertia is $I = 271.8$ in^4. For small displacements, the analytic solution of this differential equation is

$$y = \frac{wx}{24EI}\left(l^3 - 2lx^2 + x^3\right)$$

with the maximum displacement at the center:

$$y(l/2) = \frac{5wl^4}{384EI}$$

This differential equation has two boundary conditions, one at each end of the beam where it is supported:

$$y(0) = 0$$

$$y(l) = 0$$

To solve it using initial-value problem methods, you need the value and the derivative at one side. You must estimate the value of the derivative at $x = 0$, solve the problem, and then see if $y(l) = 0$. If it does not, pick another value for the derivative at $x = 0$. Note that you could also integrate this problem from $x = l$ to $x = 0$ and get the same results.

Solve this problem using the modified Euler method. First split the second-order equation into two first-order differential equations by substituting a variable u for one of the derivatives:

$$y'(x) = u(x)$$

$$u'(x) = -\frac{m}{EI}$$

Normally, using the modified Euler method, you would first calculate the solutions using the standard Euler method with

$$u(x+h) = u(x) + hu'(x)$$
$$y(x+h) = y(x) + hy'(x)$$

and then refine the values using

$$u(x+h) = u(x) + h\frac{(u'(x) + u'(x+h))}{2}$$

$$y(x+h) = y(x) + h\frac{(y'(x) + y'(x+h))}{2}$$

However, in this case, you can go directly to the final step since you know the exact value of $u'(x+h)$ from the differential equation. Create a worksheet to solve these equations, given an initial estimate of the value of $u(0)$.

1. Start with a new worksheet expanded to full size.

2. Change the width of column F to 13.

3. In cell A1, type **Deflection of a Beam; Boundary-value problem; Shooting Method**.

Create a table containing the beam parameters. The weight of the bar in cell B5 is 67 pounds per foot. To convert this to pounds per inch, divide by 12. Include the length in cell B8. To convert it to inches, multiply by 12.

4. In cell A4, type **8-WF-67 Beam parameters**.

5. In cell A5, type **w** and right-justify it.

6. Type **=67/12** in cell B5.

7. In cell C5, type **lb/in**.

8. In cell A6, type **I** and right-justify it.

9. Type **271.8** in cell B6.

10. In cell C6, type **in^4**.

11. In cell A7, type **E** and right-justify it.

12. Type **3.0E7** in cell B7.

13. In cell C7, type **psi**.

14. In cell A8, type **l** and right-justify it.

15. Type **=50*12** in cell B8.

16. In cell C8, type **in**.

17. Select cells A5:B8 and choose the Create Names command on the Formula menu. Make sure Left Column is selected and click on OK.

18. Format cell B7 as 0.00E+00.

Since you know the analytic solution of this equation, create a second table to show the analytic solution for some value of x (72 inches) and for the maximum deflection at $x = l/2$.

19. In cell E3, type **Analytic solution**.

20. In cell E4, type **x** and right-justify it.

21. Type **72** in cell F4.

22. In cell G4, type **in**.

23. Name cell F4 as **X**.

24. In cell E5, type **y** and right-justify it.

25. In cell F5, type

    =(W*X/(24*E*I))*(L^3-2*L*X^2+X^3)

26. In cell G5, type **in**.

27. In cell E6, type **y(l/2)** and right-justify it.

28. In cell F6, type

    =5*W*L^4/(384*E*I)

29. In cell G6, type **in**.

30. Format cells F5 and F6 as 0.00000.

Span the solution space, from 0 to 600 inches, with a grid of x values spaced every 12 inches.

31. In cell A10, type **x** and center it.

32. In cell A11, type **(in)** and center it.

33. Type **0** in cell A12.

34. Type **12** in cell A13.

35. Select cells A12:A13 and drag the fill handle down to cell A62.

Calculate the derivative of u for all values of x. You can get this directly from the differential equation.

36. In cell B10, type **u'(x)** and center it.

37. In cell B11, type **(1/in)** and center it.

38. In cell B12, type

    =-W*A12*(L-A12)/(2*E*I)

    and copy it to cells B13:B62.

39. Format cells B12:B62 as 0.0E+00.

Calculate the value of $u(x)$ at each step, using the average value of its derivative in the step interval between the values of x. The first value of u is the missing boundary condition. It references cell F9, where you will input your guesses.

40. In cell C10, type **u(x)** and center it.

41. In cell C11, type **(in/in)** and center it.

42. Type **=F9** in cell C12.

43. In cell C13, type

    =C12+(A13−A12)*(B12+B13)/2

    and copy it to cells C14:C62.

Calculate the value of y at each step, using the average value of $u(x)$ in the interval between the values of x. Set the first value of y to 0, which is the known boundary condition at this side of the solution space.

44. In cell D10, type **y(x)** and center it.

45. In cell D11, type **(in)** and center it.

46. Type **0** in cell D12.

47. In cell D13, type

    =D12+(A13−A12)*(C12+C13)/2

    and copy it to cells D14:D62.

Create a table to summarize the numerical results, with the value of y at $x = l$ and $x = l/2$. This is also the place where you will input your guesses for the value of $u(0)$. The value shown in cell F9 causes the value of $y(l)$ to equal 0 to four decimal places (it took me about 5 minutes to find that value).

48. In cell E8, type **Numerical solution**.

49. In cell E9, type **u(0)** and right-justify it.

50. Type **0.01** in cell F9.

51. In cell G9, type **in/in**.

52. In cell E10, type **y(l/2)** and right-justify it.

53. Type **=D37** in cell F10.

54. Type **in** in cell G10.

55. In cell E11, type **y(l)** and right-justify it.

56. Type **=D62** in cell F11.

57. In cell G11, type **in**.

58. Format cells F10 and F11 as 0.00000.

To use this worksheet, put a guess for the value of $u(0)$ into cell F9. After the worksheet recalculates, check the value of $y(l)$ that is repeated in cell F11 to see if it is 0. If it is not 0, try a different value for $u(0)$. Continue changing the value of $u(0)$ until you get $y(l)$ equal to 0 to as many decimal places as you need. When you have completed this process, the worksheet should look like Figure 11.7.

Compare the analytic values of the solution in cells F5 and F6 with the numerical solutions in cells D18 and F10, respectively. Note that even though you have hit the boundary value to four places of accuracy, the rest of the solution values have only about three places of accuracy. This loss of accuracy is due to the inherent accuracy of the method. Since the accuracy is proportional to the spacing between the grid points, decreasing this spacing increases the accuracy, until round-off error becomes significant.

FIGURE 11.7:

Bending of a simply supported beam under its own weight: boundary-value problem solved using the shooting method

	A	B	C	D	E	F	G	H	I
1	Deflection of a Beam; Boundary Value Problem; Shooting Method								
2									
3					Analytic solution				
4	8-WF-67 Beam parameters				x	72	in		
5		w	5.58333	lb/in		y	0.43170	in	
6		I	271.8	in^4		y(l/2)	1.15549	in	
7		E	3.00E+07	psi					
8		l	600	in		Numerical solution			
9						u(0)	0.00616015	in/in	
10		x	u'(x)	u(x)	y(x)	y(l/2)	1.15475	in	
11		(in)	(1/in)	(in/in)	(in)	y(l)	0.00000	in	
12		0	0.0E+00	0.00616	0				
13		12	-2.4E-06	0.00615	0.07383				
14		24	-4.7E-06	0.0061	0.14733				
15		36	-7.0E-06	0.00603	0.22014				
16		48	-9.1E-06	0.00594	0.29195				
17		60	-1.1E-05	0.00582	0.36247				
18		72	-1.3E-05	0.00567	0.43138				

Using the Finite-Difference Method

Another way to solve this problem is to write the derivatives in the differential equation as central differences. You used this method in Chapter 8 to calculate derivatives. By centering each of these differences on the grid points, you get a set of coupled equations that must be solved simultaneously. Use the following substitutions for the first and second derivatives:

$$\frac{du}{dx} = \frac{u(x+h) - u(x-h)}{2h}$$

$$\frac{d^2u}{dx^2} = \frac{u(x+h) - 2u(x) + u(x-h)}{h^2}$$

Rewrite the second derivative in the differential equation problem using the central difference substitutions:

$$\frac{y(x+h) - 2y(x) + y(x-h)}{h^2} = -\frac{m}{EI}$$

You will have one of these equations for each of the grid points except for the two at the boundaries, where the values of y are fixed by the boundary conditions.

Three methods that work well in a worksheet to solve a problem in this form are iterative, iterative with acceleration, and matrix.

Iterated Finite Differences

The iterative method is a form of the successive approximations method, which was discussed in Chapters 9 and 10. Solve the difference equation for the differential equation problem for $y(x)$:

$$y(x) = \frac{1}{2}\left[y(x+h) + y(x-h) + h^2 \frac{m}{EI} \right]$$

Use this equation for all the interior points of the problem, and use

$$y(0) = 0$$

$$y(l) = 0$$

at the endpoints. Create a worksheet to solve this problem using the iterative method. The first part of this worksheet is the same as the one you used for the shooting method example, so you can reuse part of that worksheet.

1. Start with a new worksheet expanded to full size (or a copy of the previous worksheet).

2. Switch to manual recalculation with the Calculation command on the Options menu.

3. Change the width of column F to 13.

4. In cell A1, type **Deflection of a Beam; Boundary-value problem; Finite Difference**.

Create the table containing the beam parameters.

5. In cell A4, type **8-WF-67 Beam parameters**.

6. Make the following entries in cells A5:C8:

A5: **w**	B5 **=67/12**	C5: **lb/in**
A6: **I**	B6: **271.8**	C6: **in^4**
A7: **E**	B7: **3.0E7**	C7: **psi**
A8: **l**	B8: **=50*12**	C8: **in**

7. Right-justify the contents of cells A5:A8.

8. Select cells A5:B8, choose the Create Names command on the Formula menu, make sure Left Column is selected, and click on OK.

9. Format cell B7 as 0.00E+00.

Create a second table to show the analytic solution for some value of x (72 inches) and for the maximum deflection at $x = l/2$.

10. In cell E3, type **Analytic solution**.

11. In cell E4, type **x** and right-justify it.

12. Type **72** in cell F4.

13. In cell G4, type **in**.

14. Name cell F4 as **X**.

15. In cell E5, type **y** and right-justify it.

16. In cell F5, type

$$=(W*X/(24*E*I))*(L^3-2*L*X^2+X^3)$$

17. In cell G5, type **in**.

18. In cell E6, type **y(l/2)** and right-justify it.

19. In cell F6, type

$$=5*W*L^4/(384*E*I)$$

20. Type **in** in cell G6.

21. Format cells F6 and F7 as 0.00000.

Span the solution space, from 0 to 600 inches, with a grid of *x* values spaced every 12 inches.

22. In cell A10, type **x** and center it.

23. In cell A11, type **(in)** and center it.

24. Type **0** in cell A12 and **12** in cell A13.

25. Select cells A12:A13 and drag the fill handle down to cell A62.

Put in the initialization flag so that you can reset the values in the worksheet to a known value.

26. In cell A3, type **Init Flag**.

27. Type **0** in cell B3 and **0** in cell C3.

28. Name cells B3 and C3 as **INIT** and **INIT_VAL**, respectively.

Put in the difference equation, and then enter the boundary values in the first and last cells of the range (B12 and B62). Test the initialization flag to see if the problem needs to be reset.

29. In cell B10, type **y(x)** and center it.

30. In cell B11, type **(in)** and center it.

31. Type **0** in cell B12.

32. In cell B13, type

> =IF(INIT=0,INIT_VAL,0.5*(B14+B12+((A14-A12)/2)^2*W*A13*(L-A 13)/(2*E*I)))

and copy it to cells B14:B61.

33. Type **0** in cell B62.

34. Format cells B12:B62 as 0.00000.

Copy the maximum value of y from cell B37 to the top of the worksheet to compare with the analytic value.

35. In cell E8, type **Numerical solution**.

36. In cell E9, type **y(l/2)** and right-justify it.

37. Type **=B37** In cell F9.

38. In cell G9, type **in**.

39. Format cell F9 as 0.00000.

Turn on iteration and set it to continue iterating until the changes in the values on the worksheet get smaller than 10^{-6}.

40. Choose the Calculation command on the Options menu. In dialog box, click on Iteration, set Maximum Iterations to **10000**, set Maximum Change to **1E-6**, and click on OK.

41. Save the worksheet if you want to keep a copy.

42. To use this worksheet, set the value of the initialization flag (in cell B3) to **0** and press F9 or Ctrl-= (Cmd-= on the Macintosh). After the calculation has been reset, change the initialization flag to **1**, and press F9 again to start the iteration process.

The worksheet will continue recalculating until the values change less than 10^{-6}, at which point you have the solution. This worksheet takes about 6½ minutes to converge on a 386SX-20 computer, so start it up and go have coffee. The worksheet should look like Figure 11.8 after it has converged.

Accelerated Finite Differences

A worksheet that converges as slowly as this one is just begging for some acceleration. You can use the over/under relaxation method here, just as you did in the previous chapter to speed the solution of systems of equations. Rewrite the difference equation so that you can control the amount of change in the solution at each iteration. Use the constant multiplier, Cf, to control the amount of that change:

$$y(x) = y(x) + Cf\left[\frac{1}{2}\left(y(x+h) + y(x-h) + h^2\frac{m}{EI}\right) - y(x)\right]$$

Enter this change into the existing worksheet. First enter the relaxation factor.

43. In cell A2, type **With Relaxation**.

44. In cell A9, type **Relax Fac**.

45. Type **1.9** in cell B9.

46. Name cell B9 as **Cf**.

FIGURE 11.8:

Bending of a beam; a boundary-value problem solved with iterated finite differences

	A	B	C	D	E	F	G	H	I
1	Deflection of a Beam; Boundary Value Problem; Finite Difference								
2									
3	Init Flag	1	0		Analytic solution				
4	8-WF-67 Beam parameters				x	72	in		
5		w	5.58333	lb/in		y	0.43170	in	
6		I	271.8	in^4		y(l/2)	1.15549	in	
7		E	3.00E+07	psi					
8		l	600	in		Numerical solution			
9						y(l/2)	1.15597	in	
10	x	y(x)							
11	(in)	(1/in)							
12	0	0.00000							
13	12	0.07393							
14	24	0.14751							
15	36	0.22041							
16	48	0.29231							
17	60	0.36290							
18	72	0.43189							

Change the difference formula to incorporate the relaxation factor to control the amount of change in the solution during each iteration. The value of the solution in the formula refers to the cell that contains the formula, creating a circular reference. You could also store the solution in a separate column and get the same effect.

47. In cell B13, type

=IF(INIT=0,INIT_VAL,(0.5*(B14+B12+((A14-A12)/2)^2*W*A13*(L-A13)/(2*E*I))-B13)*Cf+B13)

and copy it to cells B14:B61.

This worksheet operates in the same manner as the previous one. First, set the value of the initialization flag (B3) to 0 and press F9 or Ctrl-= (Cmd-= on the Macintosh). After the problem has reinitialized, change the value of the initialization flag to a 1 and press F9 again to start the worksheet calculating. This version of the worksheet converges in 26 seconds, nearly 1500 percent faster than with the other methods! The resulting worksheet is shown in Figure 11.9.

If you try to make the worksheet converge faster by using larger values of the relaxation factor, Cf, the worksheet diverges. With a relaxation factor of 2, the solution values get very large after a few iterations. If you have a solution that diverges, use a smaller acceleration factor. For problems that diverge with iterated finite differences, use an acceleration factor that is less than one (deceleration factor) to slow down the changes.

FIGURE 11.9:

Bending of a beam; a boundary-value problem solved with accelerated finite differences

	A	B	C	D	E	F	G	H	I
1	Deflection of a Beam; Boundary Value Problem; Finite Difference								
2	With Relaxation								
3	Init Flag	1	0		Analytic solution				
4	8-WF-67 Beam parameters								
5	w	5.58333	lb/in		x	72	in		
6	I	271.8	in^4		y	0.43170	in		
7	E	3.00E+07	psi		y(l/2)	1.15549	in		
8	l	600	in		Numerical solution				
9	Relax Fac	1.9			y(l/2)	1.15586	in		
10	x	y(x)							
11	(in)	(1/in)							
12	0	0.00000							
13	12	0.07392							
14	24	0.14749							
15	36	0.22039							
16	48	0.29228							
17	60	0.36286							
18	72	0.43185							

Using the Matrix Method

You can also use Excel's built-in matrix functions to solve a set of linear simultaneous equations. The only restriction is that there must be less than about 60 equations. Excel has no specified limit for matrix inversion, but the actual limit is around 60 x 60, depending on the amount of memory available and the contents of the matrix. If Excel can't solve the matrix because it is too large, the MINVERSE function returns #VALUE!.

For larger matrices, you need to use a macro program or an external application to do the inversions. You could write a matrix solver in Fortran and store it in a Dynamic Link Library (a CODE resource on the Macintosh). That solver could then be registered with Excel and called with the Call function.

To use the matrix solver, rewrite the difference equations as matrix equations. Rewrite the example differential equation

$$\frac{y(x+h) - 2y(x) + y(x-h)}{h^2} = -\frac{m}{EI}$$

as

$$y(x+h) - 2y(x) + y(x-h) = -h^2 \frac{m}{EI}$$

with the boundary conditions

$$y(0) = y(l) = 0$$

These can be easily rewritten into a matrix equation

Ax = b

$$
\begin{vmatrix}
1 & 0 & 0 & 0 & 0 & & . & . & . & \\
1 & -2 & 1 & 0 & 0 & & . & . & . & \\
0 & 1 & -2 & 1 & 0 & & . & . & . & \\
0 & 0 & 1 & -2 & 1 & & & & & \\
& & & & . & & & & & \\
& & & & & . & & & & \\
& & & . & . & . & 1 & -2 & 1 & 0 \\
& & & . & . & . & 0 & 1 & -2 & 1 \\
& & & . & . & . & 0 & 0 & 0 & 1 \\
\end{vmatrix}
\begin{vmatrix}
x_0 \\
x_1 \\
x_2 \\
x_3 \\
. \\
. \\
. \\
x_{n-2} \\
x_{n-1} \\
x_n
\end{vmatrix}
=
\begin{vmatrix}
b_0 \\
b_1 \\
b_2 \\
b_3 \\
. \\
. \\
. \\
b_{n-2} \\
b_{n-1} \\
b_n
\end{vmatrix}
$$

where

$$b_0 = b_n = 0$$

$$b_i = -h^2 \frac{m}{EI} \qquad i = 1, 2, 3, \cdots n-1$$

$$m_i = \frac{wx_i}{2}(l - x_i)$$

Once the equations are in this form, the solution is straightforward. Invert the matrix **A** and multiply that inverse by the vector **b** to get the solution vector **x**. Create a worksheet to solve this problem. The top part of this worksheet is the same as for the last example, so you can reuse that part and save some typing.

1. Start with a new worksheet expanded to full size (or a copy of the previous example).

2. Switch to manual recalculation with the Calculation command on the Options menu.

3. Change the width of column F to 13.

4. In cell A1, type **Deflection of a Beam; Boundary-value problem; Finite Difference**.

5. In cell A2, type **Matrix Method**.

Create the table containing the beam parameters.

6. In cell A4, type **8-WF-67 Beam parameters**.

7. Make the following entries in cells A5:B8:

A5: **w**	B5: **=67/12**	C5: **lb/in**
A6: **I**	B6: **271.8**	C6: **in^4**
A7: **E**	B7: **3.0E7**	C7: **psi**
A8: **l**	B8: **=50*12**	C8: **in**

8. Right-justify cells A5:A8.

9. Select cells A5:B8, choose the Create Names command on the Formula menu, make sure Left Column is selected, and click on OK.

10. Format cell B7 as 0.00E+00.

Create a second table to show the analytic solution for some value of x (72 inches) and for the maximum deflection at $x = l/2$.

11. In cell E3, type **Analytic solution**.

12. In cell E4, type **x** and right-justify it.

13. Type **72** in cell F4.

14. Type **in** in cell G4.

15. Name cell F4 as **X**.

16. In cell E5, type **y** and right-justify it.

17. In cell F5, type

   =(W*X/(24*E*I))*(L^3-2*L*X^2+X^3)

18. Type **in** in cell G5.

19. In cell E6, type **y(l/2)** and right-justify it.

20. In cell F6, type

   =5*W*L^4/(384*E*I)

21. Type **in** in cell G6.

22. Format cells F6 and F7 as 0.00000.

Span the solution space, from 0 to 600 inches, with a grid of x values spaced every 12 inches.

23. In cell A10, type **x** and center it.

24. In cell A11, type **(in)** and center it.

25. Type **0** in cell A12.

26. Type **12** in cell A13.

27. Select cells A12:A13 and drag the fill handle down to cell A62.

Mark a space for the solution vector.

28. In cell B10, type **y(x)** and center it.

29. In cell B11, type **(in)** and center it.

30. In cell C10, type **b** and center it.

Enter **b**, the right side of the matrix equation, including the boundary conditions.

31. Type **0** in cell C12.

32. In cell C13, type

   =(-(A13-A12)^2*W*A13*(L-A13)/(2*E*I))

   and copy it to cells C14:C61.

33. Type **0** in cell C62.

34. Name cells C12:C62 as B.

Mark and name the locations of the matrix **A** and its inverse **A**$^{-1}$.

35. In cell D11, type **A** and center it.

36. Select cells D12:BB62, name them **A**, and outline them.

37. In cell D65, type **AINV** and center it.

38. Select cells D66:BB116, name them **AINV**, and outline them.

Enter a small table to retrieve the value of the solution at the point of maximum deflection ($l/2$).

39. In cell E8, type **Numerical solution**.

40. In cell E9, type **y(l/2)** and right-justify it.

41. Type **=B37** in cell F9.

42. Format cell F9 as 0.00000.

43. Type **in** in cell G9.

The matrix contains mostly zeros, with ones and twos along the diagonal. Since you probably don't feel like typing in 2601 values, create a command macro to fill the matrix. Note that the external references contain only a !, without a worksheet sheet name. An external reference of this type always refers to the active worksheet (the topmost one), so make sure the worksheet is visible before activating the macro.

44. Open a new macro sheet.

45. In cell B1, type **Make A Matrix**.

46. With the Define Name command on the Formula menu, name cell B1 as **Make_A_Matrix** and make it a command macro.

First fill the whole matrix with zeros, then go back and fill in the values along the diagonal. The loop goes over all but the first and last rows of the matrix. The three FORMULA functions that follow insert the values 1, −2, and 1 along the diagonal. Following the loop are two more FORMULA functions that put a 1 in the first element of the first row and in the last element of the last row.

47. Type the following commands in cells B2:B10:

      B2: =FORMULA.FILL(0,!A)

      B3: =FOR("J",2,50,1)

      B4: =FORMULA(-2,INDEX(!A,J,J))

      B5: =FORMULA(1,INDEX(!A,J,J-1))

      B6: =FORMULA(1,INDEX(!A,J,J+1))

      B7: =NEXT()

      B8: =FORMULA(1,INDEX(!A,1,1))

      B9: =FORMULA(1,INDEX(!A,51,51))

    B10: =RETURN()

Run the macro to fill in the matrix. Make sure the worksheet is active before executing the macro.

48. Activate the worksheet by clicking on it, or by selecting it from the Window menu.

49. Select the Run command on the Macro menu and execute the Make_A_Matrix macro. Sit back for a moment while the macro fills in the 2601 elements of the matrix.

Invert the matrix in AINV.

50. Select the GoTo command on the Formula menu and select AINV.

51. In the top-left cell of the selection, type **=MINVERSE(A)** and press Ctrl-Shift-Enter (Cmd-Enter on the Macintosh) to insert it as an array in the whole selection.

You will need to wait several minutes for the inverse matrix to be calculated. If the calculation returns #VALUE! instead of numbers, you may have typed something wrong, or you may have hit Excel's limit on matrix size. If the matrix is too large, your only choice is to reduce the size of the matrix until it can be solved. You can do this by making the spacing between grid points wider, which reduces the total number of grid points.

Now multiply the inverse matrix by the vector **b**, in cells C12:C62, and store the result in cells B12:B62. This is the solution of the problem.

52. Select cells B12:B62. In the top cell of the selection, type **=MMULT(AINV,B)** and press Ctrl-Shift-Enter (Cmd-Enter on the Macintosh) to insert it as an array.

53. Format cells B12:C62 as 0.00000.

54. Save the worksheet and the macro sheet if you want to keep them.

The worksheet should now look like Figure 11.10, with the macro in Figure 11.11. To use the worksheet, make any changes in the input values and press F9 or Ctrl-= (Cmd-= on the Macintosh) to recalculate the matrix. It will take several minutes to calculate a solution. Most of that time is spent inverting the 51-by-51-element matrix. When the calculation is complete, the result will be in column B.

FIGURE 11.10:

Bending of a beam: a boundary-value problem solved with finite differences

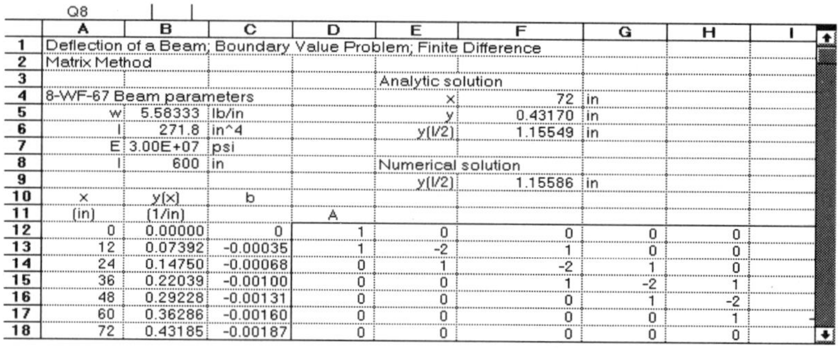

	A	B	C	D	E	F	G	H	I
1	Deflection of a Beam; Boundary Value Problem; Finite Difference								
2	Matrix Method								
3					Analytic solution				
4	8-WF-67 Beam parameters				x	72	in		
5	w	5.58333	lb/in		y	0.43170	in		
6	I	271.8	in^4		y(l/2)	1.15549	in		
7	E	3.00E+07	psi						
8	l	600	in		Numerical solution				
9					y(l/2)	1.15586	in		
10	x	y(x)	b						
11	(in)	(1/in)		A					
12	0	0.00000	0	1	0		0	0	0
13	12	0.07392	-0.00035	1	-2		1	0	0
14	24	0.14750	-0.00068	0	1		-2	1	0
15	36	0.22039	-0.00100	0	0		1	-2	1
16	48	0.29228	-0.00131	0	0		0	1	-2
17	60	0.36286	-0.00160	0	0		0	0	1
18	72	0.43185	-0.00187	0	0		0	0	0

FIGURE 11.11:

Bending of a beam: a macro program to implement a matrix solution of the finite-difference equations for the boundary-value problem

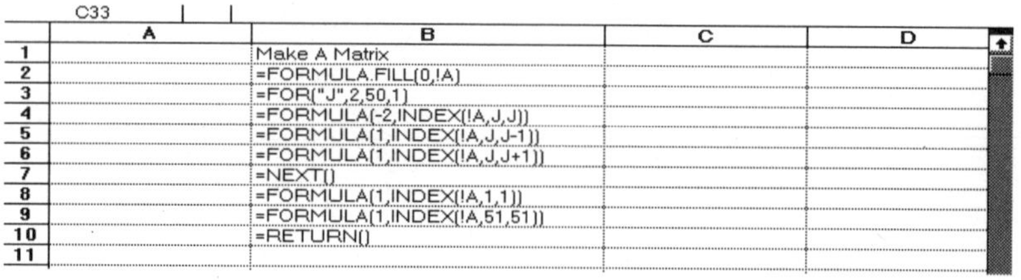

	A	B	C	D
1		Make A Matrix		
2		=FORMULA.FILL(0,!A)		
3		=FOR("J",2,50,1)		
4		=FORMULA(-2,INDEX(!A,J,J))		
5		=FORMULA(1,INDEX(!A,J,J-1))		
6		=FORMULA(1,INDEX(!A,J,J+1))		
7		=NEXT()		
8		=FORMULA(1,INDEX(!A,1,1))		
9		=FORMULA(1,INDEX(!A,51,51))		
10		=RETURN()		
11				

Handling Higher-Order Boundary Conditions

The problem you just solved had Dirichlet boundary conditions; that is, the value of the function was specified at the boundaries. The problem could just as easily have had Neumann boundary conditions, where the derivative of the function is specified on the boundaries. Or it could have had a mix of Dirichlet and Neumann boundary conditions, with the value of the function specified at one boundary and the derivative of the function specified at the other.

To handle these higher-order boundary conditions, put an extra grid point into the problem, just outside the boundary with the derivative boundary condition. Construct a central difference at the boundary using that extra point to set the value of the derivative. For example, in the previous problem, if the boundary condition at $x = 0$ was

$$y'(0) = 0.00616015$$

instead of

$$y(0) = 0$$

you would add another grid point at $x = -h$. Then write a first-order central difference at $x = 0$ and set it equal to 0.00616015.

$$\frac{y(h) - y(-h)}{2h} = 0.00616015$$

You would use this equation to define the value of the function at the extra grid point, $y(-h)$. At the actual boundary point, use the same difference equation that you used in the interior of the problem. Higher-order derivative boundary conditions are handled in the same manner—just insert the difference equation for the higher-order derivative. Alternatively, you could algebraically combine the equation above with the equation at the boundary, and achieve the same results without actually adding another grid point to the problem.

Bear in mind that problems with Neumann boundary conditions on all sides may not have unique solutions. If you can add an arbitrary constant to the function in the differential equation and not change the differential equation, a unique solution might not exist. This will happen when the function ($u(x)$) appears only in the derivatives of a differential equation.

The bending beam problem is just such an equation. If you were to add some value y_0 to the function $y(x)$, the differential equation would not change, because the derivative of a constant is zero. If there were no Dirichlet boundary conditions to fix the value of $y(x)$ at some point, the result would not be unique, and you could add any arbitrary amount to $y(x)$ and it would still be correct. Note that physically this amounts to raising or lowering the beam as a complete unit, which has no effect on the amount of bending. The beam bends the same amount whether it is in the basement or on the roof.

Summary

In this chapter, you have seen how a worksheet can be a medium for performing numerical solutions of ordinary differential equations. Initial-value problems can be solved on a worksheet using the Taylor series, the Euler or modified Euler, and the Runge-Kutta methods. Each of these methods has varying degrees of accuracy and difficulty to implement.

Boundary-value problems can be solved using the shooting method, where you pick values of the boundary condition on one side of the problem until you get the correct result on the other side. Boundary-value problems can also be rewritten using finite differences, and the resulting difference equations can be solved using iterative or matrix techniques.

Excel's Solver was not really designed to solve tens of simultaneous equations at one time, but with careful planning, you could probably solve these equations as you did the simultaneous equations in the previous chapter. The iterative methods are faster than the Solver when many equations are involved. However, future versions of the Solver may be able to handle these types of problems more efficiently.

For More Information

Bending and Stretching of Structural Materials

S. Timoshenko, D. H. Young, *Elements of Strength of Materials*, 5th. ed. (New York: D. Van Nostrand Co., 1968).

Numerical Methods for Solving Differential Equations

C. Gerald, *Applied Numerical Analysis*, 2nd. ed. (Reading, Mass.: Addison-Wesley, 1978).

W. H. Press, B. P. Flannery, S. A. Teukolsky, W. T. Vetterling, *Numerical Recipes; The Art of Scientific Computing* (Cambridge, Eng.: Cambridge University Press, 1986).

Problems

1. The charge (q) in a capacitor (C) being charged by a battery (V) in series with a resistor (R) follows the equation

$$\frac{\partial q}{\partial t} = \frac{V}{R} - \frac{q}{RC}$$

Given that $R = 1000$ ohms, $C = 10^{-5}$ f, $V = 10$ volts, and that at $t = 0, q = 0$, solve this equation using the Taylor series, Euler, and modified Euler methods for the interval $0 \leq t \leq 5 \times 10^{-2}$ s. Compare the result to the analytic solution:

$$q = CV\left(1 - e^{-\left(\frac{t}{RC}\right)}\right)$$

2. Complete problem 1 using the Runge-Kutta method for the discharging capacitor. Here, $V = 0$ and at $t = 0, q = 10^{-4}$ coul ($=CV$). Compare the result to the analytic solution:

$$q = CV e^{-\left(\frac{t}{RC}\right)}$$

3. An LCR oscillator circuit is described by the differential equation

$$L\frac{d^2q}{dt^2} + R\frac{dq}{dt} + \frac{q}{C} = 0$$

$L = 10^{-2}$ Henry, $C = 3\times10^{-6}$ farad, $R = 20$ ohms, and at $t = 0$, $q = 10^{-5}$ coul and $dq/dt = -0.01$ coul/s. Solve this equation for the interval $0 \le t \le 4\times10^{-3}$ s using the modified Euler method.

4. The motion of a simple harmonic oscillator is described by the equation

$$\frac{d^2x}{dt^2} = -\omega^2 x$$

At $t = 0$, $x = 0$ and $dx/dt = 1$. If $\theta = 6$, solve this equation over the interval $0 \le t \le 3$ using the modified Euler method.

5. The differential equation of the elastic line of a uniformly loaded cantilever beam is

$$\frac{d^2y}{dx^2} = \frac{wx^2}{2EI}$$

L is the length of the beam and x is measured from the free end of the beam. At $x = L$, $y = 0$ and $dy/dx = 0$. $E = 30\times10^6$ psi, $I = 271.8$ in^4, $w = 100$ lb/in, and $L = 10$ feet. Using the Euler method, solve for y for $0 \le x \le L$. Compare the result to the analytic solution:

$$y = \frac{w}{EI}\left(\frac{x^4}{24} - \frac{L^3x}{6} + \frac{L^4}{8}\right)$$

6. The growth rate of a colony of bacteria is described by the equation

$$\frac{dn}{dt} = kn$$

where n is the number of bacteria and k is the growth rate. If at $t = 0$ there are 10^4 bacteria and at $t = 10$ hours there are 4×10^4 bacteria, calculate k using the shooting method.

7. Given that $y(0) = 3$ and $y(1) = 7.49$, solve the following differential equation using the shooting method on the range $0 \le x \le 1$.

$$\frac{d^2 y}{dx^2} + \frac{dy}{dx} - 6y = 0$$

8. Given that $y(0) = 2$ and $y(1) = 5.288$, solve the following differential equation using the finite-difference method on the range $0 \le x \le 1$.

$$x\frac{d^2 y}{dx^2} - \frac{dy}{dx} + 4x^3 y = 0$$

Compare the result with the analytic solution:

$$y = 5\sin(x^2) + 2\cos(x^2)$$

9. Given that $y(-0.5) = 60.703$ and $y(0.5) = 9.1$, solve the following differential equation using the finite-difference method on the range $-0.5 \le x \le 0.5$.

$$\frac{d^2 y}{dx^2} + 2\frac{dy}{dx} - 18y = 0$$

10. The differential equation of the elastic line of a beam fixed at both ends and loaded at the center is

$$\frac{d^2 y}{dx^2} = \frac{wL}{2EI}\left(\frac{x}{L} - \frac{1}{4}\right) \qquad 0 < x < L/2$$

$$\frac{d^2 y}{dx^2} = \frac{wL}{2EI}\left(\frac{x}{L} - \frac{3}{4}\right) \qquad L/2 < x < L$$

L is the length of the beam, $y = 0$ at $x = 0$ and $x = L$, $E = 30 \times 10^6$ psi, $I = 271.8$ in^4, $w = 100$ lb, and $L = 200$ feet. Solve for y for $0 \leq x \leq L$ using the finite-difference method. Compare the result to the analytic solution:

$$y = \frac{wL}{2EI}\left(\frac{x^2}{8} - \frac{x^3}{6L}\right) \qquad 0 < x < L/2$$

CHAPTER

TWELVE

Solving Partial Differential Equations

Partial differential equations are part of many important science and engineering problems. Any problem involving a differential process with more than one independent variable must be described with partial differential equations rather than ordinary differential equations. For a second-order function (u) involving two independent variables (x,y), there are five possible differentials:

$$\frac{\partial u}{\partial x}, \frac{\partial^2 u}{\partial x^2}, \frac{\partial u}{\partial y}, \frac{\partial^2 u}{\partial y^2}, \frac{\partial^2 u}{\partial x \partial y}$$

These can be combined into a general partial differential equation:

$$A\frac{\partial^2 u}{\partial x^2} + B\frac{\partial^2 u}{\partial x \partial y} + C\frac{\partial^2 u}{\partial y^2} + D\frac{\partial u}{\partial x} + E\frac{\partial u}{\partial y} + F = 0$$

Each of the coefficients ($A - F$) can be functions of either of the two variables (x, y) or the function (u).

Types of Partial Differential Equations

The three categories of partial differential equations are elliptic, parabolic, and hyperbolic. The equations in these categories are distinguished by the relationships of the coefficients of the second-order terms. For example, for the second-order equation with two variables, the category is determined as follows:

- Elliptic: $B^2 - 4AC < 0$
- Parabolic: $B^2 - 4AC = 0$
- Hyperbolic: $B^2 - 4AC > 0$

The coefficients are functions of the independent variables and u, so a differential equation can move from one category to another as the variables change.

Solving Elliptic Partial Differential Equations

Elliptic partial differential equations usually arise from equilibrium problems. Poisson and Laplace equations are well-known examples of elliptic partial differential equations. In both of these equations, the coefficient of the cross term (B) is zero, which makes $B^2 - 4AC$ less than zero (assuming A and C are both positive or both negative).

You can solve elliptic partial differential equations in much the same manner as you solve iterated finite-difference problems involving ordinary differential equations, except that you must deal with at least a two-dimensional domain.

Poisson and Laplace Equations

Poisson and Laplace equations are generally used for scalar-field problems. For example, you can describe a steady-state electrostatic potential with the Poisson equation, which is written as

$$\nabla^2 \Phi = -q \frac{\rho}{\varepsilon}$$

where q is the electron charge, ρ is the charge density, and ε is the permittivity. Note that this equation uses the differential operator

$$\nabla \equiv \mathbf{i} \frac{\partial}{\partial x} + \mathbf{j} \frac{\partial}{\partial y} + \mathbf{k} \frac{\partial}{\partial z}$$

where $\mathbf{i}$, $\mathbf{j}$, and $\mathbf{k}$ are unit vectors in the x, y, and z directions. This is the definition of the differential operator in three-dimensional Cartesian coordinates. The definition differs for other coordinate systems. The square of the ∇ operator is the vector dot product of the operator on itself.

$$\nabla^2 = \nabla \cdot \nabla = \mathbf{i} \frac{\partial^2}{\partial x^2} + \mathbf{j} \frac{\partial^2}{\partial y^2} + \mathbf{k} \frac{\partial^2}{\partial z^2}$$

If no charges are present ($\rho = 0$), the Poisson equation reduces to the Laplace equation:

$$\nabla^2 \Phi = 0$$

Potential between Two Concentric Cylinders   Consider two long concentric cylinders of radii a and b in a vacuum, as illustrated in Figure 12.1. If you apply a voltage across them, the potential in the space between them is described with a two-dimensional Laplace equation.

FIGURE 12.1:

Concentric cylinders in a vacuum

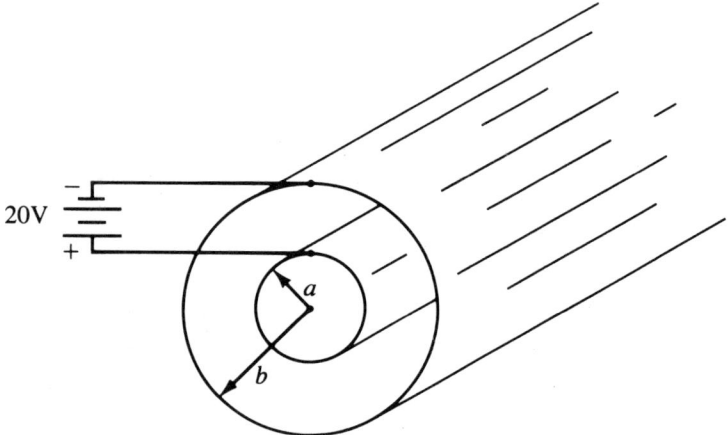

The outer conductor is grounded (0 volt) and the inner conductor is held at 20 volts. The inner diameter, a, is 5 cm, and the outer diameter, b, is 15 cm. To calculate the potential in the volume between them, you will use a two-dimensional Laplace equation. The two-dimensional domain is valid because the cylinders are infinitely long, which makes the variation of the potential in the direction parallel to the axes of the cylinders negligible:

$$\nabla^2 \Phi = \frac{\partial^2 \Phi}{\partial x^2} + \frac{\partial^2 \Phi}{\partial y^2} = 0$$

I solved this problem analytically, so that you can compare the analytical results to those that you calculate. The analytical solution for the potential at some distance r from the center of the cylinders is

$$\Phi(r) = \frac{\Phi_b \ln(r/a) - \Phi_a \ln(r/b)}{\ln(b/a)}$$

To solve the differential equation on a worksheet, replace the derivatives in the equation with central differences, centered on grid point (i,j). Assume that the grid spacing (h) is the same in both directions.

$$\frac{\Phi_{i+1,j} - 2\Phi_{i,j} + \Phi_{i-1,j}}{h^2} + \frac{\Phi_{i,j+1} - 2\Phi_{i,j} + \Phi_{i,j-1}}{h^2} = 0$$

Solve this equation for the term at the grid point $\Phi_{i,j}$:

$$\Phi_{i,j} = \left(\tfrac{1}{4}\right)\left(\Phi_{i+1,j} + \Phi_{i-1,j} + \Phi_{i,j+1} + \Phi_{i,j-1}\right)$$

The potential at any grid point is equal to the average of the potentials of the surrounding four grid points.

In the worksheet, the boundaries of the problem are set with the fixed or derivative values of the boundary conditions, and the interior points are set with the equation shown here.

You can model only a slice of the cylinder, because the solution is symmetrical about the axis of the cylinder. Model a 90-degree, pie-shaped slice of the cylinder; it is difficult to fix the boundary conditions for anything smaller. The boundary condition on the outer cylinder is fixed at 0 and that on the inner cylinder at 20. The boundary condition along the edges of the pie-shaped slice is that the derivative of the potential, perpendicular to the boundary, is zero.

1. Start with a new worksheet expanded to full size.

2. Select columns A through R and change the column width to 2.43.

3. Change the widths of columns S and T to 9.

4. Select rows 3 through 20 and change the height to 11.

5. Reduce the font size to 8 points using the Font command on the Format menu.

6. Choose the Calculation command on the Options menu and change Calculation to Manual, check Iteration, and set Maximum Iterations to **100**. Then click on OK.

7. In cell A1, type **Laplace equation between concentric cylinders; Elliptical PDE**.

Enter some arrows to locate the x- and y-axes.

8. In cell C5, type **x --->** and center it.

9. In cell B6, type **y** and center it.

10. In cells B7 and B8, type ¦ and center it.

11. In cell B9, type **+** and center it.

Create a table to contain the values of the potentials on the inner and outer cylinders.

12. In cell S9, type **Applied Potentials**.

13. Select cells S9 and T9 and click on the center across columns tool on the toolbar.

14. In cell S10, type **Inner** and center it.

15. Type **20** in cell T10.

16. In cell S11, type **Outer** and center it.

17. Type **0** in cell T11.

18. Name cells T10 and T11 as **Inner** and **Outer**, respectively.

Enter the outer and inner boundary conditions, along the edges of the outer and inner conductors. I drew two concentric circles on grid paper to see which cells to include as part of the boundary. I assumed that any cell that the circle touched was part of the boundary.

19. Type and copy **=Outer** to the following cells: Q5:Q8, P9:P12, O13, N14:N15, M16, L17, J18:K18, G19:I19, and B20:F20.

20. Type and copy **=Inner** to the following cells: G5:G7, F8, E9, and B10:D10.

Along the edges of the pie slice, the boundary condition is that the derivative is zero. To insert this boundary condition, add an extra row of cells just outside the boundary and set their values equal to those in the first row of cells, just inside the boundary. This makes the derivative zero at the cells on the boundary (H5:P5 and B11:B19). Mark those extra rows with arrows.

21. In cell C4, type **B.C. --->**.

22. In cell G4, type **=Inner**.

23. In cell H4, type **=H6** and copy it to cells I4:P4.

24. In cell Q4, type **=Outer**.

25. Type **B** in cell A6, **C** in cell A7, **|** in cell A8, and **+** in cell A9, and center cells A6:A9.

26. In cell A10, type **=Inner**.

27. In cell A11, type **=C11** and copy it to cells A12:A19.

28. In cell A20, type **=Outer**.

Fill the interior of the region between the cylinders with the finite-difference form of the differential equation. Type the equation into cell H5 and then copy it into row H5:P5. Next copy the row from H5:P5 into cells H6:P7. Continue copying the equation in blocks until it fills the region.

29. Type **=0.25*(G5+H4+I5+H6)** in cell H5.

30. Copy the contents of cell H5 into the following ranges:

H5:P5	E10:O10	B15:M15
H6:P6	B11:O11	B16:L16
H7:P7	B12:O12	B17:K17
G8:P8	B13:N13	B18:I18
F9:O9	B14:M14	B19:F19

Insert the analytic solution along the upper boundary as a comparison. The analytic solution needs the value of the radius at each cell. Enter them in a row just below the bottom of the table.

31. In cell B3, type **Analytic --->**.

32. In cells G22 and H22, type **5** and **6**, respectively.

33. Select cells G22:H22, grab the fill handle, and drag it to cell Q22.

34. In cell G3, type the formula:

$$=(Outer*LN(G22/5)- Inner*LN(G22/15))/LN(15/5)$$

and copy it to cells H3:Q3.

35. Calculate the worksheet by pressing Ctrl-= (Cmd-= on the Macintosh).

36. Save the worksheet if you want to keep it.

After a few minutes, Excel will stop calculating, and your worksheet should look like Figure 12.2. Figure 12.3 shows a comparison of the analytic equation in cells G3:Q3 with the values of the numerical solution on the boundary in cells G5:Q5. The curves in the figure are nearly identical.

FIGURE 12.2:

Potential between two concentric cylinders: solving a two-dimensional, elliptical partial differential equation

	A	B	C	D	E	F	G	H	I	J	K	L	M	N	O	P	Q	R	S	T	U
							T36														
1	Laplace equation between concentric cylinders; Elliptical PDE																				
2																					
3		Analytic --->					20	17	14	11	9	7	6	4	3	1	0				
4			B.C. --->				20	17	14	12	9	7	6	4	3	1	0				
5			x --->				20	17	14	12	10	8	6	4	3	1	0				
6	B.	y					20	17	14	12	9	7	6	4	3	1	0				
7	C.						20	16	14	11	9	7	5	4	2	1	0				
8						20	18	15	13	11	9	7	5	4	2	1	0				
9	+	+			20	18	16	14	12	10	8	6	5	3	2	0			Applied Potentials		
10	20	20	20	20	18	16	14	12	10	9	7	5	4	3	1	0			Inner	Outer	
11	17	17	17	16	15	14	12	11	9	8	6	5	3	2	1	0			20	0	
12	14	14	14	14	13	12	10	9	8	7	5	4	3	1	1	0					
13	12	12	12	11	11	10	9	8	7	5	4	3	2	1	0						
14	10	10	10	9	9	8	7	6	5	4	3	2	1	0							
15	8	8	8	7	7	6	6	5	4	3	2	2	1	0							
16	6	6	6	6	5	5	4	4	3	2	2	1	0								
17	4	4	4	4	4	3	3	2	2	1	1	0									
18	3	3	3	3	2	2	2	1	1	0	0										
19	1	1	1	1	1	1	0	0	0												
20	0	0	0	0	0	0															
21																					

FIGURE 12.3:

The finite-difference and the analytic solutions to the concentric cylinders problem

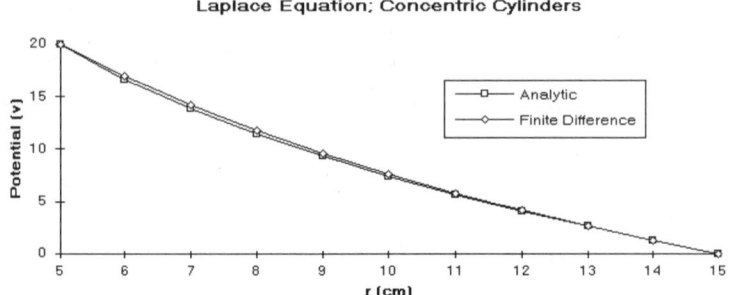

Laplace Equation; Concentric Cylinders

Once this problem is set up, you can quickly modify it for different potentials on the cylinders by simply changing the values in cells S11:T11. You can also add other conductors to the problem. For example, if you want to put a wire charged to 25 volts halfway between the two cylinders, just replace the difference equation in cell L5 with the value 25 and reexecute the macro. The result is shown in Figure 12.4 and graphed in Figure 12.5. The chart shows the situation calculated with the wire and the analytic solution without the wire.

FIGURE 12.4:

Potential between two concentric cylinders, with a wire charged to 25 volts inserted halfway between them in cell L5

	A	B	C	D	E	F	G	H	I	J	K	L	M	N	O	P	Q	R	S	T	U
1	Laplace equation between concentric cylinders; Elliptical PDE																				
2																					
3	Analytic --->						20	17	14	11	9	7	6	4	3	1	0				
4		B.C. --->					20	18	17	17	17	17	13	9	6	3	0		Wire at L5: 25 V		
5		x -->					20	19	18	18	19	25	15	10	6	3	0				
6	B.	y					20	18	17	17	17	17	13	9	6	3	0				
7	C.	I					20	18	16	15	15	13	11	8	5	2	0				
8	I	I				20	18	17	15	14	13	11	9	6	4	2	0				
9	+	+			20	18	17	15	14	12	11	9	7	5	3	0			Applied Potentials		
10	20	20	20	20	18	16	15	13	12	11	9	8	6	4	2	0			Inner	Outer	
11	17	17	17	17	15	14	13	12	10	9	8	6	5	3	2	0			20		0
12	14	14	14	14	13	12	11	10	9	8	6	5	4	2	1	0					
13	12	12	12	12	11	10	9	8	7	6	5	4	3	1	0						
14	10	10	10	9	9	8	8	7	6	5	4	3	2	0							
15	8	8	8	8	7	7	6	5	5	4	3	2	1	0							
16	6	6	6	6	5	5	4	3	2	2	1	0									
17	4	4	4	4	4	3	3	2	1	1	0										
18	3	3	3	2	2	2	1	1	0	0											
19	1	1	1	1	1	1	0	0	0												
20	0	0	0	0	0	0															
21																					

FIGURE 12.5:

Graph of the concentric cylinder problem with a wire charged to 25 volts inserted halfway between the cylinders (the analytic solution is for the case without the conductor)

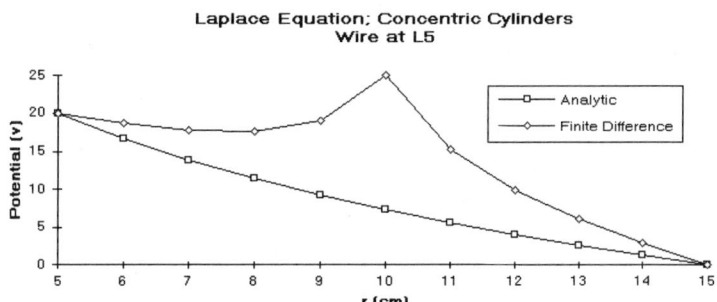

Laplace Equation; Concentric Cylinders
Wire at L5

□ Analytic
◇ Finite Difference

Solving Parabolic Partial Differential Equations

When the relationship between the coefficients, $B^2 - 4AC$, of the general partial differential equation equals zero, the equation is parabolic. Parabolic partial differential equations show up in problems involving diffusion and fluid flow. In general, these problems use the first derivative with respect to time and the second derivative with respect to the position of the concentration of some physical quantity (electron density, temperature, chemical concentration, and so on). The most important of these equations is the continuity equation.

Continuity Equations

A general continuity equation states that the time rate of change in concentration of a physical quantity in some volume is equal to the amount of that quantity flowing into the volume, minus the amount that flows out, plus the amount that is created in the volume, minus the amount that is absorbed in the volume. If the physical quantity moves at some velocity, v, the partial differential equation can be written as

$$\frac{\partial u}{\partial t} = -\nabla \cdot (u\mathbf{v}) + G - A$$

where the divergence term (the first term on the right) calculates the flow out of (or into) some volume, G is the generation term, and A is the absorption term.

The continuity equation is quite common in many branches of science and engineering. Any substance or physical quantity that can flow from one point to another can probably have that flow described with a continuity equation. It does not matter whether it is heat in a solid or tuna cans moving down a conveyor belt, the basic continuity equation is the same.

Transient Heat Flow in a Copper Bar   Consider the flow of heat Q in a solid. The velocity at which heat flows through a solid is proportional to the negative gradient of the temperature. Substituting the negative gradient of the temperature for the velocity in the continuity equation and using the chain rule on the time derivative results in this equation:

$$\frac{\partial Q}{\partial T} \frac{\partial T}{\partial t} = \nabla \cdot (K\nabla T) + G - A$$

The derivative of the heat with respect to the temperature is just the specific heat, ρC, where ρ is the density and C is the heat capacity. Inserting these, the equation becomes

$$\rho C \frac{\partial T}{\partial t} = \nabla \cdot (K \nabla T) + G - A$$

If you have simple transient heat flow in a metal bar, with no heat generation or absorption mechanisms, the equation above reduces to a one-dimensional, time-dependent partial differential equation:

$$\frac{\partial T}{\partial t} = \frac{K}{\rho C} \frac{\partial^2 T}{\partial x^2}$$

To solve this equation, first rewrite the spatial derivative as a central difference and the time derivative as a forward difference:

$$\frac{T_i^{n+1} - T_i^n}{\Delta t} = \frac{K}{\rho C} \frac{T_{i+1}^n - 2T_i^n + T_{i-1}^n}{\Delta x^2}$$

where Δx and Δt are the spatial and temporal step sizes. The superscript (n, $n+1$) indicates the time step. Solve this equation for the temperature at the future time (T_i^{n+1}):

$$T_i^{n+1} = T_i^n + \frac{K \Delta t}{\rho C \Delta x^2} \left(T_{i+1}^n - 2T_i^n + T_{i-1}^n \right)$$

The coefficient of the temperatures must be less than or equal to $1/2$ for the equation to be stable:

$$\frac{K \Delta t}{\rho C \Delta x^2} \leq \frac{1}{2}$$

If you use $1/2$, the equation reduces to

$$T_i^{n+1} = \tfrac{1}{2} \left(T_{i+1}^n + T_{i-1}^n \right)$$

For a copper bar:

$$\frac{K}{\rho C} = 1.15 \, \text{cm}^2 \, / \, \text{s}$$

This equation fixes the relationship between the time step (Δt) and the spatial grid step (Δx).

$$\Delta x^2 = 2.31 \Delta t$$

If the spatial grid step equals 1 cm, the time step must be 0.433 s.

Consider the problem with a 10 cm copper bar, initially at $0\,°C$, with one end held at $0\,°C$ and the other at $20\,°C$. Create a worksheet to calculate the change in temperature of this bar over time.

1. Start with a new worksheet expanded to full size. Turn automatic recalculation back on if it is still off from the previous example.

2. Select columns A through L and change the column width to 6.

3. In cell A1, type **Heat flow in a copper bar; Parabolic partial differential equation**.

4. In cell C3, type **Temperature versus position and time**.

Enter the time step as multiples of 0.433 second.

5. In cell A5, type **Time** and center it.

6. In cell A6, type **(s)** and center it.

7. In cell A7 type **0**, and in cell A8, type **0.433**.

8. Select cells A7:A8 and drag the fill handle to cell A20.

Enter the spatial grid, with a grid point every centimeter.

9. In cell E5, type **Position (cm)**.

10. Type **0** in cell B6 and **1** in cell C6.

11. Select cells B6:C6, grab the fill handle, and drag it to cell L6.

Enter the first boundary condition, a fixed value of 20°C. The formula in cells B8:B20 makes it simple to change the value of that boundary condition.

12. Type **20** in cell B7.

13. In cell B8, type **=B7** and copy it to cells B9:B20.

Enter the second boundary condition with a fixed value of 0°C.

14. In cell L7, type **0** and copy it to cells L8:L20.

Enter the initial condition of 0°C at t = 0.

15. In cell C7, type **0** and copy it to cells D7:K7.

Type the difference equation into the first cell of the range, and then copy it to the rest of the range.

16. In cell C8, type **=0.5*(B7+D7)** and copy it to cells C9:K20.

17. Format cells A7:L20 as 0.00.

18. Save the worksheet if you want to keep a copy.

The worksheet should now look like Figure 12.6, with the resulting temperatures versus position and time. You can see the flow of heat down the bar by observing the changes in the temperature.

FIGURE 12.6:

Heat flow in a copper bar: solution of a parabolic partial differential equation

	A	B	C	D	E	F	G	H	I	J	K	L	M
1	Heat flow in a copper bar, Parabolic partial differential equation												
2													
3				Temperature versus position and time									
4													
5	Time				Position (cm)								
6	(s)	0	1	2	3	4	5	6	7	8	9	10	
7	0.00	20.00	0.00	0.00	0.00	0.00	0.00	0.00	0.00	0.00	0.00	0.00	
8	0.43	20.00	10.00	0.00	0.00	0.00	0.00	0.00	0.00	0.00	0.00	0.00	
9	0.87	20.00	10.00	5.00	0.00	0.00	0.00	0.00	0.00	0.00	0.00	0.00	
10	1.30	20.00	12.50	5.00	2.50	0.00	0.00	0.00	0.00	0.00	0.00	0.00	
11	1.73	20.00	12.50	7.50	2.50	1.25	0.00	0.00	0.00	0.00	0.00	0.00	
12	2.17	20.00	13.75	7.50	4.38	1.25	0.63	0.00	0.00	0.00	0.00	0.00	
13	2.60	20.00	13.75	9.06	4.38	2.50	0.63	0.31	0.00	0.00	0.00	0.00	
14	3.03	20.00	14.53	9.06	5.78	2.50	1.41	0.31	0.16	0.00	0.00	0.00	
15	3.46	20.00	14.53	10.16	5.78	3.59	1.41	0.78	0.16	0.08	0.00	0.00	
16	3.90	20.00	15.08	10.16	6.88	3.59	2.19	0.78	0.43	0.08	0.04	0.00	
17	4.33	20.00	15.08	10.98	6.88	4.53	2.19	1.31	0.43	0.23	0.04	0.00	
18	4.76	20.00	15.49	10.98	7.75	4.53	2.92	1.31	0.77	0.23	0.12	0.00	

Using Iterated Time Steps

Another way to calculate a time step is by iterating the worksheet, rather than proceeding down the worksheet as time increases. The solution uses two rows of cells, creating a circular reference. One row of cells saves the values of the function from the last step, and the other row calculates the value of the function at a new time step.

Now recreate the heat flow problem, this time iterating the time steps.

1. Start with a new worksheet expanded to full size.

2. Choose the Calculation command on the Options menu. In the dialog box, change Calculation to Manual, check Iteration, and set Maximum Iterations to **1**. Then click on OK.

3. Select columns B through L and change the column width to 6.

4. Change the width of column A to 7.

5. In cell A1, type **Heat flow in a copper bar; Parabolic partial differential equation**.

Enter the initialization flag. Entering a 0 in cell B4 will cause the problem to be initialized.

6. In cell A4, type **Init Flag**.

7. Type **0** in cell B4.

8. Name cell B4 as **INIT_FLAG**.

Set up a circular reference to calculate the time of the current iteration. The formula in cell F3 checks for an initialization iteration and then adds the time step to the current time. Cell G3 stores the time for the next step.

9. In cell E3, type **Time**.

10. Type **=IF(INIT_FLAG=0,0,G3+0.433)** in cell F3.

11. Type **=F3** in cell G3.

Enter the x positions across the top of the table.

12. In cell E5, type **Position (cm)**.

13. Type **0** in cell B6 and **1** in cell C6.

14. Select cells B6:C6, grab the fill handle, and drag it to cell L6.

Enter the initial conditions of 0 and the boundary conditions of 20 at $x = 0$ and 0 at $x = 10$.

15. Type **I.C.** in cell A7.

16. In cell C7, type **0** and copy it to cells D7:K7.

17. In cell B7, type **20** and copy it to cells B8:B9.

18. In cell L7, type **0** and copy it to cells L8:L9.

Enter the finite-difference equation in row 8. The formula also checks for an initialization iteration. If the initialization flag equals 0, the value of the function is set equal to the initial conditions in row 7.

19. Type **=IF(INIT_FLAG=0,C7,0.5*(B9+D9))** in cell C8 and copy it to cells D8:K8.

20. In cell C9, type **=C8** and copy it to cells D9:K9.

21. In cell D10, type **Temperature versus position**.

22. Format cells B7:L9, F3, and G3 as 0.00.

23. Save the worksheet if you want to keep a copy.

24. To use the worksheet, set the initialization flag in cell C4 to **0** and press F9 or Ctrl-= (Cmd-= on the Macintosh). Change the value of the initialization flag to **1** and press F9 again.

The worksheet now shows the results after the first time step. Each time you press F9, the worksheet increments the time step.

25. Press F9 ten more times.

The worksheet will look like Figure 12.7, at a problem time of 4.763 seconds. These results are identical to those in row 18 of Figure 12.6.

FIGURE 12.7:

Heat flow in a bar: iterated time steps

	A	B	C	D	E	F	G	H	I	J	K	L
1	Heat flow in a copper bar; Parabolic partial differential equation											
2												
3						Time	5.196	5.196				
4	Init Flag	1										
5						Position (cm)						
6		0	1	2	3	4	5	6	7	8	9	10
7	I.C.	20.00	0.00	0.00	0.00	0.00	0.00	0.00	0.00	0.00	0.00	0.00
8		20.00	15.49	11.62	7.75	5.34	2.92	1.85	0.77	0.44	0.12	0.00
9		20.00	15.49	11.62	7.75	5.34	2.92	1.85	0.77	0.44	0.12	0.00
10					Temperature versus position							
11												
12												
13												
14												
15												
16												
17												
18												

One of the benefits of iterated time steps is that you can calculate the results for any number of time steps without using a lot of worksheet area. For example, if you wanted to know the results after 1000 time steps, the noniterated method (Figure 12.6) would use 1000 rows in the worksheet. The iterated method would use no more than it does now. To do 1000 iterations without pressing F9 1000 times, choose the Calculation command on the Options menu and set Maximum Iterations to 1000. Press F9, and the worksheet is iterated 1000 times, or until it reaches a steady-state condition (nothing is changing).

Another benefit of the iteration method is that it lends itself to two-dimensional, time-dependent calculations. Represent the two spatial dimensions in the rows and columns of the worksheet and iterate the time dimension. The setup is similar to the worksheet in Figure 12.7, except that you need three rectangular ranges of cells corresponding to the three rows of cells in the figure. The first range holds the initial conditions, the second contains the two-dimensional, finite-difference equation, and the third holds the values for the next step.

Solving Hyperbolic Partial Differential Equations

In hyperbolic differential equations, the relationship between the coefficients in the general equation ($B^2 - 4AC$) is greater than zero. These equations have second derivatives of both variables. Hyperbolic partial differential equations arise from wave mechanics and vibration, transport (of radiation, for example), diffusion, and gas dynamics problems.

The Wave Equation

Probably the most important hyperbolic partial differential equation to modern physics is the wave equation. It consists of second-order derivatives of space and time, related with speed:

$$\frac{\partial^2 y}{\partial t^2} = c^2 \nabla^2 y$$

where c is the speed of the traveling wave. An electromagnetic wave in space and a wave in a vibrating string are both described with the wave equation.

You solve the wave equation in the same manner as you solved the previous examples. Consider a one-dimensional form of the wave equation:

$$\frac{\partial^2 y}{\partial t^2} = c^2 \frac{\partial^2 y}{\partial x^2}$$

First substitute central differences for the derivatives:

$$\frac{y_i^{n+1} - 2y_i^n + y_i^{n-1}}{\Delta t^2} = c^2 \frac{y_{i+1}^n - 2y_i^n + y_{i-1}^n}{\Delta x^2}$$

Then solve the equation for the value of the function at the future time:

$$y_i^{n+1} = 2y_i^n + y_i^{n-1} + \frac{c^2 \Delta t^2}{\Delta x^2}\left(y_{i+1}^n - 2y_i^n + y_{i-1}^n\right)$$

This equation requires data from two time steps to calculate the value at the future time. This is a problem only during the first time step, where there is no history from which to get the value for y_i^{n-1}. To start the problem, you must somehow estimate the value of this term. If you are given the value of y and its derivative as your initial conditions, use them in a simple extrapolation to get the value of the function at the time $-\Delta t$:

$$y_i^{n+1} = y_i^n - \Delta t \frac{\partial y}{\partial t}$$

If you have other information, use it to get an estimate of the value of the function at $-\Delta t$.

Vibrating String   The oscillations of a vibrating string are described with a one-dimensional form of the wave equation. The boundary conditions are that the ends of the string are held fixed at zero. If the string is plucked, the extent and location that the string was pulled determine the initial conditions. Assume that you have a 70-cm string that is pulled off center by 0.1 cm at a point 20 cm from one end. The initial conditions would then be:

$$y = 0.1 \frac{x}{20} \qquad\qquad x < 20$$

$$y = 0.1 \frac{70 - x}{50} \qquad\qquad x > 20$$

For stability, the coefficient in the finite-difference equation needs to be equal to 1:

$$\frac{c^2 \Delta t^2}{\Delta x^2} = 1$$

Setting the coefficient equal to 1 also simplifies the difference equation:

$$y_i^{n+1} = y_{i+1}^n + y_{i-1}^n - y_i^{n-1}$$

Stretching the string sets the wave velocity, which then fixes the relationship between the time step and spatial step. For example, if you stretch the string until the wave velocity is 5×10^4 cm/s, the relationship between the spatial and temporal steps is:

$$\Delta x = 5 \times 10^4 \Delta t$$

If Δx is 10 cm, then Δt must be 2×10^{-4} s.

You know from the initial conditions that the string is plucked. Therefore, it is at the maximum extent of an oscillation at the time $t = 0$, which makes the value of the function at the $-\Delta t$ step equal to the value of the function at the first step (at $+\Delta t$):

$$y_i^{n-1} = y_i^{n+1}$$

Enter this value into the difference equation for the first step only:

$$y_i^{n+1} = \left(\tfrac{1}{2}\right)\left(y_{i+1}^n + y_{i-1}^n\right)$$

Create a worksheet to calculate the oscillations of the string described here.

1. Start with a new worksheet expanded to full size. Turn automatic recalculation back on if it is still off from the previous example.

2. Select columns B through M and change the column width to 6.

3. Change the width of column A to 9.

4. In cell A1, type **Vibrating String; Hyperbolic equation**.

5. In cell C2, type **Displacement of a Plucked String**.

Enter the time values with steps of 2×10^{-4} s, and the spatial values with a step of 10 cm.

6. In cell A3, type **Time** and center it.

7. In cell A4, type **(s)** and center it.

8. Type **0** in cell A5 and **0.0002** in cell A6.

9. Select cells A5:A6, grab the fill handle, and drag it to cell A35.

10. Format cells A5:A35 as 0.0E+00.

11. In cell B3, type **B.C.** and center it.

12. In cell E3, type **Length (cm)**.

13. In cell I3, type **B.C.** and center it.

14. Type **0** in cell B4 and **10** in cell C4.

15. Select cells B4:C4, grab the fill handle, and drag it to cell I4.

Enter the initial condition of the string being plucked by 0.1 cm at a point 20 cm from the end. The extension numbers are linear from the point the string is plucked to each end.

16. Make the following entries in cells B5:J5:

B5: **0**	C5: **0.05**	D5: **0.1**
E5: **0.08**	F5: **0.06**	G5: **0.04**
H5: **0.02**	I5: **0**	J5: **<--- I.C.**

Enter the boundary conditions down both sides.

17. In cell B6, type **=B5** and copy it to cells B7:B35.

18. In cell I6, type **=I5** and copy it to cells I7:I35.

Put in the special difference equation for the first step with the estimate for the back step contained in it.

19. In cell C6, type **=0.5*(B5+D5)** and copy it to cells D6:H6.

Complete the problem with the normal difference equation.

20. In cell C7, type **=B6+D6−C5** and copy it to cells C8:H35.

21. Format cells B5:H35 as 0.00.

22. Save the problem if you want to keep it.

The worksheet should look like Figure 12.8. If you follow the changes in the position of the string, you will note that it is oscillating with a period of 2.8×10^{-3} s, or a frequency of 357 Hz. The analytical equation for the oscillation frequency gives the same result:

$$f = \frac{c}{2l} = \frac{5 \times 10^4 \text{ cm/s}}{2 \cdot 70 \text{ cm}} = 357 \text{ Hz}$$

where f is the frequency and l is the length of the string.

FIGURE 12.8:

FIGURE 12.8:

A vibrating string: solution of a hyperbolic partial differential equation

	A	B	C	D	E	F	G	H	I	J	K	L
	L33											
1	Vibrating String; Hyperbolic equation											
2			Displacement of a Plucked String									
3	Time	B.C.			Length (cm)				B.C.			
4	(s)	0	10	20	30	40	50	60	70			
5	0.0E+00	0.00	0.05	0.10	0.08	0.06	0.04	0.02	0	<–I.C.		
6	2.0E-04	0.00	0.05	0.07	0.08	0.06	0.04	0.02	0			
7	4.0E-04	0.00	0.02	0.03	0.05	0.06	0.04	0.02	0			
8	6.0E-04	0.00	-0.02	-0.01	0.01	0.03	0.04	0.02	0			
9	8.0E-04	0.00	-0.02	-0.04	-0.03	-0.01	0.01	0.02	0			
10	1.0E-03	0.00	-0.02	-0.04	-0.06	-0.05	-0.03	-0.02	0			
11	1.2E-03	0.00	-0.02	-0.04	-0.06	-0.08	-0.07	-0.05	0			
12	1.4E-03	0.00	-0.02	-0.04	-0.06	-0.08	-0.10	-0.05	0			
13	1.6E-03	0.00	-0.02	-0.04	-0.06	-0.08	-0.07	-0.05	0			
14	1.8E-03	0.00	-0.02	-0.04	-0.06	-0.05	-0.03	-0.02	0			
15	2.0E-03	0.00	-0.02	-0.04	-0.03	-0.01	0.01	0.02	0			
16	2.2E-03	0.00	-0.02	0.00	0.01	0.03	0.04	0.02	0			
17	2.4E-03	0.00	0.02	0.03	0.05	0.06	0.04	0.02	0			
18	2.6E-03	0.00	0.05	0.07	0.08	0.06	0.04	0.02	0			

Summary

In this last chapter, you looked at solving multidimensional, time-dependent, partial differential equations with a worksheet. Amazingly enough, this is actually rather easy to do. The methods described here all use explicit finite differences. In explicit finite differences, the value of the function in the future time is explicitly determined by the known values of the function in the past.

The finite-difference equations can also be written as implicit finite differences, where the value of the function at the future time is a function of the value of the function in the past and in the future. The equations thus formed are sets of coupled simultaneous equations that must be solved in a matrix format, a much more complicated calculation than that required by the explicit method.

Now that you have worked through the examples in this book, you should have a good idea of what you can do with Excel. You can use the techniques developed here to work with your own scientific or engineering problems.

For More Information

Numerical Methods for Partial Differential Equations

C. Gerald, *Applied Numerical Analysis*, 2nd. ed. (Reading, Mass.: Addison-Wesley, 1978).

W. H. Press, B. P. Flannery, S. A. Teukolsky, W. T. Vetterling, *Numerical Recipes; The Art of Scientific Computing* (Cambridge, Eng.: Cambridge University Press, 1986).

General Partial Differential Equations

H. F. Weinberger, *A First Course in Partial Differential Equations* (New York: Blaisdell Publishing Co., 1965).

Problems

1. Classify the following partial differential equations as elliptic, parabolic, or hyperbolic.

   a. $\dfrac{\partial^2 u}{\partial t^2} + 2t\dfrac{\partial^2 u}{\partial x^2} + x^2\dfrac{\partial u}{\partial x} = 0$

   b. $\dfrac{\partial^2 u}{\partial t^2} + \dfrac{\partial^2 u}{\partial x^2} + xt\dfrac{\partial u}{\partial x} = 0$

   c. $x\dfrac{\partial^2 u}{\partial t^2} + \dfrac{\partial^2 u}{\partial x^2} + u = 0$

   d. $t\dfrac{\partial^2 u}{\partial t^2} + 5\dfrac{\partial^2 u}{\partial x \partial t} + x^2\dfrac{\partial^2 u}{\partial x^2} + \dfrac{\partial u}{\partial x} = 0$

   e. $xt\dfrac{\partial^2 u}{\partial t^2} + \dfrac{\partial^2 u}{\partial x \partial t} + u = 0$

2. Solve the Laplace equation between two infinite parallel plates spaced 10 cm apart. The upper plate at $x = 10$ cm is held at 200 volts, and the lower one at $x = 0$ is set at 0 volts.

3. Complete problem 2, inserting a wire charged to 50 volts at $x = 6$ cm.

4. The Poisson equation is used to calculate the potential in a volume due to applied voltages and charges.

$$\nabla^2 \varphi = -q\frac{\rho}{\varepsilon}$$

q is the charge on an electron (1.6×10^{-19} coul), ρ is the charge density, and ε is the permittivity (8.85×10^{-14} F/cm). Solve the Poisson equation ϕ between two infinite parallel plates spaced 10 cm apart, as in problem 2. Fill the lower half of the volume between the plates with fixed negative charges at a density of $\rho = -10^7$ cm^{-3}. Fill the upper half of the volume with fixed positive charges at a density of $\rho = +10^5$ cm^{-3}.

5. The decay of charge carriers (n) generated in silicon by light is described by the equation

$$\frac{\partial n}{\partial t} = -\frac{(n - n_0)}{\tau_n} + D\frac{\partial^2 n}{\partial x^2}$$

n_0 is the equilibrium carrier density (1015 cm-3), t is the lifetime (10^{-6} s), and D is the diffusion coefficient (100 cm^3/s). The initial carrier density in a 10-cm bar of silicon illuminated at one end is

$$n = 10^{17} \text{ cm}^{-3} \qquad 0 < x < 0.03 \text{ cm}$$
$$n = 10^{15} \text{cm}^{-3} \qquad 0.03 \text{ cm} < x < 0.1 \text{ cm}$$

The derivative of the carrier density is 0 at the ends of the bar. Calculate the decay of the pulse of charge carriers for the first 5 microseconds after the light is turned off.

6. The Fick equation describes the thermal diffusion of dopants into silicon.

$$\frac{\partial C}{\partial t} = D\frac{\partial^2 C}{\partial x^2}$$

where C is the concentration of the dopant. At a temperature of 1200 K, boron diffuses into silicon at a rate of $D = 8 \times 1 0^{-11}$ cm^2/s. If the surface is held at a concentration of $C_s = 10^{19}$ cm^{-3} for 1 hour, what is the doping density in the first 10 microns of the silicon? Compare the result to the analytic solution. (*erfc* is the complementary error function.)

$$c(x,t) = C_s erfc\left(\frac{x}{2\sqrt{Dt}}\right)$$

7. Complete the vibrating string example, inserting a pulse at the beginning of the string with the following initial conditions:

$$y(x) = 0.5 \qquad 0 < x \le 20 \text{ cm}$$
$$y(x) = 0 \qquad x > 20 \text{ cm}$$

The pulse will move along the string and reflect at the ends.

8. Solve Burger's equation for $T = 5$ and $n = 0.1$ using explicit finite differences. Try solving it again for values of n between 10^{-2} and 10^{-4}. You will need a predictor-corrector (modified Euler) method to achieve stability in this region.

$$\frac{\partial u}{\partial t} + u \frac{\partial u}{\partial x} = \upsilon \frac{\partial^2 u}{\partial x^2} \qquad 0 < x < 1 \qquad 0 < t < T$$

$$u(0,t) = u(1,t) = 0$$
$$u(x,0) = \sin(\pi x)$$

9. Where γ is the ratio of specific heats (7/5 for air), ρ is the density, and u is the velocity, propagation of a pressure wave in a gas is described by the equation

$$\frac{\partial u}{\partial t} + u \frac{\partial u}{\partial x} + \rho^{\gamma - 2} \frac{\partial \rho}{\partial x} = 0$$

$$\frac{\partial \rho}{\partial t} + \rho \frac{\partial u}{\partial x} + u \frac{\partial \rho}{\partial x} = 0$$

A 10-cm tube contains compressed air ($\rho = 0.0012 \text{ gm/cm}^3$) in the first 2 cm and vacuum ($\rho = 0$) in the rest. At $t = 0$, the valve is suddenly opened and the air is allowed to flow from the pressurized side into the rest of the tube. Calculate the density of the air in the tube as it begins to flow into the rest of the tube. You will need to calculate alternating solutions for both equations at each time step.

10. Calculate the solution of the following equation for $t = 0$ to 2.

$$\frac{\partial^2 u}{\partial t^2} - \frac{\partial^2 u}{\partial x^2} = e^x$$

$$u(x,0) = u'(x,0) = u'(0,t) = u'(1,t) = 0$$

11. Calculate the solution of the following equation within the square $x = \pm 1$,

$$\frac{\partial^2 u}{\partial x^2} + \frac{\partial^2 u}{\partial y^2} = x^2 + y^2 \quad -1 < x < 1 \quad -1 < y < 1$$

$y = \pm 1$. The solution is 0 on the boundary.

INDEX

This index differentiates between mentions of items, listed in regular type, and explanations of items, listed as **bold** page numbers. *Italic* page numbers refer to figures.

Symbols

* as search wildcard, 212
\$ for absolute cell reference, **8**
μ
  entering, **80**
  handled in Excel, 120
π
  entering in worksheet, 249
  PI() function for, **19**
  sine/cosine precision for, **18**
+ in value or formula, 10
? as search wildcard, **212**
"
  as alignment symbol, 62
  for minutes symbol, 62

A

ABS() function, 14, **16**. *See also* mathematical functions
absolute cell references, **8**. *See also* cell references
  for macros, 168
absolute magnitude and apparent magnitude, 76
absolute magnitude of star, table for, **75**–*78*
absolute range references, 9. *See also* cell references; range
accelerated finite differences method, for differential equations, **376**–**377**
acceleration, in free fall experiment, **290**–**295**
accuracy
  in Bessel function, 273, 276
  and calculation speed, 308
  of cubic vs. linear interpolation, 264–266
  in difference formulas, 288
  and grid points, 371
  and numeric precision, 2–3
  and round-off error, 290
  in Runge-Kutta method, 363
  and scaling, 345–346

setting criteria for, 319
ACOS() function, 15, **19**
ACOSH() function, 16, **20**
actions, command macros for, 174
active cell in data input process, 203–205. *See also* cell references
Add Arrow command for chart arrows, 124
add-in file, attaching, 13
Add Legend command for charts, 124
Add Overlay command for multiple charts, 124
address. *See also* cell reference
  for external cell reference, **5**–**6**
  setting for cell, **5**
algorithm. *See also* macros; programs
  adjusting values of, 247
  numerical, 2
  for series summation, 277
alignment
  of labels, 56
  quotation marks for, 62
Alignment command, for label alignment, 56
Alt key for extended character set, **62**
analytic equations, **48**–**57**. *See also* equations
  for extracting coefficients, **54**–**55**
  single value, **51**–**53**
  for temperature dependence of intrinsic carrier density, **65**–**68**
  for thermal conductivity of silicon, **48**–**57**
  values in list, **53**–*54*
analytic solution. *See also* solution
  for elliptic partial differential equation, 397–*398*
  in Euler method, 355, 358, 360
  in iterated finite differences method, 373
  for Laplace equation, 395
  for matrix equation, 380
  in Runge-Kutta method, 362–363
  in shooting method, 366, 368
AND() function, **25**
angular conversion functions, 21–22
annuity functions, 37
arcosecant, calculating, **19**

B

D

F

J

L

labels. *See also* text; titles
  in cells, 5, 56
  for chart curves, **128–129**, *130*
  for charts, 114, 116–117, 123–124, 147
  entering in worksheet, **55**–*58*
  for macros, 171
  text stored as, 208
Laguerre polynomials, 272
Laplace equations, **393–399**. *See also* partial differential equations
LARGE() function, 31, **34**
latitude in equatorial reference system, 59
layout of cells, 9–10
LCM() function, 15, **17**
least common multiple, function for, 15, **17**
least-squares method, 34–35. *See also* statistical functions
LEFT() function, **26**
legend, **117,** 124, 128, *129,***281**. *See also* text titles
Legend command, for legend placement, 125, 128
Legendre polynomials, 272
  analytical solution for, **279**
  calculated with macros, *281*
  equations for, **277**
  first 6 orders, *282*
LEN() function, **26,** 27
library. *See* Excel library
linear equations
  equations with 3 variables, **335–336**
  Gauss-Seidel iteration for, **336–339**
  matrix functions for, 16, **20**
  matrix methods for, **334–336**
  over/under relaxation method, **339–342**
  Solver for, **342–344**
  solving, **334–344**
linear interpolation. *See also* curve fitting
  and cubic interpolation, 264–266
  for data, **258–263**
  steam table calculations, **259–263**, *260–261*
linear regression calculations, 236–243.
     See also curve fitting;
  regression calculations
  thermal conductivity curve fit, 237–243

linear variable differential transformer (LVDT), 89–90
  calibration equations for, **90, 92**
  table creation for, **89–92**, *93*
LINEST() function, 32, **34**, **35**
list of values, calculating, **53–54**
LN() function, 15, **18**
locking titles, 82
log and semilog charts, creating, **132**–*138*
logarithmic functions, **15**, **18**
LOGEST() function, 32, **35**
LOG() function, 15, **18**
logical functions, **24,** 39
logical operators, **10**–*11*. *See also* operators
longitude in equatorial reference system, 59
LOOKUP() function, **40–41**
lookup functions, **39–41**
loop commands, controlling in macros, **173**
loop functions
  in integration macros, 305–306
  in programming macro, 182–183
  in series summation, 279
Lotus 1-2-3, day-count compatibility, 94
LVDT. See linear variable differential transformer

M

Macro Debugger, **196**–*197*
macro files for functions, 13. *See also* files; macros
macro functions, **42–43**
macros, **166–171**. *See also* programs
  buttons for, 168
  calls for, **280**
  for cell-formatting, **168–170**, *169*
  for cell references, **171–172**
  command, **166–170**
  for creating matrix, **382–383**
  for cubic interpolation, 264–266
  for curve fit adjustments, **255–257**
  for debugging programs, **195–197**
  function, **174–178**, *177*
  for gamma function, **306–309**
  global sheet for, 167
  for importing data, 211
  for input/output control, 173

N

S

U

V

W

X

Y

y coefficient in array formula, 252–254. *See also* curve fitting
y direction
in dialog box, 174
in drawings, 156
plotted as curve, 125–*127*
positioning in charts, 114, 116–117, 123–125
in 3-D charts, 138
YEAR() function, 28, **29**

Z

z direction in 3-D charts, 114
zero
argument as, 84
for underflow error, 4
zero point in magnitude scale, 76
Zoom command for drawing magnification, **156**

SYBEX

FREE BROCHURE!

Complete this form today, and we'll send you a full-color brochure of Sybex bestsellers.

Please supply the name of the Sybex book purchased.

_____

How would you rate it?

_____ Excellent   _____ Very Good   _____ Average   _____ Poor

Why did you select this particular book?

_____ Recommended to me by a friend

_____ Recommended to me by store personnel

_____ Saw an advertisement in _____

_____ Author's reputation

_____ Saw in Sybex catalog

_____ Required textbook

_____ Sybex reputation

_____ Read book review in _____

_____ In-store display

_____ Other _____

Where did you buy it?

_____ Bookstore

_____ Computer Store or Software Store

_____ Catalog (name: _____)

_____ Direct from Sybex

_____ Other: _____

Did you buy this book with your personal funds?

_____ Yes   _____ No

About how many computer books do you buy each year?

_____ 1-3   _____ 3-5   _____ 5-7   _____ 7-9   _____ 10+

About how many Sybex books do you own?

_____ 1-3   _____ 3-5   _____ 5-7   _____ 7-9   _____ 10+

Please indicate your level of experience with the software covered in this book:

_____ Beginner   _____ Intermediate   _____ Advanced

Which types of software packages do you use regularly?

_____ Accounting   _____ Databases   _____ Networks

_____ Amiga   _____ Desktop Publishing   _____ Operating Systems

_____ Apple/Mac   _____ File Utilities   _____ Spreadsheets

_____ CAD   _____ Money Management   _____ Word Processing

_____ Communications   _____ Languages   _____ Other _____

(please specify)

Which of the following best describes your job title?

_____ Administrative/Secretarial _____ President/CEO

_____ Director _____ Manager/Supervisor

_____ Engineer/Technician _____ Other _____
                                         (please specify)

Comments on the weaknesses/strengths of this book: _____

_____

_____

_____

_____

Name _____

Street _____

City/State/Zip _____

Phone _____

PLEASE FOLD, SEAL, AND MAIL TO SYBEX

SYBEX, INC.
Department M
2021 CHALLENGER DR.
ALAMEDA, CALIFORNIA USA
94501

SYBEX

SEAL

Excel 4 for Scientists and Engineers Examples Disk

If you would like to use the examples and programs in this book, but do not want to type them yourself, you can obtain them on disk (this disk contains only the examples, *not* the problems at the end of each chapter). Complete the following order form and return it along with a check or money order for $20.00 in U.S. currency. For orders from countries other than the U.S. and Canada, please add $1.00 for overseas shipping. California residents please include state sales tax.

William J. Orvis
226 Joyce St.
Livermore, CA 94550

Excel for Scientists and Engineers Examples Disk

Name: _____

Address: _____

City/State/Zip: _____

Disk: $20.00
Overseas shipping: $1.00   _____
State sales tax: $1.45   _____
(California residents only)

Total: _____

Disk size: 5.25"_____   3.5"_____
Disk format: MS DOS_____   Macintosh_____

Enclosed is my check or money order for $_____ in U.S. funds
(make checks payable to William J. Orvis). Please send me the *Excel 4 for Scientists and Engineers Examples Disk.*

SYBEX is not affiliated with William J. Orvis and assumes no responsibility for any defect in the disk programs.

Science and Engineering Applications Discussed in
Excel 4 for Scientists and Engineers (continued)

Application	Application	Page
MATHEMATICS	Shooting method solution of an ordinary differential equation	365
	Finite-difference solution of an ordinary differential equation	372
	Matrix solution of an ordinary differential equation	378
	Elliptic, parabolic, and hyperbolic partial differential equations	392
	Two-dimensional Poisson and Laplace equations	393
MECHANICAL ENGINEERING	Stress and deflection in a cantilever beam	85
	Stress and deflection in a simply supported beam	365
NUCLEAR ENGINEERING	Linear variable differential transformer (LVDT)	89
	Steam tables	259
PHYSICS	Van der Waals equation of state	72
	Spark gaps	205
	Elementary particles	208